THE THIRD REICH FROM ORIGINAL SOURCES

THE GESTAPO ON TRIAL

Evidence from Nuremberg

The Illustrated Edition

EDITED AND INTRODUCED BY
BOB CARRUTHERS

Pen & Sword
MILITARY

This edition published in 2014 by

Pen & Sword Military
An imprint of
Pen & Sword Books Ltd
47 Church Street
Barnsley
South Yorkshire
S70 2AS

First published in Great Britain in 2013 by Coda Books Ltd.

Copyright © Coda Books Ltd.
Published under licence by Pen & Sword Books Ltd.

ISBN: 9781783463190

A CIP catalogue record for this book is available from the British Library

This book includes excerpts from "The Trial of German Major War Criminals Proceedings
of the International Military Tribunal Sitting at Nuremberg, Germany" published under the
authority of H.M. Attorney-General by His Majesty's Stationery Office, London 1946/1947.

Printed and bound in England
By CPI Group (UK) Ltd, Croydon, CR0 4YY

Pen & Sword Books Ltd incorporates the imprints of Pen & Sword Aviation, Pen & Sword
Family History, Pen & Sword Maritime, Pen & Sword Military, Pen & Sword Discovery, Pen
& Sword Politics, Pen & Sword Atlas, Pen & Sword Archaeology, Wharncliffe Local History,
Wharncliffe True Crime, Wharncliffe Transport, Pen & Sword Select, Pen & Sword Military
Classics, Leo Cooper, The Praetorian Press, Claymore Press, Remember When, Seaforth
Publishing and Frontline Publishing

For a complete list of Pen & Sword titles please contact
PEN & SWORD BOOKS LIMITED
47 Church Street, Barnsley, South Yorkshire, S70 2AS, England
E-mail: enquiries@pen-and-sword.co.uk
Website: www.pen-and-sword.co.uk

Contents

Foreword

The Nuremberg Trials were held by the four victorious Allied forces in the Palace of Justice, Nuremberg from November 1945 to October 1946. Famous for prosecuting the major German war criminals, they also tried the various groups and organisations that were at the heart of Nazi Germany.

There were four counts against the accused:
- Count One: The Common Plan or Conspiracy
- Count Two: Crimes against Peace
- Count Three: War Crimes
- Count Four: Crimes against Humanity

The Rt. Hon. Sir Geoffrey Lawrence of Great Britain was the President of the court, and the United States of America, France, the United Kingdom, and the Union of Soviet Socialist Republics each provided one judge and an alternate, as well as a prosecutor and their assistants. Each defendant was given counsel, the majority of whom were German, along with a team of assistants, clerks and lawyers.

This volume is concerned with the trial of the Gestapo and includes all testimony regarding this organisation, and because of the close structural ties between the two groups, also includes some evidence regarding the S.D. (Der Sicherheitsdienst) and the defendant Ernst Kaltenbrunner, who was Obergruppenführer and General der Polizei und Waffen-SS. The defense counsel were as follows:
- Dr. Rudolf Merkel, Counsel for the Gestapo
- Ludwig Babel, Counsel for the SS and SD to 18th March 1946
- Dr Hans Gawlik, Counsel for the SD from 18th March 1946.
- Dr. Kurt Kauffmann, Counsel for Ernst Kaltenbrunner.

The witnesses called for the trial of the Gestapo and the SD include among others, Karl Hoffmann, Dr. Werner Best, Rolf-Heinz Hoeppner, Dieter Wisliceny and Walter Schellenberg

Karl Hoffmann was a senior Gestapo official who served in Koblenz and Dusseldorf, and was head of the Gestapo in Denmark from 1943. He was sentenced to death in 1948 in Copenhagen, but his sentence was transmuted to 20 years in prison. In 1952, however, he was released and deported to West Germany, where he worked as a lawyer. He died in 1975.

Dr. Werner Best (1903-1989) was a German lawyer and senior Nazi. Prior to the outbreak of the war, he was head of Department 1 of the Gestapo and oversaw organisation, administration, and legal affairs. Both Himmler and Heydrich relied on Best to develop the legalities of their actions against the enemies of the state and the Jewish problem. In 1942, he became the Third Reich's Plenipotentiary in Denmark and supervised civilian affairs there. In 1948, he was sentenced to death by a Danish court, but this sentence was

VICTIMS OF THE GESTAPO.

Row 1, left to right: *Bruno Schulz (1892-1942), Polish writer. Denise Bloch (1916–1945), French SOE agent. Edward Hamerski (1897-1941), Polish physician. Stanisław Mączewski (1892-1941), Polish physician. Violette Szabo (1921-1945), French SOE agent*

Row 2, left to right: *Józef Padewski (1894-1951), Polish bishop, imprisoned in 1942. Stanisław Estreicher (1869-1939), Polish historian. Stanisław Klimecki (1883-1942), Mayor of Krakow. Zdzisław Jachimecki (1882-1953), Polish composer, imprisoned in 1939. Ignacy Fik (1904-1942), Polish poet and critic*

Row 3, left to right: *Noor Inayat Khan (1914-1944), British SOE agent. Marc Bloch (1886-1944), French historian. Wilhelm Gaczek (1881-1941), Polish clergyman. Rudolf Hilferding (1877-1941), Austrian economist. Herschel Grynszpan (1921- declared dead 1960), German political assassin*

Row 4, left to right: *Julius Fučík (1903-1943), Czech journalist. Włodzimierz Sieradzki (1870-1941), Polish physician. Vladislav Vančura (1891-1942), Czech writer. Eliane Plewman (1917-1944), French SOE agent. Max Jacob (1876-1944), French writer*

Row 5, left to right: *Mildred Fish-Harnack (1902 -1943), American writer. Lilian Rolfe (1914–1945), British SOE agent. Antoni Łomnicki (1881-1941), Polish mathematician. Adolf Reichwein (1898-1944), German educator. Hilde Coppi (1909-1943), German resistance fighter*

reduced to twelve years, and then he was released in 1951. He was charged in 1972 after more war crimes allegations became uncovered, but he was found unfit to stand trial and released.

Rolf-Heinz Hoeppner became a member of the SD in 1934 and was an SS-Obersturmbannführer in the Reich Security Main Office (RSHA). He was head of the Central Resettlement Office in Posen and responsible for the deportation of Jews and Poles and the settlement of ethnic Germans in Wartheland. He was extradited to Poland in 1947, but reports vary as to whether he was executed or released as part of an amnesty in 1957.

Dieter Wisliceny enlisted in the SS in 1934 and rose to SS-Hauptsturmführer (captain) by 1944. He took part in the ghettoisation and liquidation of many Jewish communities in Greece, Hungary and Slovakia. His testimony at Nuremberg proved important for Adolf Eichmann's trial in Israel in 1961. Wisliceny was extradited to to Czechoslovakia, where he was tried and hanged in 1948.

Walter Schellenberg was an SS-Brigadeführer (General) who rose through the ranks to become the head of foreign intelligence in 1944. In 1940, he compiled the Informationsheft G.B., a blueprint for the occupation of Britain, and also intercepted the Duke and Duchess of Windsor in Portugal in an attempt to persuade them to work for the German cause. In 1945, he as able to persuade Himmler to try negotiating with the Western Allies. To foster goodwill Schellenberg organised the transport of 1,700 Jews out of German controlled territory, but Hitler found out and put a stop to further evacuations. Sought after as a valuable intelligence asset by the Allies, Schellenberg was captured by the British in Denmark in June 1945, and he testified against the Nazis in the Nuremberg Trials. In the 1949 Ministries Trial, he was sentenced to six years imprisonment, but was released in 1951 on the grounds of ill-health and he died of cancer in 1952 in Turin.

Bob Carruthers

Statement of Criminality of Groups and Organisations

DIE GEHEIME STAATSPOLIZEI (SECRET STATE POLICE, COMMONLY KNOWN AS THE GESTAPO)

"Die Geheime Staatspolizei (Secret State Police, commonly known as the Gestapo)" referred to in the Indictment consists of the headquarters, departments, offices, branches and all the forces and personnel of the Geheime Staatspolizei organised or existing it any time after 30th January, 1933, including the Geheime Staatspolizei of Prussia and equivalent secret or political police forces of the Reich and the components thereof.

The Gestapo was created by the Nazi conspirators immediately after their accession to power, first in Prussia by the defendant Goering and shortly thereafter in all other States in the Reich. These separate secret and political police forces were developed into a centralised, uniform organisation operating through a central headquarters and through a network of regional offices in Germany and in occupied territories. Its officials and operatives were selected on the basis of unconditional acceptance of Nazi ideology, were largely drawn from members of the SS, and were trained in SS and SD schools. It acted to suppress and eliminate tendencies, groups and individuals deemed hostile or potentially hostile to the Nazi Party, its leaders, principles and objectives, and to repress resistance and potential resistance to German control in occupied territories. In performing these functions it operated free from legal control, taking any measures it deemed necessary for the accomplishment of its missions.

Through its purposes activities and the means it used, it participated in and is responsible for the commission of the crimes set forth in Counts One, Two, Three and Four of the Indictment.

The Indictment

THURSDAY, 20TH DECEMBER, 1945

COLONEL STOREY: If the Tribunal please, the next presentation will be the Gestapo, and it will take just a few seconds to get the material here.

We are now ready to proceed if your Honour is.

THE PRESIDENT: Yes.

COLONEL STOREY: We first pass to the Tribunal Document Books marked "Exhibit AA," Your Honour will notice they are in two volumes, and I will try each time to refer to the appropriate volume. They are separated into the D Documents, the L Documents, the PS Documents, etc.

The presentation of evidence on the criminality of the Geheime Staatspolizei (Gestapo) includes evidence on the criminality of the Sicherheitsdienst (S.D.) and of the Schutzstaffeln (S.S.), which has been discussed by Major Farr, because a great deal of the criminal acts were so inter-related. In the Indictment, as your Honour knows, the S.D. is included by special reference as a part of the S.S., since it originated as a part of the S.S. and always retained its character as a Party organisation, as distinguished from the Gestapo, which was a State organisation. As will be shown by the evidence, however, the Gestapo and the S.D. were brought into very close working relationship, the S.D. serving primarily as the information gathering agency and the Gestapo as the executive agency of the police system established by the Nazis for the purpose of combating the political and ideological enemies of the Nazi regime.

In short, I think we might think of the S.D. as the intelligence organisation and the Gestapo the executive agency, the former a Party organisation and the latter a State organisation, but merged together for all practical purposes.

The first subject: The Gestapo and S.D. were formed into a powerful, centralised political police system that served Party, State and Nazi leadership.

The Geheime Staatspolizei, or Gestapo, was first established in Prussia on 26th April, 1933, by the defendant Goering, with the mission of carrying out the duties of political police, with or in place of, the ordinary police authorities. The Gestapo was given the rank of a higher police authority and was subordinated only to the Minister of the Interior, to whom was delegated the responsibility of determining its functional and territorial jurisdiction. That fact is established in the "Preussische Gesetzsammlung," of 26th April, 1933, Page 122, and it is our Document 2104-PS.

Pursuant to this law, and on the same date, the Minister of the Interior issued a decree on the reorganisation of the Police, which established a State Police Bureau in each governmental district of Prussia subordinate to the Secret State Police Bureau in Berlin, and I cite as authority, the Ministerial-

Blatt for the Internal Administration of Prussia, 1933, Page 503, and it is Document 2371-PS.

Concerning the formation of the Gestapo, the defendant in "Aufbau einer Nation," 1934, Page 87, which is our Document 2344-PS-I quote from the English translation a short paragraph, of which your Honour will take judicial notice, unless you wish to turn to it in full-the defendant Goering said:

"For weeks I had been working personally on the reorganisation, and at last I alone and upon my own decision and my own reflection created the office of the Secret State Police. This instrument, which is so feared by the enemies of the State, has contributed most to the fact that to-day there can no longer be talk of a Communist or Marxist danger in Germany and Prussia."

THE PRESIDENT: What was the date?

COLONEL STOREY: The date? 1934, sir.

On 30th November, 1933, Goering issued a decree for the Prussian State Ministry and the Reich Chancellor, placing the Gestapo under his direct supervision as chief. The Gestapo was thereby established as an independent branch of the administration of the Interior, responsible directly to Goering as Prussian Prime Minister. This decree gave the Gestapo jurisdiction over the political police matters of the general and interior administration and provided that the district, county, and local police authorities were subject to its directives, and that cites the Prussian laws of 30th November, 1933, Page 413, and Document 2105-PS.

In a speech delivered at a meeting of the Prussian State Council on 18th June, 1934, which is published in "Speeches and Essays of Hermann Goering, 1939," Page 102, our Document 3343-PS, Goering said, and I quote one paragraph:

"The creation of the Secret State Police was also a necessity. You may recognise the importance attributed to this instrument of State security from the fact that the Prime Minister has made himself head of the department of the administration, because it is precisely the observation of all currents directed against the new State which is of fundamental importance."

By a decree of 8th March, 1934, the Regional State Police Offices were separated from their organisational connection with the District Government and established as independent authorities of the Gestapo. That cites the "Preussische Gesetzsammlung" of 8th March, 1943, Page 143, our Document 2113-PS.

I now offer in evidence Document 1680-PS, Exhibit USA 477. This is an article entitled "Ten Years Security and S.D.", published in the German Police Journal, the magazine of the Security Police and S.D., of 1st February, 1943. I quote one paragraph from this article on Page 2 of the English translation, Document 1680, which is the third main paragraph:

"Parallel to that development in Prussia, the Reichsfuehrer S.S. Heinrich Himmler, created in Bavaria the Bavarian Political Police, and also suggested and directed in the other Federal States outside Prussia the establishment of political police. The unification of the political police of all the Federal States took place in the spring of 1934 when Minister President Hermann Goering appointed Reichsfuehrer S.S. Heinrich Himmler, who had meanwhile become Commander of the Political Police of all the Federal States outside Prussia, to the post of Deputy Chief of the Prussian Secret State Police."

The Prussian law about the Secret State Police, dated 10th February, 1936, then summed up the development to that date and determined the position and responsibilities of the Secret State Police in the executive regulations issued the same day.

On 10th February, 1936, the basic law for the Gestapo was promulgated by Goering as Prussian Prime Minister. I refer to Document 2107-PS. This law provided that the Secret State Police had the duty of investigating and combating, in the entire territory of the State, all tendencies inimical to the State, and declared that orders and matters of the Secret State Police were not subject to the review of the administrative courts. That is the Prussian State law of that date, cited on Pages 21-22 of the publication of the laws of 1936.

Also on that same date, 10th February, 1936, a decree for the execution of the law was issued by Goering, as Prussian Prime Minister, and by Frick, as Minister of the Interior. This decree provided that the Gestapo had authority to enact measures valid in the entire area of the State and measures affecting that area-by the way, that is found in 2108-PS and is also a published law-that it was the centralised agency for collecting political intelligence in the field of political police, and that it administered the concentration camps. The Gestapo was given authority to make police investigations in cases of criminal attacks upon the Party as well as upon the State.

Later, on 28th August, 1936, a circular of the Reichsfuehrer S.S. and Chief of the German Police provided that as on 1st October, 1936, the Political Police Forces of the German provinces were to be called the "Geheime Staatspolizei". That means the Secret State Police. The regional offices were still to be described as State Police.

The translation of that law is in Document 2372-PS, Reichsministerial-Gesetzblatt of 1936, No. 44, Page 1344.

Later, on 20th September, 1936, a circular of the Minister of the Interior, Frick, commissioned the Gestapo Bureau in Berlin with the supervision of the duties of the Political Police Commanders in all the States of Germany. That is, Reichsministerial-Gesetzblatt, 1936, Page 1,343, our Document L-297.

The law regulating and relating to financial measures in connection with the police, of igth March, 1937, provided that the officials of the Gestapo were to be considered direct officials of the Reich, and that their salaries, in addition to the operational expenses of the whole State Police, were to be borne from 1st April, 1937, by the Reich. That is shown in Document 2243-PS, which is a copy of the law of 19th March, 1937, Page 325.

Hermann Goering appointing Heinrich Himmler as head of the Gestapo, April 1934.

Thus, through the above laws and decrees, the Gestapo was established as a uniform political police system operating throughout the land and serving Party, State, and Nazi leadership.

In the course of the development of the S.D., it came into increasingly close co-operation with the Gestapo and also with the "Reichskriminalpolizei", the Criminal Police, known as Kripo, shown up there under A.M.T. V. The S.D. was called upon to furnish information to various State authorities. On

11th November, 1938, a decree of the Reich Minister of the Interior declared the S.D. to be the intelligence organisation for the State as well as for the Party, to have the particular duty of supporting the Secret State Police, and to become thereby active on a national mission. These duties necessitated a closer co-operation between the S.D. and the authorities for the general and interior administration. That law is translated in Document 1638-PS.

The Tribunal has already received evidence concerning the decrees of 17th and 26th June, 1936, under which Himmler was appointed Chief of the German Police, and by which Heydrich became the first Chief of the Security Police and S.D. Even then Goering did not relinquish his position as Chief of the Prussian Gestapo. Thus, the decree of the Reichsfuehrer S.S. and Chief of German Police which was issued on 28th August, 1936, which is our Document 2372-PS, was distributed "to the Prussian Minister President as Chief of the Prussian Secret State Police", that is, to Goering.

On 27th September, 1939, by order of Himmler in his capacity as Reichsfuehrer S.S. and Chief of the German Police, the Central Offices of the Gestapo and S.D., and also of the Criminal Police, were merged in the office of the Chief of the Security Police and S.D. under the name of R.S.H.A., which your Honour has heard described by Major Farr. Under this order the personnel and administrative sections of each agency were co-ordinated in Amt. I and II of the chart shown here, of the R.S.H.A. The operational sections of the S.D. became Amt. Ill, shown in the box Amt. III, except for foreign intelligence which was placed over in Amt. VI. The operational sections of the Gestapo became Amt. IV, as shown on the chart, and the operational sections of the Kripo, that is, the Criminal Police, became Amt. V, as shown on the chart.

Ohlendorf was named the Chief of Amt. Ill, the S.D. inside Germany; Mueller was named Chief of Amt. IV, and Nebe was named Chief of Amt. V, the Kripo.

On 27th September, 1939, Heydrich, the Chief of the Security Police and S.D., issued a directive pursuant to the order of Himmler in which he ordered that the designation and heading of R.S.H.A. was to be used exclusively in internal relations of the Reich Ministry of the Interior, and the heading "The Chief of the Security Police and S.D." in transactions with outside persons and offices. The directive provided that the Gestapo would continue to use the designation and heading "Secret State Police" according to the particular instructions.

This order is Document L-361, Exhibit USA 478, which we now offer in evidence, and refer your Honour to the first paragraph L-361. That is found in the first volume. I just direct your Honour's attention to the date and to the subject, which is the amalgamation of the "Zentral Amter" of the Sicherheitspolizei and the S.D., and the creation of the four sections, and then to the words will be joined to the R.S.H.A. in accordance with the following directives. This amalgamation carries with it no change in the position of the 'Amter' in the Party nor in their local administration.

I might say here parenthetically, if the Tribunal please, that we like to think of the R.S.H.A. as being the so-called administrative office through which a great many of these organisations were administered, and then a number of these organisations, including the Gestapo, maintaining their separate identity as an operational organisation. I think a good illustration, if your Honour will recall, is that during the war there may be a certain division or a certain air force which is administratively under a certain headquarters, but operationally, when they had an invasion, may be under the general supervision of somebody else who was operating a task force. So the R.S.H.A. was really the administrative office of a great many of these alleged criminal organisations.

The Gestapo and the S.D. were therefore organised functionally on the basis of the opponents to be combated and the matters to be investigated.

I now invite the attention of the Tribunal to this chart which has already been identified, and I believe it is Exhibit 53. This chart - I am in error; that is the original identification number. This chart shows the main chain of command from Himmler, who was the Reich Leader of the S.S. and Chief of the German Police, to Kaltenbrunner, who was Chief of the Security Police and S.D., and from Kaltenbrunner to the various field offices of the Gestapo and the S.D.

We now formally offer in evidence this chart, Document L-219, as Exhibit USA 479.

This chart, from which the one on the wall is taken, has been certified by Otto Ohlendorf, Chief of Amt III of the R.S.H.A., and by Walter Schellenberg, Chief of Amt VI of the R.S.H.A., and has been officially identified by both of those former officials.

The chart shows that the principal flow of command in police matters came from Himmler as Reich Leader of the S.S. and Chief of the German Police directly to Kaltenbrunner, who was Chief of the Security Police and S.D., and as such was also head of the R.S.H.A., which is the administrative office to which I have referred.

Kaltenbrunner's headquarters organisation was composed of seven Amter, plus a military office; the seven Amter shown here.

Under subsection D was Obersturmbannfuehrer Rauff, who handled technical matters, including motor vehicles of the Sipo and the S.D., to which we will refer later.

Amt III was the S.D. inside Germany and was charged with investigations into spheres of German national life. It was the Internal Intelligence Organisation of the police system and its interests extended into all areas occupied by Germany during the course of the war. In 1943 it contained four sections. I would like to mention them briefly. It shows their scope of authority.

Section A dealt with questions of legal order and structure of the Reich.

Section B dealt with nationality, including minorities, race, and health of the people.

(Left to right) Ernst Kaltenbrunner, Heinrich Himmler and Franz Ziereis at Mauthausen Concentration Camp, April 1941.

Section C dealt with culture, including science, education, religion, Press, folk culture, and art.

Section D dealt with economics, including food, commerce, finance, industry, labour, colonial economics, and occupied regions.

Now, Amt IV, with which we are dealing here, was the Gestapo, and was charged with combating opposition. In 1945, as identified by these two former officials, it contained six subsections.

1. Subsection A dealt with opponents, sabotage, and protective service, including Communism, Marxism, Reaction and Liberalism.

2. Subsection B dealt with political churches, sects and Jews, including political Catholicism, political Protestantism, other Churches, Freemasonry, and a special section, B-4, that had to do with Jewish affairs, matters of evacuation, means of suppressing enemies of the people and State, and dispossession of rights of German citizenship. The head of this office was Eichmann.

3. Subsection C dealt with protective custody.

4. Subsection D dealt with regions under German domination.

5. Subsection E dealt with security.

6. Subsection F dealt with passport matters and alien police.

Now, Amt V, which will be referred to as the Kripo was charged with combating crime. For example, Subsection D was the criminological institute for the: Sipo and handled matters of identification, chemical and biological investigations, and technical research.

Amt VI was the S.D. outside Germany and was concerned primarily with foreign political intelligence. In 1944, the "Abwehr," or Military Intelligence, was joined with Amt VI as military "Amt." Your Honour will recall that the witness Lahousen was in the "Abwehr." Amt VI maintained its own regional organisation.

And finally, Amt VII handled ideological research among enemies such as Freemasonry, Judaism, Political Churches, Marxism and Liberalism.

Within Germany there were regional offices of the S.D., the Gestapo, and the Kripo, shown on the chart at the right. The Gestapo and Kripo offices were often located in the same place and were always collectively referred to as the Sipo. You see that shaded line around the Secret Police, and kripo the Criminal Police. These regional offices all maintained their separate identity and reported directly to the section of the R.S.H.A., that is, under Kaltenbrunner, which had the jurisdiction of the subject matter. They were, however, co-ordinated by Inspectors of the Security Police and S.D., as shown at the top of the chart. The Inspectors were also under the supervision of Higher S.S. and Police Leaders appointed for each "Wehrkreis." The Higher S.S. and Police Leaders reported to Himmler and supervised not only the Inspectors of the Security Police and S.D., but also the Inspectors of the Order Police and various sub-divisions of the S.S.

In the occupied territories, the organisation developed as the German armies advanced. Combined operational units of the Security Police and the S.D., known as Einsatz Groups, about which your Honour will hear in a few minutes, operated with and in the rear of the army. These groups were officered by personnel of the Gestapo, Kripo and the S.D., and the enlisted men were composed of Order Police and "Waffen S.S." They functioned with various Army groups.. The Einsatz Groups - and, if your Honour will recall, they are simply task force groups for special projects - were divided into "Einsatzkommandos," "Sonderkommandos," and "Teilkommandos," all of which performed the functions of the Security Police and the S.D., with or closely behind the Army.

After the occupied territories had been consolidated, these Einsatz Groups and their subordinate parts were formed into permanent combined offices of the Security Police and S.D. within the particular geographical location. These combined forces were placed under the Kommandeurs of the Security Police and S.D., and the offices were organised in sections similar to this R.S.H.A. headquarters. The Kommandeurs of the Security Police and S.D. reported directly to Befehlshaber of the Security Police and S.D. who in turn reported directly to the Chief of the Security Police and S.D.

In the occupied countries, the Higher S.S. and Police Leaders were more directly controlled by the Befehlshabers and the Kommandeurs of the Security Police and S.D. than within the Reich. They had authority to issue direct orders so long as they did not conflict with the Chief of the Security Police and S.D. who exercised controlling authority.

The above chart and the remarks concerning it are based upon two documents which I now offer in evidence. They are Document L-219, which is the organisation plan of the R.S.H.A. of 1st October, 1943, and document 2346-PS, which is Exhibit USA 480.

Now the primary mission of the Gestapo and the S.D. was to combat the actual and ideological enemies of the Nazi regime and to keep Hitler and the Nazi leadership in power as specified in Count 1 of the Indictment. The tasks and methods of the Secret State Police were well described in an article which is translated in Document 1956-PS, Volume 2 of the document book, which is an article published in January, 1936, in Das Archiv, at Page 1342, which I now offer in evidence and quote from. It is on Page 1 of the English translation, 1956. I will first read the first paragraph and then the third and fourth paragraphs. That is in January 1936:

"In order to refute the malicious rumours spread abroad, the Voelkischer Beobachter published on 22nd January, 1936, an article on the origin, meaning and tasks of the Secret Police; extracts from this read as follows:"

Now passing to the third paragraph:

"The Secret State Police is an official machine on the lines of the Criminal Police, whose special task is the prosecution of crimes and offences against the State, above all the prosecution of high treason and treason. The task of the Secret State Police is to detect these crimes and offences, to ascertain the perpetrators and to bring them to judicial punishment. The number of criminal proceedings continually pending in the People's Court on account of high treasonable actions and of treason is the result of this work. The next most important field of operations for the Secret State Police is the preventive combating of all dangers threatening the State and the leadership of the State. As, since the National Socialist Revolution, all open struggle and all open opposition to the State and to the leadership of the State is forbidden, a Secret State Police as a preventive instrument in the struggle against all dangers threatening the State is indissolubly bound up with the National Socialist Leader State. The opponents of National Socialism were not removed by the prohibition of their organisations and their newspapers, but have withdrawn to other forms of struggle against the State. Therefore, the National Socialist State has to trace out, to watch over and to render harmless the underground opponents fighting against it in illegal organisations, in camouflaged associations, in the coalitions of well-meaning fellow Germans and even in the organisations of Party and State before they have succeeded in actually executing an action directed against the interest of the State. This task of fighting with all means the secret enemies of the State will be spared no Leader State, because powers hostile to the State from their foreign headquarters, always make use of some persons in such a State and employ them in underground activity against the State.

The preventive activity of the Secret State Police consists primarily in the thorough observation of all enemies of the State in the Reich

Territory. As the Secret State Police cannot carry out, in addition to its primary executive tasks, this observation of the enemies of the State, to the extent necessary, there marches by its side, to supplement it, the Security Service of the Reichsfuehrer of the S.S., set up by his deputy as the Political Intelligence Service of the movement, which puts a large part of the forces of the movement mobilised by it into the service of the security of the State.

The Secret State Police takes the necessary police preventive measures against the enemies of the State on the basis of the results of the observation. The most effective preventive measure is, without doubt, the withdrawal of freedom, which is covered in the form of protective custody, if it is to be feared that the free activity of the persons in question might endanger the security of the State in any way. The employment of protective custody is so organised by directions of the Reich and Prussian Minister of the Interior and by a special arrest procedure of the Secret State Police that, as far as the preventive fight against the enemies of the State permits, continuous guarantees against the mis-use of the protective custody are also provided."

THE PRESIDENT: Have we not really got enough now as to the organisation of the Gestapo and its Objective?

COLONEL STOREY: Your Honour, I had finished with the organisation. I was just going into the question of the action of protective custody, for which the Gestapo was famous, and showing how they went into that field of activity and the authority for taking people into protective custody - alleged protective custody.

THE PRESIDENT: I think that has been proved more than once in the preceding evidence that we have heard.

COLONEL STOREY: There is one more law I would like to refer to, to the effect that that action is not subject to judicial review, ... unless that has already been established. I do not know whether Major Farr did that, or not.

THE PRESIDENT: They are not subject to judicial review?

COLONEL STOREY: Review, yes.

THE PRESIDENT: I think you have told us that already this afternoon.

COLONEL STOREY: The citation is in the Reichsgesetzblatt of 1935 Page 577, which is Document 2347-PS.

I would like, if your Honour pleases, to refer to this quotation from that law.

The decision of the Prussian High Court of Administration on 2nd May, 1935, held that the status of the Gestapo as a special Police authority removed its orders from the jurisdiction of the administrative tribunal, and the Court said in that law that the only redress available was by appeal to the next higher authority within the Gestapo itself.

THE PRESIDENT: I think you told us that, apropos of the document of 10th February, 1936, where you said the Secret State Police was not subject to review by any of the State Courts.

COLONEL STOREY: I just did not want there to be any question about the authority. I refer your Honour to Document 1825-B-PS, which is already in evidence as Exhibit USA 449, also stating that theory, and also Document 1723-PS, and that is the decree, your Honour, of 1st February, 1938, which relates to the protective custody and the issuance of new regulations, and I would like to quote just one sentence from that law - "as a coercive measure of the Secret State Police against persons who endanger the security of the people and the State through their attitude, in order to counter all aspirations of the enemies of the people and the State". The Gestapo had the exclusive right to order protective custody and that protective custody was to be executed in the State concentration camps.

Now, I pass to another phase where the S.D. created an organisation of agents and informers who operated through the various regional offices throughout the Reich and later in conjunction with the Gestapo and the Criminal Police throughout the occupied countries. The S.D. operated secretly. One of the things it did was to mark ballots secretly in order to discover the identity of persons who cast "No" and "invalid" votes in the referendum. I now offer in evidence Document R-142, second volume. I believe it is toward the end of Document R-142, Exhibit USA 481.

This document contains a letter from the branch office of the S.D. at Kochem to the S.D. at Koblenz. The letter is dated 7th May, 1938, and refers to the plebiscite of 10th April, 1938. It refers to a letter previously received from the Koblenz office and apparently is a reply to a request for information concerning the way in which people voted in the supposedly secret plebiscite. It is on Page 1 of Document R-142.

THE PRESIDENT: Colonel Storey, I am told that that has been read before.

COLONEL STOREY: I did not know it had, if your Honour pleases. We will then just offer it without reading it.

With reference to National Socialism and the contribution of the Sipo and the S.D., I refer to an article of 7th September, 1942, which is shown in Document 3344-PS. It is the first paragraph, Volume 2. It is the official journal. Quoting:

"Even before the taking over of power, the S.D. had added its part to the success of the National Socialist Revolution. After the taking over of power, the Security Police and the S.D. have borne the responsibility for the inner security of the Reich, and have paved the way for a powerful fulfilment of National Socialism against all resistance."

In connection with the criminal responsibility of the S.D. and the Gestapo, it will be considered with respect to certain War Crimes and Crimes Against Humanity, which were in the principal part committed by the centralised political police system. The development, organisation and tasks have been considered before. In some instances the crimes were committed in co-operation or in conjunction with other groups or organisations.

Now, in order to look into the strength of these various organisations, I have some figures here that I would like to quote to your Honour. The Sipo and S.D. were composed of the Gestapo, Kripo and S.D. The Gestapo was the largest, and it had a membership of about 40,000 to 50,000 in 1934 and 1935. That is an error; it is 1943 to 1945. It was the political force of the Reich.

THE PRESIDENT: Did you say the date was wrong?

COLONEL STOREY: Yes, it is '43 to '45.

THE PRESIDENT: Very well.

THE TRIBUNAL (MR. BIDDLE): Where are you reading from?

COLONEL STOREY: Document 3033-PS, and it is an affidavit of Walter Schellenberg, one of the former officials I referred to a moment ago.

I think, if your Honour pleases, in order to get it in the record, I will read the whole affidavit. Document 3033-PS, Exhibit USA 488:

> "The Sipo and S.D. were composed of the Gestapo, Kripo and S.D. In 1943-45 the Gestapo had a membership of about 40,000 to 50,000; the Kripo had a membership of about 15,000 and the S.D. had a membership of about 3,000. In common usage, and even in orders and decrees, the term 'S.D.' was used as an abbreviation for the term 'Sipo' and 'S.D.' In most cases actual executive action was carried out by personnel of the Gestapo rather than of the S.D. or the Kripo. In occupied territories, members of the Gestapo frequently wore S.S. uniforms with S.D. insignia. New members of the Gestapo and the S.D. were taken on a voluntary basis. This has been stated and sworn to by me today the 21st November, 1945." And then, "Subscribed and sworn to before Lt. Harris, 21st November, 1945."

I think I ought to say here, if your Honour pleases, that it is our information that a great many of the members of the Gestapo were also members of the S.S. We have heard various estimates of the numbers, but have no direct authority. Some authorities say as much as 75 per cent, but still we have no direct evidence on that.

I now offer in evidence Document 2751-PS, which is Exhibit USA 482. It is an affidavit of Alfred Helmut Naujocks, dated 20th November, 1945. This affidavit particularly refers to the actual occurrences in connection with the Polish Border incident. I believe it was referred to by the witness Lahousen when he was on the stand.

> "I, Alfred Helmut Naujocks, being first duly sworn, depose and state as follows:
>
> 1. I was a member of the S.S. from 1931 to 19th October, 1944, and a member of the S.D. from its creation in 1934 to January, 1941. I served as a member of the 'Waffen S.S.' from February, 1941, until the middle of 1942. Thereafter, I served in the Economic Department of the Military Administration of Belgium from September, 1942 to September, 1944. I surrendered to the Allies on 19th October, 1944,
>
> 2. On or about 10th August, 1939, the Chief of the Sipo and S.D. Heydrich, personally ordered me to simulate an attack on the radio

station near Gleiwitz, near the Polish border, and to make it appear that the attacking force consisted of Poles. Heydrich said, 'Practical proof is needed for these attacks of the Poles for the foreign Press, as well as for German propaganda purposes.' I was directed to go to Gleiwitz with five or six other S.D. men and wait there until I received a code word from Heydrich indicating that the attack should take place. My instructions were to seize the radio station and to hold it long enough to permit a Polish-speaking German, who would be put at my disposal, to broadcast a speech in Polish. Heydrich told me that this speech should state that the time had come for the conflict between Germans and Poles, and that the Poles should get together and smash down any Germans from whom they met resistance. Heydrich also told me at this time that he expected an attack on Poland by Germany in a few days.

3. I went to Gleiwitz and waited there 14 days. Then I requested permission from Heydrich to return to Berlin, but was told to stay in Gleiwitz. Between 25th and 31st August, I went to see Heinrich Mueller, head of the Gestapo, who was then nearby at Oppeln. In my presence Mueller discussed with a man named Mohlhorn plans for another border incident, in which it should be made to appear that Polish soldiers were attacking German troops. Germans in the approximate strength of a company were to be used. Mueller stated that he had 12 or 13 condemned criminals who were to be dressed in Polish uniforms and left dead on the ground of the scene of the incident, to show that they had been killed while attacking. For this purpose they were to be given fatal injections by a doctor employed by Heydrich. Then they were also to be given gunshot wounds. After the incident, members of the Press and other persons were to be taken to the scene of the incident. A police report was subsequently to be prepared.

4. Mueller told me that he had an order from Heydrich to make one of those criminals available to me for the action at Gleiwitz. The code name by which he referred to these criminals was 'Canned goods'.

5. The incident at Gleiwitz in which I participated was carried out on the evening preceding the German attack on Poland. As I recall, war broke out on 1st September, 1939. At noon on 31st August, I received by telephone from Heydrich the code word for the attack which was to take place at 8 o'clock that evening. Heydrich said, 'In order to carry out this attack, report to Mueller for Canned Goods.' I did this and gave Mueller instructions to deliver the man near the radio station. I received this man and had him laid down at the entrance to the station. He was alive but he was completely unconscious. I tried to open his eyes. I could not recognise by his eyes that he was alive, only by his breathing. I did not see the shot wounds but a lot of blood was smeared across his face. He was in civilian clothes.

6. We seized the radio station as ordered, broadcast a speech of three to four minutes over an emergency transmitter, fired some pistol shots and left."

And that was sworn to and subscribed before Lt. Martin.

The Gestapo and the S.D. carried out mass murders of hundreds of thousands of civilians of occupied countries as a part of the Nazi programme to exterminate political and racial undesirables, by the so-called Einsatz Groups. Your Honour will recall evidence concerning the activity of these Einsatz Groups or Einsatzkommandos. I now refer to Document R-102.

If your Honour pleases, I understand Major Farr introduced this document this morning, but I want to refer to just one brief statement which he did not include, concerning the S.D. and the Einsatz Groups and Security Police. It is on Page 4 of R-102.: Quoting:

"During the period covered by this report the stations of the Einsatz Groups of the Security Police and the S.D. have changed only in the Northern Sector."

THE PRESIDENT: What was the document?

COLONEL STOREY: R-102, which is already introduced in evidence by Major Farr, and it is in Volume 2 toward the end of the book.

THE PRESIDENT: I have a document here. Page 4, is it?

COLONEL STOREY: Page 4, Yes, Sir. There are two reports submitted by the Chief of the Einsatz Group A available. The first report is Document L-180, which has already been received as Exhibit USA 276.

THE PRESIDENT: Colonel Storey, will you not pass quite so fast from one document to another?

COLONEL STOREY: Yes, Sir, pardon me, Sir. L-180, and I want to quote from Page 13. It is on Page 5 of the English translation. It is the beginning of the first paragraph, near the bottom of the page. Quoting:

"In view of the extension of the area of operations and of the great number of duties which had to be performed by the Security Police, it was intended from the very beginning to obtain the co-operation of the reliable population for the fight against vermin; that is, mainly the Jews and Communists."

And also in that same document, Page 30 of the original, Page 8 of the English translation. Quoting:

"From the beginning it was to be expected that the Jewish problem could not be solved by pogroms alone."

THE PRESIDENT: I am told that that has been read already.

COLONEL STOREY: I had it checked, and we did not find that it had, your Honour. I will pass on them.

Now, if your Honour pleases, we will pass to Document 2273-PS next. I offer in evidence now just portions of Document 2273-PS, which is Exhibit USA 487. This document was captured by the U.S.S.R. and will be offered in detail by our Soviet colleagues later. But with their consent, I want to introduce in evidence a chart which is identified by that document, and we have an enlargement which we would like to put on the board, and we will pass to the Tribunal photostatic copies.

If your Honour pleases, this chart is identified by the photostatic copy attached to the original report which will be dealt with in detail later. I want to quote just one statement from Page 2 of the English translation of that document. It is the third paragraph from the bottom on Page 2 of the English translation:

> "The Esthonian self-protection movement formed as the Germans advanced and began to arrest Jews, but there were no spontaneous pogroms. Only by the Security Police and the S.D. were the Jews gradually executed as they became no longer required for work. Today there are no longer any Jews in Estonia."

That document is a top secret document by Einsatz Group A, which was a special projects group. This chart, of which the photostatic copy is attached to the original in the German translation on the wall, shows the progress of the extermination of the Jews in the area in which this Einsatz Kommando Group operated.

If your Honour will refer to the top, next to St. Petersburg, or Leningrad as we know it, you will see down below the picture of a coffin, and that is described in the report as 3,600 having been killed.

Next over, at the left, is another coffin in one of the small Baltic States, showing that 963 in that area have been put in the coffin.

Then next, down near Riga, you will note that 35,238 were put away in the coffins, and it refers to the ghetto there as still having 2,500.

You come down to the next square or the next State showing 136,421 were put in their coffins, and then in the next area near Minsk, and just above it there were 41,828 put in their coffins.

THE PRESIDENT: Are you sure that they were executed, the 136,000, because there is no coffin there.

COLONEL STOREY: Here are the totals from the documents.

THE PRESIDENT: These photostatic copies are different from what you have there. In the area which is marked 136,421 there is no coffin.

COLONEL STOREY: Well, I am sorry. The one that I have is a true and correct copy.

THE PRESIDENT: Mine has not got it and Mr. Biddle's has not got it.

COLONEL STOREY: Will you hand this to the President, please?

THE PRESIDENT: I suppose the document itself will show it.

COLONEL STOREY: I will turn to the original and verify it. Apparently there is a typographical error. If your Honour pleases, here it is, 136,421, with the coffin.

THE PRESIDENT: Mr. Parker points out it is in the document itself too.

COLONEL STOREY: Yes, sir, it is in the document itself. There is an error on that.

The 128,000 at the bottom shows that at that time there were 128,000 on hand; and the literal translation of the statement, as I understand, means "Still on hand in the Minsk area."

I next refer to Document 1104-PS, Volume 2, Exhibit USA 483, which I now offer in evidence.

THE PRESIDENT: Colonel Storey, did you tell us what the document was? There is nothing on the translation to show what the document is.

COLONEL STOREY: If your Honour pleases, it is a report of the special purpose Group A, or the Einsatz Group A, a top secret report, in other words, making a record of their activities in these areas, and this chart was attached showing the areas covered.

THE PRESIDENT: Special group of the Gestapo?

COLONEL STOREY: The special group that was organised of the Gestapo and the S.D. in that area. In other words, a Commando Group.

As I mentioned, your Honour, they organised these special commando groups to work with and behind the armies as they consolidated their gains in occupied territories, and your Honour will hear from other reports of these "Einsatz" groups as we go along in this presentation. In other words, "Einsatz" means special action or action groups, and they were organised to cover certain geographical areas behind the immediate front lines.

THE PRESIDENT: Yes, but they were groups, were they, of the Gestapo?

COLONEL STOREY: The Gestapo and the S.D.

THE PRESIDENT: Well, that is part of the Gestapo.

COLONEL STOREY: There were some of the Kripo in it, too.

Now, the next document is 1104-PS, dated 30th October, 1941. This document shows on that date the Commissioner of the territory of Sluzk wrote a report to the Commissioner of Minsk, in which he severely criticised the actions of the Einsatz Commandos of the Sipo and the S.D. operating in his area for the murder of the Jewish population of that area, and I quote the English translation, on Page 4 of that document beginning at the first paragraph:

> "On 27th October in the morning, at about 8 o'clock a first lieutenant of the Police Battalion No. 11, from Kauen (Lithuania) appeared and introduced himself as the adjutant of the Battalion Commander of the Security Police. The first lieutenant explained that the Police Battalion had received the assignment to effect the liquidation of all Jews here in the town of Sluzk within two days. The Battalion Commander, with his battalion in strength of four companies, two of which were made up of Lithuanian partisans, was on the march here and the action would have to begin instantly. I replied to the first lieutenant that I had to discuss the action in any case first with the Commander. About half an hour later the Police Battalion arrived in Sluzk. Immediately after the arrival, a conference with the Battalion Commander took place according to my request. I first explained to the Commander that it would not very well be possible to effect the action without previous preparation, because everybody had been sent to work and it would lead to a terrible

confusion. At least it would have been his duty to inform me a day ahead of time. Then I requested him to postpone the action one day. However, he rejected this with the remark that he had to carry out this action everywhere and in all two days, the town of Sluzk had to be cleared of Jews by all means."

That report was made to the Reich Commissioner for the Eastern Territories through Gauleiter Heinrich Lusch at Riga. Your Honour will recall that he was referred to in another presentation.

Now, skipping over to Page 5. The first paragraph, I would like to quote it:
"For the rest, as regards the execution of the action, I must point out to my deepest regret that the matter bordered on sadism. The town itself offered a picture of horror during the action. With indescribable brutality on the part of both the German Police officers, and particularly the Lithuanian partisans, not only the Jewish people, but also White Ruthenians, were taken out of their dwellings and herded together. Everywhere in the town shots were to be heard, and in different streets the corpses of shot Jews accumulated. The White Ruthenians were in the greatest distress to free themselves from the encirclement. Regardless of the fact that the Jewish people, among whom were also tradesmen were mistreated in a terribly barbarous way, in front of the White Ruthenian people, the White Ruthenians themselves were also worked over with rubber clubs and rifle butts. There was no question of an action against the Jews any more. It rather looked like a revolution."

And then I skip down to the next to the last paragraph on that same page; quoting:
"In conclusion, I find myself obliged to point out that the Police Battalion has looted in an unheard of manner during the action, and that not only in Jewish houses but just the same in those of the White Ruthenians, anything of use such as boots, leather, cloth, gold and other valuables, has been taken away. On the basis of statements of members of the Armed Forces, watches were torn off the arms of Jews in public, on the street, and rings were pulled off the fingers in the most brutal manner. A major of the Finance Department reported that a Jewish girl was asked by the police to obtain immediately 5,000 roubles to have her father released. This girl is said to have actually gone everywhere in order to obtain the money."

There is another paragraph with reference to the number of copies - on the third page of the translation - to which I would like to call your Honour's attention. The last paragraph on Page 3 of the translation, quoting:
"I am submitting this report in duplicate so that one copy may be forwarded to the Reich Minister. Peace and order cannot be maintained in White Ruthenia with methods of that sort. To bury seriously wounded people alive who worked their way out of their graves again, is such a base and filthy act that the incident as such, should be reported to the Fuehrer and Reich Marshal.

The civil administration of White Ruthenia makes very strenuous efforts to win the population over to Germany, in accordance with the instructions of the Fuehrer. These efforts cannot be brought in harmony with the methods described herein."

Signed by the Commissioner General for White Ruthenia.

And then on 11th November, 1941, he forwarded it on to the Reich Minister for Occupied Countries, in Berlin.

THE PRESIDENT: Who was that at that time?

COLONEL STOREY: The Reich Commissionere (I believe it was shown for the Easter occupied country) was the defendant Rosenberg. I think that is correct. On the same date by separate letter the Commissioner General of White Ruthenia reported to the Reich Commissioner for the Eastern Territories that he had received money, valuables, and other objects taken by the police in the action at Sluzk, and other regions, all of which had been deposited with the Reich Credit Institute, for the disposal of the Reich Commissioner.

On 21st November, 1941, a report on the Sluzk incident was sent to the personal reviewer of the permanent deputy of the Minister of the Reich with a copy to Heydrich, who was the Chief of the Security Police and the S.D. That is shown on the first page of Document 1104.

The activities of the Einsatz Groups continued throughout 1943 and 1944 under Kaltenbrunner as Chief of the Security Police and S.D. Under adverse war conditions, however, the programme of extermination was to a large extent changed to one of rounding up slave labour for Germany.

I next refer to Document 3012-PS, which has heretofore been introduced as Exhibit USA igo. This is a letter from the headquarters of one of the Commando Groups, a section known as Einsatz Group C, dated 19th March, 1943. This letter summarises the real activities and methods of the Gestapo and S.D., and I should like to refer to additional portions of the letter, to those previously quoted on Page 2, of Document 3012-PS, and I think I will read the first page beginning with the first paragraph:

"It is the task of the Security Police and of the Security Service (S.D.) to discover all enemies of the Reich, and to fight them in the interest of security and, in the zone of operations, especially to guarantee the security of the Army. Besides the annihilation of active opponents all other elements who by virtue of their convictions or their past may prove to be active enemies, favourable circumstances provided, are to be eliminated through preventive measures. The Security Police carries out this task according to the general directives of the Fuehrer, with all of the required toughness. Energetic measures are especially necessary in territories endangered by the activity of hostile gangs.

The competence of the Security Police within the zone of operations is based on the 'Barbarossa' decrees."

The Tribunal will recall the famous "Barbarossa" code, namely, the decrees that were issued in connection with the invasion of Russia:

"I deem the measures of the Security Police carried out on a considerable scale during recent times necessary for the two following reasons:

1. The situation at the front in my sector had become so serious, with the population partly influenced by Hungarians and Italians who streamed back in chaotic condition and took, openly, positions against us.

2. The strong expeditions by hostile gangs who came especially from the Forest of Bryansk were another reason. Besides that, other partisan groups formed by the population appeared suddenly in all districts. The providing of arms was evidently no difficulty at all. It would have been irresponsible if we had observed this whole activity without acting against it. It is obvious that all such measures necessitate some harshness."

I want to take up the significant point of the harsh measures.

1. Shooting of Hungarian Jews
2. Shooting of Agronoms.
3. Shooting of children.
4. Total burning down of villages.
5. "Shooting" - I quote -"while trying to escape", of Security Service (S.D.) prisoners.

"Chief of Einsatz group C confirmed once more the correctness of the measures taken, and expressed his recognition of the energetic action. With regard to the current political situation, especially in the armament industry in the Fatherland, the measures of the Security Police have to be subordinated to the greatest extent to the recruiting of labour for Germany. In the shortest possible time the Ukraine has to put at the disposal of the armament industry 1,000,000 workers, Some of whom have to be sent from the territory daily."

Your Honour, please, I believe the numbers have been quoted before by Mr. Dodd. I refer on the next page, to the first order in sub-paragraphs 1 and 2:

"1. Special treatment is to be limited to the minimum.

2. Communist functionaries, agitators, and so on, will only be listed for the time being, without being arrested. It is, for instance, no longer feasible to arrest all the close relatives of a member of the Communist Party. Also members of the Konisomolz are to be arrested only if they occupied leading positions."

The next paragraphs have been read into evidence, 3 and 4, in a previous presentation. I will read:

"No. 5. The reporting of hostile gangs, as well as drives against them, is not affected hereby. All drives against those hostile gangs can take place only after my approval has been obtained. The prisons have to be kept empty as a rule, and we have to be aware of the fact that the Slavs will interpret the soft treatment on our part as weakness, and that they will act accordingly right away. If we limit our harsh measures of the Security Police through the above orders for the time being, that is only done for the reason that the most important thing is the recruiting of workers. No check of persons to be sent into the Reich will be made. No written certificates of political reliability check, or similar things, will be issued. Signed by Christensen, S.S. Sturmbannfuehrer and commanding officer."

I understood that your Honour wanted to adjourn at four o'clock, and I believe that I can introduce one more statement. It was the Einsatz Groups of the Security Police and S.D. that operated the infamous death vans. Document 501-PS, which was received as Exhibit USA 288, has previously referred to this operation. The letter from Becker, which is a part of this exhibit, was addressed to Obersturmbannfuehrer Rauff at Berlin. We now refer to Document L-185. I simply refer to Document 501-PS as a reference to the death vans. The Document L-185, Exhibit USA 484, is the one I am now offering in evidence, Page 7 of the English translation, L-185. It will be observed that the Chief of Amt. II D of the R.S.H.A. in charge of technical matters was Obersturmbahnfuehrer Rauff. Mr. Harris advises me that the only point to be proved by that is that Amt. II of the R.S.H.A., who made this report on technical matters, was the Obersturmbahnfuehrer Rauff, and then he refers in the same connection to Document 2348-PS, which is Exhibit USA 485. The previous one was to identify Rauff, and then to offer his affidavit, which is Document 2348-PS, second volume. Reading from the beginning of the affidavit, which was made on 19th October, 1945, in Ancona, Italy,

"I hereby acknowledge the attached letter written by Dr. Becker on 16th May, 1942, and received by me on 29th May, 1942, as a genuine letter. I did, on 18th October, 1945, write on the side of this letter a statement to the effect that it was genuine. I do not know the number of death vans being operated, and cannot give an approximate figure. The vans were built by the Saurer Works, Germany, located, I believe, in Berlin. Some other firms built these vans also. In so far as I am aware these vans operated only in Russia. In so far as I can state these vans were probably operating in 1941, and I personally believe that they were operating up to the termination of the war."

If your Honour pleases, I do not think that we will have time to go into the next exhibit.

THE PRESIDENT: Very well. Then the Tribunal will now adjourn until Wednesday, 2nd January.

(The Tribunal adjourned to 2nd January, 1946, at 1000 hours.)

WEDNESDAY, 2ND JANUARY, 1946

THE PRESIDENT: I call on the Counsel for the United States.

COLONEL STOREY: If the Tribunal please, when your Honours adjourned on 20th December we were presenting the Gestapo, and had referred to the use of the death vans by the Einsatz Groups in the Eastern Occupied Territories and had almost concluded that phase of the presentation. Your

Honours will recall that we had referred to the use of some death vans made by the Saurer Works, and the final reference that I want to make in that connection is to a telegram attached to Document 501-PS, which it is not necessary to read, establishing the fact that the same make of truck or vans was the death van used by the Einsatz Groups.

The final document in connection with the Einsatz Groups in the Eastern Occupied Territories which we desire to offer is Document 2992-PS, and I believe it is in the second volume of the Document Book. This is an affidavit made by Hermann Graebe. Hermann Graebe is at present employed by the United States Government in Frankfurt. The affidavit was made at Wiesbaden, and I offer excerpts from Document 2992-PS, Exhibit USA 494.

This witness was at the head of a construction firm that was doing some building in the Ukraine and he was an eye-witness of the anti-Jewish actions at the town of Rowno, Ukraine, on 13th July, 1942, and I refer to the part of the affidavit which is on Page 5 of the English translation. Beginning at the first paragraph :

"From September, 1941, until January, 1944, I was manager and engineer-in-charge of a branch office in Sdolbunow, Ukraine, of the Solingen building firm of Josef Jung. In this capacity it was my job to visit the building sites of the firm. The firm had, among others, a site in Rowno, Ukraine.

During the night of 13th July, 1942, all inhabitants of the Rowno Ghetto, where there were still about 5,000 Jews, were liquidated.

I should describe the circumstances of my being a witness of the dissolution of the Ghetto and the carrying out of the pogrom during the night and morning, as follows :

I employed for the firm, in Rowno, in addition to Poles, Germans and Ukrainians, about 100 Jews from Sdolbunow, Ostrog and Mysotch. The men were quartered in a building, 5 Bahnhofstrasse, inside the Ghetto, and the women in a house at the corner of Deutsche Strasse, 98.

On Saturday, 11th July, 1942, my foreman, Fritz Einsporn, told me of a rumour that on Monday all Jews in Rowno were to be liquidated. Although the vast majority of the Jews employed by my firm in Rowno were not natives of this town, I still feared that they might be included in this pogrom which had been reported. I therefore ordered Einsporn at noon of the same day to march all the Jews employed by us - men as well as women - in the direction of Sdolbunow, about 12 km from Rowno. This was done.

The senior Jew had learned of the departure of the Jewish workers of my firm. He went to see the Commanding Officer of the Rowne, Sipo and S.D., S.S. Major (S.S. Sturmbannfuehrer) Dr. Putz. as early as Saturday afternoon to find out whether the rumour of a forthcoming Jewish pogrom - which had gained further credence by reason of the departure of Jews of my firm - was true. Dr. Putz dismissed the rumour as a clumsy lie and, for the rest, had the Polish personnel of my firm in

Rowno arrested. Einsporn avoided arrest by escaping to Sdolbunow. When I learned of this incident I gave orders that all Jews who had left Rowno were to report back to work in Rowno on Monday, 13th July, 1942. On Monday morning I myself went to see the Commanding Officer, Dr. Putz, in order to learn, for one thing, the truth about the rumoured Jewish pogrom and, for another, to obtain information on the arrest of the Polish office personnel. S.S. Major Putz stated to me that no pogrom whatever was planned. Moreover, such a pogrom would be stupid because the firms and the Reichsbahn would lose valuable workers.

An hour later I received a summons to appear before the Area Commissioner of Rowno. His deputy Stabsleiter and Cadet Officer Beck, subjected me to the same questions as I had undergone at the S.D. My explanation that I had sent the Jews home for urgent delousing appeared plausible to him. He then told me - making me promise to keep it a secret - that a pogrom would, in fact, take place in the evening of Monday, 13th July, 1945. After lengthy negotiation I managed to persuade him to give me permission to take my Jewish workers to Sdolbunow - but only after the pogrom had been carried out. During the night it would be up to me to protect the house in the Ghetto against the entry of Ukrainian Militia and S.S. As confirmation of the discussion he gave me a document, which stated that the Jewish employees of Messrs. Jung were not affected by the pogrom."

And this original which I hold in my hand, I will now pass to the translator for reading. I call the attention of your Honour to the fact that it has the letterhead of "Der Gebietskommissar in Rowno," and it is dated 13th July, 1942, and is signed by this area commissioner. I now read this document:

"The Area Commissioner" - which means Gebietskommissar - Rowno.
"Secret.

Addressed: Messrs. Jung, Rowno.

The Jewish workers employed by your firm are not affected by the pogrom - in parenthesis "Aktion."

As I understand, that means action.

"You must transfer them to their new place of work by Wednesday, 15th July, 1942, at the latest."

Signed by the Area Commissioner Beck. And then the stamp - the official stamp of the area commissioner at Rowno.

Now, just the following paragraph on the original, Page 5 or 6, I believe it is, one more paragraph I would like to read after the reference "Original attached ":

"On the evening of this day I drove to Rowno and posted myself with Fritz Einsporn in front of the house in the Bahnhoffstrasse in which the Jewish workers of my firm slept. Shortly after 22.00 hours the Ghetto was encircled by a large S.S. detachment and about three times as many members of the Ukrainian Militia. Then the electric arclights which had been erected in and around the Ghetto were switched on. S.S. and Militia squads of 4 to 6 men entered or at least tried to enter the house. Where the doors and windows were closed and the inhabitants did not open at the knocking, the S.S. men and Militia broke the windows, forced the doors with beams and crowbars and entered the houses. The people living there were driven into the street just as they were, regardless of whether they were dressed or in bed. Since the Jews in most cases refused to leave their houses and resisted, the S.S. and Militia applied force. They finally succeeded, with strokes of the whip, kicks and blows with rifle butts in clearing the houses. The people were driven out of their houses in such haste that in several instances, small children in bed had been left behind. In the streets women cried out for their children and children for their parents. That did not prevent the S.S. from driving the people along the road, at running pace, and hitting them, until they reached a waiting freight train. Car after car was filled, and the screaming of women and children, and the cracking of whips and rifle shots resounded unceasingly.

Since several families or groups had barricaded themselves in especially strong buildings and the doors could not be forced with crowbars or beams, these houses were now blown open with hand grenades. Since the Ghetto was near the railroad tracks in Rowno, the younger people tried to get across the tracks and over a small river, to get away from the Ghetto area. As this stretch of country was beyond the range of the electric lights, it was illuminated by signal rockets. All through the night these beaten, hounded and wounded people moved along the lighted streets. Women carried their dead children in their arms, children pulled and dragged their dead parents by their arms and legs down the road toward the train. Again and again the cries 'Open the door!' Open the door!' echoed through the Ghetto."

I will not read any more of this affidavit. It is a very long one. There is also a second affidavit, but the part I wanted to emphasise is the fact that the original exemption was signed by the Area Commissioner, and that the S.D. and the S.S. participated in this action.

THE PRESIDENT: Ought you not to read the rest of that page, Colonel Storey?

COLONEL STOREY: All right, sir. I really had eliminated that because I thought it might be cumulative.

"About 6 o'clock in the morning I went away for a moment, leaving behind Einsporn and several other German workers who had returned in the meantime. I thought the greatest danger was past and that I could risk it. Shortly after I left, Ukrainian Militia men forced their way into 5 Bahnhoffstrasse and brought seven Jews out and took them to a collecting point inside the Ghetto. On my return I was able to prevent further Jews from being taken out. I went to the collecting point to save these seven men. I saw dozens of corpses of all ages and both sexes in the streets I had to walk along. The doors of the houses stood open, windows were smashed. Pieces of clothing, shoes, stockings, jackets, caps, hats, coats, etc., were lying in the street. At the corner of a house lay a baby, less than a year old, with his skull crushed. Blood and brains were spattered over the house wall and covered the area immediately around the child. The child was dressed only in a little shirt. The commander, S.S. Major Putz, was walking up and down a row of about 80 - 100 male Jews who were crouching on the ground. He had a heavy dog whip in his hand. I walked up to him, showed him the written permit of Stabsleiter Beck, and demanded the seven men whom I recognised among those who were crouching on the ground. Dr. Putz was furious about Beck's concession and nothing could persuade him to release the seven men. He made a motion with his hand encircling the square and said that anyone who was once here would not get away. Although he was very angry with Beck, he ordered me to take the people from 5 Bahnhofstrasse out of Rowno by 8 o'clock at the latest. When I left Dr. Putz, I noticed a Ukrainian farm cart with two horses. Dead people with stiff limbs were lying on the cart. Legs and arms projected over the side boards. The cart was making for the freight train. I took the remaining 74 Jews who had been locked in the house to Sdolbunow. Several days after 13th July, 1942, the Area Commissioner of Sdolbunow, Georg Marschall, called a meeting of all firm managers, railroad superintendents, and leaders of the Organisation Todt and informed them that the firms etc. should prepare themselves for the 'resettlement' of the Jews which was to take place almost immediately. He referred to the pogrom in Rowno where all the Jews had been liquidated, i.e., had been shot near Kostolpol."

Finally, his signature is sworn to on 10th November, 1945.

THE PRESIDENT: What nationality is Graebe?

COLONEL STOREY: He is German. Graebe is a German, and is now in the employ of the Military Government at Frankfurt - the United States Military Government.

Your Honour, in that connection there is another separate affidavit, which I will not attempt to read, attached to this, a part of the same document. But it has to do with the execution of some people in another area and is along the same line. I am not reading it because it would be cumulative, but it is a part of this same document.

I now pass from that subject to the next one.

The Gestapo and S.D. stationed special units in prisoner-of-war camps for the purpose of screening racial and political undesirables and executing those who were screened. The programme of mass murder of political and racial undesirables carried on against civilians was also applied against prisoners of war who were captured on the Eastern Front. In this connection I call the attention of the Tribunal to the testimony of General Lahousen, which your Honours will recall, of the 30th November, 1945. Lahousen testified to a conference which took place in the summer of 1941, shortly after the beginning of the campaign against the Soviet Union, which he attended; and I want to emphasise this, because we will later have a document that emanated from this conference, attended by Lahousen himself, General Reinecke, Colonel Breuer, and Mueller, the Head of the Gestapo. At this conference the command to kill Soviet functionaries and Communists among the Soviet prisoners-of-war was discussed. The executions were to be carried out by Einsatz Commandos of the Sipo and the S.D.

Lahousen further recalled that Mueller, who was the head of the Gestapo, insisted on carrying out the programme, and that the only concession he made was that, in deference to the sensibilities of the German troops, the executions would not take place in their presence. Mueller also made some concessions as to the selection of the persons to be murdered; but, according to Lahousen, the selection was left entirely to the commanders of these screening units. I refer to Page 281 of the transcript.

Now I offer Document 502-PS as the next exhibit, Exhibit USA 486. This document is a Gestapo directive of 17th July, 1941.

If you will recall, Lahousen said this conference was in the summer of 1941.

It is addressed to commanders of the Sipo and S.D. stationed in camps and provides in part as follows, and I read from the first page of the English translation.

Now, if the Tribunal please, our colleagues, the Soviet prosecutors, will present most of that document, and I am only going to read enough to show that the Gestapo were the ones that took part in it. From the beginning :

"The action of commandos will take place in accordance with the agreement of the Chief of the Security Police and Security Service and the Supreme Command of the Armed Forces as of 16th July, 1941. Enclosure I.

The commandos will work independently according to special authorisation and according to the general directive given to them in the limits of the camp regulations. Naturally the commandos will keep close contact with the camp commander and the intelligence officer assigned to him.

This mission of the commandos is the political investigation of all camp inmates, the elimination and further treatment:

(a) of all political, criminal, or in some other way undesirable elements among them;

(b) of those persons who could be used for the reconstruction of the occupied countries."

Now I pass to the beginning of the fourth paragraph:

"The commandos must use for their work as far as possible now, and even later, the experiences of. the camp commanders, which the latter have gathered from observation of the prisoners and examination of the camp inmates. Further, the commandos must make efforts from the beginning to seek out among the prisoners elements which would

General Erwin von Lahousen during his testimony at the Nuremberg war crimes trial in 1946. He was involved in two plots to assassinate Hitler, but escaped punishment as he was in the Eastern Front.

appear reliable, regardless whether there are communists concerned or not, in order to use them for intelligence purposes inside the camp, and, if advisable, later in the occupied territories also.

By using such informers, and by use of all other existing possibilities, the discovery of all elements to be eliminated among the prisoners must follow step by step. The commandos must learn for themselves in every case by means of short questioning of the informer and possible questioning of other prisoners. The information of one informer is not sufficient to designate a camp inmate to be a suspect without further proof. It must be confirmed in some way, if possible."

Now I pass to Page 4, the 3rd paragraph of the English translation, quoting:

"Executions are not to be held in the camp or in the immediate vicinity of the camp. If the camps in the Government General are in the immediate vicinity of the border, then the prisoners are to be taken for special treatment, if possible, into the former Soviet territory."

And then the 5th paragraph:

"In regard to executions to be carried out and to the possible removal of reliable civilians and the removal of informers for the Einsatzgruppe in the occupied territories, the leader of the Einsatzkommandos must make an agreement with the nearest State Police Office, as well as with the commandant of the Security Police unit and Security Service, and beyond these, with the Chief of the Einsatzgruppe concerned in the occupied territories."

Proof that persons so screened out of the prisoner of war camps by the Gestapo were executed is to be found in Document 1165-PS, from which I do not intend to quote, and which has been previously introduced as Exhibit USA 244. Document 1165-PS shows that those that had been screened out were executed.

The first page of that document, is a letter from the Camp Commandant of the concentration camp Gross-Rosen to Mueller, who was the Chief of the Gestapo, dated the 23rd of October, 1941, referring to a previous oral conference with Mueller and setting forth the names of 20 Soviet prisoners of war executed the previous day.

The second page - I am still referring to Document 1165 but not reading from it, because it has already been quoted from - is a directive issued by Mueller on the 9th of November, 1941, to all Gestapo offices, in which he ordered that all diseased prisoners of war should be excluded from transports to concentration camps for execution, because 5 to 10 per cent. of those destined for execution were arriving in the camps dead or half dead.

I now offer Document 3542-PS, Exhibit USA 489, which is in the second volume. This is an affidavit of Kurt Lindow, a former Gestapo official, which was taken on the 30th of September, 1945, at Oberursel, Germany, in the course of an official military investigation by the United States Army, and I quote from that document from the beginning:

"I was Kriminaldirektor in Section IV of the R.S.H.A." -

I call your Honour's attention to the chart on the board that he was Director of Section IV and head of the Sub-section IV A I -

"From the middle of 1942 until the middle of 1944. I had the rank of S.S.-Sturmbannfuehrer.

From 1941 until the middle of 1943, there was attached to Subsection IV A i (which is not shown on this chart, but was described in the beginning) a special department that was headed by the Regierungsoberinspektor, later Regierungsamtmann, and S.S.-Hauptsturmbannfuehrer Franz Koenigshaus. In this department were handled matters concerning prisoners of war. I learned from this department that instructions and orders by Reichsfuehrer Himmler, dating from 1941 to 1942, existed, according to which captured Soviet political Commissars and Jewish soldiers were to be executed. As far as I know, proposals for execution of such P.W.'s. were received from the various P.W. camps. Koenigshaus had to prepare the orders for execution and submitted them to the Chief of Section IV, Mueller, for signature (Mueller being the Head of the Gestapo). These orders were made out so that one order was to be sent to the agency making the request, and a second one to the concentration camp designated to carry out the execution. The P.W.'s. in question were at first formally released from P.W. status, then transferred to a concentration camp for execution.

The Department Chief, Koenigshaus, was under me in disciplinary questions from the middle of 1942 until about the beginning of 1943, and worked, in matters of his department, directly with the chief of Group IV A, Regierungsrat Panzinger. Early in 1943 the department was dissolved, and absorbed into the departments in Sub-section IV B. The work concerning Russian P.W.'s. must then have been done by IV B 2a. Head of Department IV B 2a was Regierungsrat and Sturmbannfuehrer Hans Helmut Wolf.

There existed in the P.M. camps on the Eastern Front small screening teams (Einsatzkommandos), headed by a lower ranking member of the Secret Police or Gestapo. These teams were assigned to the camp commandos and had the job of segregating the P.W.'s. who were candidates for execution, according to the orders that had been given, and to report them to the Office of the Secret Police."
I will not read the remainder of that affidavit.

Passing from that phase of the case: The Gestapo and S.S. sent re-captured prisoners of war to concentration camps, where they were executed, that is, prisoners of war who had escaped and were recaptured. The Tribunal will recall that in a document heretofore introduced, 1650-PS, was an order in which the Chief of the Security Police and S.S. instructed regional Gestapo offices to take certain classes of recaptured officers from camps, and to transport them to Mauthausen. Concentration Camp, under the operation known as "Kugel." That, if your Honour recalls, means "Bullet." That is the famous "Bullet" Decree that has been previously introduced. On the journey the prisoners of war were to be placed in irons. The Gestapo officers were to make semi-annual reports, giving numbers only, of the sending of these prisoners of war to Mauthausen. On the 27th of July, 1944, an order was issued from the VI Corps Area Command on the treatment of prisoners of war. That is Document 1514-PS in the second volume, which I offer as Exhibit USA 491. This document provided that prisoners of war were to be discharged from prisoner of war status and transferred to the Gestapo under certain circumstances, and I quote from the first page:

"Subject: Delivery of prisoners of war to the Secret State Police."
Enclosed is the decree (I) referred to

"The following summarising ruling is issued with respect to the delivery to the Secret State Police:

1. (a) According to the decrees (2) and (3), the commander of the camp has to deliver Soviet prisoners of war in case of punishable offences to the Secret State Police and to dismiss them from imprisonment of war, if he does not believe that disciplinary functions are sufficient to prescribe punishment for violations committed. Report of the facts is not necessary.

(b) Recaptured Soviet prisoners of war have to be delivered first to the nearest police office in order to ascertain whether punishable offences have been committed during the escape. The dismissal from imprisonment of war takes place upon suggestion of the police office (Section A6 of the decree No. 4) regarding the compilation of all regulations on the Arbeitseinsatz of prisoners of war who have been recaptured and refuse to work.

(c) Recaptured Soviet officers who are prisoners of war have to be delivered to the Gestapo and to be dismissed from imprisonment of war. (Section C1 of Decree No. 4 and Decree No. 5.)

(d) Soviet officer prisoners of war who refuse to work and those who distinguish themselves as agitators and have an unfavourable influence upon the willingness to work of the other prisoners of war, have to be delivered by the responsible Stalag to the nearest State Police office and to be dismissed from imprisonment of war. (Section C1 of Decree No. 4 and Decree No. 5.)

(e) Soviet enlisted prisoners of war refusing to work who are ring-leaders and those who distinguish themselves as agitators and therefore have an unfavourable influence upon the willingness to work of the other prisoners of war, have to be delivered to the nearest State Police Office and to be dismissed from imprisonment of war. (Section C2 of Decree No. 4.)

(f) Soviet prisoners of war (enlisted men and officers), who with respect to their political attitude have been sifted out by Einsatzkommando of the Security Police and the Security Service, have to be delivered upon request by the camp commander to the Einsatzkommando and to be dismissed from imprisonment of war. (Decree No. 6.)

(g) Polish prisoners of war have to be delivered, if acts of sabotage are proven, to the nearest State Police Office and to be dismissed from imprisonment of war. The decision rests with the camp commander. Report on this is not necessary. (Decree No. 7.)

2. A report on the delivery and dismissal from imprisonment of war in the cases mentioned under paragraph 1of this decree to the Mil. District Command VI, Dept. of Prisoners of War, is not necessary.

3. Prisoners of war from all nations have to be delivered to the Secret State Police and to be dismissed from imprisonment of war, if a special

order of the O.K.W. or of the Mil. District Command VI, Dept. for Prisoners of War, is issued.

4. Prisoners of war under suspicion of participating in illegal organisations and resistance movements have to be left to the Gestapo, upon request, for the purpose of interrogation. They remain prisoners of war and have to be treated as such. The delivery to the Gestapo and their dismissal from imprisonment of war has to take place only by order of the O.K.W. or of the Mil. District Command VI, Dept. of Prisoners of War.

In case of French and Belgian prisoners of war and interned Italian military personnel, approval of Mil. District Command VI Dept. of Prisoners of War, has to be obtained - if necessary by phone - before delivery to the Gestapo for the purposes of interrogation."

This decree was known as the "Bullet Decree." Prisoners of war, sent to Mauthausen Concentration Camp under the decree, were executed. I now offer in support of that statement Document 2285-PS, Exhibit USA 490. It is in the second volume. Document 2285-PS is an affidavit of Lt.-Col. Guivante de Saint Gast, and Lt. Jean Veith, both of the French Army, which was taken on the 13th May, 1945, in the course of an official military investigation by the United States Army. The affidavit discloses that Lt.-Col. Gast was confined at Mauthausen from 15th March, 1944, to 22nd April, 1945, and that Lt. Veith was confined from 22nd April, 1943 until 22nd April, 1945. I quote from the affidavit, beginning with the third paragraph of Page 1, quoting :

"In Mauthausen existed several treatments of prisoners, amongst them the 'action K or Kugel' (Bullet action). Upon the arrival of transports, prisoners with the mention 'K' were not registered, and received no numbers, and their names remained unknown except to the officials of the 'Politische Abteilung.' (Lt. Veith had the opportunity of hearing upon the arrival of a transport the following conversation between the Untersturmfuehrer Streitwieser and chief of the convoy: 'How many prisoners?' '15 but two K.' 'Well, that makes 13').

The prisoners were taken directly to the prison, where they were unclothed and taken to the 'Bathroom.' This bathroom in the cellars of the prison building near the crematory was specially designed for execution (shooting and gassing). The shooting took place by means of a measuring apparatus. The prisoners being backed towards a metrical measure with an automatic contraption releasing a bullet in his neck as soon as the moving plank determining his height touched the top of his head.

If a transport consisted of too many 'K' prisoners, instead of losing time for the measurement they were exterminated by gas, laid on to the bathrooms instead of water."

I now pass to another subject, namely "The Gestapo was responsible for establishing and classifying concentration camps and for committing racial and political undesirables to concentration and annihilation camps for slave labour and mass murder."

The Tribunal has already received evidence concerning the responsibility of the Gestapo for the administration of concentration camps, and the authority of the Gestapo for taking persons into protective custody to be carried out in the state concentration camps. The Gestapo also issued orders establishing concentration camps, transforming prisoner of war camps into concentration camps as internment camps, changing labour camps into concentration camps, setting up special sections for female prisoners, and so forth.

The Chief of the Security Police and S.S. ordered the classification of concentration camps according to the seriousness of the accusation and the chances for reforming the prisoners, from the Nazi viewpoint. I now refer to Documents 1063A and 1063B in the second volume, Exhibit USA 492. The concentration camps were classified as Class I, II or III. Class I was for the least serious prisoners, and Class III was for the most serious. Now Document 1063A is signed by Heydrich and it is dated 2nd January, 1941. I quote from the beginning:

Subject: Classification of the Concentration Camps.

The Reichsfuehrer S.S. and Chief of the German Police has given his approval to classify the concentration camps into various categories, which take into account the personality of the prisoner as well as the degree of his danger to the State. Accordingly, the concentration camps will be classified into the following categories :

Category I - for all prisoners charged with minor offences only and definitely qualified for correction; also for special cases and solitary confinement - Camps Dachau, Sachsenhausen and Auschwitz 1. The latter also applies in part to Category II.

Category 1a - for all old prisoners unconditionally qualified for work, who could still be used in the medicinal herb gardens - the Camp Dachau.

Category II - for prisoners charged with major offences but still qualified for re-education and correction - the Camps Buchenwald, Flossenburg, Auschwitz II.

Category III - for prisoners under most serious charges, also for those who have been previously convicted for criminal offences; at the same time for asocial prisoners, that is to say, those who can hardly be corrected - the Camp Mauthausen."

I call your Honour's attention to the fact that we have been talking about Mauthausen, where the "K" action took place.

The Chief of the Security Police and S.D. had authority to fix the length of the period of custody. During the war it was the policy not to permit the prisoners to know the period of custody and merely to announce the term as "Until further notice." That was established by Document 1531-PS, which has previously been introduced as Exhibit USA 248, and the only reason for referring to it is to show that they had the right to fix the period of custody.

The local Gestapo offices, which made the arrests, maintained a register called the "Haftbuch," and, as I understand, "Haftbuch" simply means a block or police register. In this register the names of all persons arrested were listed, together with personal data, grounds of arrest and disposition. When orders were received from the Gestapo Headquarters in Berlin to commit persons who had been arrested to concentration camps, an entry was made in the "Haftbuch" to that effect.

I now offer in evidence the original of one of these books, and it is Document L-358, Exhibit USA 495. This book was collected by the 3rd Army when it overran an area, and it was captured by the T Force on 22nd April, 1945, near Bad Sulze, Germany. This book is the original register used by the Gestapo at Tomassow, Poland, to record the names of the persons arrested, the grounds for arrest and the disposition made, of cases during the period from 1st June, 1943, to 20th December, 1944.

In the register are approximately 3,500 names of persons. Approximately 2,200 were arrested for membership in the resistance movements and partisan unit. This is a very large book, and I am going to ask the clerk to pass it to your Honours so that you might get a look at it. It is too big to photograph. And if your Honours will just turn to one of the pages, I will read what the different columns provide - just any one of the pages. There is a double column. It starts on the left and goes over to the other side. In the first column that heading is simply a number of the man when he comes in. The next column is his name. The third column is the family - a brief family history and his religion. The fourth is the domicile. The next shows the date he was arrested and by whom - that is the fifth column. The next column, the place of arrest. And then the next column, the reason for arrest. And then the next is another number which is apparently a serial number for delivery. And next to the last column is the disposition. And the final column, remarks.

Now, out of the 3,500 names that are shown in that book, your Honours will notice a number of red marks. Those apparently meant the ones that were shot. Of those, 325 were shot. Only 35 of that 325 had first been tried. 950 out of this list were sent to concentration camps and 155 sent to the Reich for forced labour. According to this register, similar treatment was accorded persons who were arrested on other grounds, for instance, Communists, Jews, hostages, and persons taken in reprisal. A large number are shown to have been arrested during raids, no further grounds being stated.

I particularly refer your Honours to entries 286, 287 and 288, that is, the numbers in the first column of the register, where the crime charged to the person arrested was "als Juden"; in other words, he was a Jew. And by that you will find a red cross mark, and the punishment given was death.

I now pass from this document and merely call attention to Document L-215, which was heretofore introduced as Exhibit USA 243. I do not intend to read from it unless your Honours want to turn to L-215. This is a file of original dossiers on 25 Luxembourgers taken into protective custody for commitment to concentration camps. I will just refer to a sentence of the language in the document. Quoting:

"According to the finding of the State Police he endangers by his attitude the existence and security of the People and the State."

And in each case, with reference to those dossiers, that appears as the reason for the execution of these 25 Luxembourgers. And in connection -

THE PRESIDENT:: Colonel Storey, you said execution, did you not?

COLONEL STOREY: I beg your pardon - sending to concentration camps.

THE PRESIDENT:: Yes. There is no evidence they were executed.

COLONEL STOREY: No, sir; they were committed to concentration camps. And also in connection with that same document there is a form provided by which the Gestapo Headquarters in Berlin were notified when the persons were received by the concentration camps.

Another document - which has heretofore been received as Exhibit USA 279, Document 1472-PS, in the second volume - I am simply going to refer to it as a predicate for another. That was a telegram of 16th December, 1942, in which Mueller reported that the Gestapo could round up some 45,000 Jews in connection with the programme of obtaining additional labour in concentration camps. And with reference to the same subject there is Document 1063-D-PS, which has heretofore been offered as Exhibit USA 219, Mueller sent a directive to the commanders and inspectors of the Security Police and S.D. and to the directors of the Gestapo regional offices, in which he stated that Himmler had ordered on 14th December, ordered on 14th December, 1942, that at least 35,000 persons, who were fit for work, had to be put into concentration camps not later than the end of January.

Now, in that same connection I offer Document L-41, volume 1, as Exhibit USA 496. This document contains a further directive from Mueller dated 23rd March, 1943, and supplements the directive of 17th December, 1942, to which I referred, and in this he states that the measures are to be carried out until 30th April, 1943. And I would like to quote from the second paragraph on page 3 of the exhibit.

"Care must, however, be taken that only prisoners who are fit for work are transferred to concentration camps, and adolescents only in accordance with the given directives; otherwise, the concentration camps would become overcrowded, and this would defeat the intended object."

In that same connection I offer Document 701-PS, Exhibit USA 497. This is a letter dated 1st April, 1943, from the Minister of Justice to the Public Prosecutors and also addressed to the Commissioner of the Reich Minister of Justice for the penal camps in Emsland. Quoting :

"Regarding Poles and Jews who are released from the penal institutions of the Department of Justice. Instructions for the independent penal institutions.

1. With reference to the new guiding principles for the application of Article 1, Section 2, of the decree of 11th June, 1940, Reich Legal Gazette I S. 887 - Attachment I of decree (RV) of 27th January, 1943 - 913-2 enclosure I-IIIa 2-2629 - the Reich Chief Security Office has directed by the decree of 11th March, 1943 - 11 A 2 number 100-43-176:

(a) Jews, who in accordance with number VI of the guiding principles are released from a penal institution, are to be taken by the State Police (Chief) Office competent for the district in which the penal institution is located, to be detained for the rest of their lives in the concentration camps Auschwitz or Lublin in accordance with the regulations for protective custody that have been issued.

The same applies to Jews who in future are released from a penal institution after serving sentence of confinement.

(b) Poles, who in accordance with Number VI of the guiding principles are released from a penal institution, are to be taken by the State Police (Chief) Office competent for the district in which the penal institution is located, to be placed for the duration of the war in a concentration camp in accordance with the regulations on protective custody that have been issued.

The same applies in the future to Poles, who after serving a term of imprisonment of more than six months, are to be discharged by a penal institution.

Conforming to the request of the Chief Office for Reich Security, I ask that in the future:

(a) All Jews to be discharged;

(b) All Poles to be discharged;

who have served a sentence of more than six months, be transferred for further confinement to the State Police (Chief) Office competent for the district, and are to be placed promptly at its disposal before the end of sentence, for collection."

And the last paragraph states that this ruling replaces the hitherto ordered return of all Polish prisoners undergoing imprisonment in the Old Reich condemned in the annexed Eastern territory.

The next subject: "The Gestapo and the S.D. Participated in Deportation of Citizens of Occupied Countries for Forced Labour and Handled the Disciplining of Forced Labour."

With reference to the presentation heretofore made concerning forced labour, I do not intend to repeat this. However, there were several references to the important position played by the Gestapo and the S.D. in rounding up persons to be brought into the Reich for forced labour, and references in two or three documents that were introduced. I simply want to cite those documents as showing the part that the Gestapo and S.D. played. Document L-61, Exhibit USA 177. It is set out in this document book - I am simply citing it - it is a letter of the 26th of November, 1942, from Fritz Sauckel, in which he stated that he had been advised by the Chief of the Security Police and S.D. under date of 26th October, 1942, that during the month of November the evacuation of Poles in the Lublin district would begin, in order to make room for the settlement of persons of the German race. The Poles who were evacuated as a result of this measure were to be put into concentration camps for labour, so far as they were criminal or anti-social.

The Tribunal will also recall the Christensen letter, which is our Document 3012-PS, Exhibit USA 190. In that letter it is stated that during the year 1943 the programme of mass murder carried out by the Einsatz Groups in the East should be modified in order to round up hundreds of thousands of persons for labour in the armament industry. That was in 3012-PS, which has heretofore been introduced as Exhibit USA 190. And that force was to be used when necessary. Prisoners were to be released so that they could be used for forced labour. When villages were burned down the whole population was to be placed at the disposal of the labour commissioners.

Now in that connection the direct responsibility of the Gestapo for disciplining forced workers is shown in our next exhibit, Document 1573-PS, Exhibit USA 498. This is a secret order signed by Mueller himself to the regional Gestapo Offices on the 18th June, 1941, and I quote from the document from the beginning. It is addressed:

"To all State Police Administrative Offices, attention S.S. Sturmbahnfuehrer Nosske or representative at Aachen.

Subject: Measures to be taken against emigrants and civilian workers who came from the great Russian areas and against foreign workers.

Reference: None.

To prevent the unauthorised and arbitrary return of Russian, Ukrainian, White Ruthenian, Cossack, and Caucasian emigrants and civilian workers from the territory of the Reich to the East, and to prevent attempts at disorder by foreign workers in the German production, I decide as follows:

(1) The managers of the branch offices of the Russian, Ukrainian, White Ruthenian, and Caucasian trustee office, as well as the relief committee and the leading members of the Russian, Ukrainian, White Ruthenian, Cossack, and Caucasian emigration organisations are to be notified immediately that, until further notice, they are not allowed to leave their domicile without permission of the Security Police. Also they are to be told to apply the same measures to the members who are under their care. Their attention is to be called to the fact that they will be arrested in case of unauthorised leaving place of work and domicile. I request to have a check on the presence of branch office leaders if possible by daily inquiries under pretext.

(2) Emigrants and foreign workers are to be arrested if it is warranted by the situation, in case they were charged with similar offences previously and are under the suspicion of having been active as informers for the U.S.S.R. This measure has to be prepared. It should,

however, not be taken before the pass word 'Fremdvoelker' has been transmitted by means of 'urgent' telegram."

THE PRESIDENT: Do you think you should read the rest of that?

COLONEL STOREY: Sir?

THE PRESIDENT: Is it necessary to read the rest of that?

COLONEL STOREY: I do not think so, your Honour.

THE PRESIDENT: We will adjourn now for ten minutes.

(A recess was taken.)

COLONEL STOREY: If the Tribunal please, I next offer in evidence Document 3330-PS, Exhibit USA 499, the second volume. Before I hand this document to the translator I should like to exhibit it to your Honours. It is an original telegram that was sent to the Gestapo office at Nuremberg. It was discovered by the C.I.C., by a Lieutenant Stevens, near Herzburg, Germany, and your Honours will notice that parts of it have been burned. It was in connection with some documents that had been buried and they were partially burned when they were buried. This is one of the telegrams. It is from the Secret State Police, the State Police Station at Nuremberg and Furth, and it is dated the 12th February, 1944. I quote from the telegram:

"R.S.H.A. IV F1 45-44.

The Border Inspector General.

Urgent - Submit immediately.

Treatment, of recaptured escaped eastern labourers (Ostarbeiter).

By order of the R.F.S.S. all recaptured escaped Eastern labourers without exception are to be sent to concentration camps, effective immediately. In regard to reporting to R.F.S.S., I request only one report by teletype to Section IV D (Foreign labourers) on 10th March, 1944, as to how many of such male or female Eastern labourers were turned over to a concentration camp, between to-day and 10th March, 1944."

By these methods the Gestapo and S.D. maintained control over forced labour brought into the Reich.

The next subject I go into is that the Gestapo and S.D. executed captured commandos and paratroopers and protected civilians who lynched Allied fliers.

On 4th August, 1942, Keitel issued an order which provided that the Gestapo and S.D. were responsible for taking counter-measures against single parachutists or small groups of them with special missions. In substantiation I offer now Document 513-PS as the exhibit next in order, Exhibit USA 500. I read from the first page of the translation, the first part of paragraph 3:

"Single parachutists captured by members of the Armed Forces are to be delivered to the nearest agency of the Chief of the Security Police and S.D. without delay."

Now, if the Tribunal please, to digress from the text: Colonel Taylor will present the Nazi High Command and a few of their orders. This is one thing and there is also another one, with which he is going to deal extensively. My purpose in introducing these orders now is to show the part that the Gestapo and S.D. played in connection with them.

The next order that I introduce is Document 498-PS, in the first volume, Exhibit USA 501. That is the celebrated commando order signed by the Fuehrer himself on 18th October, 1942. There were only 12 copies of this made and it bears the original personal signature of Adolf Hitler. One copy was sent to the Reichsfuehrer S.S. and Chief of the Security Police. That order, without reading it, and getting down to the part from which I want to quote, simply provides that all commandos, whether or not in uniform or unarmed, are to be slaughtered to the last man. I want to read down at the bottom, the beginning of paragraph 4, to show the part of the S.D.:

"If individual members of such commandos, such as agents, saboteurs, etc., fall into the hands of the military forces by some other means, through the police in occupied territories for instance, they are to be handed over immediately to the S.D."

Another one of those orders is Document 526-PS, Exhibit USA 502, to which I would like to refer. That document has to do with some alleged saboteurs landing in Norway. It is dated the 10th May, 1943, and is Top Secret. I quote the first paragraph as identifying a crew:

"On the 30th March, 1943, on Toftefjord (70 deg. lat.) an enemy cutter was sighted. Cutter was blown up by the enemy. Crew two dead men, 10 prisoners."

That is the crew. Near the bottom of that order, the third sentence from the bottom, is this statement

"Fuehrer order executed by S.D. (Security Service)."

We have heretofore introduced Document R-110, Exhibit USA 333, and that was the Himmler order of 10th August, 1943, which was sent to Security Police. That order provided that it was not the task of the Police to interfere in clashes between Germans and English and American terror fliers who had baled out. It was personally signed by Himmler and here is the signature. It has already been introduced in evidence, but I wanted to call the attention of the Court to it again.

May I next go to the subject where the Gestapo and the S.D. took civilians of occupied countries to Germany for secret trial and punishment. That is the so-called "Night and Fog Decree," issued on 7th December, 1941, by Hitler. That decree has not been introduced in evidence.

I now refer to Document L-90, in the first volume, Exhibit USA 503. Under that decree persons who committed offences against the Reich or occupation forces in occupied territory, except where death sentence was certain, were to be taken secretly to Germany and surrendered to the Security

Police and S.D. for trial or punishment in Germany itself. And this is the original from which we quote, beginning on the first page of the translation. It is on the stationery of the Reichsfuehrer S.S. and Chief of German Police, Munich, 4th February, 1942. Subject: Prosecution of Offences against the Reich or the Occupation Forces.

"1. The following regulations published by the Chief of the Armed Forces High Command, dated 12th December, 1941, are being made known herewith:

(1) The Chief of the Armed Forces High Command.

After thoughtful consideration, it is the will of the Fuehrer that the measures taken against those who are guilty of offences against the Reich or against the occupation forces in occupied areas should be altered. The Fuehrer thinks that in the case of such offences life imprisonment, even life imprisonment with hard labour, is regarded as a sign of weakness. An effective and lasting deterrent can be achieved only by the death penalty or by taking measures which will leave the family and the population uncertain as to the fate of the offender. The deportation to Germany serves this purpose.

The directives for the prosecution of offences as outlined below correspond with the Fuehrer's conception. They have been examined and approved by him. (Signed) Keitel."

And then follow some of the directives and descriptions.

This is a very long document, with enclosures, and we next turn to Page 4 of the English translation, near the bottom:

"In so far as the S.S. and the police are the competent authorities for dealing with offences committed under 1, they should proceed accordingly."

Next, in connection with the same document, on Page 20, Part II of the English translation, which is the secret letter addressed to the "Abwehr," I quote from Page 2. It is the letter dated 2nd February, 1942, passing down to the words "Enclosed please find:

"1. Decree of the Fuehrer and Supreme Commander of the Armed Forces of 7th December, 1941.

2. Executive order of the same date.

3. Communication of the Chief of the High Command of the Armed Forces of 12th December, 1941.

The decree introduces a fundamental innovation. The Fuehrer and Supreme Commander of the Armed Forces orders that offences committed by civilians in the occupied territories and of the kind mentioned above, are to be dealt with by the competent Military Courts in the occupied territories only if (a) the death penalty is pronounced, and (b) sentence is pronounced within eight days of the prisoner's arrest.

Unless both these conditions are fulfilled, the Fuehrer and Supreme Commander does not anticipate that criminal proceedings within the occupied territories will have the necessary deterrent effect.

In all other cases the prisoners are in future to be transported to Germany secretly, and further dealings with the offences will take place there; these measures will have a deterrent effect because (a) the prisoners will vanish without leaving a trace, (b) no information may be given as to their whereabouts or their fate."

The Gestapo Headquarters in Prinz-Albrecht-Strasse, Berlin.

Now, skipping the next paragraph, to the second paragraph below:

"In case the competent Military Court, and the Military Commander respectively are of the opinion that an immediate decision on the spot is impossible, and the prisoners are therefore to be transported to Germany, the Counter Intelligence Offices have to report this fact directly to the R.S.H.A. in Berlin, SW11, Prinz Albrecht Street 7, c-o Dr. Fischer, Director of Criminal Police, stating the exact number of prisoners and of the group or groups which belong together as the case may be. Isolated cases, where the superior commander has an urgent interest in the case being dealt with by a military court, are to be reported to the R.S.H.A. Copy of the entire report has to be sent to Office Foreign Countries Intelligence Department, Abwehr III.

The R.S.H.A., on the basis of available accommodation, will determine which office of the State Police has to accept the prisoners. The latter office will communicate with the competent Counter Intelligence Office and determine with it the particulars of the removal, particularly whether this will be carried out by the Secret Field Police, the Field Gendarmerie, or the Gestapo itself, as well as on the place and the manner of the actual handing over."

After the civilians arrived in Germany no word of the disposition of their cases was permitted to reach the country from which they came or their relatives.

I now offer Document 668-PS, Exhibit USA 504. This is a letter of the Chief of the Security Police and the S.D., dated 24th June, 1942, and I quote from the first page of the English translation:

"It is the intent of the directive of the Fuehrer and Commander-in-Chief of the Wehrmacht concerning prosecution of criminal acts against the Reich or the occupation forces in occupied territories, dated 7th December, 1941" - that is the order that I first referred to - "to create, for deterrent purposes, uncertainty over the fate of prisoners among their relatives and acquaintances, through the deportation into Reich territory of persons arrested in occupied areas on account of activity inimical to Germany. This goal would be jeopardised if the relatives were to be notified in cases of death. Release of the body for burial at home is inadvisable for the same reason, and beyond that also because the place of burial could be misused for demonstrations.

I therefore propose that the following rules be observed in the handling of cases of death:

(a) Notification of relatives is not to take place.

(b) The body will be buried at the place of decease in the Reich.

(c) The place of burial will, for the time being, not be made known."

Now passing to the next activity of the S.D. and Gestapo, which was that they arrested, tried and punished citizens of occupied countries under special criminal procedure and by summary methods. And I next offer in evidence Document 674-PS, Exhibit USA 505.

The Gestapo, under certain circumstances, arrested, placed in protective custody, and executed civilians of occupied countries. Even where there were courts capable of handling emergency cases the Gestapo conducted its own proceedings without regard to normal judicial processes.

This document, 674-PS, Exhibit USA 505, is a letter from the Chief Public Prosecutor at Kattowitz, dated 3rd December, 1941, and it is addressed to the Reich Minister of Justice, attention Chief Councillor to the Government Stadermann or representative in office, Berlin. The subject is "Executions by the Police and Expediting of Penal Procedure, without Order; Enclosure: 1 copy of report." I quote from the beginning:

"About three weeks ago, six ringleaders (some of them German) were hanged by the Police, in connection with the destruction of a treasonable organisation of 350 members in Tarnowitz, without notification to the Ministry of Justice. Such executions of criminal agents have previously taken place also in the Bielitz district without the knowledge of the public prosecutor. On 2nd December, 1941, the head of the State Police at Kattowitz, chief councillor to the government Mildner, reported orally to the undersigned that he had ordered, with authority from the Reichsfuehrer of the S. S., as necessary immediate action, these executions by public hanging at the place of the crime, and that deterrents would also have to be continued in future until the criminal and actively anti-German elements in the occupied Eastern territories have been destroyed, or until other immediate actions, perhaps also by the courts, would guarantee equally deterrent effect. Accordingly, six leaders.of another Polish organisation guilty of high treason in the district in and around Sosnowitz were to be hanged publicly to-day as an example.

About this procedure the undersigned expressed considerable concern.

Besides the fact that such measures have been withdrawn from the jurisdiction of the ordinary courts and are contradictory to laws still in force, a justified emergency for the exceptional proceedings by the police alone cannot, in our opinion, be lawfully recognised.

The penal justice in our district within the limits of our jurisdiction is quite capable of fulfilling its duty of immediate penal retribution by means of a special form of special judicial activity established by a so-called 'Rapid Special Court.' Indictment and trial could be speeded up in such a way that between turning the case over to the public prosecutor and the execution no more than three days would elapse, if the practice of reprieve is simplified and if the decision, if necessary, can be obtained by telephone. This was expressed yesterday to the head of the State police at Kattowitz by the undersigned.

We cannot believe that execution by the police of criminals, especially German criminals, can be considered more effective in view of the shaken sense of justice of many Germans. In the long run they might, in spite of public deterrent, lead even more to further brutality of mind, which is contrary to the intended purpose of pacification. These deliberations, however, do not apply to future legal competence of a drumhead court-martial for Poles and Jews."

I next refer to document 654-PS, Exhibit USA 218, which has previously been introduced in evidence, but it bears on this subject, and I will merely summarise in a word what it provided.

It states that on 18th of September, 1942, Thierack, the Reich Minister of Justice, and Himmler came to an understanding by which anti-social elements were to be turned over to Himmler to be worked to death. That is in Document 654-PS, and a special criminal procedure was to be applied by the police to the Jews, Poles, Gypsies, Russians, and Ukrainians, who were not to be tried in ordinary criminal courts.

I refer to that document merely as bearing on the same subject.

Another document from which I will not quote, but will cite to your Honour, is the order of 5th November, 1942, issued by the R.S.H.A., and that is Document L-316, Exhibit USA 346. I do not think it is necessary to quote from that except to state that that letter provides that the administration - in fact, the last statement in it just before the signature provides:

"The administration of penal law for persons of alien race must be transferred from the hands of the administrators of justice into the hands of the police."

That is the part that connects the police with it, and I will not quote from the document otherwise.

Now I next come to the subject where the Gestapo and the S.D. executed or confined persons in concentration camps for crimes allegedly committed by their relatives and in that connection I offer Document L-37 in the first volume, Exhibit USA 506.

That is a letter dated 19th July, 1944. I call your Honour's attention to the fact that it is dated in 1944, sent by the Commander of the Sipo and S.D. for the District of Radom to the Foreign Service Office in Tomassow.

Parenthetically, that big Haftbuch that we introduced in evidence has a number of cases in connection with the District of Radom, and your Honour will remember that it is a list of the people in the District of Tomassow.

The subject of this letter is "Collective responsibility of members of families of assassins and saboteurs." I will read after the word "precedents."

"The Higher S.S. and Police Fuehrer Ost has issued on 28th June, 1944, the following order:

The security situation in the Government General has in the last nine months grown so much worse that from now on the most radical means and the harshest measures must be enforced against the alien assassins and saboteurs. The Reichsfuehrer S.S., in agreement with the Governor General, has ordered that, in all cases where assassinations of Germans or attempts at such have occurred, or saboteurs have destroyed vital installations, not only the perpetrators who are caught are to be shot but also all male relatives are to be executed and their female relatives who are over 16 years are to be put into concentration camps. It is of course strictly understood that, if the perpetrator or the perpetrators are not apprehended, their names and addresses must be correctly ascertained. Among male relatives can be considered for example: the father, sons (in so far as they are over 16 years of age), brothers, brothers-in-law, cousins and uncles of the perpetrator. Proceedings must take place in the same manner against the women. By this procedure it is intended to secure collective responsibility of all men and women relatives of the perpetrator. It furthermore affects. to the utmost the family circle of the political criminal. This practice has already shown, for example, by the end of 1939, the best results in the new Eastern territories, especially in the Warthe district. As soon as this new method for combating assassins and saboteurs becomes known to these foreign people - this may be achieved by oral propaganda - the female members of a family to which members of the resistance movement or bands belong, as shown by experience, will exert a curbing influence."

Now the S.D. and Gestapo also conducted third degree interrogations of prisoners of war, and I refer to Document 1531-PS, Exhibit USA 248. This document contains an order of 12th June, 1942, signed by Mueller, which authorised the use of third degree methods in interrogations where preliminary investigation indicated that the prisoners could give information on important facts such as subversive activities, but did not authorise their use to extort confessions of the prisoner's own crimes.

Now I quote from Page 2 of the English translation, paragraph 2:

"Third degree may, under this supposition, only be employed against Communists, Marxists, Jehovah's Witnesses, saboteurs, terrorists, members of resistance movements, parachute agents, anti-social elements, Polish or Soviet-Russian loafers or tramps. In all other cases, my permission must first be obtained."

Then I pass to paragraph 4 at the end:

"Third degree can, according to the circumstances, employ, among other methods:

Very simple diet (bread and water); hard bunk; dark cell; deprivation of sleep; exhaustive drilling; also flogging (for more than 20 strokes a doctor must be consulted)."

On 24th February, 1944, the Commander of the Sipo and the S.D. for the district of Radom published an order issued by the Befehlshaber of the Sipo and the S.D. at Cracow, which is Document L-89, Exhibit U.S.A. 507, in the first volume. This followed closely the provisions of the previous decree that I have just quoted from, and I quote the first paragraph after the list of offices on the first page:

"In view of the variety of methods used to date in intensified interrogations and in order to avoid excesses, also to protect officials against eventual criminal proceedings, the Befehlshaber of the Security Police and of the S.D. in Cracow has issued the following order for the Security Police in the Government General, which is based on the regulations in force for the Reich."

And then the regulations are quoted. The significance of this document is that it proves that as late as 1944 third degree interrogations were still being conducted by the Gestapo.

I next pass to the activity of the Gestapo and the S.D. as being primary agencies for the persecution of the Jews, and I do not intend to go into any of the evidence previously introduced, except to refer to the participation of these organisations.

The responsibility of the Gestapo and S.D. for the mass extermination programme carried out by the Einsatz Groups of the Sipo and S.D. annihilation camps to which Jews were sent by the Sipo and S.D. has already been considered, and I simply cite to the Tribunal the Document 2615-PS, which has previously been introduced, and in which the number of Jews executed was referred to by Eichmann. I simply recall to your attention the fact that Eichmann was head of Section B 4 of the Gestapo. That section of the Gestapo dealt with Jewish affairs, including matters of evacuation, means of suppressing enemies of the People and the State, and the dispossession of rights of German citizenship.

The Gestapo was also charged with the enforcement of discriminatory laws, which have heretofore been introduced.

I now invite your Honour's attention to Document 3058-PS, Exhibit USA 508. I should like to point out to your Honour that it is a red-bordered document signed by Heydrich himself and addressed to the defendant Goering. It is dated 11th November, 1938. I pass this to the reporter, and before it is passed to the reporter it is to be noted that there is an appendix attached to it to the effect that the matter had been called to the attention of the defendant Goering.

Now this concerns a report of activities of the Gestapo in connection with the anti-Jewish demonstrations which you will recall were in the fall of 1938. This is a report from Heydrich personally to the defendant Goring. It is addressed to the Prime Minister, General Field- Marshal Goering, and is dated 11th November, 1938, and the previous documents showed that these activities occurred just before, and the order for it in connection with the Jewish uprooting or extermination:

"The extent of the destruction of Jewish shops and houses cannot yet be verified by figures. The figures given in the reports: 815 shops destroyed, 171 dwelling houses set on fire or destroyed, only indicate a fraction of the actual damage caused, as far as arson is concerned. Due to the urgency of the reports, those received to date are entirely limited to general statements such as 'numerous' or 'most shops destroyed.' Therefore the figures given must have been exceeded considerably.

191 synagogues were set on fire and another 76 completely destroyed. In addition, 11 parish halls, cemetery chapels and similar buildings were set on fire and 3 more completely destroyed.

Twenty thousand Jews were arrested, also seven Aryans and three foreigners. The latter were arrested for their own safety.

Thirty-six deaths were reported and those seriously injured were also numbered at thirty-six. Those killed and injured are Jews. One Jew is still missing. The Jews killed include one Polish national, and those injuries include two Poles."

I want to call your Honour's special attention to the paper appended to that document:

"The General Field Marshal" - that is Goering - "has been informed.

No steps are to be taken. By order."

It is dated 15th November, 1938, and signed. The signature is illegible.

Now in that same connection Heydrich was charged by the defendant Goering with this entire programme, and we next offer in evidence the original of that order, Document 710-PS, Exhibit USA 509. That is an order dated 31st July, 1941. It is written on the stationery of the Reich Marshal of the Greater German Reich, Commissioner for the Four Year Plan, Chairman of the Ministerial Council for National Defence, and it is dated at Berlin 31st July, 1941, and directed to the Chief of the Security Police and the Security Service, S.S. Gruppenfuehrer Heydrich.

"Complementary to the task that was assigned to you on 24th January, 1939, which dealt with arriving at - through furtherance of emigration and evacuation - a solution of the Jewish problem, as advantageous as possible, I hereby charge you with making all necessary preparations in regard to organisational and financial matters for bringing about a complete solution of the Jewish question in the German sphere of influence in Europe.

Wherever other Government agencies are involved, these are to co-operate with you.

I charge you furthermore to send me, before long, an overall plan concerning the organisational, factual and material measures necessary for the accomplishment of the desired solution of the Jewish question."

Signed, "Goering."

The Tribunal has already received the evidence as to what was the final solution of the Jewish problem as conceived by Heydrich, and executed by the Security Police and S.D. under him and under the defendant Kaltenbrunner. It was enslavement and mass murder.

Now, finally, in this presentation the last activity of the Gestapo and S.D. to which I will refer is that these organisations were the primary agencies for the persecution of the churches. Already evidence has been received concerning the persecution of the churches. In this struggle the Gestapo and the S.D. played a secret but very highly significant part.

Section C2 of the S.D. dealt with education and religious life. Section Bi of the Gestapo dealt with political Catholicism, Section B2 with political Protestantism, and Section B3 with other churches and Freemasonry.

The Church was one of the enemies of the Nazi State, and it was a peculiar function of the Gestapo to combat it. It issued restrictions against church activities, dissolved church organisations, and placed clergymen in protective custody.

I now want to offer in evidence Document 1815.-PS, Exhibit USA 510. This is a very large file, this original document, and I want to quote only portions of it. This was a file of the Gestapo regional office at Aachen. It discloses that the purpose of the Gestapo in combating the churches was to destroy them, and I want to read the first page of the English translation from the beginning.

This is dated "12th May, 1941, at Berlin, from the R.S.H.A., Section IV, B, 2, to all Staatspolizeileitsteller. For information: The S.D. Leit-Abschnitte; the Inspectors of the Sipo and S.D."

I understand this word "Abschnitte" means sub-divisions.

The subject is "Concerning the study and treatment of political Churches.

"The chief of the R.S.H.A. has issued an order, effective immediately, in which the S.D. and Sipo Study and Treatment of Political Churches, which has hitherto been divided between the S.D.-Abschnitte and Stapostellen, shall now be taken over entirely by the Stapostellen"

- which I understand means Regional Offices of the Gestapo.

Then it refers to the plan for the division of work issued by the R.S.H.A. on 1st March, 1941.

"In addition to combating opposition, the Stapostellen thus take over the entire Gegnernachrichtendienst"

- I understand that word means counter-intelligence

"in this sphere.

In order that the Stapostellen should be in a position to take over this work, the Chief of the Sipo and S.D. has ordered that the Church Specialists, hitherto employed in the S.D.-Abschnitte, should be temporarily transferred to the same posts at the Stapo Offices and operate the "Nachrichtendienstliche Arbielt"

- which, means Intelligence Service in the Church. -

"On the orders of the Chief of the R.S.H.A., and in agreement with the heads of Amt III, II, and I, those Church Specialists specified in the attached list" -

THE PRESIDENT: Is it necessary to give us the details of this?

COLONEL STOREY: No, Sir, I do not think so.

At any rate, if your Honour pleases, we quote from it, and it is simply a direction as to how they will proceed.

Now then, later, on 22nd and 23rd September, 1941, they called a conference of these so-called Church Specialists attached to the Gestapo Regional Offices which I have mentioned. This was held in the lecture hall of the R.S.H.A. in Berlin. Notes were taken, and this same document contains notes of that conference. The programme is shown and the plan worked out, in connection with the churches. I will just read the closing statement to these so-called Church Specialists; it is very short:

"Each one of you must go to work with your whole heart and a true fanaticism. Should a mistake or two be made in the execution of this work, this should in no way discourage you, since mistakes are made everywhere. The main thing is that the enemy" - meaning the church - "should be constantly tackled with determination, will, and effective initiative."

And then, finally, the last thing I would like to refer to in this document is on the eighth page of the English translation, which sets out their immediate aim and their ultimate aim; it is on Page 8 of the English translation:

"The immediate aim: The Church must not regain one inch of the ground it has lost.

The ultimate aim: Destruction of the Confessional Churches to be brought about by the collection of all material obtained through Nachrichtendienst activities, which will, at a given time, be produced as evidence for the charge of treasonable activities during the German fight for existence."

I understand that long German word means intelligence activities.

Now, if your Honour pleases, this concludes the factual, documentary presentation which I shall make in connection with the S.D. and Gestapo. Closely allied with it is the case against Kaltenbrunner, as the representative of these organisations, which will be presented immediately after lunch by Lieutenant Whitney Harris. Also, there will be one or two witnesses who will be introduced in connection with these organisations and in connection with Kaltenbrunner.

There I should like to conclude, with just these remarks.

The evidence shows that the Gestapo was created by the defendant Goering in Prussia in April, 1933, for the specific purpose of serving as a police agency to strike down the actual and ideological enemies of the Nazi regime, and that henceforward the Gestapo in Prussia and in the other states of the Reich carried out a programme of terror against all who were thought to be dangerous to the domination of the Conspirators over the people of Germany. Its methods were utterly ruthless. It operated outside the law and sent its victims to the concentration camps. The term "Gestapo" became the symbol of the Nazi regime of force and terror.

Behind the scenes, operating secretly, the S.D., through its vast network of informants, spied upon the German people in their daily lives, on the streets, in the shops, and even within the sanctity of the churches.

The most casual remark of the German citizen might bring him before the Gestapo where his fate and freedom were decided without recourse to law. In this government, in which the rule of law was replaced by a tyrannical rule of men, the Gestapo was the primary instrument of oppression.

The Gestapo and the S.D. played an important part in almost every criminal act of the Conspiracy. The category of these crimes, apart from the thousands of specific instances of torture and cruelty in policing Germany for the benefit of the Conspirators, reads like a page from the Devil's notebook:

They fabricated the border incidents which Hitler used as an excuse for attacking Poland.

They murdered hundreds of thousands of defenceless men, women and children by the infamous Einsatz Groups.

They removed Jews, political leaders, and scientists from prisoner of war camps and murdered them.

They took recaptured prisoners of war to concentration camps and murdered them.

They established and classified the concentration camps and sent thousands of people into them for extermination and slave labour.

They cleared Europe of the Jews, and were responsible for sending hundreds of thousands to their deaths in annihilation camps.

They rounded up hundreds of thousands of citizens of occupied countries and shipped them to Germany for forced labour and sent slave labourers to labour reformatory camps.

Reinhard Heydrich with Secretary Karl Hermann Frank (right) and Horst Böhme (left) in Prague, late September 1941.

They executed captured commandos and paratroopers and protected civilians who lynched allied fliers.

They took civilians of occupied countries to Germany for secret trial and punishment.

They arrested, tried and punished citizens of occupied countries under special crimifial procedures which did not accord fair trails, and by summary methods.

They murdered or sent to concentration camps the relatives of persons who had allegedly committed crimes.

They ordered the murder of prisoners in Sipo and S.D. prisons to prevent their release by Allied armies.

They participated in the seizure and spoliation of public and private property.

They were primary agencies for the persecution of the Jews and churches.

In carrying out these crimes the Gestapo operated as an organisation closely centralised and controlled from Berlin headquarters. Reports were submitted to Berlin and all important decisions emanated from Berlin. The regional offices had only limited power to commit persons to concentration camps. All cases, other than short of duration, had to be submitted to Berlin for approval.

The Gestapo was organised on a functional basis. Its principal divisions dealt with groups and institutions against which it committed the worst crimes - which I have enumerated.

Thus, in perpetrating these crimes, the Gestapo acted as an entity, each section performing its parts in the general criminal enterprises ordered by Berlin. The Secret State Police should be held responsible as an organisation for the vast crimes in which it participated.

The S.D. was at all times a department of the S.S. Its criminality directly concerns and contributes to the criminality of the S.S.

And as to the Gestapo, it is submitted that it was an organisation in the sense in which that term is used in Article 9 of the Charter, that the defendants Goering and Kaltenbrunner committed the crimes defined in Article 6 of the Charter in their capacity as members and leaders of the Gestapo, and that the Gestapo, as an organisation, participated in and aided the conspiracy which contemplated and involved the commission of the crimes defined in Article 6 of the Charter.

And finally, I have in my hand here a brochure published in honour of the famous Heydrich, the former Chief of the Security Police and S.D., and I quote from a speech delivered by Heydrich on German Police Day, 1941, of which I ask the Tribunal to take judicial notice:

"Secret State Police, Criminal Police, and S.D. are still adorned with the furtive and whispered secrecy of a political detective story. In a mixture of fear and shuddering-and yet at home with a certain feeling of security because of their presence - brutality, inhumanity bordering on the sadistic, and ruthlessness are attributed abroad to the men of this profession."

Those are the words of Heydrich, who was the former head of this organisation.

Does your Honour want to go ahead?

DR. KURT KAUFMANN (Counsel for defendant Kaltenbrunner): I have just heard that during the afternoon the evidence will concern the defendant Kaltenbrunner. I therefore regard it as advisable to make a proposition regarding Kaltenbrunner immediately, before the recess, and not in the afternoon.

My suggestion is the following:

I ask that the trial against Kaltenbrunner be postponed during his absence. Kaltenbrunner, so far as the proceedings thus far have been concerned, has taken only a small part. The reason for his absence is an illness which, according to my opinion, is of a serious nature, for it is obvious that in so important a trial only a very serious illness can bring about the absence of a defendant and justify it. I have no doctor's report on his present condition. It therefore appears to me dubious whether he will be capable of attending the hearing at all in the future.

Be that as it may, my present suggestion that the trial of Kaltenbrunner be postponed is not in contradiction to paragraph 12 of the Charter. If a defendant is alive and cannot be brought to trial in person, then the trial can proceed against him in his absence. This is particularly justified if the defendant is concealing himself and if he thus is obliged to submit to the trial even in his absence.

But Kaltenbrunner is here in prison. He did not withdraw himself from the trial and he wishes nothing more than that he may be able to take a position as regards the accusation. But if such a defendant is absent through no fault of his own, it would hardly be consistent with justice if his trial were nevertheless carried out.

I should regret the procedure of the trial all the more since it is precisely now that Kaltenbrunner must have an opportunity to give me information in my capacity as his defence counsel. The particular indictment is not even known to him; it was given to him just before the Christmas recess.

I do not need to emphasise how much more difficult the defence's task is made by a continuation of the trial - indeed, it is made almost impossible.

THE PRESIDENT: The Tribunal will consider the application which has been made on behalf of counsel for the defendant Kaltenbrunner and will give its decision shortly.

The Tribunal will now adjourn until 2 o'clock.

COLONEL STOREY: If I may make just one statement in connection with that, if your Honour pleases?

THE PRESIDENT: Yes, certainly.

COLONEL STOREY: The evidence against Kaltenbrunner will be in connection with the part he played in these organisations, and we thought that, in the interest of time, the individual case against Kaltenbrunner could be presented simultaneously. Now, if it were not presented in this connection, it would be within a few days, early next week, in connection with the other individual defendants. Counsel mentions that he probably will not be able to be here for some time, and I thought I would make that statement.

THE PRESIDENT: Yes.

(A recess was taken until 1400 hours.)

THE PRESIDENT: The Tribunal has considered the motion made by counsel on behalf of Kaltenbrunner, and it considers that any evidence which you were intending to produce, which is directed against Kaltenbrunner individually and not against the organisations, ought to be postponed until the prosecution come to deal, as the Tribunal understands you do propose to deal, with each defendant individually; and the Tribunal thinks that Kaltenbrunner's case might properly be kept to the end of the individual defendants, and that the evidence which is especially brought against Kaltenbrunner might then be adduced. If Kaltenbrunner is then still unable to be in Court, that evidence will have to be given in his absence.

COLONEL STOREY: If your Honour pleases, I do not believe that the case, as we have it prepared now, can be separated as between the organisations and the individuals.

THE PRESIDENT: No, but if it bears against the organisations it can be adduced now.

COLONEL STOREY: I understand that, but if your Honour pleases, I say that the preparation that we have made is in connection both with the organisations and the individuals. In other words, it is a joint presentation. Therefore, under your Honour's ruling, as taken, it would have to go over until next week with the individual defendants' cases, because we prepared it so that it will affect the organisations as well as the defendant individually, because his acts are in connection with what he has done with the organisations included; in other words, we have not got it separated.

THE PRESIDENT: How will that affect you for this afternoon?

COLONEL STOREY: We can introduce a witness, next, but if your Honour pleases, in reference to the witness, he, of course, would affect the organisations, and incidentally would affect Kaltenbrunner, too. I do not see how you could separate that, except that for the witnesses this afternoon the questions could be confined to the organisations.

THE PRESIDENT: Now, of course, all the evidence which has been given up to date, much of it in Kaltenbrunner's absence, has in one sense been against Kaltenbrunner in being evidence against the organisation of which he was the head.

COLONEL STOREY: Colonel Amen is going to examine the witness orally, and it is primarily evidence against the organisations; and, incidentally, it would affect Kaltenbrunner's individual liability.

THE PRESIDENT: I think the Tribunal would like you to go on with the evidence.

COLONEL STOREY: Yes. It has been suggested, if your Honour pleases, that we might have a few minutes to confer about the situation, about the witnesses.

THE PRESIDENT: You wish to adjourn for a few minutes?

COLONEL STOREY: Just a few minutes so that we can confer, as it changes our order of proof.

THE PRESIDENT: Very well.

COLONEL STOREY: Just ten minutes will be sufficient.

THE PRESIDENT: Yes, we will adjourn now.

(A recess was taken.)

THE PRESIDENT: The Tribunal will now hear the evidence which the prosecution desires to call, and in so far as it consists of oral testimony, the Tribunal will afford counsel for Kaltenbrunner the opportunity of cross-examining the witnesses now called, at a later stage if he wishes to do so.

DR. LUDWIG BABEL (Counsel for S.S. and S.D.): I was first appointed counsel for the members of the S.S. and S.D., who in these proceedings have asked for leave to be heard. My duties were circumscribed in such a manner that I was to present to the Court the motions in suitable form. Not until the Tribunal made its announcement of 17th December, 1945, was I appointed as defence counsel for the organisations of the S.S. and the S.D. As such I am not working on behalf of a client who could give me information or instructions for carrying on the defence. In order to obtain the necessary information I am, therefore, restricted to communicating with members of the organisations I am representing, most of which members are in prisoner of war camps or have been arrested. Thus far, because of the shortness of time, I have not been able to get the necessary information.

After 17th December, 1945, thousands of requests were submitted to me by the Court and in the short period of time, since then, I have not been able to work on all of them.

According to Article 16 of the Charter, a copy of the Indictment and of all pertaining documents - written in a language he understands - is to be handed to the defendant within a reasonable time prior to the beginning of the trial. This provision should, presumably, be also applied to the indicted organisations. To serve the Indictment on the organisations is not provided for in the rules of procedure nor has the Tribunal so far ordered it.

In view of the very extensive work involved I personally was not in a position to have copies prepared in a number sufficient for distribution to the members of the organisations in the various camps so that they could express their views and give me the needed information.

In face of these circumstances, for which neither I nor the organisations which I am representing are responsible, I am not in a position to cross-examine a witness. who would be heard to-day thereby making use of the right accorded to me as defence counsel. To hear a witness against the defendant Kaltenbrunner likewise concerns the organisations which I represent, the S.S. and the S.D. To hear this witness at this point would mean limiting the defence.

I therefore submit a motion to postpone the further discussion of the charges against the organisations of the S.S. and the S.D. By visiting the camps, in which there are members of the organisations of the S.S. and S.D., and after discussions with them, I shall be able to obtain the information needed for the defence. I should like to add that thereby no delay in the proceedings would be caused and, I presume, this would in no way place a burden upon the prosecution.

THE PRESIDENT: If you will allow me to interrupt you, I understand your application to be, that you are not in a position to cross-examine these witnesses this afternoon, and that you wish for an opportunity similar to that which I have already accorded to the counsel for Kaltenbrunner, to be accorded to you. You wish for an opportunity to cross-examine these witnesses at a later stage, is that right?

DR. BABEL: Yes. At the same time, however, I should like to point out at this moment that, through the peculiarity of the task that has been allotted to me, my defence is being made so difficult that to cover questions subsequently -

THE PRESIDENT: Let us not take up time by that. Was your application that you might have an opportunity of cross-examining these witnesses at a later date?

DR. BABEL: My motion had that meaning but its purpose was also to make the defence practicable and ensure that the witnesses should not be heard at a time when I cannot make use to the fullest extent of the privileges granted me by the Charter.

THE PRESIDENT: The Tribunal is ready to give you the opportunity of cross-examining these witnesses at a later date.

LT. WHITNEY R. HARRIS: May it please the Tribunal.

We submit Document Book BB as a separate Document Book, relating to the defendant Kaltenbrunner. This book contains our documents, from which quotations will be made during this presentation. Reference will be made to three or four other documents contained in the Document Book on the Gestapo and the S.D.

During the past three Court days, the Tribunal has heard evidence of the criminality of the S.S., the S.D. and the Gestapo. The fusion of these organisations into the shock formations of the Hitler Police-State has been explained from an organisational standpoint. There is before the Tribunal a defendant who represents these organisations through the official positions which he held in the S.S. and the German Police, and whose career gives added significance to this unity of the S.S. and the Nazi Police. The name of this defendant is Ernst Kaltenbrunner.

I now offer Document 2938-PS as the Exhibit next in order, USA 511. This is an article which appeared in Die Deutsche Polizei, the magazine of the Security Police and S.D., on 15th May, 1943, at Page 193, entitled, "Dr. Ernst Kaltenbrunner, the New Chief the Security Police and S.D." and I quote the beginning of the article:

"S.S. Gruppenfuehrer Dr. jur. Kaltenbrunner was born the son of the lawyer Dr. Hugo Kaltenbrunner, on 4th October, 1903, at Ried on Inn, near Braunau. He spent his youth in the native district of the Fuehrer, with whom his kinsfolk, originally a hereditary farming clan, had been closely connected since olden times. Later he moved with his parents to the little market-town Raab, and then to Linz, on the Danube, where he attended the State Realgymnasium, and there he passed his final examination in 1921."

The next paragraph describes Kaltenbrunner's legal education, his nationalistic activities and his opposition to Catholic-Christian-Social student groups. It states that after 1928 Kaltenbrunner worked as a lawyer-candidate in Linz. The article continues, and I quote, reading the third paragraph:

"As early as January, 1934, Dr. Kaltenbrunner was imprisoned by the Dollfuss Government on account of his Nazi views and sent with other leading National Socialists into the concentration camp Kaisersteinbruch. He caused and led a hunger strike and forced the Government to dismiss 490 National Socialist prisoners. In the following year he was imprisoned again, because of suspicion of high treason and committed to the Court-Martial of Wels (Upper Danube). After an investigation of many months, the accusation of high treason collapsed, but he was sentenced to six months' imprisonment for conspiracy. After the spring of 1935, Dr. Kaltenbrunner was the leader of the Austrian S.S., the right to practise his profession having been suspended because of his National Socialist views. It redounds to his credit that in this important position he succeeded, through energetic leadership, in maintaining the unity of the Austrian S.S., which he had built up, in spite of all persecution, and succeeded in committing it successfully at the right moment.

After the annexation, in which the S.S. was a decisive factor, he was appointed State Secretary for Security Matters on 11th March, 1938, in the new National Socialist Cabinet of Dr. Seyss-Inquart. A few hours later he was able to report to the Reichsfuehrer S.S. Heinrich Himmler, who had landed at Aspern, the Vienna Airport, on 12th March, 1938, 3 a.m., as the first National Socialist leader, that the Movement had achieved complete victory and that" - the article quotes Kaltenbrunner - "the S.S. is in formation awaiting further orders" - closing Kaltenbrunner's statement.

"The Fuehrer promoted Dr. Kaltenbrunner on the day of the annexation, to S.S. Brigadefuehrer and leader of the S.S.-Abschnitt Ober Donau. On 11th September, 1938, this was followed by his promotion to S.S. Gruppenfuehrer."

The Tribunal will recall evidence heretofore received, and I refer to Page 254 (Part I) of the transcript of these proceedings, of the telephone conversation between Goering and Seyss- Inquart, in which Goering stated that Kaltenbrunner was to have the Department of Security.

I continue quoting the last paragraph from this article:

"During the liquidation of the Austrian National Government and the reorganisation of Austria into Alps and Danube Districts, he was appointed Higher S.S. and Police Leader with the Reich Government in Vienna, Lower Danube and Upper Danube in Corps Area 17, and in April, 1941, he was promoted to Major General of Police."

Kaltenbrunner thereby became the little Himmler of Austria.

According to Der Grossdeutsche Reichstag, Vierte Wahlperiode, 1938, published by F. Kienast, at Page 262, our Document 2892-PS, Kaltenbrunner joined the Nazi Party and the S.S. in Austria in 1932. He was Party Member 300179 and S.S. Member 13039. Prior to 1933 he was the "Gauredner" and legal adviser to S.S. Division 8. After 1933, he was the leader of S.S. Regiment 37, and later the leader of S.S. Division 8. Kaltenbrunner was given the highest Nazi Party decorations, the Golden Insignia of Honour and the Blutorden. He was a member of the Reichstag after 1938.

I now offer Document 3427-PS, as Exhibit next in order USA 512. This is also an article which appeared in Die Deutsche Polizei, the magazine of the Security Police and S.D., 12th February, 1943, at Page 65, and I quote:

"S.S. Gruppenfuehrer Kaltenbrunner Appointed Chief of the Security Police and of the S.D.

Berlin, 30th January, 1943.

Upon suggestion of the Reichsfuehrer S.S. and Chief of German Police, the Fuehrer has appointed S.S. Gruppenfuehrer and Major General of Police Dr. Ernst Kaltenbrunner as Chief of the Security Police and of the S.D. as successor of S.S. Obergruppenfuehrer and Lieutenant General of Police Reinhard Heydrich, who passed away 4th June, 1942."

The Tribunal has heard frequent references made to the speech of Himmler delivered on 4th October, 1943, at Posen, Poland, to Gruppenfuehrers of the S.S., our Document 1919-PS, heretofore received as Exhibit USA170, in which, with unmatched frankness, Himmler discussed the barbaric programme and criminal activities of the S.S. and the Security Police. Near the beginning of the speech Himmler referred to, and I quote merely this one sentence: "Our comrade, S.S. Gruppenfuehrer Ernst Kaltenbrunner, who has succeeded our fallen friend Heydrich."

Kaltenbrunner carried out the responsibilities as Chief of the Security Police and S. D. to the satisfaction of Himmler and Hitler, for on 9th December 1944, according to the "Befehlsblatt" of the Security Police and S.D.

DR. KAUFMANN (Counsel for defendant Kaltenbrunner): May I interrupt just for a second? I understood the decision of the Tribunal to be that the proceedings against Kaltenbrunner were to be postponed until Kaltenbrunner is fit for trial and now the matter of Kaltenbrunner is being discussed.

THE PRESIDENT: No, the decision which the Tribunal indicated before was based upon the view that the evidence could be divided between evidence which bore directly against Kaltenbrunner and evidence which bore against the organisation of the Gestapo, but, when you attended before us in closed session, it was explained that it was impossible to do that and that the evidence was so inextricably mingled that it was impossible to direct the evidence solely to the organisation and not to include that against Kaltenbrunner. Accordingly the Tribunal decided that they would go on with the evidence, which the prosecution desired to present, in its entirety, but that they would give you the opportunity of cross-examining any witnesses who might be called, at a later date. Of course, you will, in addition to that, have the fullest opportunity of dealing with any documentary evidence which bears against Kaltenbrunner when the time comes for you to present the defence on behalf of Kaltenbrunner.

Do you follow that?

DR. KAUMANN: Of course.

THE PRESIDENT: You will have the opportunity of cross-examining any witness who is called this afternoon or to-morrow, at a later date, a date which will be convenient to yourself. And in addition, with reference to any documentary evidence such as is now being presented by counsel for the United States, you will have full opportunity at a future date of dealing any way that it seems right to you to do.

DR. KAUFMANN: Yes. May I just say one word more? The misunderstanding from which I am suffering is probably due to the fact that I was of the opinion that witnesses were now to be heard, but now I hear that the evidence - that is to say, a vastly greater complex of evidence - is to be put forward. Now that I hear that the Tribunal is also admitting the evidence in its entirety I shall, of course, have to submit to this decision.

LT. HARRIS: Kaltenbrunner carried out the responsibilities as Chief of the Security Police and S.D. to the satisfaction of Himmler and Hitler, it for on 9th December, 1944, according to the "Befehlsblatt" of the Security Police and S.D., No. 51, Page 361, our 2770-PS, he received, as Chief of the Security Police and S.D., the decoration known as the Knight's Cross of the War Merit with Crossed Swords, one of the highest military decorations. By that time Kaltenbrunner had been promoted to the high rank of S.S. Obergruppenfuehrer and General of the Police.

I invite the attention of the Tribunal to the organisation chart entitled "The Position of Kaltenbrunner and the Gestapo and S.D. in the German Police System," Exhibit USA 493. As Chief of the Security Police and S.D., Kaltenbrunner was the Head of the Gestapo, the Kripo and the S.D. and of the R.S.H.A., which was a department of the S.S. and the Reich Ministry of the Interior. He was in charge of the regional offices of the Gestapo, the S.D. and the Kripo within Germany, and of the Einsatz Groups and Einsatz Commandos in the occupied territories.

Directly under Kaltenbrunner were the Chiefs of the main offices of the R.S.H.A., including Amt III (the S.D. within Germany), Amt IV (the Gestapo), Amt V (the Kripo), and Amt VI (Foreign Intelligence).

I offer Document 2939-PS as Exhibit next in order, Exhibit USA 513. This is the affidavit of Walter Schellenberg, who was chief of Amt VI of the R.S.H.A. from the autumn of 1941 to the end of the war. I am going to read a very small portion of this affidavit, beginning with the sixth sentence of the first paragraph:

"On or about 25th January, 1943, I went together with Kaltenbrunner to Himmler's headquarters at Loetzen in East Prussia. All of the Amt Chiefs of the R.S.H.A. were present at this meeting, and Himmler informed us that Kaltenbrunner was to be appointed Chief of the Security Police and S.D. (R.S.H.A.) as successor to Heydrich. His appointment was effective as from 30th January, 1943. I know of no limitation placed on Kaltenbrunner's authority as Chief of the Security Police and S.D. He promptly entered upon the duties of the office and assumed direct charge of the office and control over the Amt. All important matters of all Amter had to clear through Kaltenbrunner."

During Kaltenbrunner's term in office as Chief of the Security Police and S.D., many crimes were committed by the Security Police and S.D. pursuant to policy established by the R.S.H.A. or upon orders issued out of the R.S.H.A., for all of which Kaltenbrunner was responsible by virtue of his office. Each of these crimes has been discussed in detail in the case against the Gestapo and S.D., and reference is here made to that presentation. Evidence now will be offered only to show that these crimes continued after Kaltenbrunner became Chief of the Security Police and S.D. on 30th January, 1943.

The first crime for which Kaltenbrunner is responsible as Chief of the Security Police and S.D. is the murder and mistreatment of civilians of occupied countries by the Einsatz Groups. There were at least five Einsatz Groups operating in the East during Kaltenbrunner's term in office.

The "Befehlsblatt" of the Security Police and S.D. - and this is contained in our Document 2890-PS, of which I ask the Tribunal to take judicial notice - contains reference to Einsatz Groups A, B, D, G and Croatia during the period of August, 1943, to January, 1945.

I shall not read from the document which contains those excerpts, but the Tribunal will note those references to the name "Einsatz Groups," indicating that they were operating during the time that Kaltenbrunner was Chief of the Security Police and S.D. The Tribunal will recall Document 1104-PS, which has heretofore been received as Exhibit USA 483. I will only refer in passing to this document, which contained a lengthy and critical report on the conduct of the Security Police in exterminating the Jewish population of Sluzk, White Ruthenia. That report was submitted to Heydrich on 21st November, 1941. Yet, the same conditions of horror and cruelty continued to characterise the operations of Einsatzkommandos in the East while Kaltenbrunner was Chief of the Security Police and S.D. I refer to Document R-135, which has heretofore been received as Exhibit USA 289, and I will not read anything from that but simply refresh the Tribunal's recollection of the report of Gunther, the prison warden at Minsk, under date of 31st May, 1943, to the General Commissioner for White Ruthenia, in which he pointed out that after 13th April, 1943, the S.D. had pursued a policy of removing all gold teeth, bridgework and fillings of Jews, an hour or two before they were murdered.

The Tribunal will also recall in this Exhibit the report of 18th June, 1943, to the Reich Minister for the occupied territories describing the practice of the police battalions of locking men, women and children into barns which were then set on fire.

The second crime for which Kaltenbrunner is responsible as Chief of the Security Police and S.D. is the execution of racial and political undesirables.

THE PRESIDENT: Lieutenant Harris, I think you are going perhaps a little bit too fast, and it is difficult for us to follow you when you are referring so quickly to these documents.

LIEUTENANT HARRIS: Thank you, sir.

The second crime for which Kaltenbrunner is responsible as Chief of the Security Police and S.D. is the execution of racial and political undesirables screened out of prisoner-of-war camps by the Gestapo. The Tribunal will recall Document 2542-PS, heretofore received as Exhibit USA 489.

I believe, you will find that document in the Gestapo Document Book. It was introduced this morning.

THE PRESIDENT: The Lindow affidavit?

LIEUTENANT HARRIS: Yes. That is the Lindow affidavit that indicates that the programme of screening prisoner of war camps continued during 1943.

The third crime for which Kaltenbrunner is responsible as Chief of the Security Police and S.D. was the taking of recaptured prisoners of war -

THE PRESIDENT: Wait a minute. You have not yet drawn our attention to any specific paragraph which shows that this programme was in operation after 1943; you are passing on to something else whilst I am looking at the document to see what I have got.

LIEUTENANT HARRIS: Referring specifically to the third paragraph, if the Tribunal please, which has heretofore been read into evidence.

THE PRESIDENT: That only says until about the beginning of 1943.

LIEUTENANT HARRIS: It says early in 1943 the department was dissolved and it went into the departments in Subsection IV B. The work concerning Russian prisoners of war must then have been done by IV B2a.

THE PRESIDENT: Yes. Well, that is all you want it for, is it not

LIEUTENANT HARRIS: Yes.

The third crime for which Kaltenbrunner is responsible as Chief of the Security Police and S.D. was the taking of recaptured prisoners-of-war to concentration camps where they were executed. I invite the attention of the Tribunal to Document 1650-PS, which has heretofore been received as Exhibit USA 246. This is the secret Gestapo order, the "Kugel Erlass," or "Bullet Decree," under which escaped prisoners-of-war were sent to concentration camps by the Security Police and S.D. for execution.

This order, dated 4th March, 1944, was signed - and I quote - "Chief of the Security Police and of the Security Service, for the Chief," (signed) "Mueller."

I now offer Document L-158 as Exhibit next in order. This is Exhibit USA 54. I am not going to read this document since it is similar to the previous document offered, but I do wish to refer to the marked passages. First: "On 2nd March, 1944, the Chief of the Security Police and S.D., Berlin, forwarded the following O.K.W. order." Then follows the statement that upon recapture certain escaped prisoners of war should be turned over to the Chief of the Security Police and S.D.

The document goes on to say - and I quote - "In this connection the Chief of the Security Police and S.D. has issued the following instructions." Detailed instructions follow concerning the turning over of such prisoners to the commandant of Mauthausen under the operation "Bullet." Further, this order states - and I quote - this is at the very end of the order - "The list of the recaptured officers and non-working N.C.O. prisoners of war will be kept here by IV A I. To enable a report to be made punctually to the Chief of the Sipo and S.D., Berlin, statements of the numbers involved must reach Radom by 20th June, 1944."

I recall the attention of the Tribunal to Document 2285-PS, which was received this morning as Exhibit USA 490.

THE PRESIDENT: Has that Document L-158 already been put in evidence?

LT. HARRIS: No, Sir, I have just put in those portions. I have just put the document in evidence at this time, Sir. The document has not been read in its entirety for the reason that the contents, other than the quoted portions, are substantially the same as Document 1650, which has been read at length.

THE PRESIDENT: You say it is the same as 1650?

LT. HARRIS: It is, Sir, substantially the same. It relates to the same subject. It was, however, addressed to a different party, and I particularly wish to place before the Tribunal the last paragraph which has been quoted and read into evidence.

THE PRESIDENT: The last paragraph does not mean very much by itself, does it?

LT. HARRIS: Very well, Sir. Then, if the Tribunal will permit it, I would like to read the document in its entirety.

THE PRESIDENT: Do you mean that 1650 has got these paragraphs 1, 2 and 3 in it?

LT. HARRIS: Yes, Sir. That is exactly what I do mean, Sir.

I will call the attention of the Tribunal to Document 2285-PS, which was received in evidence this morning as Exhibit USA 490. That was the affidavit of Lt. Colonel Gast and Lt. Veith of the French Army, who stated that during 1943 and 1944 prisoners of war were murdered at Mauthausen under the "Bullet Decree." I am sure the Tribunal will recall that document.

The fourth crime for which Kaltenbrunner is responsible as Chief of the Security Police and S.D. was the commitment of racial and political undesirables to concentration camps and annihilation camps, for slave labour and mass murder. Before Kaltenbrunner became Chief of the Security Police and S.D., on 30th January, 1943, he was fully cognisant of conditions in concentration camps and of the fact that concentration camps were used for slave labour and mass murder. The Tribunal will recall from previous evidence that Mauthausen concentration camp was established in Austria and that Kaltenbrunner was the Higher S.S. and Police Leader for Austria.

This concentration camp, as shown by Document 1063A-PS, which was received this morning as Exhibit USA 492, was classified by Heydrich in January, 1941, in Category III, a camp for the most heavily accused prisoners and for asocial prisoners who were considered incapable of being reformed. The Tribunal will recall that prisoners of war to be executed under the "Bullet Decree" were sent to Mauthausen. As will be shown hereafter, Kaltenbrunner was a frequent visitor to Mauthausen concentration camp. On one such visit in 1942 Kaltenbrunner personally observed the gas chamber in action. I now offer Document 2753-PS as Exhibit next in order, Exhibit USA515. This is the affidavit of Alois Hoellriegl, former guard at Mauthausen concentration camp. The affidavit states, and I quote:

"I, Alois Hoellriegl, being first duly sworn, declare I was a member of the Totenkopf S. S. and stationed at the Mauthausen concentration camp from January, 1940, until the end of the war. On one occasion, I believe it was in the fall of 1942, Ernst Kaltenbrunner visited Mauthausen. I was on guard duty at the time and saw him twice. He went down into the gas chamber with Ziereis, commandant of the camp, at a time when prisoners were being gassed. The sound accompanying the gassing operation was well known to me. I heard the gassing taking place while Kaltenbrunner was present.

I saw Kaltenbrunner come up from the gas cellar after the gassing operation had been completed.

(Signed) Hoellriegl"

On one occasion Kaltenbrunner made an inspection of the camp grounds at Mauthausen with Himmler and had his photograph taken during the course of the inspection. I offer Document 2641-PS as exhibit next in order, Exhibit USA 5 16.

This exhibit consists of two affidavits and a series of photographs. Here are the original photographs in my hand. The original photographs are the small ones which have been enlarged, and those in the Document Book are not very good reproductions, but the Tribunal will see better reproductions which are being handed to it.

DR. KAUFMANN (Counsel for defendant Kaltenbrunner): Since the whole accusation against Kaltenbrunner has nevertheless been brought forward, I feel bound to make a motion on a matter of principle. I could have made this motion this morning just as well. It is in reference to the question of whether affidavits may be read or not. I know that this question has already been the subject of consultation by the Tribunal and that the Tribunal has already decided this question in a definite manner. When I ask that this question be decided once more, it is for a special reason.

Every trial is something dynamic. What was correct at that time may at a later date be wrong. The most important and most significant trial in history rests in many important points on the mere reading of affidavits which have been taken down by the prosecution exclusively, according to its own maxims.

The reading of affidavits is not satisfactory in the long run. It is becoming more necessary from hour to hour to see, to hear for once a witness for the prosecution and to test his credibility and the reliability of his memory. There are many witnesses standing, so to speak, at the door of this Courtroom, and they need only be called in. To hear the witness at a later stage is not sufficient; nor is it certain that the Tribunal will permit a hearing on the same evidential subject. I therefore oppose the further reading of the affidavit just announced. The meaning of Article 19 of the Charter should not be killed by a literal interpretation.

THE PRESIDENT: Is your application that you want to cross-examine the witness or is your application that the affidavit should not be read?

DR. KAUFMANN: The latter.

THE PRESIDENT: That the affidavit should not be read?

DR. KAUFMANN: Yes.

THE PRESIDENT: Are you referring to the affidavit of Hoellriegl, Document 2753-PS?

DR. KAUFMANN: Yes.

THE PRESIDENT: The Tribunal is of the opinion that the affidavit, which is upon a relevant point, upon a material point, is evidence which ought to be admitted under Article 19 of the Charter, but they will consider any motion which counsel for Kaltenbrunner may think fit to make for cross-examination of the witness who made the affidavit, if he is available and could be called.

LT. HARRIS: Yes, Sir. They have been offered in evidence as the exhibit next in order, and I wish to refer to the first affidavit accompanying them, which appears in the Document Book.

THE PRESIDENT: Yes.

LT. HARRIS: It being the affidavit of Alois Hoellriegl.

THE PRESIDENT: Yes. You had handed up the affidavit at the same time, had you not?

LT. HARRIS: Yes, Sir, I did, Sir. That affidavit states, and I quote:
"I was a member of the Totenkopf S.S. and stationed in the Mauthausen concentration camp from January, 1940, until the end of the war. I am thoroughly familiar with all of the buildings and grounds at Mauthausen concentration camp. I have been shown Document 2641-PS, which is a series of six photographs. I recognise all these photographs as having been taken at Mauthausen concentration camp. With respect to the first photograph I positively identify Heinrich Himmler as the man on the left, Ziereis, the commandant of Mauthausen concentration camp, in the centre, and Ernst Kaltenbrunner as the man on the right."

THE PRESIDENT: He does not say, does he, at what date the photographs were taken?

LT. HARRIS: No, Sir. I have no evidence as to what date the photographs were taken, Sir.

THE PRESIDENT: Just that Kaltenbrunner was there?

LT. HARRIS: Just that Kaltenbrunner was there, at some time, in the company of Ziereis and Himmler.

THE PRESIDENT: Yes.

LT. HARRIS: With full knowledge of conditions in and the purpose of concentration camps, Kaltenbrunner ordered or permitted to be ordered in his name, the commitment of persons to concentration camps.

I offer Document L-38 as exhibit next in order, Exhibit USA S17. This is the affidavit of Herman Pister, the former commandant of Buchenwald concentration camp, which was taken on 1st August, 1945, at Freising, Germany, in the course of an official military investigation by the United States Army, and I quote from it as follows, beginning with the second paragraph:

"With exception of the mass delivery of prisoners from the concentration camps of the occupied territory all prisoners were sent to the concentration camp Buchenwald by order of the Reichssicherheitshauptamt - Reich Security Main Office - Berlin. These orders for protective custody (red forms) were in most cases signed with the name 'Kaltenbrunner.' The few remaining protective custody orders were signed by 'Foerster.'"

I now offer Document 2477-PS as exhibit next in order, Exhibit USA 5 18. This is the affidavit of Willy Litzenberg, former Chief of Department IV A Ib in the R.S.H.A. This document reads in part as follows, and I quote, beginning with the second paragraph:

"The right of summary taking into protective custody belongs to the Directors of the State Police H.Q's or State Police Offices; previously for a period of 21 days; later, I think, for a period of 56 days. Custody exceeding this time had to be sanctioned by the competent Office for Protective Custody in the R.S.H.A. The Regulations for Protective Custody or the signing of the Protective Custody Order could only be issued through the Director of the R.S.H.A. as Chief of the Sipo and S.D. All Regulations and Protective Custody Orders that I have seen bore a facsimile stamp of Heydrich or Kaltenbrunner. As far as I can remember, I have never seen a document of this kind with another name as signature. How far and to whom the Chief of the Sipo and S.D. possibly gave authority for the use of his facsimile stamp, I do not know. Perhaps the Chief of Amt IV possessed a similar authority.

The greater part of the Protective Custody Office was transferred to Prague. Only one staff remained in Berlin."

I now offer Document 2745-PS as exhibit next in order, Exhibit USA 519.

This is an order under date 7th July, 1943, which was found at the former office of the section of the Gestapo which handled protective custody matters in Prague. It was an order to the Prague Office to send a teletype message to the Gestapo office in Koeslin, ordering protective custody of one Racke, and her commitment to the concentration camp at Ravensbruck for refusing to work. The order carried the facsimile signature of Kaltenbrunner and I invite the attention of the Tribunal to the original which has that facsimile for the arrest. Orders of this type were the basis for the orders actually sent out to the Prague office, which carried the teletype signature of Kaltenbrunner. At the bottom of the page the Tribunal will note the facsimile stamp of Kaltenbrunner.

I next refer to Document L-215, which has heretofore been received as Exhibit USA 243, and which contains 25 orders for arrest issued out of the Prague office of the R.S.H.A. to the Einsatz.

THE PRESIDENT: Which number are you dealing with now?

LT. HARRIS: I am dealing with Document L-215. I believe the Tribunal will recall this document, which has heretofore been received in evidence, and which contains 25 orders for arrest issued out of the Prague office of the R.S.H.A. to the Einsatz Commando of Luxembourg, all of which carry the typed signature of Kaltenbrunner. And the Court will remember, and I am holding up the original document, that these arrest orders were the red forms which the Commandant of Buchenwald referred to in his affidavit as being the forms which he saw coming from R.S.H.A. committing persons to Buchenwald.

The concentration camps to which persons were committed, according to Document L-215, by Kaltenbrunner, included Dachau, Natzweiler, Sachsenhausen, and Buchenwald.

THE PRESIDENT: What was the date of it?

LT. HARRIS: Most of these, Sir, were in 1944. I believe they are all in 1944.

THE PRESIDENT: It does not appear on the document does it?

LT. HARRIS: It does appear, Sir, on the original document. The first page of this translation is a summary of all of these. There is only one of the dossiers which has been translated in full, and the date on that one is 15th February, 1944.

THE PRESIDENT: Yes; I see.

LT. HARRIS: Among the grounds specified on these orders carrying the typed signature of Kaltenbrunner were, quoting:

"Strongly suspected of working to the detriment of the Reich; spiteful statements inimical to Germany, as well as aspersions and threats against persons active in the National Socialist Movement; strongly suspected of aiding deserters."

I now offer Document 2239-PS as exhibit next in order, Exhibit USA 520. This is a file of 42 telegrams sent by the Prague office of the R.S.H.A. to the Gestapo office at Darmstadt, and they all carry the teletype signature of Kaltenbrunner. These commitment orders were issued during the period from 20th September, 1944, to 2nd February, 1945. The concentration camps to which Kaltenbrunner sent these people included Sachsenhausen, Ravensbruck, Buchenwald, Bergen-Belsen, Flossenburg, and Theresienstadt. Nationalities included Czech, German, French, Dutch, Italian, Corsican, Lithuanian, Greek and Jews. Grounds included refusal to work, religious propaganda, sex relations with prisoners of war, communist statements, loafing on the job, working against the Reich, spreading of rumours detrimental to morale, "action Gitter," breach of work contracts, statements against Germany, assault of foremen, defeatist statements, and theft and escape from gaol.

Not only did Kaltenbrunner commit persons to concentration camps, but he authorised executions in concentration camps. I now offer Document L-51 as exhibit next in order, Exhibit USA 521. This is the affidavit of Adolf Zutter, the former adjutant of Mauthausen concentration camp, in the course of an official military investigation of the United States Army, on 2nd August, 1945, at Linz, Austria. This affidavit states, and I am quoting from paragraph 3:

> "Standartenfuehrer Ziereis, the commander of Camp Mauthausen, gave me a large number of execution orders after opening the secret mail, because I was the adjutant and I had to deliver these to Obersturmfuehrer Schulz. These orders of execution were written approximately in the following form."

There follows in the affidavit a description of the order for execution issued by the R.S.H.A. to the commander of the concentration camp Mauthausen. I omit quoting that description and continue at the next paragraph:

> "Orders for execution also came without the name of the court of justice. Until the assassination of Heydrich, these orders were signed by him or by his competent deputy. Later on the orders were signed by Kaltenbrunner, but mostly they were signed by his deputy, Gruppenfuehrer Mueller.
>
> Dr. Kaltenbrunner, who signed the above- mentioned orders, had the rank of S.S. General (S.S. Obergruppenfuehrer) and was the Chief of the Reich Security Main Office.
>
> Dr. Kaltenbrunner is about 40 years old, height about 1.76 to 1.80 metres, and has deep fencing scars on his face. When Dr. Kaltenbrunner was only a Higher S.S. and Police Officer, he visited the camp several times, later on as the Chief of Reich Security Main Office (R.S.H.A.) he visited the camp too, though much less frequently. During these visits, the commander usually received him outside the building of the camp headquarters and reported.
>
> Concerning the American military mission, which landed behind the German front in the Slovakian or Hungarian area in January, 1945, I remember when these officers were brought to Camp Mauthausen. I suppose the number of the arrivals was about 12 to 15 men. They wore a uniform, which was American or Canadian, brown-green colour shirt and cloth cap. Eight or ten days after their arrival the execution order came in by telegraph or teletype. Standartenfuehrer Ziereis came to me, into my office, and told me: 'Now Kaltenbrunner has given permission for the execution.' This letter was secret and had the signature 'signed Kaltenbrunner.' Then these people were shot according to martial

law and their belongings were given to me by Oberscharfuehrer Niedermeier."

The fifth crime for which Kaltenbrunner is responsible as Chief of the Security Police and S.D. was the deportation of citizens of occupied territories for forced labour and the disciplining of forced labour.

I am sure the Tribunal will recall, without referring to it, Document 3012-PS. which has heretofore been received as Exhibit USA 190. That was the letter from the head of the Sonderkommando of the Sipo and S.D., which stated that the Ukraine would have to provide a million workers for the armament industry and that force should be used where necessary. That letter was dated 19th March, 1943.

Kaltenbrunner's responsibility for the disciplining of foreign labour is shown by Document 1063B-PS, which has heretofore been received as Exhibit USA 492. No part of this letter has been read into the record. This letter dated 26th July, 1943, was addressed to Higher S.S. and Police Leaders, Commanders and Inspectors of the Sipo and S.D., and to the Chiefs of Einsatz Groups B and D.

The Tribunal will recall that Einsatz Groups A, B, C, and D, operating in the East, carried out the extermination of Jews and communist leaders. This document proves Kaltenbrunner's control over Einsatz Groups B and D. It is signed "Kaltenbrunner." The first paragraph provides as follows:

"The Reichsfuehrer S.S. has given his consent that besides concentration camps, which come under the jurisdiction of the S.S. Economic Administration Main Office, further labour reformatory camps may be created, for which the Security Police alone is competent. These labour reformatory camps are dependent on the authorisation of the Reich Security Main Office, which can only be granted in case of emergency (great number of foreign workers, and so forth)."

I now offer Document D-473 as exhibit next in order, Exhibit USA 522. It should be right at the beginning of the Document Book. This letter signed "Kaltenbrunner" was sent by him under date of 4th December, 1944, to Regional Offices of the Criminal Police.

The Tribunal will recall that Kaltenbrunner's responsibility covered the Criminal Police as well as the Gestapo. It provides in part, and I quote, reading at the beginning of the letter:

"According to the Decree of 30th June, 1943, crimes committed by Polish and Soviet- Russian civilian labourers are being prosecuted by the State Police (Head) Offices, and even in those cases, where for the time being the Criminal Police had, within the sphere of its competence, carried on the inquiries. For the purpose of speeding up the process and in order to save manpower, the Decree of 30th June, 1943, is altered, and the Criminal Police (Head) Offices are authorised as from now on to prosecute, themselves, the crimes they are inquiring into, within the sphere of their competence, in so far as they are cases of minor or medium crimes."

I begin with the second paragraph:

"The following are available to the Criminal Police as a means of prosecution:

Police imprisonment.

Admission into a concentration camp for preventive custody as being anti-social or dangerous to the community."

And next to the last paragraph:

"Their stay in the concentration camp is normally to be for the duration of the war. Besides this, the Criminal Police (Head) Offices are authorised to hand over Polish and Soviet-Russian civilian labourers in suitable cases and with the agreement of the competent State Police (Head) Offices to the Gestapo's penal camps for the 'education for labour.' Where the possibilities of prosecuting an individual case are insufficient because of the peculiarity of the case, the case is to be handed over to the competent State Police (Head) Office.

Signed: Dr. Kaltenbrunner."

In addition to sending foreign workers to Gestapo labour camps, Kaltenbrunner punished foreign workers by committing them to concentration camps. I offer Document 2582-PS as the exhibit next in order, USA 523.

This is a series of four teletype orders committing individuals to concentration camps. I invite the attention of the Tribunal to the second order dated the 18th of June, 1943, under which the Gestapo at Saarbrucken was ordered to deliver a Pole to the concentration camp Natzweiler as a skilled workman, and to the third teletype dated the 12th of December, 1944, in which the Gestapo at Darmstadt was ordered to commit a Greek to the concentration camp Buchenwald because he was drifting around without occupation, and to the fourth teletype dated the 9th of February, 1945, in which the Gestapo at Darmstadt in Benslein was ordered to commit a French citizen to Buchenwald for shirking work and insubordination. All of those orders are signed, Kaltenbrunner.

I offer document 2580-PS as Exhibit next in order, USA 524. This document contains three more of these red-form orders for protective custody, all signed Kaltenbrunner. The first one shows that a citizen of the Netherlands was taken into protective custody for work sabotage, and the second one shows that a French citizen was taken into protective custody for work sabotage and insubordination, both under date 2 December, 1944.

The sixth crime for which Kaltenbrunner is responsible as Chief of the Security Police and S.D. is the executing of captured commandos and paratroopers and the protecting of civilians who lynched Allied fliers.

The Tribunal will recall, I am sure, without referring to it, the Hitler Order of 18 October, 1942, which was introduced this morning, Document 498-PS, Exhibit USA 501, to the effect that commandos, even in uniform, were to be exterminated to the last man, and that individual members captured by the police in occupied territory were to be handed over to the S.D.

I now offer document 1276-PS as Exhibit next in order, USA 525. This is an express top secret letter from the Chief of the Security Police and S.D. signed "Mueller, by order," to the Supreme Command of the Armed Forces, in which the Chief of the Security Police and S.D. states, and I quote from the third paragraph of the second page of the English translation:

"I have instructed the 'Befehlshaber' of the Security Police and the S.D. in Paris to treat such parachutists in English uniform as members of the commando operations in accordance with the Fuehrer's order of 18 October, 1942, and to inform the military authorities in France that there must be corresponding treatment at the hands of the armed forces."

This letter was dated 17th June, 1944. That executions were carried out by the S.D. pursuant to the said Hitler order of 18th October, 1942, while Kaltenbrunner was Chief of the Security Police and S.D., is indicated by Document 526-PS heretofore received as Exhibit USA 502; that was the order introduced this morning; I am sure the Tribunal recalls it.

The policy of the police to protect civilians who lynched Allied fliers was effective during the period that Kaltenbrunner served as Chief of the Security Police and S.D. I now offer Document 2990-PS as Exhibit next in order, USA 526. This is an affidavit of Walter Schellenberg, the former Chief of Amt VI of the R.S.H.A., and provides in paragraph 7 - this is all I am going to read from the affidavit:

"In 1944, on another occasion but also in the course of an Amtschef conference, I heard fragments of a conversation between Kaltenbrunner and Muller. I remember distinctly the following remarks of Kaltenbrunner:

'All officers of the S.D. and the Security Police are to be informed that pogroms of the populace against English and American terror fliers are not to be interfered with. On the contrary, this hostile mood is to be fostered.'"

The seventh crime for which Kaltenbrunner is responsible as Chief of the Security Police and S.D. is the taking of civilians of occupied countries to Germany for secret trial and punishment and the punishment of civilians of occupied territories by "summary methods." The fact that this crime continued after the 30th of January, 1943, is shown by Document 835-PS, which is offered as Exhibit next in order, USA 527. This is a letter from the High Command of the Armed Forces to the German Armistice commission under date 2nd September, 1944. The document begins, and I quote:

"Conforming to the decrees, all non-German civilians in occupied territories who have endangered the security and readiness for action of the occupying power by acts of terror and sabotage or in other ways, are to be surrendered to the Security Police and S.D. Only those prisoners are to be accepted who were legally sentenced to death or were serving a sentence of confinement prior to the announcement of these decrees. Included in the punishable acts which endanger the security or readiness of action of the garrison power, are those of a political nature."

The eighth crime for which Kaltenbrunner is responsible as Chief of the Security Police and S.D. is the crime of executing and confining persons in concentration camps for crimes allegedly committed by their relatives.

That this crime continued after the 30th January, 1943, is indicated by Document L-37, heretofore received in evidence as Exhibit USA 506. That was received this morning. It is the letter of the Kommandeur of Sipo and S.D. at Radom, dated the 19th of July, 1944, in which it was stated that the male relatives of assassins and saboteurs should be shot and the female relatives over 16 years of age sent to concentration camps. I refer again to Document L-215, which has heretofore been received in evidence as Exhibit USA 243, and specifically to the case of Junker, who was ordered by Kaltenbrunner to be committed to Sachsenhausen concentration camp by the Gestapo "because as a relative of a deserter, he is expected to endanger the interest of the German Reich if allowed to go free."

The ninth crime for which Kaltenbrunner is responsible as Chief of the Security Police and S.D. is the clearance of Sipo and S.D. prisons and concentration camps. I refer the Tribunal to Document L-53, which was received in evidence as Exhibit USA 291. This was the letter from the Kommandeur of the Sipo and S.D. Radom, dated 21St July, 1944, in which it is stated that the Kommandeur of the Sipo and S.D. of the Government General had ordered all Sipo and S.D. prisons to be cleared and, if necessary, the inmates to be liquidated. I now offer Document 3462-PS as Exhibit next in order, USA 528. This is the sworn interrogation of Bertus Gerdes, the former Gaustabsanitsleiter under the Gauleiter of Munich. This interrogation was taken in the course of an official military investigation of the U.S. Army. In this interrogation Gerdes was ordered to state all he knew about Kaltenbrunner. I am only going to read a very small portion of his reply, beginning on the third paragraph of page 2:

"Giesler told me that Kaltenbrunner was in constant touch with him because he was greatly worried about the attitude of the foreign workers and especially inmates of concentration camps Dachau, Muehldorf and Landsberg, which were in the path of the approaching Allied armies. On a Tuesday in the middle of April 1945, I received a telephone call from Gauleiter Giesler asking me to be available for a conversation that night. In the course of our personal conversation that night, I was told by Giesler that he had received a directive from Kaltenbrunner by order of the Fuehrer, to work out a plan without delay for the liquidation of the concentration camp at Dachau and the two Jewish labour camps in Landsberg and Muehldorf. The directive proposed to liquidate the two Jewish labour camps at Landsberg and Muehldorf, by use of the German Luftwaffe, since the construction area of these camps had previously been the targets of repeated enemy air attacks. This action received the code name of 'Wolke A- I.'"

I now pass to the second paragraph on page 3, continuing quoting from this interrogation:

"I was certain that I would never let this directive be carried out. As the action 'Wolke A-I' should already have become operational for some time, I was literally swamped by couriers from Kaltenbrunner and moreover I was supposed to have discussed the details of the Muehldorf and Landsberg actions in detail with the two Kreisleiter concerned. The couriers who were in most cases S.S. officers, usually S.S. lieutenants, gave me terse and strict orders to read and initial. The orders threatened me with the most terrible punishment, including execution, if I did not comply with them. However, I could always excuse my failure to execute the plan because of bad flying weather and lack of gasoline and bombs. Therefore, Kaltenbrunner ordered the Jews in Landsberg to be marched to Dachau in order to include them in the Dachau extermination operations, and the Muehldorf action to be carried out by the Gestapo.

Kaltenbrunner also ordered an operation - 'Wolkenbrand' - for the concentration camp at Dachau, which provided that the inmates of the concentration camp at Dachau were to be liquidated by poison with the exception of Aryan nationals of the Western Powers.

Gauleiter Giesler received this order direct from Kaltenbrunner an discussed, in my presence, the procurement of the required amounts poison with Dr. Hartfeld, the Gau Health Chief. Dr. Hartfeld promise to procure these quantities when ordered and was advised to await my further directions. As I was determined to prevent the execution this plan in any event, I gave no further instructions to Dr. Hartfeld.

The inmates of Landsberg had hardly been delivered at Dachau when Kaltenbrunner sent a courier declaring the action Wolkenbran was operational.

I prevented the execution of the Wolke A-I and Wolkenbrand by giving Giesler the reason that the Front was too close and asked him transmit this on to Kaltenbrunner.

Kaltenbrunner therefore issued directives in writing to Dachau transport all Western European prisoners by truck to Switzerland an to march the remaining inmates into the Tyrol, where the final liquidation of these prisoners was to take place without fail."

THE PRESIDENT: The Court will adjourn now.

(The Tribunal adjourned until 1000 hours on 3rd January, 1946)

THURSDAY, 3RD JANUARY, 1946

LT. HARRIS: If the Tribunal will recall, at the end of the last session we had finished reading a portion of the sworn interrogation of the Gaustabsamtsleiter under the Gauleiter of Munich and had touched on the point where he said that Kaltenbrunner issued directives to Dachau to transport Western European prisoners by truck to Switzerland and to march the remaining inmates into the Tyrol.

I now offer as Exhibit next in order the first five pages of the interrogation report of Gottlieb Berger, Chief of the head office of the S.S., made under oath on 20th September, 1945, in the course of these proceedings. You will find these pages at the end of the Document Book and this is offered as Exhibit US.A. 529. These pages have been translated into German and made available to the defendants.

THE PRESIDENT: Does it have a number?

LT. HARRIS: It has no PS number, Sir. It is at the very end of the Document Book. I wish to read only one question and answer from these pages; and I refer to the last question and answer Page 3 of the Exhibit:

"Q: Assuming, only for the purposes of this discussion, that these atrocities that we hear about are true, who do you think is primarily responsible?

"A: The first one, the Commandant; the second one, Gluecks; because he was practically responsible for all the interior direction of the camps. If one wants to be exact, one would have to find out how the information service between the camp Commandant and Gluecks actually operated. I want to give you the following example: During the night of the 22nd and 23rd April I was sent to Munich. As I entered the city, I met a group of perhaps 120 men dressed in the suits of the concentration camps. I asked the guard who was with them, 'What about these men?' He told me that these men were marching by foot to the Alps. Firstly, I sent him back to Dachau. Then I wrote a letter to the Commandant, to send no more people by foot to any place, but, whenever the Allies advanced any further, to give over the camp completely. I did that on my own responsibility and I told him that I came straight from Berlin and that I can be found in my service post in Munich. The Commandant, or his deputy, telephoned at about twelve o'clock and told me that he had received this order from Kaltenbrunner after he had been asked by the Gauleiter of Munich, the Reichskommissar."

The tenth crime for which Kaltenbrunner is responsible as Chief of the Security Police and S.D. is the persecution of the Jews. This crime, of course, continued after 30th January, 1943, and evidence has heretofore been received that the persecutions continued until and were accelerated toward the end of the war. Kaltenbrunner took a personal interest in such matters, as is indicated by Document 2519-PS, which is offered as Exhibit next in order, Exhibit US.A. 530. This exhibit consists of a memorandum and an affidavit, and I invite the attention of the Tribunal to the affidavit. Quoting from the affidavit:

"I, Henri Monneray, being first duly sworn, depose and say that since 12th September, 1945, I have been and I am the member of the French staff for the prosecution of Axis Criminality and have been pursuing my official duties in this connection in Nuremberg, Germany, since 12th October, 1945.

In the course of my official duties, at the instruction of the French Chief Prosecutor, I examined the personal document of the defendant-"

THE PRESIDENT: Is it necessary to read all of this? What is the object of this affidavit?

LT. HARRIS: To show that this document was derived from the personal effects of the defendant Kaltenbrunner.

THE PRESIDENT: You can leave out the immaterial parts.

LT. HARRIS: Very good, Sir. Passing to the last sentence of the affidavit:
"Said Document 2519-PS is the document which I found in the envelope containing Kaltenbrunner's personal papers."

I now read the memorandum:
"Radio message to Gruppenfuehrer S.S. Major General Fegelein, Headquarters of the Fuehrer, through Sturmbannfuehrer S.S. Major Sansoni, Berlin:

Please inform the Reichsfuehrer S.S. and report to the Fuehrer that all arrangements against Jews, political and concentration camp internees in the Protectorate have been taken care of by me personally to-day. The situation there is one of calmness, fear of Soviet successes and hope of an occupation by the Western enemies.

Kaltenbrunner."

THE TRIBUNAL (Mr. BIDDLE): That is not dated?

LT. HARRIS: This is not dated.

The eleventh crime for which Kaltenbrunner is responsible is the persecution of the Churches. It is unnecessary to present specific evidence that this crime continued after 30th January, 1943, since this was one of the fundamental purposes of the Security Police and S.D., as has already been shown.

These are the crimes for which the defendant Kaltenbrunner must answer. As to his criminal intent, there is no need to go outside the record before this Tribunal. On 1st December, 1945, in these proceedings the witness Lahousen was asked on cross-examination, "Do you know Mr. Kaltenbrunner?"

After describing his meeting with Kaltenbrunner on a day in Munich when a university student and his sister were arrested and executed for distributing leaflets from the auditorium, Lahousen said - and I wish to quote only to two sentences on Page 324 (Part I.) of the transcript:
"I can easily reconstruct that day. It was the first and last time that I saw Kaltenbrunner, with whose name was known to me. Of course, Kaltenbrunner mentioned this subject to Canaris, and witnesses were there, and everybody was under the terrible impression of what had happened, and Kaltenbrunner spoke about that to Canaris in a manner for which cynicism would be a very mild description. This is the only thing I can say to this question."

Kaltenbrunner was a life-long fanatical Nazi. He was the leader of the S.S. in Austria prior to the Anschluss and played a principal role in the betrayal of his native country to the Nazi Conspirators. As higher S.S. and Police Leader in

Otto Ohlendorf was the commanding officer of Einsatzgruppe D, and was hanged in Landsberg Prison in 1951.

Austria after the Anschluss, he supervised and had knowledge of the activities of the Gestapo and the S.D. in Austria. The Mauthausen concentration camp was established in his jurisdiction and he visited it several times. On at least one occasion he observed the gas chamber in action. With this knowledge and background he accepted, in January, 1943, appointment as Chief of the Security Police and S.D., the very agencies which sent such victims to their deaths. He held that office to the end, rising to great prominence in the S.S. and the German Police and receiving high honours from Hitler. Like other leading Nazis, Kaltenbrunner sought power; to gain it, he made his covenant with crime.

COL. STOREY: If the Tribunal please, next will be some witnesses and Colonel Amen will handle the interrogation.

COLONEL JOHN H. AMEN: May it please the Tribunal, I wish to call, as a witness for the prosecution, Mr. Otto Ohlendorf. Your Lordship will note that his name appears under Amt III on the chart on the wall.

THE PRESIDENT: What did you say appeared?

COLONEL AMEN: The name of this witness appears under Amt III of the chart, R.S.H.A., the large square, the third section down.

THE PRESIDENT: I see it.

Otto Ohlendorf, will you repeat this oath after me: I swear by God, the Almighty and Omniscient, that I will speak the pure truth and will withhold and add nothing.

(The witness repeated the oath.)

BY COLONEL AMEN:

Q. Where were you born?

A. In Hohen Egelsen.

Q. How old are you?

A. Thirty-eight years old.

Q. When, if ever, did you become a member of the National Socialist Party?

A. 1925.

Q. When, if ever, did you become a member of the S.A.?

A. For the first time in 1926.

Q. When, if ever, did you become a member of the S.S.?

A. I must correct myself. I answered the first question as if I were speaking of my membership in the S.S.

Q. When did you become a member of the S.A.?

A. In the year 1923.

Q. When, if ever, did you join the S.D.?

A. In 1936.

Q. What was your last position in the S.D.?

A. Amt Chief of Amt III in the R.S.H.A..

Q. Turning to the chart on the wall behind your back, will you tell the Tribunal whether you can identify that chart in any way?

A. This chart was seen previously by me and worked on by me and I can consequently identify it.

Q. What, if anything, did you have to do with making up that chart?

A. This chart was made during my interrogation.

COLONEL AMEN: For the information of the Tribunal, the chart of which the witness speaks is Exhibit US.A. 493.

Q. Will you tell the Tribunal whether that chart correctly portrays the basic organisation of the R.S.H.A., as well as the position of Kaltenbrunner, the Gestapo, and the S.D. in the German Police system?

A. The organisation, as represented in that chart, is a correct representation of the organisation of the R.S.H.A. It shows correctly the position of the S.A. as well as the State Police, the Criminal Police, and the S.D.

Q. Referring once more to the chart, please indicate your position in the R.S.H.A. and state for what period you continued to serve in that capacity.

(At this point the witness pointed to Amt III on the chart.)

Q. What were the positions of Kaltenbrunner, Mueller, and Eichmann in the R.S.H.A., and state for what periods of time each of them continued to serve in his respective capacity?

A. Kaltenbrunner was Chief of the Sicherheitspolizei and the S.D.; as such, he was also Chief of the R.S.H.A., the internal organisational term for the office of the chief of the Sicherheitspolizei and the S.D.

Kaltenbrunner occupied this position from 30th January, 1943, until the end of the war. Mueller was Chief of Amt IV, the Gestapo. When the Gestapo was established, he became Deputy Chief, and as such he subsequently was appointed Chief of Amt IV of the R.S.H.A.. He occupied this position until the end of the war.

Eichmann occupied a position in Amt IV under Mueller and worked on the Jewish problem from 1940 on. To my knowledge, he also occupied this position until the end of the war.

Q. Will you tell us for what period of time you continued to serve as Chief of Amt III?

A. I was Chief of Amt III from 1939 to 1945.

Q. Turning now to the designation "Mobile Units" with the Army, shown in the lower right-hand corner of the chart, please explain to the Tribunal the significance of the terms "Einsatzgruppe" and "Einsatzkommando".

A. The concept "Einsatzgruppe" was established after an agreement between the Chiefs of the R.S.H.A., O.K.W., and O.K.H., in regard to the use of the Sipo in the area of operation. The concept "Einsatzgruppe" first appeared during the Polish campaign.

The agreement with the O.K.H. and O.K.W., however, was first arrived at before the beginning of the Russian campaign. This agreement specified that an official of the Sipo and the S.D. should be assigned to the Army Groups, or the Armies, and that this official would have at his disposal mobile units of the Sipo and the S.D. in the form of Einsatzgruppen, subdivided into Einsatzkommandos. The Einsatzkommandos should be assigned to the Army Units as needed, to the particular Army Group or Army.

Q. State, if you know, whether prior to the campaign against Soviet Russia, any agreement was entered into between the O.K.W., O.K.H., and R.S.H.A.?

A. Yes, the Einsatzgruppen, just described by me, and the Einsatzkommandos were used in the Russian campaign, according to a written agreement between the O.K.W., O.K.H., and R.S.H.A..

Q. How do you know that there was such a written agreement?

A. I was often present when the negotiations which Schellenberg conducted with the O.K.H. and OKW were being discussed, and I also had a written copy of this agreement in my own hands when I took over the Einsatzgruppen.

Q. Explain to the Tribunal who Schellenberg was. What position, if any, did he occupy?

A. Schellenberg was finally the Chief of Amt VI in the R.S.H.A.; at the time when he was conducting these negotiations as ordered by Heydrich, he belonged to the Amt.

Q. On approximately what date did these negotiations take place?

A. The negotiations took several weeks. The agreement must have been reached about one or two weeks before the beginning of the Russian campaign.

Q. Did you yourself ever see a copy of this written agreement?

A. Yes.

Q. Did you have occasion to work with this written agreement?

A. Yes.

Q. On more than one occasion?

A. Yes; and in regard to more than one question which had to do with the use of Einsatzgruppen in the Army.

Q. Do you know where the original or any copy of that agreement is located to-day?

A. No, I do not.

Q. To the best of your knowledge and recollection, please explain to the Tribunal the entire substance of this written agreement.

A. First of all, the agreement stated the fact that Einsatzgruppen should be set up and that Einsatzkommandos should be used for joint efforts in this operation. Up to that time the Army had completely taken over the tasks that the Sipo should have done itself.

THE PRESIDENT: What is it that you say the Einsatzkommandos did under the agreement?

A. The second was the authority of the Army in regard to the Einsatzgruppen and the Einsatzkommandos. The agreement specified that the Army Groups or Armies should be responsible for marching and maintenance so far as the Einsatzgruppen were concerned. Particular instructions came from the Chief of the Sipo and S.D.

COL. AMEN:

Q. Let us understand. Is it correct that an Einsatz Group was to be attached to each Army Group or Army?

A. Every Army Group was to have attached to it an Einsatzgruppe. The Einsatzkommandos, in their turn, were to be attached to the Armies by the Army Group.

Q. And was the Army Command to determine the area within which the Einsatz Group was to operate?

A. The operational region of the Einsatzgruppe was determined by the fact that the Einsatzgruppe was attached to a specific Army Group and therefore marched with it, whereas the Einsatzkommandos functioned in territories as determined by the Army Group or Army.

Q. Did the agreement also provide that the Army Command was to direct the time during which they were to operate?

A. That was included under the concept "March."

Map used to illustrate Franz Stahlecker's report to Heydrich on January 31, 1942. entitled "Jewish Executions Carried Out by Einsatzgruppe A" and stamped "Secret Reich Matter." It shows the number of Jews executed in the Baltic States and Belarus in 1941. The legend at the bottom states that "the estimated number of Jews still on hand is 128,000." Estonia is marked as "judenfrei".

Q. And also to direct any additional tasks they were to perform?

A. Yes. As far as the actual instructions of the Chiefs of the Sipo and S.D. were concerned, they were guided by the general practice that they could issue orders to the Army if the operational situation made it necessary.

Q. What did this agreement provide with respect to the attachment of the Einsatz Group Command to the Army Command?

A. I cannot remember whether anything specific was said about that. At any rate, an attachment was established.

Q. Do you recall any other provisions of this written agreement?

A. I believe I can state the essential content of that agreement.

Q. What position did you occupy with respect to this agreement?

A. From June, 1941, to the death of Heydrich in June, 1942, I led Einsatzgruppe D, and was the Deputy of the Chief of the Sipo and the S.D. with the 11th Army.

Q. And when was Heydrich's death?

A. Heydrich was wounded at the end of May, 1942, and died on 4th June, 1942.

Q. How much advance notice, if any, did you have of the campaign against Soviet Russia?

A. About four weeks.

Q. How many Einsatz Groups were there, and who were their respective leaders?

A. There were four Einsatzgruppen, Group A, B, C and D. Chief of Einsatzgruppe A was Stahlecker; Chief of Einsatzgruppe B was Nebe; Chief of Einsatzgruppe C Dr. Rausche, and later, Dr. Thomas; Chief of Einsatzgruppe D, Bierkamp.

Q. To which army was Group D attached?

A. Group D was not attached to any Army Group, but was attached directly to the 11th Army.

Q. Where did Group D operate?

A. Group D operated in the Southern Ukraine.

Q. Will you describe in more detail the nature and extent of the area in which Group D originally operated, naming the cities or territories?

A. The most Northern city was Czernowitz; then Southward to Mogilev-Podelsk; South-west to Odessa; North-east of that, Melitopol, Mariupol, Taganrog, Rostov and the Crimea.

Q. What was the ultimate objective of Group D?

A. Group D was held in reserve for the Caucasus. An Army Group was provided for this operation.

Q. When did Group D commence its move into Soviet Russia?

A. Group D left Duegen on 21st June, reaching Romania in 21 days. There the first Einsatzkommandos were already being demanded by the Army, and they marched at once to the goals set by the Army. The entire Einsatzgruppe was made use of at the beginning of July.

Q. You are referring to the 11th Army?

A. Yes.

Q. In what respects, if any, were the official duties of the Einsatz Groups concerned with Jews and Communist Commissars?

A. As far as the question of Jews and Communists is concerned, the Einsatzgruppen and Einsatzkommandos were orally instructed by their leaders before the march.

Q. What were their instructions with respect to the Jews and the Communist functionaries?

A. They were instructed that in the field of activity of the Einsatzgruppe in Russian territory the Jews, as well as the political Soviet Commissars, were to be liquidated.

Q. And when you say "liquidated" do you mean "killed?"

A. I mean "killed."

Q. Prior to the opening of the Soviet campaign, did you attend a conference at Pretz?

A. Yes, it was a discussion at which the Einsatzgruppen and the Einsatzkommandos were informed of the goals of their activity and were given the necessary commands.

Q. Who was present at that conference?

A. The Chiefs of the Einsatzgruppen and the leaders of the Einsatzkommandos and Streckenbach of the R.S.H.A., who transmitted the orders of Heydrich and Himmler.

Q. What were those orders?

A. Those were the general orders regarding the work of the Sipo, which aided the liquidation order which I have already mentioned.

Q. And that conference took place on approximately what date?

A. About three or four days before our march.

Q. So that before you commenced to march into Soviet Russia, you received orders at this conference to exterminate the Jews and Communist functionaries, in addition to the regular professional work of the Security Police and SD; is that correct?

A. That is right.

Q. Did you, personally, have any conversation with Himmler, respecting any communication from Himmler to the Chiefs of Army Groups and Armies concerning this mission?

A. Yes. Himmler informed me that before the beginning of the Russian campaign Hitler, in a conference with the Commander of the Army, had stated this task and had instructed the High Commander to provide the necessary support in regard to it.

Q. So that you can testify that the Chiefs of the Army Groups and the Armies had been similarly informed of those orders for the liquidation of the Jews and Soviet functionaries?

A. I believe that it is not correct in this particular form. They had no orders for liquidation. The order for the liquidation originated with Himmler, but since this liquidation took place in the operational region of the High Command, of the Army Groups or the Army, the Army was ordered to support these measures. Without these instructions to the Army, the Einsatzgruppe in this sense would not have been possible.

Q. Did you have any other conversation with Himmler concerning this order?

A. Yes, in the late summer of 1941 Himmler was in Nikolaiev. He assembled the leaders and men of the Einsatzgruppen and Kommandos and repeated to them the orders for liquidation with the remark that the leaders and men who were taking part in the liquidation bore no personal responsibility for the execution of these orders. The responsibility was his, alone, as well, of course, as that of the Fuehrer.

Q. And you yourself heard that said?

A. Yes.

Q. Do you know whether this mission of the Einsatz Group was known to the Army Group Commanders?

A. This order and the execution of these orders were known to the High Commander of the Army.

Q. How do you know that?

A. Through conferences with the Army and through instructions which were given by the Army in reference to this execution.

Q. Was the mission of the Einsatz Groups and the agreement between O.K.W., O.K.H. and R.S.H.A. known to the other leaders in the R.S.H.A.?

A. At least some of them knew, since some of the leaders were also active in the Einsatzgruppen and Einsatzkommandos in the course of time. Furthermore, the leaders who had to do with organisation also knew it.

Q. Most of the leaders came from the R.S.H.A., did they not?

A. Which leaders?

Q. Of the Einsatz Groups.

A. No, one cannot say that. The leaders in the Einsatzgruppen and Einsatzkommandos came from the entire Reich.

Q. Do you know whether the mission and the agreement were also known to Kaltenbrunner?

A. After his entry into service Kaltenbrunner had to concern himself with these questions and consequently must have known the background of the Einsatzgruppen which were dealt with in his own office.

Q. Who was the commanding officer of the 11th Army?

A. At first, Ritter von Schober; later, von Mannstein.

Q. Will you tell the Tribunal in what way or ways the commanding officers of the 11th Army directed or supervised Einsatz Group D in carrying out its liquidation activities?

A. An order from the 1st Army came to Nikolaiev, stating that liquidations were to take place only at a distance of not less than 200 kilometers from the Headquarters of the High Commander Mannheim.

Q. Do you recall any other occasion?

A. In Simferopol, the Army High Command gave the proper Einsatzkommandos further orders to hasten the liquidation, on the grounds that in this region there was a great housing shortage.

Q. Do you know how many persons were liquidated by Einsatz Group D, under your direction?

A. In the year between June, 1941, to June, 1942, the Einsatzkommandos announced 90,000 people liquidated.

Q. Did that include men, women, and children?

A. Yes.

Q. On what do you base those figures?

A. On reports sent by the Einsatzkommandos to the Einsatzgruppen.

Q. Were those reports submitted to you?

A. Yes.

Q. And you saw them and read them?

A. I beg your pardon?

Q. And you saw and read those reports, personally?

A. Yes.

Q. And it is on those reports that you base the figures you have given the Tribunal?

A. Yes.

Q. Do you know how those figures compare with the number of persons liquidated by other Einsatz Groups?

A. The figures known to me from other Einsatzgruppen are materially larger.

Q. That was due to what factor?

A. I believe that to a large extent the figures submitted by the other Einsatzgruppen were exaggerated.

Q. Did you see reports of liquidations from the other Einsatz Groups from time to time?

A. Yes.

Q. And those reports showed liquidations exceeding those of Group D; is that correct?

A. Yes.

Q. Did you personally supervise mass executions of these individuals?

A. I was present at mass executions for purposes of inspection.

Q. Will you explain to the Tribunal in detail how an individual mass execution was carried out?

A. A local Einsatzkommando attempted to collect all the Jews in one area. The registration of the Jews was performed by the Jews themselves.

Q. On what pretext, if any, were they rounded up?

A. On the pretext that they were to be re-located.

Q. Will you continue?

A. After the registration, the Jews were collected at a certain place. From there they were later led to the place of execution. The execution was carried out in a military fashion.

Q. In what way were they transported to the place of execution?

A. They were transported to the place of execution in a wagon - always only as many as could be executed immediately. In this way the attempt was made to keep the span of time in which the victims knew what was about to happen to them until the time of their actual execution as short as possible.

Q. Was that your idea?

A. Yes.

Q. And after they were shot what was done with the bodies?

A. The bodies were buried in the trenches.

Q. What determination, if any, was made as to whether the persons were actually dead?

A. The unit leaders had the order to watch out for that and to administer the coup de grace themselves if necessary.

Q. And who would do that?

A. Either the unit leader himself or somebody designated by him.

Q. In what positions were the victims shot?

A. Standing or kneeling.

Q. What was done with the personal property and clothing of the persons executed?

A. All personal property of value was collected at the time of the shooting, confiscated and handed over to the R.S.H.A. or the Finance Minister. At first the clothing was divided up, but in the winter of 1942 it was taken by the N.S.V. and disposed of by that organisation.

Q. All their personal property was registered at the time?

A. Only the objects of value were registered. The other objects were not.

Q. What happened to the garments which the victims were wearing when they went to the place of execution?

A. They were obliged to take off their outer garments immediately before the execution.

Q. All of them?

A. The outer garments, yes.

Q. How about the rest of the garments they were wearing?

A. They were allowed to keep their underclothing.

Q. Was that true of not only your group but of the other Einsatz Groups?

A. That was the order in my Einsatzgruppe. Other Einsatzgruppen handled the matter differently.

Q. In what way did they handle it?

A. A few of the Einsatz leaders did not employ the military way of liquidation and killed the victims simply by shooting them in the back of the neck.

Q. And you objected to that procedure?

A. I was against that procedure, yes.

Q. For what reason?

A. Because for the victims as well as those who carried out the executions that was an unnecessary spiritual suffering.

Q. Now, what was done with the property collected by the Einsatzkommandos from these victims?

A. In so far as it was a question of objects of value, they were sent to the R.S.H.A. in Berlin or to the Reich Ministry of Finance. The articles which could be used in the operational area were used there immediately.

Q. For example, what happened to gold and silver taken from the victims?

A. That was, as I have just said, turned over to the Reich Ministry of Finance in Berlin.

Q. How do you know that?

A. I can remember that it was actually handled in that way in Simferopol.

Q. How about watches, for example, taken from the victims?

A. At the request of the Army watches were put at the disposal of the Front.

Q. Were all victims, including men, women, and children, executed in the same manner?

A. Until the spring of 1942, yes. Then an order came from Himmler that in the future women and children should be killed only in gas vans.

Q. How had the women and children been killed previously?

A. In the same way as the men - by shooting.

Q. What, if anything, was done about burying the victims after they had been executed?

A. At first the Kommandos filled the graves so that signs of the execution could not be seen any more, and then levelled the graves with Arbeitskommandos from the population.

Q. Referring to the gas vans which you said you received in the spring of 1942, what order did you receive with respect to the use of these vans?

A. That these gas vans should be used in the future for the killing of women and children.

Q. Will you explain to the Tribunal the construction of these vans and their appearance?

A. The actual purpose of these vans could not be recognised from the outside. They were practically closed trucks. They were so constructed that when the motor ran, the gas was conducted into the van causing death of the occupants in 10 to 15 minutes.

Q. Explain in detail just how one of these vans was used for an execution.

A. The vans were loaded with the victims and driven to the place of burial, which was usually the same as that used for the mass executions. The time needed for transportation was long enough to insure the death of the passengers.

Q. How were the victims induced to enter the vans?

A. They were told that they were to be transported to another locality.

Q. How was the gas turned on?

A. I am not familiar with the technical details.

Q. How long did it take to kill the victims ordinarily?

A. About 10 to 15 minutes, the victims did not notice what was going on.

Q. How many persons could be killed simultaneously one such van?

A. The vans were of various sizes, anywhere from 15 to 25 persons.

Q. Did you receive reports from those persons operating these vans from time to time?

A. I did not understand the question.

Q. Did you receive reports from those who were working on the vans?

A. I received the report that the Einsatzkommandos did not like to use the vans.

Q. Why not?

A. Because the burial of the occupants was a great ordeal for the members of the Einsatzkommandos.

Q. Now, will you tell the Tribunal who furnished these vans to the Einsatz Groups?

A. The gas vans did not belong to the motor pool of the Einsatzgruppen but came from a special Kommando of the Einsatzgruppe. This Kommando also had charge of the construction of the vans. These vans were assigned to the Einsatzgruppen by the R.S.H.A.

Q. Were the vans supplied to all of the different Einsatz Groups?

A. I cannot say that. I only know about Einsatzgruppe D, and indirectly about Einsatzgruppe C, both of which had such vans.

Q. Are you familiar with the letter from Becker to Rauf with respect to these gas vans?

A. I saw this letter during my interrogation.

COLONEL AMEN: May it please the Tribunal, I am referring to Document 501-PS, Exhibit USA 288, being a letter already in evidence, a letter from Becker to Rauf.

Q. Will you tell the Tribunal who Becker was?

A. As far as I recall, Becker was the builder of the vans. It was he who was in charge of the vans for Einsatzgruppe D.

Q. Who was Rauf?

A. Rauf was group leader in Amt II of the R.S.H.A. He was in charge of motor vehicles and other things at that time.

Q. Can you identify that letter in any way?

A. The contents seem to bear out my experiences and are therefore probably correct. (Document 501-PS was handed to the witness.) Yes.

Q. Will you look at the letter before you and tell us whether you can identify it in any way?

A. I recognise the external appearance of the letter as well as the sign "R" (Rauf) on it, and the reference to the man who took care of the motor vehicles under Rauf seems to testify to its authenticity. The contents bear out the experiences which I had at that time.

Q. So that you believe it to be an authentic document?

A. Yes, I do.

Q. Will you now lay it aside on the table there?

Referring to your previous testimony, will you explain to the Tribunal why you believe that the type of execution ordered by you, namely, military, was preferable to the shooting in the neck procedure adopted by the other Einsatz Groups?

A. On the one hand, the aim was that the individual leaders and men should be able to carry out the executions in a military fashion acting on order and should have to make no decision of their own. That is, it should take place only by order. On the other hand, it was known to me that in the case of individual executions emotional disturbances could not be avoided since the victims discovered too soon that they were to be executed and thereby were subjected to prolonged nervous strain. Likewise, it seemed intolerable to me that the individual leaders and men were forced in this way to form their own decisions in the killing of a large number of people.

Q. In what manner did you determine which were the Jews to be executed?

A. That was not part up to me, but the identification of the Jews was done by the Jews themselves, since the registration was carried out by a Jewish Council of Elders.

Q. Did the amount of Jewish blood have anything to do with it?

A. I cannot remember the details, but I believe that in this case half-Jews were also included in the concept "Jew."

Q. What organisations furnished most of the officer personnel of the Einsatz Groups and Einsatzkommandos?

A. I did not understand the question.

Q. What organisations furnished most of the officer personnel of the Einsatz Groups?

A. The leadership personnel was furnished by the State Police, the Kripo, and, to a lesser extent, by the S.D.

Q. Kripo?

A. Yes, the Kripo. The State Police, the Criminal Police and, and to a lesser extent, the S.D.

Q. Were there any other sources of personnel?

A. Yes; the great masses of men employed were furnished by the Waffen S.S. and the Ordinary Police. The State Police and the Kripo furnished the experts for the most part and the troops were furnished by the Waffen S.S. and the Ordinary Police.

Q. How about the Waffen S.S.?

A. The Waffen S.S. was supposed to supply the Einsatzgruppen with one company, just as was the Ordinary Police.

Q. How about the Ordinary Police?

A. The Ordinary Police [Ordnungspolizei] also furnished a company to the Einsatzgruppen.

Q. What was the size of Einsatz Group D and its operating area as compared with the other Einsatz Groups?

A. I estimate that Einsatzgruppe D was two-thirds to one- half as large as the other Einsatzgruppen. That changed in the course of time. Individual Einsatzgruppen were in the course of time greatly enlarged.

COLONEL AMEN: May it please the Tribunal, I have other questions relating to organisational matters which I think would clarify some of the evidence which has already been in part received by the Tribunal; but I don't want to take the time of the Tribunal unless they feel that they want any more such testimony. I thought, perhaps, if any members of the Tribunal had questions they would ask this witness directly, because he is the best informed on these organisational matters of anyone who will be presented in Court.

THE PRESIDENT: We will adjourn now for 10 minutes.

(A recess was taken.)

THE PRESIDENT: Colonel Amen, the Tribunal does not think that it is necessary to go further into the organisational questions at this stage, but it is a matter which must be really decided by you because you know what the nature of the evidence which you are considering is. So far as the Tribunal is concerned, they are satisfied at the present stage to leave the matter where it is. But there is one aspect of the witness's evidence which the Tribunal would like you to investigate, and that is whether the practices of which he has been speaking continued after 1942, and for how long.

BY COLONEL AMEN:

Q. Can you state whether the liquidation practices which you have described continued after 1942 and, if so, for how long a period of time thereafter?

A. I do not think that the basic order was ever lifted. But I cannot remember sufficient details to enable me to make concrete statements on this subject, at least not in reference to Russia; for very shortly thereafter the retreat began, so that the operational region of the Einsatzgruppen became smaller and smaller. I do know whether other Einsatzgruppen with similar orders were provided for other areas.

Q. The question was up to what date does your personal knowledge of these liquidation activities go.

A. As far as the liquidation of Jews is concerned, I know that appropriate withdrawals of the order were made about six months before the conclusion of the war. Furthermore, I saw a document according to which the liquidation of Soviet Commissars was to be terminated. I cannot recall a specific date.

Q. Do you know whether in fact it was so terminated?

A. Yes, I believe so.

BY THE PRESIDENT:

Q. The Tribunal would like to know the number of men in your Einsatz Group.

A. There were about five hundred people in my Einsatzgruppe, besides those who were added to the group from the country itself to help out.

Q. Including them, did you say?

A. Excluding those who were brought into the group from the land itself.

Q. Do you know how many there would be in other groups?

A. I should estimate that at the beginning, seven to eight hundred men; but, as I said before, this number changed rapidly in the course of time for this reason, that individual Einsatzgruppen themselves acquired new people or succeeded in getting additional personnel from the R.S.H.A..

Q. The numbers increased, did they?

A. Yes, the numbers increased.

THE PRESIDENT: All right.

COLONEL AMEN: Now, here are perhaps just a half dozen of these questions I would like to ask, because I do think they might clear up, in the minds of the Tribunal, some of the evidence which has gone before. I shall be very brief, if that is satisfactory to the Tribunal.

THE PRESIDENT: Yes.

BY COLONEL AMEN:

Q. Will you explain the significance of the different widths of the blue lines on the chart?

A. The thick blue line between the name Himmler, as Reichsfuehrer S.S. and Chief of the German Police and the initials R.S.H.A. is designed to show the

A sub-unit of the Einsatzgruppe A in Lithuania, July 1941. The condemned men were forced to dig their own graves.

identity of the offices of the chiefs of the Sicherheitspolizei and the S.D. and their tasks. This is a department in which ministerial questions of leadership as well as individual executive matters were treated, that is to say, the closed circle of operations of the Sipo and the S.D. The organisational scheme, however, seen from the legal administrative point of view, represents an illegal state of affairs since the R.S.H.A. never actually had official validity.

The formal, legal situation was different from that which appears on this chart. Party and State offices were amalgamated here with different channels. Under this designation neither orders nor laws with a legal basis were issued. That is due to the fact that the State Police, in its ministerial capacity, was subordinate to the Ministry of the Interior just as before, whereas the S.D., despite this organisation, was an organ of the Party.

Therefore if I wished to reproduce this scheme legally according to the administrative situation, I should have to put, for example, in place of Amt IV the Amt Political Police of the former Sicherheitspolizei Hauptamt. This Amt Political Police existed formally to the very end and had its origin in the Police Department of the Ministry of the Interior. At the same time, the Secret State Police Amt, the Central Office of the Prussian Secret State Police, the leading organ of all the political police offices of the different provinces, continued to exist formally.

Thus, ministerial questions continued to be handled under the leadership of the Minister of the Interior; in so far as the emphasis on the formal competence of the Ministry of the Interior was necessary, it appeared under the heading "Reich Minister of the Interior" with the filing notice "Pol," the former designation of the Police Department of the Ministry of the Interior and the appropriate filing notice of the competent department of the former Sicherheitspolizei Hauptamt. For example, filing notice "Pol-S" meant Sicherheitspolizei; "V" meant Amt Verwaltung und Recht (Department Administration and Law).

The R.S.H.A. was therefore nothing more than a camouflage designation which did not correctly represent the actual conditions but gave the Chief of the Sipo and the S.D. as a collective designation for the Chief of the Sicherheitspolizei Hauptamt and the Chief of the S.D. Hauptamt (an office held until 1939) the opportunity of using one or the other letterhead at any given time.

At the same time it gave him the opportunity of an internal amalgamation of all forces and the opportunity of a division of activity-areas according to the point of view of practical effectiveness. But the fact remains that in this department State offices did remain in a way dependent on the Ministry of the Interior, and similarly the departments of the S.D. remained Party departments.

The S.D. Hauptamt, or the R.S.H.A., had formally only the significance of an S.S. Main Office, a main office in which the S.S. members of the Sipo and the S.D. belonged to the S.S. But the S.S., that is to say, Himmler, as Reichsfuehrer S.S., gave these state offices no official authority to issue orders.

BY THE PRESIDENT:

Q. I am not sure that I follow altogether what you have been saying, but is what you have been saying the reason why you are shown on the chart as concerned with Amt III, which refers, apparently, only to inside Germany, while, according to your evidence, you were the head of Einsatz Group D, which was operating outside Germany?

A. The fact that I led an Einsatzgruppe had nothing to do with the fact that I was also Chief of Amt III. I was given that as an individual, not as Chief of Amt III; and in my capacity as leader of an Einsatzgruppe I came into a completely new function and into an office completely separate from the former one.

Q. I see. And did it involve that you left Germany and went into the area invaded in the Soviet Union?

A. Yes.

BY COLONEL AMEN:

Q. Will you explain the significance of the dotted blue lines, as compared with the solid blue lines on the right hand side of the chart?

A. The solid lines indicate a direct official channels, whereas the dotted lines signify that here as a rule there were no direct channels.

Q. Was the term "S.D." ever used to include both the Sipo and the S.D.?

A. In the course of years the term "S.D." was used more and more incorrectly. It came to be established as an abbreviation for Sipo and S.D., without actually being suitable for that. "S.D." was originally simply a designation for the fact that someone belonged to the S.S. via the S.D. Main

Office. When the S.D. Main Office was dissolved and was taken over into the R.S.H.A., the question arose as to whether the designation S.D., which was also worn as insignia on the sleeve of the particular S.S. man, should be replaced by another insignia or a new abbreviation, e.g. R.S.H.A.. Things did not reach that point because the camouflage of the R.S.H.A. would thereby have been endangered. But when, for example, I read in a Fuehrer order that in France people were to be turned over to the S.D., that was a case in point of the false use of the designation S.D., since there were no such offices in France, and, on the other hand, the S.D., in so far as it functioned in departments, e.g., Amt III, in offices, had no executive power but was purely an intelligence organ.

Q. Briefly, what was the relationship between the S.S. and the Gestapo?

A. The relationship between the S.S. and Gestapo was this: The Reichsfuehrer S.S., as such, took over the tasks of the police and attempted to combine more closely the State Police and the S.S., that is to say, on the one hand to employ only those members of the State Police who were eligible for the S.S., and, on the other hand, to use the institutions of the S.S., e.g., education and training of the younger generation by the Waffen-S.S., in order in this way to draw the younger generation into the State Police. This amalgamation was later extended by him in an attempt to bring about the same relationship between the S.S. and the Ministry of the Interior, i.e., the whole internal administration.

Q. About how many full-time agents and honourary auxiliary personnel did the S.D. employ?

A. One cannot use the concept SD in this connection either. It is necessary to distinguish here between Amt III and Amt VI. Amt III, as the interior intelligence service, had about three thousand main office members, including men and women. On the other hand, the interior intelligence service worked essentially with honourary personnel, that is to say, with men and women who could serve the internal intelligence services with their professional experiences and with experiences based on their surroundings. I would judge that the number of these persons was roughly thirty thousand.

Q. Will you briefly give the Tribunal a general example of how a typical transaction was handled through the channels indicated on the chart?

A. First, a general example, invented to make things clear. Himmler discovered through experience that more and more saboteurs were being dropped from planes into Germany and were endangering transportation and factory sites. He told this to Kaltenbrunner in the latter's capacity as Chief of the Sipo and instructed him to make his organisation aware of this state of affairs and to take measures to see to it that these saboteurs would be seized as soon and as completely as possible.

Kaltenbrunner instructed Amt IV, that is to say, the State Police, with the preparation of the necessary order to the regional offices. This order was drawn up by the competent office of experts in Amt IV and was either transmitted by Mueller directly to the State Police offices in the Reich or, what is more probable because of the importance of the question and because of necessity and in order to bring to the attention of the other offices and officials to this fact, was given by him to Kaltenbrunner, who signed it and issued it to the regional offices in the Reich.

On the basis of this order it was, for example, determined that the State Police offices should report the measures they were taking as well as any successes they might have. These reports went back through the same channels from the regional offices to the offices of experts in Amt IV, thence to the Chief of Amt IV, thence to the Chief of the R.S.H.A., Kaltenbrunner, and thence to the Chief of the German Police Himmler.

Q. And, finally, will you give a specific example of typical transaction handled through the channels indicated on the chart?

A. The example of the arrest of the leaders of the leftist parties after the event of the 20th of July: This order was also transmitted from Himmler to Kaltenbrunner; Kaltenbrunner passed it on to Amt IV and an appropriate draft for a decree was formulated by Amt IV, signed by Kaltenbrunner and sent to the regional offices. The reports were returned from the subordinate offices back to the higher offices along the same channels.

COLONEL AMEN: May it please the Tribunal. The witness is now available to other counsel. I understand that Colonel Pokrovsky has some questions that he wishes to ask on behalf of the Soviets.

DIRECT EXAMINATION BY COLONEL POKROVSKY:

The testimony of the witness is important for the clarification of such questions, on the report of which the Soviet Delegation is at present working. Therefore, with the permission of the Court, I would like to ask the witness Ohlendorf a number of questions.

Q. You, witness, said that you were present twice at the mass executions. On whose orders were you an inspector at the executions?

A. I was present at the executions on my own initiative.

Q. But you said that you attended as inspector.

A. I said that I attended for inspection purposes.

Q. That was your initiative?

A. Yes.

Q. Did one of your chiefs always attend the executions for purposes of inspection?

A. Whenever possible I sent some leader of the Einsatzgruppe, but this was not always possible because of the great distance from the Einsatzgruppe.

Q. For what reasons was a person sent for purposes of inspection?

A. Please repeat the question?

Q. For what purpose was an inspector sent?

A. To determine whether or not my instructions regarding the manner of the execution were actually being carried out.

Q. Am I to understand that the inspector was to make certain that the execution had actually been carried out?

A. No, that is not a correct statement of the fact. He should simply ascertain whether the conditions which I set for the execution were actually being carried out.

Q. What manner of conditions had you in mind?

A. (1) The absence of publicity; (2) The carrying out of the execution in a military fashion. (3) The arrival of the transports and the carrying out of the liquidation without any hitch, in order to avoid unnecessary excitement. (4) The control of the property, in order to prevent appropriation by any person. There may have been other details which I no longer remember. At any rate any mistreatment, whether physical or spiritual, was to be prevented by means of these measures.

Q. You wished to make sure that, according to your opinion, a more equitable distribution of this property was effected, or did you aspire to a complete acquisition of the valuables?

A. Yes. *[Note: Only the first half of the preceding question, originally spoken in Russian, was transmitted to the witness in German by the interpreter. The answer of the witness, therefore, refers only to the first half of the question.]*

Q. You spoke of ill-treatment. What did you mean by ill- treatment at the executions?

A. If, for instance, the manner in which the executions were carried out was not able to prevent excitement and disobedience among the victims and the consequent execution of the order by means of violence.

Q. What do you mean by "execution of the order by means of violence"? What do you mean by violent suppression of the excitement arising amongst the victims?

A. When, as I have already stated, in order to carry out the liquidation as ordered it was necessary, for example, to resort to beating.

Q. Was it absolutely necessary to beat the victims?

A. I myself never saw such a case, but I heard of such.

Q. From whom?

A. In conversations held with members of other Kommandos.

Q. You said that cars, auto-cars, were used for the executions?

A. Yes.

Q. Do you know where, and with whose assistance, the inventor, Becker, was able to materialise his inventions?

A. I remember only that it took place within Amt II of the R.S.H.A.; but I can no longer say definitely.

Q. How many were executed in these cars?

A. I did not understand the question.

Q. How many persons were executed by means of these cars?

A. I cannot give you any precise figures. The number was comparatively small - about a few hundred.

Q. You said that mostly women and children were executed in these vans. For what reason?

A. There was a special order from Himmler to that effect.

According to this order women and children were not to be executed in this manner in order to avoid the spiritual strain arising from other forms of execution and likewise not to force the soldiers, mostly married men, to shoot down women and children.

Q. Did anybody observe the behaviour of the persons executed in these vans?

A. Yes, the doctor.

Q. Did you know that Becker had reported that death in these vans was particularly agonising?

A. No. I only learned about Becker from the letter which was shown to me here in the Court. On the contrary, I know that according to the doctor's reports the victims felt nothing at the time of death.

Q. Did any military units - I should say, Army units - take part in these mass executions?

A. As a rule, no.

Q. And as an exception?

A. In so far as I remember, in Nikolaiev and in Simferopol an observer from the Army High Command was there for a short time.

Q. For what purpose?

A. I do not know. Probably for personal information.

Q. Were military units assigned for carrying out the executions in these towns?

A. Officially, the Army did not assign any units for this purpose, since the Army as such was opposed to the liquidation.

Q. But factually?

A. Individual units voluntarily made themselves available. However, I know of no such case in the Army itself, only in the units attached to the Army (Heeresgefolge).

Q. You were the man by whose orders people were sent to their death. Were Jews only handed over for the execution by the Einsatzgruppe or were Communists - "Communist Officials" you call them in your instructions - handed over for execution along with the Jews?

A. Yes, "Communist Officials" was the name for political commissars and for those who were politically active. The mere fact of belonging to the Communist Party was not sufficient grounds for sending a man to his death.

Q. Were any special investigations made concerning the part played by persons in the Communist Party?

A. No, I said precisely the contrary, i.e., that the fact of belonging to the Communist Party was not, in itself, a determining factor in regard to persecution or in regard to execution - unless it implied a special political function.

Q. Did you hold any conversations regarding the murder vans sent from Berlin and on their work?

A. I do not understand the question.

Q. Had you any occasion to discuss, with your chiefs and your colleagues, the fact that motor vans had been sent to your own particular Einsatzgruppe from Berlin for carrying out the executions? Do you remember any such conversations?

A. I do not remember any specific conversation.

Q. Had you any information concerning the fact that members of the execution squad in charge of the executions were unwilling to use the vans?

A. I knew that the Einsatzkommandos used these gas vans.

Q. No, I have something else in mind. I wish to discover whether you received any information whether members of the execution squads were unwilling to choose the vans or whether they preferred other means of execution?

A. In other words, that they would killing by gas vans rather than by shooting?

Q. On the contrary, that they preferred execution by shooting to rather than by the gas vans.

A. Yes, I have already said so, that the gas van-

Q. And why did they prefer execution by shooting to killing in the gas vans?

A. I have already said: because, according to the opinion of the Einsatzkommandos, the unloading of the corpses was an unnecessary spiritual strain.

Q. What do you mean "an unnecessary spiritual strain"?

A. As far as I can remember the actual conditions, for instance, the state of the bodies, certain functions of the body took place which left the corpses lying in filth.

Q. You wish to say that the sufferings endured prior to death were clearly visible on the victims? Have I understood you correctly?

A. Do you mean during that moment when the gas killed them in the van?

Q. Yes.

A. I can only repeat what the doctor told me, namely, that the victims at the time of death, felt nothing.

Q. In that case your reply to my previous question, namely, that the unloading of the bodies made a very terrible impression on the members of the execution squad, becomes entirely incomprehensible.

A. As I have already said, the terrible impression was created by the whole situation and by the fouling of the vans by excreta.

COLONEL POKROVSKY: I have no further questions to ask this witness at the present stage of the Trial.

THE PRESIDENT: Does the Prosecutor for the French Republic desire to put any questions to the witness?

M. DE MENTHON: No.

THE PRESIDENT: Does the counsel for Kaltenbrunner desire to cross-examine now or at a later date?

DR. KAUFFMANN (Counsel for defendant Kaltenbrunner): Perhaps I could ask a few questions now and request that I be allowed to make my cross-examination later after I have already spoken with Kaltenbrunner.

An execution of Poles by an Einsatzgruppe in Leszno, October 1939.

THE PRESIDENT: Certainly.

CROSS-EXAMINATION BY DR. KAUFFMANN:

Q. Since when have you known Kaltenbrunner?

A. May I address a request to the Tribunal? May I sit down?

Q. Yes.

THE WITNESS: I saw Kaltenbrunner for the first time on a trip from Berlin to Himmler's headquarters at the time when Kaltenbrunner was to be appointed Chief of the Sipo and S.D. Previously to that I simply knew the fact of his existence.

BY DR. KAUFFMANN:

Q. Did you come into personal contact with Kaltenbrunner through private or official conversations after he had become Chief of the R.S.H.A.?

A. Yes, of course.

Q. Do you know his attitude, as for example, on the Jewish question?

A. I am not familiar with any particular attitude of Kaltenbrunner's.

Q. How about the question of the Church?

A. The question of the church - he deplored the anti-church course taken by Germany. We agreed that an understanding should be reached with the Church.

Q. Do you know what his thoughts were on the liquidation of civilian prisoners, parachute troops, and so on?

A. No.

Q. Do you know that Kaltenbrunner made special efforts to make use of the S.D., in order to supply the Fuehrerstab with the criticism it otherwise lacked?

A. Yes, that was the duty of the S.D. and he also gave this task his official support.

Q. A little bit more slowly.

A. It was the duty of the S.D. even before Kaltenbrunner came and he supported and officially approved the direction of this work.

Q. Do you know, either directly or indirectly, that Kaltenbrunner had no authority to give executive orders, for example, that he had no authority to put people into concentration camps or to take them from concentration camps, that all these things were handled exclusively by Himmler and Mueller?

A. I believe this question is too general for me to be able to answer correctly. The question will have to be broken down, I believe.

If you ask the question whether Kaltenbrunner could bring about executive actions, I must answer in the affirmative. If you then name Himmler and Mueller to the exclusion of Kaltenbrunner, then I must point out that according to the organisation of the R.S.H.A. Mueller was a subordinate of Kaltenbrunner, and consequently orders from Himmler to Mueller were also orders to Kaltenbrunner and Mueller was obliged to inform Kaltenbrunner of them.

On the other hand, it is certain that, particularly in regard to the concentration camps, the final decision regarding entry into or departure from was determined by Himmler. I can say that I know absolutely that - I refer to the expression that often came up, namely, "to the last washerwoman" - Himmler reserved the final decision for himself. As to whether Kaltenbrunner had no authority at all in this regard, I can make no statement.

Q. Have you personally seen the original orders and original signatures of Kaltenbrunner's that ordered the liquidation of sabotage troops and so on?

A. No.

Q. Do you know, either directly or indirectly, that after Heydrich's death a change, which to be sure was not a formal change, took place and that another milder course was taken by Kaltenbrunner?

A. I could not answer that question concretely.

Q. I withdraw the question. Here is another question. Did Kaltenbrunner know that you were an Einsatz Leader in the East?

A. Yes.

Q. Who gave you this command?

A. Heydrich gave it to me.

Q. Heydrich gave it to you? That was before this time?

A. Yes, of course.

DR. KAUFFMANN: I have no further questions at this time.

BY THE TRIBUNAL (GENERAL NIKITCHENKO):

Q. Witness Ohlendorf, can you answer up to what date the Einsatzgruppe under your command was operating?

A. The staff of the Einsatzgruppe went to the Caucasus and was then led back. As far as I can remember, a Combat Command (Kampfkommando) was formed out of it under the name "Bierkamp" which was used in fighting the Partisans. Then the Einsatzgruppe was entirely disbanded, Bierkamp went into the Government General and took a large number of his men with him.

Q. What was your occupation after Bierkamp left?

A. I think I can say that the Einsatzgruppe ceased to exist after the retreat from the Caucasus. It took over tasks similar in the Wehrmacht under the immediate command of the Commander of the Ukraine and particularly under the command of the Higher S.S. and Police Leaders.

Q. In other words, you merely entered a different circle of activity, under a different leadership, and that is all there was to it. Such functions as were performed by the Einsatzgruppe in the past continued to be carried out in the new circle?

A. No, it actually became a Combat Unit.

Q. What does that mean? Against whom were the military activities directed?

A. Within the scope of the operations which were directed against the Partisan movement.

Q. Or can you say more particularly what this group was actually doing?

A. After the retreat?

Q. When you say that the function of this group had changed when it conducted operations against the Partisans.

A. I have no concrete experiences myself. It was probably used, I believe, for reconnaissance against the Partisans and also was actually used as a military fighting unit.

Q. But did it carry out any executions?

A. I cannot make any definite statement about that as regards this period of time, for it now entered into territories in which that sort of activity no longer came into question.

Q. In your testimony you said that the Einsatz Group had the object of annihilation of the Jews and the commissars; is that correct?

A. Yes.

Q. And in what category did you consider the children? For what reason were the children massacred?

A. The order was that the Jewish population should be liquidated in its entirety.

Q. Including the children?

A. Yes.

Q. Were all the Jewish children murdered?

A. Yes.

Q. But the children of those whom you considered as belonging to the category of commissars, were they also destroyed?

A. I am do not know that the families of Soviet commissars were ever inquired after.

Q. Were you sending anywhere the reports of those executions which the group carried out?

A. The reports on the executions were regularly submitted to the R.S.H.A..

Q. No; did you personally send any reports with reference to the annihilation of thousands of people effected by you? You, personally, did you submit any report?

A. Yes, the reports came from the Einsatzkommandos who carried out the actions, to the Einsatzgruppe, and the Einsatzgruppe informed the R.S.H.A.

Q. Where to?

A. They went to the Chief of the Sipo personally.

Q. Personally.

A. Yes, personally.

Q. What was the name of this police officer? Can you give his name?

A. At the time, Heydrich.

Q. After Heydrich?

A. I did not mention any time, but that was the standing order.

Q. I am asking of you whether you continued to submit reports after Heydrich left or not?

A. After Heydrich's death I was no longer in the Einsatz, but the order, of course, continued in effect.

Q. Have you any information whether the reports were continued after Heydrich left or were discontinued?

A. Yes, they were continued.

Q. Was the order concerning the annihilation of the Soviet people in conformity with the policy of the German Government or the Nazi Party or was it against it?

Do you understand the question?

A. Yes. One must distinguish. The order for the liquidation came from the Fuehrer of the Reich and it was to be carried out by the Reichsfuehrer S.S. Himmler.

Q. But was it in conformity with the policy which was conducted by the Nazi Party and the German Government, or was it contrary to it?

A. Politics expresses itself in activity, in so far it was thus a policy that was determined by the Fuehrer. If you ask whether this activity was in conformity with the idea of National Socialism, then I should deny that.

Q. I am talking about the practice.

BY THE PRESIDENT:

Q. I understood you to say that objects of value were taken from the Jewish victims by the Jewish Council of Elders.

A. Yes.

Q. Did the Jewish Council of Elders settle who were to be killed?

A. No.

Q. How did they know who was to be killed?

A. The Jewish Council of Elders determined who were Jews and registered them individually.

Q. And when they registered them did they take their valuables from them?

A. That was done in various ways. As far as I remember, the Council of Elders was given the order to collect valuables at the same time.

Q. So that the Jewish Council of Elders would not know whether or not they were to be killed?

A. That is true.

THE PRESIDENT: We will adjourn now until five minutes past two.

(A recess was taken until 1405 hours.)

CROSS-EXAMINATION BY DR. KAUFFMANN:

Since when have you known Kaltenbrunner?

A. May I address a request to the Tribunal? May I sit down?

Q. Yes.

THE WITNESS: I saw Kaltenbrunner for the first time on a trip from Berlin to Himmler's headquarters at the time when Kaltenbrunner was to be appointed Chief of the Sipo and S.D. Previously to that I simply knew the fact of his existence.

BY DR. KAUFFMANN:

Q. Did you come into personal contact with Kaltenbrunner through private or official conversations after he had become Chief of the R.S.H.A.?

A. Yes, of course.

Q. Do you know his attitude, as for example, on the Jewish question?

A. I am not familiar with any particular attitude of Kaltenbrunner's.

Q. How about the question of the Church?

A. The question of the church - he deplored the anti-church course taken by Germany. We agreed that an understanding should be reached with the Church.

Q. Do you know what his thoughts were on the liquidation of civilian prisoners, parachute troops, and so on?

A. No.

Q. Do you know that Kaltenbrunner made special efforts to make use of the S.D., in order to supply the Fuehrerstab with the criticism it otherwise lacked?

A. Yes, that was the duty of the S.D. and he also gave this task his official support.

Q. A little bit more slowly.

A. It was the duty of the S.D. even before Kaltenbrunner came and he supported and officially approved the direction of this work.

Q. Do you know, either directly or indirectly, that Kaltenbrunner had no authority to give executive orders, for example, that he had no authority to put people into concentration camps or to take them from concentration camps, that all these things were handled exclusively by Himmler and Mueller?

A. I believe this question is too general for me to be able to answer correctly. The question will have to be broken down, I believe.

If you ask the question whether Kaltenbrunner could bring about executive actions, I must answer in the affirmative. If you then name Himmler and Mueller to the exclusion of Kaltenbrunner, then I must point out that according to the organisation of the R.S.H.A. Mueller was a subordinate of

Kaltenbrunner, and consequently orders from Himmler to Mueller were also orders to Kaltenbrunner and Mueller was obliged to inform Kaltenbrunner of them.

On the other hand, it is certain that, particularly in regard to the concentration camps, the final decision regarding entry into or departure from was determined by Himmler. I can say that I know absolutely that - I refer to the expression that often came up, namely, "to the last washerwoman" - Himmler reserved the final decision for himself. As to whether Kaltenbrunner had no authority at all in this regard, I can make no statement.

Q. Have you personally seen the original orders and original signatures of Kaltenbrunner's that ordered the liquidation of sabotage troops and so on?

A. No.

Q. Do you know, either directly or indirectly, that after Heydrich's death a change, which to be sure was not a formal change, took place and that another milder course was taken by Kaltenbrunner?

A. I could not answer that question concretely.

Q. I withdraw the question. Here is another question. Did Kaltenbrunner know that you were an Einsatz Leader in the East?

A. Yes.

Q. Who gave you this command?

A. Heydrich gave it to me.

Q. Heydrich gave it to you? That was before this time?

A. Yes, of course.

DR. KAUFFMANN: I have no further questions at this time.

BY THE TRIBUNAL (GENERAL NIKITCHENKO):

Q. Witness Ohlendorf, can you answer up to what date the Einsatzgruppe under your command was operating?

A. The staff of the Einsatzgruppe went to the Caucasus and was then led back. As far as I can remember, a Combat Command (Kampfkommando) was formed out of it under the name "Bierkamp" which was used in fighting the Partisans. Then the Einsatzgruppe was entirely disbanded, Bierkamp went into the Government General and took a large number of his men with him.

Q. What was your occupation after Bierkamp left?

A. I think I can say that the Einsatzgruppe ceased to exist after the retreat from the Caucasus. It took over tasks similar in the Wehrmacht under the immediate command of the Commander of the Ukraine and particularly under the command of the Higher S.S. and Police Leaders.

Q. In other words, you merely entered a different circle of activity, under a different leadership, and that is all there was to it. Such functions as were performed by the Einsatzgruppe in the past continued to be carried out in the new circle?

A. No, it actually became a Combat Unit.

Q. What does that mean? Against whom were the military activities directed?

A. Within the scope of the operations which were directed against the Partisan movement.

Q. Or can you say more particularly what this group was actually doing?

A. After the retreat?

Q. When you say that the function of this group had changed when it conducted operations against the Partisans.

A. I have no concrete experiences myself. It was probably used, I believe, for reconnaissance against the Partisans and also was actually used as a military fighting unit.

Q. But did it carry out any executions?

A. I cannot make any definite statement about that as regards this period of time, for it now entered into territories in which that sort of activity no longer came into question.

Q. In your testimony you said that the Einsatz Group had the object of annihilation of the Jews and the commissars; is that correct?

A. Yes.

Q. And in what category did you consider the children? For what reason were the children massacred?

A. The order was that the Jewish population should be liquidated in its entirety.

Q. Including the children?

A. Yes.

Q. Were all the Jewish children murdered?

A. Yes.

Q. But the children of those whom you considered as belonging to the category of commissars, were they also destroyed?

A. I am do not know that the families of Soviet commissars were ever inquired after.

Q. Were you sending anywhere the reports of those executions which the group carried out?

A. The reports on the executions were regularly submitted to the R.S.H.A..

Q. No; did you personally send any reports with reference to the annihilation of thousands of people effected by you? You, personally, did you submit any report?

A. Yes, the reports came from the Einsatzkommandos who carried out the actions, to the Einsatzgruppe, and the Einsatzgruppe informed the R.S.H.A.

Q. Where to?

A. They went to the Chief of the Sipo personally.

Q. Personally.

A. Yes, personally.

Q. What was the name of this police officer? Can you give his name?

A. At the time, Heydrich.

Q. After Heydrich?

A. I did not mention any time, but that was the standing order.

Q. I am asking of you whether you continued to submit reports after Heydrich left or not?

A. After Heydrich's death I was no longer in the Einsatz, but the order, of course, continued in effect.

Q. Have you any information whether the reports were continued after Heydrich left or were discontinued?

A. Yes, they were continued.

Q. Was the order concerning the annihilation of the Soviet people in conformity with the policy of the German Government or the Nazi Party or was it against it?

Do you understand the question?

A. Yes. One must distinguish. The order for the liquidation came from the Fuehrer of the Reich and it was to be carried out by the Reichsfuehrer S.S. Himmler.

Q. But was it in conformity with the policy which was conducted by the Nazi Party and the German Government, or was it contrary to it?

A. Politics expresses itself in activity, in so far it was thus a policy that was determined by the Fuehrer. If you ask whether this activity was in conformity with the idea of National Socialism, then I should deny that.

Q. I am talking about the practice.

BY THE PRESIDENT:

Q. I understood you to say that objects of value were taken from the Jewish victims by the Jewish Council of Elders.

A. Yes.

Q. Did the Jewish Council of Elders settle who were to be killed?

A. No.

Q. How did they know who was to be killed?

A. The Jewish Council of Elders determined who were Jews and registered them individually.

Q. And when they registered them did they take their valuables from them?

A. That was done in various ways. As far as I remember, the Council of Elders was given the order to collect valuables at the same time.

Q. So that the Jewish Council of Elders would not know whether or not they were to be killed?

A. That is true.

THE PRESIDENT: We will adjourn now until five minutes past two.

DR. RUDOLF MERKEL (Counsel for the Gestapo):

Q. Witness, do you know that in April 1933 the Gestapo was created in Prussia?

A. I do not know the month, but I do know the year.

Q. Do you know what was the purpose of creating this institution?

A. To fight political opponents potentially dangerous to the State.

Q. Do you know how this institution, which was intended originally for Prussia only, was extended to the rest of the Reich?

A. Either in 1933 or in 1934, the institution of the Political Police was created in all of the States (Laender). These political police agencies were officially subordinated, in 1934, as far as I remember, to the Reichsfuehrer S.S. as Political Police Chief of the States. The Prussian Secret State Police Office represented the first central headquarters. After the creation of the "Main Office Security Police" the command tasks were delegated by Himmler to Heydrich who carried them out through the "Main Office Security Police."

Q. Who created and instituted the Gestapo in the individual States?

A. I cannot give you an answer to this question.

Q. Do you know whether before 1933, in the area which then constituted the Reich, there had existed a similar institution, a political police force?

A. Yes, that existed, as far as I remember, at Police headquarters, Berlin, for instance, and I believe it was Department IA. At any rate political police organisations did exist.

Q. Do you know anything about the sphere of activities of this organisation which existed before 1933?

A. Yes. They were the same; at any rate their activities were fundamentally the same.

Q. Do you know anything about the recruiting of the Gestapo personnel, which, on the whole, was a new institution and consequently not constituted merely by transfer of personnel already in existence.

A. When I got acquainted with the State Police it was certainly true that the nucleus of expert personnel had been taken from the Criminal Police, and the majority of the leading men in the State Police Offices, i.e., in the regional offices of the State police, had risen from the ranks of the Department of the Interior, possibly also from the State Police Administrations, and that they had, in part, even been detailed from this Department of the Interior civil. The same was also true for the experts within Amt IV, i.e., the Gestapo.

Q. You say the majority of the officials were detailed?

A. I did not say the majority were detailed, but I said "in part."

Q. Detailed in part! Could any of these members of the Gestapo possibly resist being taken over into the Gestapo if they did not wish it, or could they not?

A. I would not affirm that a definite resistance was possible. Some of them might have succeeded, by cunning, in avoiding it had they not wanted to go. But if one was detailed to such an office from the Department of the Interior, then, as an official, one simply had to obey. As an official he had to....

Q. The members of the Gestapo evidently consisted almost exclusively, or exclusively, of officials? Do you know anything about that?

A. That probably was no longer the case during the war. But as a rule it should be assumed that they were officials in as far as the experts were concerned. Some of them, of course, while in training, were not yet officials, and others again were merely employees, especially in the Auxiliary Forces.

Q. Can you tell me the approximate number of the members of the Gestapo towards the end of the war?

A. I estimate the total organisation of the Gestapo, including the regional offices and the Occupied Territories, at about 30,000.

Q. There was therefore within the Gestapo, a considerable percentage of officials who were merely administrative officials and had nothing to do with executive powers?

A. Yes, of course.

Q. And what was the percentage of these administrative officials who performed purely administrative functions?

A. We must, in the first instance, take into consideration that this number included the auxiliaries, as well as the women, and I cannot, offhand, immediately give you any figures. But it is certain that a proportion of one expert to three or four persons not employed in an executive capacity could not be considered excessive.

Q. Do you know anything about who was responsible for the direction and administration of the concentration camps?

A. It was Obergruppenfuehrer Pohl.

Q. Did the Gestapo have anything to do with the leadership and with the administration of the concentration camps or not?

A. According to my knowledge, no.

Q. Therefore, no members of the Gestapo were active, or in any way involved in the measures carried out in the concentration camps?

A. As far as I could judge, from a distance, only investigating officials of the State Police were active in the concentration camps.

Q. Did the Gestapo in any way participate in the mass executions undertaken by your Einsatzgruppe, which you described this morning?

A. Only as much as every other person present in the Einsatzgruppe.

DR. MERKEL: I ask the Tribunal to give me the opportunity of questioning this witness again after the return of the defendant Kaltenbrunner, since I am obliged to rely exclusively on information received from Kaltenbrunner.

THE PRESIDENT: I think that the Tribunal will be prepared to allow you to put further questions at a later stage.

DR. MERKEL: Thank you.

BY DR. EXNER (Counsel for the General Staff and the O.K.W.):

Q. Witness, you mentioned the negotiations which took place in the O.K.W., which later led to an agreement between O.K.W. and O.K.H. on the one side, and the Main Security Office of the Reich (R.S.H.A.) on the other. I am interested in this point: Can you state that during the negotiations on this agreement there was any mention made regarding the extermination and the killing of Jews?

A. I cannot say anything concrete on this particular subject, but I do not believe it.

Q. You do not believe it?

A. No.

Q. In addition, you have told us that the Commander-in-Chief of the 11th Army knew about the liquidations, and I should like to ask you first of all:

Do you know anything regarding the Commanders-in-Chief of the other armies?

A. In general, they must have been informed, through the speech of the Fuehrer, before the beginning of the Russian campaign.

Q. That is a conclusion that you have drawn?

A. No, it is not a conclusion that I have drawn; it is merely a report on the contents of the speech which, according to Himmler's statement, Hitler had made to the Commanders-in-Chief.

Q. Now, you have spoken about directives given by the Commander-in-Chief of the 11th Army. What kind of directives were they?

A. I once spoke about the Commander-in-Chief in the case of Nikolaiev, i.e., that the order given at that time, for the liquidations to take place 200 kilometers away from the headquarters of the Army. On the second occasion, I did not speak about the Commander-in-Chief of the Army, but about the High Command of the Army at Simferopol, because I cannot say, with any certainty, who had requested the competent Einsatzkommando at Simferopol to speed up the liquidation.

Q. That is the very question I should like to put to you: With whom in the 11th Army did you negotiate at that time?

A. I did not personally negotiate at all with anyone on this subject, since I was not the person directly concerned with these matters; but the High Command of the Army negotiated with the competent local Einsatzkommando either through the responsible army office, which at all times was in touch with the Einsatzkommandos, namely the I-C or the I-CAO, or else through the staff of the O.Q.

Q. Who gave you directives for the march?

A. The directives for the march came, as a rule, from the Chief of Staff.

Q. From the Chief of Staff? The Commander-in-Chief of the Army at the time referred to was von Manstein. Was there ever an order in this case signed by von Manstein?

A. I cannot remember any such order, but when the march was discussed there were oral consultations with von Manstein, the Chief of Staff and myself.

Q. When discussing the march?

A. Yes.

Q. You said that the Army was opposed to these liquidations. Can you state how this became evident?

A. Not the Army, but the Leaders were secretly opposed to the liquidations.

Q. Yes. But I mean, how did you recognise that fact?

A. By our conversations. Not only the leaders of the Army but also most of those who had to carry them out were opposed to the liquidations.

DR. EXNER: I thank you.

BY PROFESSOR KRAUS (Counsel for defendant Schacht):

Q. Were you acquainted with the personal records kept in your department on Reichsbank President Schacht?

A. No.

Q. Do you know why, after the 20th July, 1944, the former Reichsbank President Schacht was arrested and interned in a concentration camp?

A. Probably the occasion of the 20th of July was also favorable for a possible conviction of Reichsbank President Schacht, who was known to be inimical to the Party, whilst by means of witnesses or other methods he could be prosecuted in connection with the events of the 20th of July.

Q. Then defendant Schacht was known to your people as being inimical to the Party?

A. Yes, at least since the year 1937 or 1938.

Q. Since the year 1937 or 1938? And you also suspected him of participating in "putsches"?

A. Personally I did not suspect this, because I was not concerned with these matters at all; He was mainly under suspicion mainly because of his well-known enmity. But, as far as I know, this suspicion was never confirmed.

Q. Can you tell me, who caused Schacht to be arrested?

A. That I cannot say.

Q. Then you do not know whether the arrest was ordered by the Fuehrer, by Himmler or by some subordinate authority.

A. I consider it impossible that it should emanate from any subordinate authority.

Q. Then you assume that it had been ordered by the Fuehrer?

A. At least by Himmler.

BY DR. STAHMER (Counsel for defendant Goering):

Q. Witness, if I have understood you correctly, you said that at the beginning of 1933, after the seizure of power by Hitler, the Gestapo was created in Prussia; but before that time there had already existed in Prussia an organisation with similar tasks; for instance at the Police Headquarters in Berlin with Department IA; only this organisation was opposed to National Socialism, whereas now the contrary is true. But you also had the task of keeping political opponents under observation and possibly of arresting them, thus protecting the State from these political opponents.

A. Yes.

Q. You said further that in 1933, after the seizure of power, a political police with identical tasks was also instituted in all the other States (Laender).

A. Yes, in the year 1933-1934.

Q. This political police, which existed in the various States was then centralised in 1934 and its direction handed over to Himmler?

A. It was not at first centralised, but Himmler did become Chief of Police of all the States.

Q. Now one more question. Did the Prussian Gestapo play a leading role, as far as the other States were concerned, as early as 1933 or only after Himmler took over the leadership in 1934?

A. I do not believe that the Prussian State Police, which after all was under the leadership of Reichsmarshal Goering, became, at that time, the competent authority for the other States as well.

BY DR. KRANZBUEHLER (Counsel for defendant Doenitz):

I am speaking as the representative of the counsel for defendant Grand Admiral Raeder.

Q. Witness, you just mentioned a speech of the Fuehrer before the Commanders-in-Chief, in which the he is supposed to have instructed the Commanders-in-Chief regarding the liquidation of Jews. Which conference do you mean by that?

A. A conference took place, shortly before the Russian campaign, with the Commanders-in-Chief of the Army Groups and the Armies, at the Fuehrer's quarters.

Q. Were the of the Commanders-in-Chief of the divisions of the Armed Forces absent?

A. I do not know that.

Q. Were you yourself present at this conference?

A. No. I have recounted this conference on the basis of a conversation I had with Himmler.

Q. Did this conversation with Himmler take place in a large circle of people or was it a private conversation?

A. It was a private conversation.

Q. Did you have the impression that Himmler stated facts, or do you consider it possible that he wished to encourage you in your difficult task?

A. No. The conversation took place much later and did not spring from such motives, but from resentment at the attitude of certain generals of the Armed Forces; Himmler wanted to say that these generals of the Armed Forces could not disassociate themselves from the events that had taken place, as they were just as responsible as all the rest.

Q. And when did this conversation with Himmler take place?

A. In May, 1945, at Flensburg.

DR. KRANZBUHLER: Thank you.

(A recess was taken until 1405 hours.)

BY DR. SERVATIUS (Counsel for the Political Leaders and for defendant Sauckel).

Q. Witness, with regard to the command channels at the disposal of the R.S.H.A. for the execution of their orders and measures and for the transmission of these orders to tactical organisations, such as the S.D. and the concentration camps, did the R.S.H.A. possess their own official channels or did they rely on the channels of the Political Leaders Organisation, i.e., were these orders forwarded via the Gauleitung and the Kreisleitung?

A. I know nothing at all about it. I consider it entirely out of the question.

Q. You consider it entirely out of the question that the Gauleitung and the Kreisleitung had been informed? How was it, for instance...

A. One moment, please. You asked me whether the channels passed their way; you did not ask me whether they had been informed.

Q. Were these offices informed of the orders?

A. The Inspectors, the Gestapo, or the S.D. Leaders were considered as police or political reporters (Referenten) of the Gauleiter or the Reichsstatthalter, and these official chiefs had to report to the Gauleiter on their respective fields of activity. Just how extensively this was done, I am unable to judge. It depends on the activities and on the nature of the co-operation between the Gauleiter and these offices, but it is, in any case, inconceivable that the State Police could carry on these activities, for any length of time, without the knowledge of the responsible Party Organisations.

Q. Does this also refer to reports from lower to higher units, i.e., to the activities of the concentration camps?

A. The concentration camps were not subordinate to the State Police; I am convinced - since these were purely affairs of the Reich - that there was no such close connection between the Gauleiter and the concentration camps as there was between the Gauleiter and the permanent activities of the State Police.

Q. I also represent the defendant Sauckel. Do you know of the impressment of foreign workers by the S.S.? Foreign workers who, as a matter of fact, came from the concentration camps?

A. Only superficially.

BY HERR BABEL (Counsel for the S.S. and the S.D.).

Q. Witness, this morning you mentioned the figures of 3,000 and 30,000 for the Security Service. I should now like to know for certain how these figures are to be understood. Do the 3,000 members of the S.D., whom you mentioned this morning, represent the entire personnel of the S.D. at that time, or did they only represent that part of the units which were employed in the field with the mobile units also mentioned by you this morning?

A. No, the figures represent the total personnel including employees and women auxiliaries.

Q. Including employees and women auxiliaries. And the 30,000, which we also discussed, were they honorary members (ehrenamtliche Mitglieder) employed only in the interior of Germany?

A. Yes, as a rule, in any case...

Q. And who, to a considerable extent, belonged neither to the S.S. nor to the Party?

A. Yes.

Q. How large were the mobile units of the S.D. employed in these executions?

A. The S.D. had no mobile units and only individual members of the S.D. were detailed to regional offices elsewhere. The S.D., as a separate entity, did not act independently anywhere.

Q. In your opinion and judging by your own experience, what figure did this detailed personnel attain?

A. The figure was quite a low one.

Q. Will you please give an approximate figure.

A. I place the figure at an average of about two to three S.D. experts per Einsatzkommando.

Q. I should like to be informed of the total number of the S.S. Do you know anything about that?

A. No, I have no idea at all.

Q. No idea at all. Did any units of the S.S. Armed Forces (Waffen S.S.) and other subordinate S.S. Groups in any way participate in the Einsatzgruppen?

A. As I said this morning, in each Einsatzgruppe there was, or rather there should have been, one company of the S.S. Armed Forces (Waffen S.S.).

Q. One company. And what, at that time, was the exact strength of one company?

A. I do not know about the Waffen S.S. serving with the other Einsatzgruppen, but I estimate that my particular group employed approximately 100 men of the S.S. Armed Forces.

Q. Were "Death's Head Units" (Totenkopf Verbaende) also involved?

A. No.

Q. Was the "Adolf Hitler Bodyguard" (Leibstandarte Adolf Hitler) employed in any fashion?

A. That was purely a matter of chance. I cannot name a single formation from which these S.S. Armed Forces had been seconded.

Q. Another question that was touched upon this morning: When was the S.D. created and what, at first, were their duties?

A. As far as I know, the S.D. was created in 1932.

Q. And what were their duties at that time?

A. They constituted, so to speak, the I-C [Intelligence Corps] of the Party. They were supposed to give information about Party opponents and, if necessary, to deceive them.

Q. Did these duties change in the course of time. and, if so, when?

A. Yes, after the seizure of power, the combating of political opponents was, in certain spheres, one of their principal duties, and supplying the required information on certain individuals was considered their main task. At that time an Intelligence Service, in the true sense of the word, did not yet exist; the real evolution of the S.D. machine within the field of the Home Intelligence Service only followed as from 1936-1937. From that time onwards the work changed, from the observation of individuals to technical matters. With the 1939 reorganisation, when the Main Office of the S.D. was dissolved, the handling of political opponents was completely eliminated from the work of the S.D., which work was thereafter limited to technical matters. Its duties now consisted in observing the effects of the measures carried out by the leading authorities of the Reich and the States (Laender) and in determining how the circles affected reacted to them; in addition, they had to determine what shape the moods and attitude of the people and various classes of society assumed during the course of the war. It was, as a matter of fact, the only authority supplying criticism within the Reich and reporting facts on objective lines to the highest authorities. It should also be pointed out that the Party did not, at any stage, legitimise this work until 1945. The only legal recognition of this critical work came from Reichsmarshal Goering, and that only after the beginning of the war, since he could, in this way, draw the attention of the other departments, at meetings of the Reich Defence Council, to faulty developments. This unbiased and critical work became, in fact, after 1939 the main function of the S.D. Home Intelligence Service.

Q. Another question. To what extent were units of the S.D. committed for duty in the concentration camps?

A. I would ask you, at all times to distinguish between the Home Front S.D. (Inland) working under the Head Office (Amt III) and the Foreign S.D. (Ausland). I cannot give you any information about the Foreign S.D. (Ausland), but their Chief, Schellenberg, is present in this courthouse. As far as Amt III is concerned, I know of no single case in which the representatives of the Home Front S.D. (Inland) had anything at all to do with concentration camps.

Q. Now, a question concerning you personally. From whom did you receive your orders for the liquidation of the Jews and so forth? And in what form?

A. My duty was not the task of liquidation, but I did head the staff which led the Einsatzkommandos in the field, whilst the Einsatzkommandos themselves had already received this order in Berlin, on behalf of Himmler and Heydrich, from Streckenbach. This order was renewed by Himmler at Nikolaiev.

Q. You personally were not concerned with the execution of these orders?

A. I led the Einsatzgruppe, and therefore I had the task of seeing how the Einsatzkommandos executed the orders received.

Q. But did you have no scruples in regard to the execution of these orders?

A. Yes, of course.

Q. And how is it that they were carried out regardless of these scruples?

A. Because to me it is inconceivable that a subordinate leader should not carry out orders given by the Leaders of the State.

Q. This is your own opinion. But this must have been not only your point of view but also the point of view of the majority of the people involved. Did not some of the men appointed to execute these orders ask you to be relieved of such tasks?

A. I cannot remember any one concrete case. I excluded some whom I did not consider emotionally suitable for executing these tasks and I sent some of them home.

Q. Was the legality of the orders explained to these people under false pretences?

A. I do not understand your question; since the order was issued by the superior authorities, the question of legality could not arise in the minds of these individuals, for they had sworn obedience to the people who had issued the orders.

Q. Could any individual expect to succeed in evading the execution of these orders?

A. No, the result would have been a court martial with a corresponding sentence.

THE PRESIDENT: Colonel Amen, do you wish to re-examine?

COLONEL AMEN: Just a very few questions, Your Honor.

RE-EXAMINATION BY COLONEL AMEN:

Q. What organisation furnished the supplies to the Einsatz Groups?

A. The Reichssicherheitshauptamt furnished supplies.

Q. What organisation furnished weapons to the Einsatz Groups?

A. The weapons were also furnished through the R.S.H.A.

Q. What organisation assigned personnel to the Einsatz Groups?

A. The Organisation and Personnel Department of the Reichssicher-heitshauptamt.

Q. And all these activities of supplies required personnel in addition to the operating members?

A. Yes.

COLONEL AMEN: I have no more questions.

THE PRESIDENT: That will do; thank you.

(The witness withdrew.)

Q. The next witness to be called by the prosecution is Dieter Wisliceny. That witness will be examined by Lieutenant-Colonel Smith W. Brookhart, Jr.

BY THE PRESIDENT:

Q. What is your name?

A. Dieter Wisliceny.

Q. Will you repeat this oath? I swear by God, the Almighty and Omniscient, that I will speak the pure truth and will withhold and add nothing.

(The witness repeated the oath in German.)

Q. Please speak slowly and pause between each sentence.

BY LIEUTENANT COLONEL BROOKHART:

Q. How old are you?

A. I am thirty-four years old.

Q. Where were you born?

A. I was born at Regulowken in East Prussia.

Q. Were you a member of the N.S.D.A.P.?

A. Yes, I was a member of the N.S.D.A.P..

Q. Since what year?

A. I entered the N.S.D.A.P. first in 1931, was then struck off the list and finally entered in 1933.

Q. Were you a member of the S.S.?

A. Yes, I entered the S.S. in 1934.

Q. Were you a member of the Gestapo?

A. In 1934 I entered the S.D.

Q. What rank did you achieve?

A. In 1940 I was promoted to S.S. Hauptsturmfuehrer.

Q. Do you know Adolf Eichmann?

A. Yes, I have known Eichmann since 1934.

Q. Under what circumstances?

Adolf Eichmann in 1942.

A. We joined the S.D. about the same time, in 1934. Until 1937 we were together in the same department.

Q. How well did you know Eichmann personally?

A. We knew each other very well. We used the intimate "Du," and I also knew his family very well.

Q. What was his position?

A. Eichmann was in the R.S.H.A., Chief of Department IV, Gestapo.

Q. Do you mean Section IV or a subsection, and, if so, which subsection?

A. He led Section IV-A-4. This department comprised two subsections: one for Church and another for Jewish matters.

Q. You have before you a diagram showing the position of Subsection IV-A-4-b in the R.S.H.A.

A. Yes.

Q. Did you prepare this diagram?

A. Yes, I made the diagram myself.

Q. Does it correctly portray the organisational set-up showing the section dealing with Jewish problems?

A. Yes, this was approximately the personnel of the section at the beginning of 1944.

Q. Referring to this chart and the list of leading personnel, as shown in the lower section of the paper, were you personally acquainted with each of the individuals named therein?

A. Yes; I knew all of them personally.

Q. What was the particular mission of IV-A-4-b of the R.S.H.A.?

A. This Section IV-A-4-b was concerned with the Jewish question on behalf of the R.S.H.A. Eichmann had special powers from Gruppenfuehrer Mueller, the Chief of Amt IV, and from the Chief of the Security Police. He was responsible for the so-called solution of the Jewish question in Germany and in all countries occupied by Germany.

Q. Were there distinct periods of activity affecting the Jews?

A. Yes.

Q. Will you describe to the Tribunal the approximate periods and the different types of activity?

A. Yes. Until 1940 the general policy within the section was to settle the Jewish question in Germany and in areas occupied by Germany by means of a planned emigration. The second phase, from that time on, was the concentration of all Jews in Poland and in other territories occupied by Germany in the East, by concentration in ghettos. This period lasted approximately until the beginning of 1942. The third period was the so-called "final solution" of the Jewish question, that is, the planned extermination and destruction of the Jewish race; this period lasted until October, 1944, when Himmler gave the order to stop their destruction.

(A recess was taken.)

LT. COLONEL BROOKHART:

Q. When did you first become associated with Section IV-A-4 of the R.S.H.A.?

A. That was in 1940. I accidentally met Eichmann....

Q. What was your position?

A. Eichmann suggested that I should go to Bratislava as adviser on the Jewish question to the Slovakian Government.

Q. Thereafter how long did you hold that position?

A. I was at Bratislava until the spring of 1943; then, almost a year in Greece and later, from March, 1944, until December, 1944, I was with Eichmann in Hungary. In January, 1945, I left Eichmann's department.

Q. In your official connection with Section IV-A-4, did you learn of any order which directed the annihilation of all Jews?

A. Yes, I learned of such an order for the first time from Eichmann in the summer of 1942.

Q. Will you tell the Tribunal under what circumstances, and what was the substance of the order?

A. In the spring of 1942 about 17,000 Jews were taken from Slovakia to Poland as workers. It was a question of an agreement with the Slovakian

Government. The Slovakian Government further asked whether the families of these workers could not be taken to Poland as well. At first Eichmann declined this request.

In April, or at the beginning of May, 1942, Eichmann told me that henceforward whole families could also be taken to Poland. Eichmann himself was at Bratislava in May, 1942, and had discussed the matter with competent members of the Slovakian Government. He visited Minister Mach and the then Prime Minister, Professor Tuka. At that time he assured the Slovakian Government that these Jews would be humanely and decently treated in the Polish ghettos. This was the special wish of the Slovakian Government. As a result of this assurance about 35,000 Jews were taken from Slovakia into Poland. The Slovakian Government, however, made efforts to see that these Jews were, in fact, humanely treated; they particularly tried to help such Jews as had been converted to Christianity. Prime Minister Tuka repeatedly asked me to visit him, and expressed the wish that a Slovakian delegation be allowed to enter the areas to which the Slovakian Jews were supposed to have been sent. I transmitted this wish to Eichmann, and the Slovakian Government even sent a note on the matter to the German Government. Eichmann, for the time being, gave evasive answers.

Then at the end of July or the beginning of August, I went to see him in Berlin and implored him once more to grant the request of the Slovakian Government. I pointed out to him that abroad there were rumours to the effect that all Jews in Poland were being exterminated. I pointed out to him that the Pope had intervened with the Slovakian Government on their behalf. I advised him that such a proceeding, if really true, would seriously injure our prestige, i.e., the prestige of Germany, abroad. For all these reasons I begged him to permit the inspection in question. After a lengthy discussion, Eichmann told me that this request to visit the Polish ghettos could not be granted under any circumstances whatsoever. In reply to my question "Why?" he said that most of these Jews were no longer alive. I asked him who had given such instructions and he referred me to an order of Himmler's. I then begged him to show me this order, because I could not believe that it actually existed in writing. He....

Q. Where were you at that time? Where were you at the time of this meeting with Eichmann?

A. This meeting with Eichmann took place in Berlin, Kurfuerstenstrasse 116, in Eichmann's office.

Q. Proceed with the answer to the previous question. Proceed with the discussion of the circumstances and the order.

A. Eichmann told me he could show me this order in writing if it would soothe my conscience. He took a small volume of documents from his safe, turned over the pages, and showed me a letter from Himmler to the Chief of the Security Police and the S.D. The gist of the letter was roughly as follows:

The Fuehrer had ordered the "final solution" of the Jewish question; the Chief of the Security Police and the S.D. and the Inspector of the

Concentration Camps were entrusted with carrying out this so-called "final solution." All Jewish men and women who were able to work were to be temporarily exempted from the so-called "final solution" and used for work in the concentration camps. This letter was signed by Himmler in person. I could not possibly be mistaken since Himmler's signature was well known to me. I....

Q. To whom was the order addressed?

A. To the Chief of the Security Police and S.D., i.e. , to the office of the Chief of the Security Police and S.D.

Q. Was there any other addressee on this order?

A. Yes, the Inspector of the Concentration Camps. The order was addressed to both these offices.

Q. Did the order bear any classification for security purposes?

A. It was classified as "Top Secret."

Q. What was the approximate date of this order?

A. This order was dated April, 1942.

Q. By whom was it signed?

A. By Himmler personally.

Q. And you personally examined this order in Eichmann's office?

A. Yes, Eichmann handed me the document and I saw the order myself.

Q. Was any question asked by you as to the meaning of the words "final solution" as used in the order?

A. Eichmann went on to explain the meaning of the concept to me. He said that the planned biological destruction of the Jewish race in the Eastern Territories was disguised by the concept and wording "final solution." In later discussions on this subject the same words "final solution" re-appeared over and over again.

Q. Was anything said by you to Eichmann in regard to the power given him under this order?

A. Eichmann told me that within the R.S.H.A. he personally was entrusted with the execution of this order. For this purpose, he had received every authority from the Chief of the Security Police; he himself was personally responsible for the execution of this order.

Q. Did you make any comment to Eichmann about his authority?

A. Yes. It was perfectly clear to me that this order spelled death to millions of people. I said to Eichmann, "God grant that our enemies never have the opportunity of doing the same to the German people," in reply to which Eichmann told me not to be sentimental; it was an order of the Fuehrer's and would have to be carried out.

Q. Do you know whether that order continued in force and under the operation of Eichmann's department?

A. Yes.

Q. For how long?

A. This order was in force until October, 1944. At that time Himmler gave a counter-order which forbade the annihilation of the Jews.

Q. Who was Chief of the Reichssicherheitshauptamt at the time the order was first issued?

A. That would be Heydrich.

Q. Did the program under this order continue with equal force under Kaltenbrunner?

A. Yes; there was no alleviation or change of any kind.

Q. State, if you know, how long Kaltenbrunner knew Eichmann.

A. From various statements by Eichmann I gathered that Kaltenbrunner and Eichmann had known each other for a long time. Both came from Linz, and when Kaltenbrunner was made Chief of the Security Police, Eichmann expressed his satisfaction. He told me at that time that he knew Kaltenbrunner very well personally, and that Kaltenbrunner was very well acquainted with Eichmann's family in Linz.

Q. Did Eichmann ever refer to his friendship or standing with Kaltenbrunner as being helpful to him?

A. Yes, he repeatedly said that, if he had any serious trouble, he could, at any time, go to Kaltenbrunner personally. He did not have to do that very often, since his relations with his immediate superior, Gruppenfuehrer Mueller, were very good.

Q. Have you been present when Eichmann and Kaltenbrunner met?

A. Yes; once I saw how cordially Kaltenbrunner greeted Eichmann. That was in February, 1945, in Eichmann's office in Berlin. Kaltenbrunner came to lunch every day at Kurfuerstenstrasse 116; there the Chiefs met for their mid-day meal with Kaltenbrunner; and it was on one such occasion that I saw how cordially Kaltenbrunner greeted Eichmann and how he inquired after the health of Eichmann's family in Linz.

Q. In connection with the administration of his Office, do you know to what extent Eichmann submitted matters to Heydrich, and later to Kaltenbrunner for approval?

A. The routine channel from Eichmann to Kaltenbrunner lay through Gruppenfuehrer Mueller. To my knowledge reports to Kaltenbrunner were drawn up at regular intervals by Eichmann and submitted to him. I also know that in the summer of 1944 he made a personal report to Kaltenbrunner.

Q. Did you have an opportunity to examine files in Eichmann's office?

A. Yes; I frequently had occasion to examine the files in Eichmann's office. I know that he handled all files pertaining to questions with this particular order very carefully. He was in every respect a definite bureaucrat; he immediately recorded in the files every discussion he ever had with any of his superiors. He always pointed out to me that the most important thing was for him to be covered by his superiors at all times. He shunned all personal responsibility and took good care to take shelter behind his superiors - in this case Mueller and Kaltenbrunner - and to inveigle them into accepting the responsibility for all his actions.

Q. In the case of a typical report going from Eichmann's department through Mueller, Kaltenbrunner to Himmler - have you seen copies of such reports in Eichmann's file?

A. Yes, such copies were naturally very often in the files. The regular channel was as follows: Eichmann had a draft made by an expert or he prepared it himself; this draft went to Gruppenfuehrer Mueller, his Chief of Department; Mueller either signed this draft himself or left the signing to Eichmann. In most cases, when reports to Kaltenbrunner and Himmler were concerned, Mueller signed them himself. Whenever reports were signed unchanged by Mueller, they were returned to Eichmann's office, where a fair copy and one carbon copy were prepared. The fair copy then went back to Mueller for his signature, and thence it was forwarded either to Kaltenbrunner or to Himmler. In individual cases where reports to Himmler were involved, Kaltenbrunner signed them himself. I myself have seen carbon copies with Kaltenbrunner's signature.

Q. Turning now to areas and countries in which measures were taken affecting the Jews, will you state as to which countries you have personal knowledge of such operations?

A. Firstly, I have personal knowledge of all measures taken in Slovakia. I also know full particulars of the evacuation of Jews from Greece and especially from Hungary. Further, I know about certain measures taken in Bulgaria and in Croatia. I naturally heard about the measures adopted in other countries, but was unable from my own observations or from detailed reports, to gain a clear picture of the situation.

Q. Considering the case of Slovakia, you have already made reference to the 17,000 Jews specially selected who were sent from Slovakia. Will you tell the Tribunal of the other measures that followed concerning Jews in Slovakia?

A. I mentioned before that these first 17,000 labourers were followed by about 35,000 Jews, including entire families. In August, or the beginning of September, 1942, an end was put to this action in Slovakia. The reasons for this were that a large number of Jews still in Slovakia had been granted - either by the President or by various Ministries - special permission to remain in the country. A further reason might have been the unsatisfactory answer I gave the Slovakian Government in reply to their request for the inspection of the Jewish camps in Poland. This state of affairs lasted until September, 1944; from August, 1942, until September, 1944, no Jews were removed from Slovakia. From 25,000 to 30,000 Jews still remained in the country.

Q. What happened to the first group of 17,000 specially selected workers?

A. This group was not annihilated, but all were employed for enforced labor in the Auschwitz and Lublin concentration Camps.

Q. How do you know this?

A. I know this detail because the Commandant of Auschwitz, Hoess, made a remark to this effect to me in Hungary, in 1944. He told me, at that time, that these 17,000 Jews were his best workers in Auschwitz.

Q. What was the name of that Commandant?

A. The Commandant of Auschwitz was Hoess.

Q. What happened to the approximately 35,000 members of the families of the Jewish workers that were also sent to Poland?

A. They were treated according to the order which Eichmann had shown me in August, 1942. Part of them were left alive if they were able to work. The others were killed.

Q. How do you know this?

A. I know that from Eichmann and, naturally, also from Hoess, during conversations in Hungary.

Q. What proportion of this group remained alive?

A. Hoess, at that time, in a conversation with Eichmann, at which I was present, gave the figure of the surviving Jews who had been put to work at about 25 to 30 per cent.

Q. Referring now to the 25,000 Jews that remained in Slovakia until September, 1944, do you know what was done with those Jews?

A. After the outbreak of the Slovakian insurrection in the fall of 1944, Hauptsturmfuehrer Brunner, one of Eichmann's assistants, was sent to Slovakia. My wish to go to Slovakia was refused by Eichmann. Brunner then, with the help of German police forces and also with forces of the Slovakian Gendarmerie, assembled these Jews in several camps and transported them to Auschwitz. According to Brunner's statement, about 14,000 people were involved. A small group which remained in Camp Szered was, as far as I know, sent to Theresienstadt in the spring of 1945.

Q. What happened to these Jews after they were deported from Slovakia, this group of 25,000?

A. I assume that they also met with the so-called "final solution," because Himmler's order to suspend this action was not issued until several weeks later.

Q. Considering now actions in Greece about which you have personal knowledge, will you tell the Tribunal of the actions there in a chronological sequence?

A. In January, 1943, I was summoned by Eichmann to Berlin, where he told me that I was to proceed to Salonika, there to solve the Jewish problem there in co-operation with the German Military Administration in Macedonia. Eichmann's permanent representative, Sturmbannfuehrer Wolf, had previously been to Salonika. My departure had been scheduled for February, 1942. At the end of January, 1942, I was told by Eichmann that Hauptsturmfuehrer Brunner had been nominated by him for the technical execution of all operations in Greece, and that he was to accompany me to Salonika. Brunner was not subordinate to me; he worked independently. In February, 1942, we went to Salonika and there contacted the Military Administration. As first action....

Q. With whom in the Military Administration did you deal?

A. War Administration Counsellor (Kriegsverwaltungsrat) Dr. Merten, Chief of the Military Administration with the Commander of the Armed Forces in the Salonika-Aegean theatre.

Q. I believe you used 1942 once or more in reference; did you at all times refer to 1943 in dealing with Greece?

A. That is an error. These events occurred in 1943.

Q. What arrangements were made through Dr. Merten and what actions were taken?

A. In Salonika the Jews were first of all concentrated in certain quarters of the city. There were, in Salonika, about 50,000 Jews of Spanish descent. At the beginning of March, after this concentration had taken place, a teletype arrived from Eichmann to Brunner, ordering the immediate evacuation of all Jews from Salonika and Macedonia to Auschwitz. Armed with this order Brunner and I went to the Military Administration; no objections were raised by the Administration and measures were prepared and executed. Brunner directed the entire action in Salonika in person. The trains necessary for the evacuation were requisitioned from the Transport Command of the Armed Forces. All Brunner had to do was to indicate the number of railway cars needed and the exact time at which they were required.

Q. Were any of the Jewish workers retained at the request of Dr. Merten or the Military Administration?

A. The Military Administration had requisitioned about 3,000 Jews for construction work on the railroad, which number was duly delivered. Once the work was ended, these Jews were returned to Brunner and were, like all the others, dispatched to Auschwitz. The work in question was carried out within the programme of the Todt Organisation.

Q. What was the number of Jewish workers retained for the Organisation Todt?

A. Three to four thousand.

Q. Was there any illness among the Jews that were concentrated for transport?

A. In the camp proper, i.e., the concentration camp, there were no incidence of disease to report. However, in certain quarters of the city inhabited by the Jews there was a prevalence of typhus and other contagious diseases, especially tuberculosis of the lungs.

Q. What, if any, communication did you have with Eichmann concerning this typhus?

A. On receipt of the teletype concerning the evacuation from Salonika, I drew Eichmann's attention over the telephone to the prevalence of typhus. He ignored my objections and gave orders for the evacuation to proceed immediately.

Q. Altogether, how many Jews were collected and shipped from Greece?

A. There were over 50,000 Jews; I believe that about 54,000 were evacuated from Salonika and Macedonia.

Q. What is the basis for your figure?

A. I myself read a comprehensive report from Brunner to Eichmann on completion of the evacuation. Brunner left Salonika at the end of May 1943.

I personally was not in Salonika from the beginning of April until the end of May, so that the action was carried out by Brunner alone.

Q. How many transports were used for shipping Jews from Salonika?

A. From 20 to 25 transport trains.

Q. And how many were shipped in each transport?

A. There were at least 2,000, and in many cases 2,500.

Q. What kind of railway equipment was used for these shipments?

A. Sealed freight cars were used. The evacuees were given sufficient food to last them for about ten days, consisting mostly of bread, olives and other dry food. They also received water and various sanitary facilities.

Q. Who furnished this railway transportation?

A. Transport was supplied by the Rail Transport Command of the Armed Forces, i.e., the cars and locomotives. The food was furnished by the Military Administration.

Q. What did the Subsection IV-A-4 have to do with obtaining this transportation, and who in that sub-section dealt with transportation?

THE PRESIDENT: Colonel Brookhart, you need not go into this in such great detail.

LIEUTENANT-COLONEL BROOKHART: If Your Honour pleases, this particular question, I believe, will have a bearing on the implications involving the military; I can cut down on the other details.

THE PRESIDENT: Well, you spent some considerable time in describing how many of them were concentrated. Whether it was 60,000, or how many were kept for the Todt Organisation - all those details are really unnecessary.

LIEUTENANT-COLONEL BROOKHART: Very well, Sir.

THE PRESIDENT: I mean, you must use your own discretion about how you cut down. I do not know what details or what facts you are going to prove.

LIEUTENANT-COLONEL BROOKHART: If Your Honour pleases, this witness, as he has testified, is competent to cover practically all details in these Balkan countries. It is not our wish to add cumulative evidence, but his testimony does furnish a complete story from the Head Office of the Reichssicherheitshauptamt through the field operations to the "final solution."

THE PRESIDENT: Well, what is he going to prove about these 50,000 Jews?

LIEUTENANT-COLONEL BROOKHART: Their ultimate disposition at Auschwitz, as far as he knows.

THE PRESIDENT: Well, you can go on to what ultimately happened to them then.

LIEUTENANT-COLONEL BROOKHART: Yes, Sir.

Q. What was the destination of these transports of Jews from Greece?

A. In every case to Auschwitz.

Q. And what was the ultimate disposition of the Jews sent to Auschwitz from Greece?

A. They were without exception destined for the so-called "final solution."

Q. During the collection period were these Jews called upon to furnish their own subsistence?

A. I did not understand the question exactly.

THE PRESIDENT: Colonel Brookhart, does it matter, if they were "brought to the "final solution"" which I suppose means death?

LIEUTENANT-COLONEL BROOKHART: Your Honour, this witness will testify that 280,000,000 drachmas were deposited in the Greek National Bank for the subsistence of these people and that this amount was later appropriated by the German Military Administration. That is all I have hoped to prove by this question.

LIEUTENANT-COLONEL BROOKHART (to the Witness): Is that a correct statement of your testimony?

A. Yes. The cash which the Jews possessed was taken away and put into a common account at the Bank of Greece. After the Jews had been evacuated from Salonika this account was taken over by the German Military Administration. About 280,000,000 drachmas were involved.

Q. When you say the Jews taken to Auschwitz were submitted to the "final solution," what do you mean by that?

A. By that I mean what Eichmann had explained to me under the term "final solution," that is, they were destroyed biologically. As far as I could gather from my conversations with him, this annihilation took place in the gas chambers and the bodies were subsequently destroyed in the crematories.

LIEUTENANT-COLONEL BROOKHART: If Your Honour pleases, this witness is able to testify as to actions in Hungary, involving approximately 500,000 Jews.

THE PRESIDENT: Go on, then. You must use your own discretion. I cannot present your case for you.

LIEUTENANT-COLONEL BROOKHART: I have no desire to submit cumulative evidence.

Q. Turning to actions in Hungary, will you briefly outline the actions taken there and your participation?

A. After the entry of the German troops into Hungary, Eichmann went there personally with a large command. By an order signed by the head of the Security Police, I was assigned to Eichmann's Command. Eichmann began his activities in Hungary at the end of March 1944. He contacted members of the then Hungarian Government, especially Secretaries of State Endre and von Baky. The first measures adopted by Eichmann in co-operation with these Hungarian Government officials were the concentration of the Hungarian Jews in special places and special localities. These measures were carried out zone-wise, beginning in Ruthenia and Transylvania. The action was initiated in mid-April 1944.

In Ruthenia over 200,000 Jews were affected by these measures. In consequence, impossible food and housing conditions developed in the small towns and rural communities where the Jews were assembled. On the strength of this situation Eichmann suggested to the Hungarians that these

Jews be transported to Auschwitz and other camps. He insisted, however, that a request to this effect be submitted to him either by the Hungarian Government or by a member thereof. This request was submitted by Secretary of State von Baky. The evacuation was carried out by the Hungarian Police.

Eichmann appointed me Liaison Officer to Lieutenant-Colonel Ferency, charged by the Hungarian Minister of the Interior with this operation. The evacuation of Jews from Hungary began in May, 1944, and was also carried out zone by zone, first starting in Ruthenia, then in Transylvania, Northern Hungary, Southern, and Western Hungary. Budapest was to be cleared of Jews by the end of June. This evacuation, however, was never carried out, as the Regent, Horthy, would not permit it. This operation affected some 450,000 Jews. A second operation was then...

Q. Before you go into that, please, will you tell the Tribunal what, if anything, was done about organising an Einsatz Group to act in Hungary on the Jewish question?

A. At the beginning of March, 1944, a so-called Einsatzgruppe consisting of Security Police and S.D., was formed at Mauthausen near Linz. Eichmann himself headed a so-called "Sondereinsatz-Kommando" (Execution Squad) to which he detailed everybody who, in his department, had occupied some position or other. This "Sondereinsatz-Kommando" was likewise assembled at Mauthausen. All questions of personnel devolved on the then Standartenfuehrer, Dr. Geschke, Leader of the Einsatzgruppe. In technical matters Eichmann was subordinate only to the Chief of the Security Police and the S.D.

Q. What was the meaning of the designation "Special Action Commando Eichmann" in relation to the movement into Hungary?

A. Eichmann's activities in Hungary comprised all matters connected with the Jewish problem.

Q. Under whose direct supervision was Special-Action Commando Eichmann organised?

A. I have already said that in all matters of personnel and economy Eichmann was subordinate to Standartenfuehrer, Dr. Geschke, Leader of the Einsatzgruppe. In technical matters he could give no orders to Eichmann. Eichmann likewise reported direct to Berlin on all the special operations undertaken by him.

Q. To whom?

A. Either to Gruppenfuehrer Mueller, or, in more important cases, to the Chief of the Security Police and S.D., i.e., to Kaltenbrunner.

Q. During the period in which Hungarian Jews were being collected, what, if any, contact was made by the Joint Distribution Committee for Jewish Affairs with Eichmann's representative?

A. The Joint Distribution Committee made efforts to contact Eichmann and to try to ward off the fate of the Hungarian Jews. I myself established this contact with Eichmann, since I wanted to discover some means of protecting the half million Jews in Hungary from the measures already in force. The

Joint Distribution Committee made certain proposals to Eichmann and, in return, requested that the Jews should remain in Hungary. These proposals were particularly of a financial nature. Eichmann felt himself, much against his will, obliged to forward these proposals to Himmler. Himmler thereupon entrusted a certain Standartenfuehrer Becher with further negotiations. Standartenfuehrer Becher then continued the negotiations with Dr. Kastner, Delegate of the J.D.C. But Eichmann, from the very first, endeavoured to wreck the negotiations. Before any concrete results were obtained he attempted to face us with a fait accompli: in other words, he tried to transport as many Jews as possible to Auschwitz.

THE PRESIDENT: Need we go into all these conferences? Can you take us on to the conclusion of the matter?

LIEUTENANT-COLONEL BROOKHART: The witness is inclined to be lengthy in his answers. That has been true in his pre-trial examination I will try...

THE PRESIDENT: You are examining him.

LIEUTENANT-COLONEL BROOKHART: Yes, Sir.

Q. Was there any money involved in the meeting between Dr. Kastner and Eichmann?

A. Yes.

Q. How much?

A. In the first conversation Dr. Kastner gave Eichmann about 3,000,000 pengoes. What the sums mentioned in further conversations amounted to, I do not exactly know.

Q. To whom did Dr. Kastner give this money and what became of it?

A. It was given to Eichmann, who then turned it over to his trustee; the sum was, in turn, handed to the Commander of the Security Police and the S.D. in Hungary.

Q. These actions that you have described involving approximately 450,000 Jews being moved from Hungary - were there any official communications sent to Berlin concerning these movements?

A. Yes, as each transport left, Berlin was informed by teletype. From time to time Eichmann also dispatched a comprehensive report to the R.S.H.A. and to the Chief of the Security Police.

Q. Now, with reference to the Jews that remained in Budapest, what, if any, action was taken against them?

A. After Szalasi had taken over the Government of Hungary.

THE PRESIDENT: Colonel Brookhart, we have not yet heard have we, what happened to these Jews from Hungary? If we have, I have missed it.

LIEUTENANT-COLONEL BROOKHART: I will ask that question now, Sir.

Q. What became of the Jews to whom you have already referred - approximately 450,000?

A. They were, without exception, taken to Auschwitz and brought to the "final solution".

Rudolf Hoess at the Supreme National Tribunal of Poland. He was hanged in April 1947.

Q. Do you mean they were killed?

A. Yes, with the exception of perhaps 25 to 30 per cent. who were used for labour purposes. I here refer to a previously mentioned conversation on this matter between Hoess and Eichmann in Budapest.

Q. Turning now to the Jews remaining in Budapest, what happened to them?

A. In October-November, 1944, about 30,000 of these Jews, perhaps a few thousand more, were removed from Budapest and sent to Germany. They were to be used to work on the construction of the so-called South-East-Wall, a fortification near Vienna. They were mostly women.

They had to walk from Hungary to the German border - almost 200 kilometers. They were assembled in marching formations and followed a route specially designated for them. Their shelter and nutrition on this march was extremely bad. Most of them fell ill and lost strength. I had been ordered by Eichmann to take over these groups at the German border and direct them further to the "Lower Danube" Gauleitung for labour purposes. In many cases I refused to take over these so-called workers, because the people were completely exhausted and emaciated by disease. Eichmann, however, forced me to take them over and in this case even threatened to turn me over to Himmler to be put into a concentration camp if I caused him further political difficulties. For this same reason I was later removed from Eichmann's department.

A large proportion of these people then died in the so-called "Lower Danube" Work Camp from exhaustion and epidemics. A small percentage, perhaps 12,000, were taken to Vienna and the surrounding area, and a group of about 3,000 were taken to Bergen-Belsen, and from there to Switzerland. Those were Jews who had been released from Germany as a result of the negotiations with the "Joint."

Q. Summarising the countries of Greece, Hungary, and Slovakia, approximately how many Jews were affected by measures of the Secret Police and S.D. in those countries about which you have personal knowledge?

A. In Slovakia there were about 66,000, in Greece about 64,000, and in Hungary more than half a million.

Q. In the countries of Croatia and Bulgaria, about which you have some knowledge, how many Jews were thus affected?

A. In Bulgaria, to my knowledge, about 8,000; in Croatia I know of only 3,000 Jews who were brought to Auschwitz from Agram in the summer of 1942.

Q. Were meetings held of the specialists on the Jewish problem from Amt IV-A, for the names which appear on this sheet, to which we made reference earlier?

A. Yes. Eichmann was accustomed to calling a large annual meeting of all his experts in Berlin. This meeting was usually in November. At these meetings all the men who were working for him in foreign countries had to report on their activities In 1944, to my knowledge, such a meeting did not take place, because in November, 1944, Eichmann was still in Hungary.

Q. In connection with the Jews about whom you have personal knowledge, how many were subjected to the "final solution", i.e., to being killed?

A. The exact number is extremely hard for me to determine. I have only one basis for a possible estimate, that is a conversation between Eichmann and Hoess in Vienna, in which he said that only a very few of them had been fit for work. Of the Slovakian and Hungarian Jews about 20 to 30 per cent. have been able to work. It is, therefore, very hard for me to give a reliable total.

Q. In your meetings with the other specialists on the Jewish problem and Eichmann did you gain any knowledge or information as to the total number of Jews killed under this program?

A. Eichmann personally always talked about at least 4,000,000 Jews. Sometimes he even mentioned 5,000,000. According to my own estimate I should say that at least 4,000,000 must have been affected by the so-called "final solution". How many of those actually survived, I am not in a position to say.

Q. When did you last see Eichmann?

A. I last saw Eichmann towards the end of February, 1945, in Berlin. At that time he said that if the war were lost he would commit suicide.

Q. Did he say anything at that time as to the number of Jews that had been killed?

A. Yes, he expressed this in a particularly cynical manner. He said "he would leap laughing into the grave because the feeling that he had 5,000,000 people on his conscience would be, for him, a source of extraordinary satisfaction."

LIEUTENANT-COLONEL BROOKHART: The witness is available for other counsel.

THE PRESIDENT: Do any of the other prosecuting counsel wish to examine the witness?

MR. ROBERTS: My Lord, I have no desire to ask any questions.

THE PRESIDENT: Does the Soviet prosecutor wish to ask any questions?

COLONEL POKROVSKY: At this stage the Soviet Union does not wish to ask any questions.

THE PRESIDENT: Does the French prosecutor?

(No response.)

CROSS-EXAMINATION BY DR. SERVATIUS (Counsel for the defendant Sauckel.):

Q. Witness, you mentioned the labour impressment of the Jews and named two cases, one of Jews from Slovakia, who were brought to Auschwitz and of whom those fit for work were so used; the other when, later, you spoke of such Jews who were brought from Hungary to the "South-East Wall." Do you know whether the Plenipotentiary for Labor, Sauckel, had any connection with these actions, whether this happened on his orders and whether he otherwise had anything to do with these matters?

A. As far as the Jews from Slovakia were concerned, the Plenipotentiary for Labor had nothing to do with these matters. It was a purely internal affair for the Inspector of Concentration Camps who committed these Jews for his own purposes. Concerning the impressment of Jews for the construction of the "South-East Wall," I cannot definitely answer this question. I do not know to what extent the construction of the "South-East Wall" was directed by the Plenipotentiary for Labor. The Jews who came up from Hungary for this construction work were turned over to the "Lower Danube" Gauleitung.

DR. SERVATIUS: I have no further questions to ask the witness.

THE PRESIDENT: Any other?

BY DR. BABEL (Counsel for S.S. and S.D.):

Q. Witness, you mentioned measures taken by the Security Police and the S.D., and you spoke about these organisations several times in your testimony. Is this merely an official designation or are we justified in concluding from your statement that the Security Service, the S.D., was participating in any way?

A. The actions mentioned were executed by Amt IV, i.e., the Gestapo. If I mentioned the Chief of the Security Police and the S.D., I did so because it was the correct designation of thier office and not because I wished mention the S.D. as such.

Q. Did the S.D. therefore participate, in any way, in the measures against the Jews mentioned by you: (1) numerically, and (2) with regard to the execution of these measures?

A. The S.D. as an organisation, was not involved. Some of the leaders, including myself, had risen from the S.D., but they had been detailed to Amt IV, i.e., the Gestapo.

Q. Did former members of the S.S. and S.D., who later became active in the Gestapo, still remain members of their original organisation, or were they exclusively members of the Gestapo?

A. No, they still remained with the S.D.

Q. And were they acting as members of the S.D. or actually by order of the Gestapo?

A. We belonged to the Gestapo for the duration of the detail. We merely remained on the S.D. payroll and were taken care of as members of their personnel. Orders were received exclusively from the Gestapo, i.e., Amt IV.

Q. In this connection I should like to ask one more question. Could an outsider ever know his way about in this maze of offices?

A. No; that was practically impossible.

THE PRESIDENT: Is there any other of the defendants' counsel who wishes to cross-examine this witness? Colonel Amen? Do you wish, or Colonel Brookhart, does he wish to re- examine the witness?

COLONEL AMEN: No further questions, Your Lordship.

THE PRESIDENT: Very well. That will do.

(The witness withdrew.)

COLONEL AMEN: It will take about 10 minutes, sir, to get the next witness up. I had not anticipated we would finish quite so quickly. Do you still want me to get him up this afternoon?

THE PRESIDENT: Have you any other witnesses on these subjects?

COLONEL AMEN: Not on this subject, Sir. I have two very short witnesses: one on the written agreement, as to which testimony was given this morning, between the O.K.W., and O.K.H. and the R.S.H.A., a witness who can answer the questions which the members of the Tribunal asked this morning, very briefly; and one other witness who is on a totally different subject.

THE PRESIDENT: On what subject is the other witness?

COLONEL AMEN: Well, he is on the subject of identifying two of the defendants at one of the concentration camps. I prefer not to mention these names to the defence unless you wish me to.

THE PRESIDENT: Very well. Then you will call those two witnesses to-morrow?

COLONEL AMEN: Yes, Your Lordship. I do not think either of them will take more than twenty minutes.

THE PRESIDENT: Very well. Then you will go on with the evidence against the High Command?

COLONEL AMEN: Yes, Sir.

THE PRESIDENT: We will adjourn now.

(The Tribunal adjourned until 4th January, 1946, at 1000 hours.)

Walter Schellenberg (1910-1952) as a SS-Oberführer.

FRIDAY, 4TH JANUARY, 1946

COL. AMEN: I would like to call as a witness for the prosecution Walter Schellenberg.

THE PRESIDENT: Is your name Walter Schellenberg?

THE WITNESS SCHELLENBERG: My name is Walter Schellenberg.

THE PRESIDENT: Will you take this oath: I swear to God, the Almighty and Omniscient, that I will speak the pure truth and will withhold and add nothing.

(The witness repeated the oath in German.)

COL. AMEN:

Q. Where were you born?

A. In Saarbruecken.

Q. How old are you?

A. Thirty-five years.

Q. You were a member of the N.S.D.A.P.?

A. Yes.

Q. And of the S.S.?

A. Yes; the S.S. also.

Q. And of the Waffen S.S.?

A. And the Waffen S.S.

Q. And the S.D.?

A. And the S.D.

Q. What rank did you hold?

A. The highest rank that I held was that of S.S. Brigadefuehrer in the S.S. and of Major-General in the Waffen S.S.

Q. You were Chief of Amt VI?

A. I was Chief of Amt VI and ...

Q. During what period of time?

A. I was Deputy Chief of Amt VI in July, 1941, and the final confirmation of my appointment as Chief was in June of 1942.

Q. State briefly the functions of Amt VI of the R.S.H.A.

A. Amt VI was the political secret service of the Reich and worked basically in foreign countries.

Q. Do you know of an agreement between O.K.W., O.K.H. and the R.S.H.A. concerning the use of Einsatz Groups and Einsatz Commandos in the Russian campaign?

A. At the end of May, 1941, conferences took place between the then head of the Security Police and the Quartermaster-General, General Wagner.

Q. And who?

A. The Quartermaster-General of the Army, General Wagner.

Q. Did you personally attend those conferences?

A. Yes. I kept the minutes of the final meetings.

Q. Have you given us the names of all persons present during those negotiations?

A. The conferences took place principally between Obergruppenfuehrer Heydrich, who was then the Chief of the Security Police and, the S.D., and the Quartermaster-General of the Army.

Q. Was anyone else present during any of the negotiations?

A. Not during the conferences themselves, but at a later meeting other persons took part.

Q. And did those negotiations result in the signing of an agreement?

A. A written agreement was concluded.

Q. Were you there when the written agreement was signed?

A. I kept the minutes and was present when both gentlemen signed.

Q. By whom was this agreement signed?

A. It was signed by the then Chief of the Security Police, S.S. Obergruppenfuehrer Heydrich, and the Quartermaster-General of the Army, General Wagner.

Q. Do you know where the original agreement, or any copy thereof, is located to-day?

A. No, that I cannot say. I know nothing about that.

Q. But you are familiar with the contents of that written agreement?

A. Yes; for the most part I recollect that.

Q. To the best of your knowledge and recollection, please tell the Tribunal exactly what was contained in that written agreement.

A. The first part of this agreement began with the quotation of a basic decree by the Fuehrer. It read somewhat as follows:

"For the safety of the fighting troops in the Russian campaign that is now at hand, all means are to be used to keep the rear safe and protected. On the basis of this consideration every resistance is to be broken by every means. In order to support the fighting unit of the Army, the Security Police and the Security Service are also to be called in for this task."

If I remember correctly, as a special example of something to be protected, the safeguarding of the so-called great routes of supply, also called "Rollbahnen," was mentioned.

Q. Do you recall anything else contained in that agreement?

A. In the second part of this agreement the organisation of the Army Groups was mentioned ...

Q. And what was said about that?

A. ... and the corresponding organisation of the Einsatz Groups and the Einsatzkommandos of the Security Police and the S.D. Four different spheres of activity were distinguished.

I remember the following: first, the front area; second, the operational zone - it was also divided into an Army area and a rear Army area; third, the rear Army area; and fourth, the area for the Civil Administration "Reichskommissariate" to be set up.

To cover these different spheres, questions of subordination and command were settled exactly. In the front areas or fighting areas, the Einsatzkommandos of the Security Police and the S.D. were tactically and operationally under the command of the Army, that is, they were completely under the command of the Army.

In the operational zones only subordination in respect to operations should apply and this same rule should apply in the rear Army area. In the zone intended for the Civil Administration (Reichskommissariate) the same conditions of subordination and command were to apply as in the area of the Reich.

In a third part was explained what was meant by tactical and operational, or rather only the concept "operational" was explained in detail.

By "operational" was meant the subordination to the Army in respect to discipline and provisions. Special mention was made of the fact that the operational subordination also included all supplies - especially supplies of petrol, food and the making available of technical routes of intelligence transmission.

Q. Have you now told us everything which you can recall about that agreement?

A. Yes; I cannot remember anything else contained in the agreement.

COL. AMEN: If your Honour pleases, that is all.

THE PRESIDENT: Has the English prosecution any questions to ask?

SIR DAVID MAXWELL FYFE: No.

THE PRESIDENT: Has the Russian prosecution any questions to ask?

COL. POKROVSKY: No.

THE PRESIDENT: Has the French prosecution any questions to ask?

(There was no response.)

THE PRESIDENT: Do the defendants' counsel wish to ask any questions?

CROSS-EXAMINATION BY DR. KAUFFMANN (Counsel for defendant Kaltenbrunner)

Q. Is it correct that Dr. Kaltenbrunner was your superior?

A. Dr. Kaltenbrunner was my immediate superior.

Q. During what time?

A. From the 30th January, 1943, until the end.

Q. Do you know his attitude towards the important views of life entertained by National Socialism, for instance, towards the question of the treatment of the Jews or the question of the treatment of the Church?

A. I personally did not have a chance to converse with him on these problems. What I know about him is the result of my own few personal observations.

Q. Did you see original orders from Kaltenbrunner dealing with the execution of saboteurs, the confinement of people in concentration camps and the like?

A. No. I had only oral orders from him in respect to this - commands which he gave to the Chief of the State Police, the Chief of Amt IV of the R.S.H.A.

Q. Did Kaltenbrunner ever indicate to you that he had agreed with Himmler that everything concerning concentration camps and the entire executive power was to be taken away from him, and that only the S.D., as an Intelligence Service, was to be entrusted to you and him, and that he wanted to expand this Intelligence Service, in order to supply the criticism that was otherwise lacking?

A. I never heard of any such agreements. and what I found out later to be the fact is to the contrary.

Q. Now, since you have given a negative answer, I must ask you the following question, in order to make this one point clear: What fact do you mean?

A. I mean, for instance, the fact that, after the Reichsfuehrer S.S., persuaded by me, had very reluctantly agreed not to evacuate the concentration camps, Kaltenbrunner, in direct contact with Hitler, circumvented this decree of Himmler's and broke his word in respect to international promises.

Q. Were there any international decisions in respect to this, decisions which referred to existing laws, or decisions which referred to international agreements?

A. I would like to explain that, if in regard to internationally known persons the then Reichsfuehrer S.S. promised the official Allied authorities not to evacuate the concentration camps in case of emergency, this promise was humanly binding.

Q. What do you mean by evacuate?

A. Arbitrarily to evacuate the camps before the approaching enemy troops and to transplant them to other parts of Germany still unoccupied by the enemy troops.

Q. What was your opinion?

A. That no further evacuation should take place, because human right simply did not allow it; that the camps should therefore be surrendered to the approaching enemy.

Q. Did you know that your activity could also contribute to the suffering caused to many people who were innocent?

A. Yes.

Q. Did you know that your activity, too, could bring suffering to many people, to people who were per se innocent?

A. I did not understand the question. Will you please repeat it?

Q. Did you ever think that your activity, too, and the activity of your fellow workers, was a cause for the great suffering of many people - let us say Jews - even though these people were innocent?

A. I cannot imagine that the activity of my office could cause any such thing. I was merely in an information service.

Q. Then your information service had no connection at all with such crimes?

A. No.

Q. Then Kaltenbrunner too would not be guilty in regard to this point?

A. But he was, at the same time, the Chief of Amt IV of the State Police.

Q. I asked in regard to this point, and by that I meant your sector.

A. I only represented the sector Amt VI and Amt Mil.

Q. But Kaltenbrunner, at the same time, was Chief of Amt VI?

A. Kaltenbrunner was the Chief of the R.S.H.A. Eight departments were under him. One or two of them I headed, namely, Amt VI and Amt Mil. These two offices had nothing to do with the executive power of the State Police.

THE PRESIDENT: What I understood you to say was that you were only in a branch which was an information centre; is that right?

THE WITNESS: Yes.

THE PRESIDENT: And that Kaltenbrunner was your immediate chief; is that right?

THE PRESIDENT: Yes, he was the Chief not only of your branch but of the whole organisation.

THE WITNESS: Yes, this is correct.

DR. KAUFMANN: I should like to question this witness later on. I should like to reserve these important questions for later on, after I have talked with Kaltenbrunner.

BY DR. KUBUSCHOF (Counsel for defendant von Papen)

Q. In the summer of 1943 were you in Ankara, and did you then pay a visit to the German Embassy?

A. Yes.

Q. Did you during this visit criticise German foreign policy in various respects, and did you in this regard mention that it was absolutely advisable to establish better relations with the Holy See? Did Herr von Papen then answer: "That would be possible only if, in accordance with the demands that I have made repeatedly, the Church policy is revised completely and the persecution of the Church ceases"?

A. Yes, that is the correct gist of the conversation, and I spoke with the then Ambassador von Papen to that effect.

BY DR. THOMA (Counsel for defendant Rosenberg):

Q. You said a little while ago that the same regulations applied in the area of the Civil Administration as in the Reich.

A. I said they were to apply.

Q. Please answer my question again.

A. I will repeat: I described the agreement which contained the pro vision that in the areas intended for Civil Administration (Reichskommissariate) the same relations to the Security Police and the S.D., in regard to subordination and command, were applicable as in the Reich.

Q. Do you know how that was done in practice?

A. No, later on I did not concern myself with these questions any more.

Q. Thank you.

BY DR. BABEL (Counsel for S.S. and S.D.):

Q. You were a member of the S.S. and of the S.D., and in leading positions ...

THE PRESIDENT: Will you state, for the purposes of the record, on behalf of which organisation you appear?

DR. BABEL: I represent the organisations of the S.S. and S.D.

Q. In the R.S.H.A. there were departments of the Security Police and the S.D. How were these two departments related, and what was the purpose of the S.D.?

A. That is a question that I cannot answer in one sentence.

Q. I can withdraw the question for the moment and ask a concrete one:

Was the S.D. used with the "Einsatzgruppen" in the East? To what extent? And with what tasks?

A. I believe that the largest employment of personnel in the East was undertaken by the Security Police, that is, by the Secret State Police and the Criminal Police, and that from the personnel of the S.D. only supplementary contingents were formed.

Q. How large were these contingents? How large was the S.D.?

A. I believe that I can estimate the figures: excluding female help, the State Police - perhaps 40,000 to 45,000; the Criminal Police - 15,000 to 20,000; the S.D. of the Interior, that is, Amt Ill with its organisational subsidiaries - 2,000 to 2,500; and the S.D. outside Germany, that is my Amt VI - about 400.

Q. And how was the S.D. used in the East with the Einsatz Groups?

A. I cannot give you the particulars, since that was a concern of the Personnel Administration, and subject directly,to the instructions of the then Chief of the Security Police.

Q. Did the figures you mentioned include male members of the S.D. exclusively, or was female help also included?

A. Only male members. I excluded the female help.

Q. Yesterday a witness gave us approximately the same figure of 3,000, but he included the female help in this figure.

A. I mentioned a figure of 2,000 to 2,500 for the S.D. in the Interior.

Q. What was the organisational structure of the Waffen S.S.?

A. As for the organisational structure of the Waffen S.S., I cannot give you a detailed reply that is reliable.

Q. You were a member of the Waffen S.S. and of the S.D.

A. I was appointed a member of the Waffen S.S. only in January, 1945, by higher orders, so to speak. There I had more military units under my command through the Amt Mil and had to have a military rank to justify my activities.

Q. Do you know whether that also happened to a large extent in other cases?

A. That question is beyond me to answer.

DR. BABEL: Thank you.

RE-EXAMINATION BY COLONEL AMEN:

Q. Do you know of any particular case in which Kaltenbrunner had ordered the evacuation of any one concentration camp, in direct contradiction to Himmler's wishes?

A. Yes.

Q. Will you tell the Tribunal about that?

A. I cannot give you the exact date, but I believe it was in the beginning of April, 1945. The son of the former Swiss President, Muesi, who had taken his father to Switzerland, returned by car to the Buchenwald Concentration Camp, in order to call for a Jewish family which I myself had set free. He found the camp in complete evacuation and under the most deplorable conditions. As he had, three days previously, driven his father to Switzerland, with the final decision that the camps would not be evacuated, and since this declaration was also intended for General Eisenhower, he was doubly disappointed at this breach of promise. Muesi Jr. called on me personally at my office. He was deeply offended and reproached me bitterly. I could not understand the situation and at once contacted Himmler's secretary, protesting against this sort of procedure. Shortly after the truth of the facts, as depicted by Muesi Jr., was confirmed, although it was still incomprehensible, since Himmler had not given these orders. An immediate halt to the evacuations by every available method was assured. This was certified personally by Himmler by telephone a few hours later. I believe it was on the same day, after a meeting of office chiefs, that I informed Kaltenbrunner of the situation and expressed my profound concern at this new breach of international assurances. As I paused in the conversation, the Chief of the State Police, Gruppenfuehrer Mueller, interrupted and explained that he had started the evacuation of the more important internees of the individual camps, three days ago at Kaltenbrunner's orders. Kaltenbrunner replied with these words:

"Yes, that is correct, it was an order of the Fuehrer which was also recently confirmed by the Fuehrer in person. All the important internees are to be evacuated at his order to the South of the Reich."

He then turned to me mockingly and, speaking in dialect, said :

"Tell your old gentleman (i.e., Muesi Jr.) that there are still enough left in the camps. With that you, too, can be satisfied."

I think this was on the 10th April, 1945.

COL. AMEN: That is all, may it please the Tribunal.

QUESTIONS BY THE TRIBUNAL (GENERAL NIKITCHENKO):

Q. Can you say what the functions of the Chief Amt of the Security Police were?

A. That I cannot answer in one sentence. I believe ...

Q. Be brief, be brief! What were the aims?

A. The R.S.H.A. was a comprehensive grouping of a Security Police, that is, a State Police ...

Q. We know about this organisation on the basis of the documents which are at the disposal of the Court, but what were its functions?

A. I just wanted to explain its functions. Its functions consisted of security, that is, State Police activity, of Criminal Police activity, and of intelligence activity at home and abroad.

Q. Would it be correct to formulate the functions as follows: to suppress those whom the Nazi Party considered its enemies?

A. No, I think that statement is too one-sided.

Q. But these functions were included?

A. They were, perhaps, a certain part of the activities of the State Police.

Q. Had this part of the functions, then, been changed after Kaltenbrunner took office?

A. No, there was no change.

Q. Had those functions, to which you referred just now, been changed since the time that Kaltenbrunner took office as Chief of the Security Police?

A. The functions, as I formulated them, did not change after Kaltenbrunner assumed office.

Q. I have one more question: What were the aims and purposes of the operation groups which were to have been created on the basis of the agreement between the S.D. and the High Command?

A. As far as the agreement was covered at that time, the first part, as I mentioned before, referred to the task laid down of protecting the rear of the troops, and using all means against opposition and against resistance.

Q. To repress or to crush resistance?

A. The words were: "All resistance is to be crushed with every means."

Q. By what means was the resistance suppressed?

A. The agreement did not mention nor discuss this in any way.

Q. But you know what means were used for that suppression, do you not?

A. Later I heard that because of the bitterness of the struggle, harsh means were chosen, but I know this only by hearsay.

Q. What does it mean more exactly?

A. That in Partisan fighting and in the treatment of the civilian population many shootings took place.

Q. Including the children?

A. That I did not hear.

Q. You have not heard it?

A. *(No response.)*

Q. That is all.

SIR DAVID MAXWELL FYFE: Since your Lordship was good enough to ask me whether I wanted to put any questions, I have had some further information and I should be very grateful if you would be good enough to allow me to ask one or two questions.

RE-EXAMINATION BY SIR DAVID MAXWELL FYFE:

Q. Would you direct your mind to a conversation between the defendant Kaltenbrunner, Gruppenfuehrer Nebe and Gruppenfuehrer Mueller, in the Spring of 1944, in Berlin at Wilhelmstrasse 102?

A. Yes.

Q. With what was that conversation concerned?

A. That conversation, as far as I could gather - since I took no part in it - concerned the subsequent invention of excuses for the shooting of about 50 English and American prisoners of war. The conversation in its particulars and to the best of my recollection, was as follows: there had evidently been a request from the International Red Cross inquiring as to the whereabouts of 50 English and American prisoners of war. This request for information by the International Red Cross appears to have been passed on to the Chief of the Security Police and the S.D. via the Foreign Office. From the conversation I could ...

Q. Just one moment: was it already in the form of a protest against the shooting of prisoners of war?

A. I believe it was lodged in the form of a protest, since from fragments of this conversation I gathered that there was a discussion as to how the shooting of these prisoners of war, which had already taken place, could be covered up or disguised.

Q. How this could be done?

A. Or had been done.

Q. Did Kaltenbrunner discuss this with Mueller and Nebe?

A. Kaltenbrunner discussed this matter with Mueller and Nebe, but I merely heard fragments of the conversation. I heard, incidentally, that they meant to discuss the details in the course of the afternoon.

Q. Did you hear any suggestion put forward as to what explanations should be offered to explain away the shooting of these prisoners?

A. Yes, Kaltenbrunner himself offered these suggestions.

Q. What were the suggestions?

A. That the greatest part be treated as individual cases, as "having perished in air raids"; some, I believe, because they "offered resistance" i.e., "physical resistance", while others were "pursued when escaping".

Q. You mean - shot while trying to escape?

A. Yes, shot in flight.

Q. And these were the excuses which Kaltenbrunner suggested?

A. Yes. these were the excuses that Kaltenbrunner suggested.

Q. Now, I want you to try and remember as well as you can about these prisoners. Does any number remain in your mind? Can you remember any number of prisoners that they were discussing or how these explanations arose? About how many?

A. I remember only that the number 50 was mentioned over and over again, but how the particulars went I cannot say because I just followed fragments of the conversation, I could not follow the exact conversation.

Q. But the number 50 remains in your mind?

A. Yes, I heard 50.

Q. Can you remember anything of the place or the camp in which these people had been, who were said to have been shot?

A. I cannot tell you under oath. There is a possibility that I might add a little bit. I believe it was Breslau, but I cannot state it exactly, as a fact.

Q. Can you remember anything of what service the people belonged to? Were they Air Force or Army? Have you any recollection on that point?

A. I believe they were all officers.

Q. Were officers?

A. Yes.

Q. But you cannot remember what service?

A. No, that I cannot tell you.

SIR DAVID MAXWELL FYFE: I am very grateful to the Tribunal for letting me ask these questions.

COLONEL AMEN: That is all for this witness.

THE PRESIDENT: Very well, the witness can go then.

(The witness withdrew.)

COLONEL AMEN: I wish to call as the next witness Alois Hoellriegel.

THE PRESIDENT: What is your name?

THE WITNESS: Alois Hoellriegel.

THE PRESIDENT: Will you take this oath?

I swear by God, the Almighty and Omniscient, that I will speak the pure truth and will withhold and add nothing.

(The witness repeated the oath in German.)

THE PRESIDENT: You can sit down if you want to.

DIRECT EXAMINATION BY COLONEL AMEN:

Q. What position did you hold at the end of the war?

A. At the end of the war I was Unterscharfuehrer at Mauthausen.

Q. Were you a member of the Totenkopf S.S.?

A. Yes; in the year 1939 I was drafted into the S.S.

Q. What were your duties at the Mauthausen Concentration Camp?

A. I was, until the winter of 1942, with a guard company and I stood guard. From 1942 until the end of the war I was detailed to the inner service of the concentration camp.

Q. And you therefore had occasion to witness the extermination of inmates of that camp by shooting, gassing and so forth?

A. Yes, I saw that.

Q. And did you make an affidavit in this case to the effect that you saw Kaltenbrunner at that camp?

A. Yes.

Q. And that he saw and was familiar with the operation of the gas chamber there?

A. Yes.

Q. Did you also have occasion to see nay other important personages visiting that concentration camp?

A. I remember Pohl, Gluecks, Kaltenbrunner, Schirach and Gauleiter of the Steyermark, Uiberreuther.

Q. And did you personally see Schirach at that concentration camp at Mauthausen?

A. Yes.

Q. Do you remember what he looks like so that you could identify him

A. I think that he has probably changed a little in recent times, but I would certainly remember him.

Q. How long ago was it that you saw him there

A. It was in the fall of 1942. Since then I have not seen him.

Q. Will you look around the Courtroom and see whether you can see Schirach in the Courtroom?

A. Yes.

Q. Which person is it?

A. In the second row, the third person from the left.

COLONEL AMEN: The affidavit to which I referred was Exhibit USA 515.

THE PRESIDENT: What is the PS number?

COLONEL AMEN: 2753-PS.

BY COLONEL AMEN:

Q. I now show you a copy of Document 2641-PS and ask you whether you can recognise the place where those individuals are standing?

A. As far as I can recognise it at a glance, it is a quarry; whether it is at Mauthausen or not one cannot determine exactly, because the view is too small.

Q. Would you repeat that answer please?

A. Certainly, as far as can be seen from this picture, I cannot see clearly if this is the Wiener-Graben quarry near Mauthausen. It might easily be another quarry. A larger range of vision is required. But I think that visits were often made there. I assume that this is the Wiener-Graben quarry.

Q. Very good. Just lay the picture aside for the time being.

Did you have occasion to observe the killing of inmates of the concentration camp by their being pushed off a cliff?

A. Yes.

Q. Will you tell the Tribunal what you saw with respect to that practice?

A. I remember it was in 1941. At that time I was with a guard company on the tower which closed off the area of the quarry. I was able to observe in the morning about six to eight prisoners who came with two S.S. men of my acquaintance. One was Spatzenecker and the other, Unterscharfuehrer Eichenhofer; they moved ...

THE PRESIDENT: Wait, you are going too fast. You should go slower.

A. I saw that they were approaching the precipice near the quarry. I saw, from my watch-tower, that these two S.S. men were beating the prisoners and I realised immediately that they intended to force them to throw themselves over the precipice or else to push them over. I noticed how one of the prisoners was kicked while lying on the ground, and the gestures showed that he was supposed to throw himself down the precipice. This the prisoner promptly did under the pressure of the blows - presumably in despair.

A. I estimate that it was 30 to 40 metres.

Q. Was there a term used amongst you guards for this practice of having the prisoners fall from the top of the precipice?

A. Yes. In Mauthausen Camp they were called paratroopers.

COLONEL AMEN: The witness is available to other counsel.

THE PRESIDENT: Has the Russian Prosecutor or the French Prosecutor or any defence counsel any questions?

CROSS-EXAMINATION BY DR. SAUTER (Counsel for defendant von Schirach):

Q. Witness, I am interested in the following points.

You said previously that in 1939 you were taken into the S.S.?

A. That is true, on 6th September....

Q. One moment, please repeat your answer.

A. That is right. On 6th September, 1939, I was taken into the S.S. at Ebersberg near Linz.

Q. Had you no connection at all with the Party before then?

A. Yes. In April, 1938, I enlisted in the Civilian S.S., because I was out of work and without any support, and I thought, I will join the Civilian S.S.; there I will get work, in order to be able to marry.

Q. Then, if I understood you correctly, you were drafted into the S.S. in 1939, because you had already enlisted in the Civilian S.S. in the spring of 1938?

A. I cannot say that exactly. Many were drafted into the Armed Forces, into the Air Force and into the General S.S.

Q. Are you an Austrian?

A. Yes.

Q. Then at that time you lived in Austria

A. Yes, at Graz.

Q. I am interested in a certain point in regard to the defendant von Schirach. You saw the defendant von Schirach at Mauthausen. How often did you see him there?

A. I cannot remember so exactly - once.

Q. Once?

A. Yes.

Q. Was von Schirach alone at Mauthausen, or was he with other people?

A. He was accompanied by other gentlemen. There was a group of about ten people, and among them I recognised von Schirach and Gauleiter Niberreuter.

Q. There are supposed to have been 20 persons at least and not 10, on that occasion.

A. I did not know at that time that I might have to give these figures I did not count them.

Q. This point is important to me, because the defendant Schirach told me it was a, visit of inspection, an official inspection tour of the concentration camp Mauthausen, occasioned by a meeting of the Economic Advisors of all six Gaue of the Ostmark.

A. Yes, I naturally did not know why he came to the camp, but I remember that this group came with von Schirach and Schutzhaftlagerfuehrer (Protective Custody-Camp Leader) Bachmeyer. At any rate I could see that it looked like an inspection.

Q. Did you know that this inspection was announced in we camp several days before and that certain preparations were made in the camp because of it?

A. I cannot remember any specific preparations, but I do remember it was during the evening hours. I cannot tell you the exact hour; it was the time of the evening roll-call. The prisoners had assembled for roll-call and all the troops on duty also had to fall in. Then this group came in.

Q. Did you or your comrades not know on the day before that this inspection would take place the very next day?

A. I cannot remember that.

Q. And did it not strike you that certain definite preparations had been made in this camp?

A. I cannot remember that any preparations were made.

DR. SAUTER: I have no further questions to ask this witness.

BY DR. STEINBAUER (Counsel for defendant Seyss-Inquart):

Q. Witness, you described an incident which, according to the conception entertained by civilised people, cannot be designated anything but murder - i.e., the hurling of people over the side of the quarry. Did you report this incident to your superiors?

A. These incidents happened frequently and it is to be assumed with a 100 per cent. degree of accuracy, that the superiors knew about them

Q. In other words, you did not report this. Is it true that on pain of death not only the internees but also the guards were forbidden to report incidents of this sort to a third person?

A. Yes.

DR. STEINBAUER: I have no other questions.

RE-EXAMINATION BY COLONEL AMEN:

Q. Would you just look at that picture again?

A. Yes.

Q. Will you look at it carefully and tell me whether that is the quarry underneath the cliff which you have just described?

A Yes, as far as I can tell from this picture, I assume with a 100 per cent. degree of accuracy that it is the quarry Wiener-Graben; but one would have to see more, more background, to decide whether it is really this quarry. One sees too little, but I think quite certainly ...

Q. Do you recognise the individuals whose faces appear in the picture?

A. Yes.

Q. Will you tell the Tribunal the ones whom you recognise?

A. I recognise of course Reichsfuehrer S.S. Himmler first of all, next to him the Commandant of Mauthausen Concentration Camp and away to the right I recognise Kaltenbrunner.

COLONEL AMEN: That is all, may it please the Tribunal.

THE PRESIDENT: The witness can go and we will adjourn for ten minutes.

(A recess was taken.)

The Case for the Gestapo

WEDNESDAY, 31st JULY, 1946

DR. MERKEL (on behalf of the Secret State Police - the GESTAPO):
Mr. President, may it please the Tribunal, first of all I should like to submit documentary proof. For the first one I am submitting my two document books, Document Book I, containing Nos. 1 to 31, and Document Book 2, Containing Nos. 32 to 62.

Mr. President, shall I give my opinion on the individual documents now or only after the conclusion of the hearing of witnesses?

THE PRESIDENT: When it is convenient to you.

DR. MERKEL: I should prefer to do it after the hearing of witnesses.

THE PRESIDENT: Very well.

DR. MERKEL: First of all, I would like to submit a list of thirteen witnesses who nave been heard before the Commission. Furthermore, I should like to submit a German copy of these thirteen records and would ask you first of all to accept them as evidence. I will then deal with the argumentation myself at the conclusion of the hearing of witnesses. Finally I should like to submit a list of the names and a summary of the affidavits given to the Commission, numbered i to 85, which I should also like to offer in evidence.

The three records of the Commission sessions, in which these affidavits were discussed, I shall submit later as soon as I have them.

Further, I have still about fifteen hundred affidavits to submit, which I would like to hand over in one collective affidavit. As the summary has not yet been quite completed, I should like to ask permission to submit this after the conclusion of the hearing of witnesses.

With the permission of the Tribunal, I should like to call the witness Dr. Best.

THE PRESIDENT: Bring in the witness.

(DR. KARL RUDOLF WERNER BEST, witness, took the stand and testified as follows):

BY THE PRESIDENT:

Q. Will you state your full name?

A. Dr. Karl Rudolf Werner Best.

Q. Will you repeat this oath after me:

I swear by God, the Almighty and Omniscient, that I will speak the pure truth and will withhold and add nothing.

(The witness repeated the oath.)

DIRECT EXAMINATION OF THE WITNESS DR. KARL BEST BY DR. MERKEL:

Q. Witness, please describe your professional career.

A. I am a jurist and a professional civil servant. I have been a judge since the beginning of 1929 and since 1933 I have been an administrative official, and since 1942 I have been a diplomat.

Q. When and how did you join the Gestapo?

A. From 1st January, 1935, onward as Oberregierungsrat and departmental chief (Abteilungsleiter) for administration and law, I was employed in the Gestapo in Berlin from 1936, in the Reich Ministry for the Interior and in the Special Department of the Security Police, until 1940. From 1940 and until 1942 I was a military administrative official, and since 1942 Reich Plenipotentiary in Denmark.

Q. Was the Gestapo a union of people?

A. No.

Q. What was the Gestapo?

A. The Gestapo was a multiplicity of State offices.

Q. However, the prosecution seems to consider the Gestapo as a union of people joined together voluntarily in order to realise certain aims; what have you to say about it?

Witness, you must always leave a slight pause between question and answer.

A. An organisation has members. The officials of the Secret State Police were officials employed by the State, and they occupied a public position. An organisation sets its own aims. The officials of the Secret State Police received their orders from the State and from the State leaders.

Q. Did the Gestapo belong in any way to the NSDAP or to the National Socialist organisation?

A. No, the officials of the Gestapo were purely and simply State officials.

Q. Witness, please speak a little more slowly. Otherwise, the interpreters cannot keep up.

A. Very well.

Q. Was there a uniform Secret State Police set up in January, 1933, throughout the territory of the German Reich?

A. No. In the individual German States, political police systems were set up which were created by the various State governments concerned.

Q. Were these police systems entirely new?

A. No, they were brought about through the regrouping and reorganisation of the political police systems which already existed.

Q. In what way did this take place?

A. Through the orders or decrees of the State governments concerned.

Q. For what reasons were these new authorities created by the State governments?

A. I can state from my own personal experience that in the State of Hesse a State police system was created, as the authority of the police had been shaken by the events that occurred before 1933, and the authority of these officials had to be restored once more, through a new kind of political police, especially in relation to the members of the National Socialist movement. I assume that this motive also carried weight in other German States.

Dr. Werner Best (1903-1989).

Q. Were these new authorities issued with new instructions?

A. No. No, they were issued with the same duties as the political police had been given in the past.

Q. What were these duties

A. In the first place, the prosecution for political crimes, that is to say, for actions which were actually political or with a political motive which were in violation of the criminal law, and in the second place, the taking of police measures as a precaution against such crimes.

Q. What do you understand by "Precautionary police preventive measures "?

A. Precautionary police preventive measures are those which influence groups of perpetrators or individual perpetrators in such. a way that they do not undertake the feared criminal act.

Q. When and how did Himmler become political police chief of the German States (Polizeikommandeur)?

A. Between March of 1933 and March of 1934 Himmler gradually came to an agreement with the governments of the various German States regarding his appointment as political Chief of Police of each individual State in Germany.

Q. Did Himmler's power arise from his police work or from his political work on the whole?

A. He had never had anything to do with the police, and he also never went into the matter of police ideas and methods.

Q. Were the authorities and the officials of the various political police responsible for Himmler's coming to power?

A. No, they were notified of the appointment as a fait accompli.

Q. When and how were the political police systems of the various German States formed into a uniform German Secret State Police?

A. After Himmler's appointment in 1936 as Chief of the German Police in the Reich Ministry of the Interior, the political police systems of the various German States were formed into a uniform Secret State Police, by means of several orders and decrees issued by the Reich Ministry of the Interior.

Q. Did the NSDAP establish a political police anywhere in the German Reich?

A. No, nowhere.

Q. Was there anywhere an establishment or an organisation of the Party taken over by the State as a political police system?

A. No, nowhere.

Q. Were the political police posts of the German States occupied by Party members in 1933?

A. No, those posts were occupied by former police. Only a few officials were newly taken on at that time.

Q. Were the leading officials members of the Party?

A. That varied in the various States. There were even officials who had formerly held quite different views and belonged to other parties.

Q. Can you give an example of this?

A. There are several well-known examples. It is well known that Herr Diels, the Chief of the Prussian Secret State Police, had formerly held other political opinions.

The closest colleagues of Himmler and Heydrich from Munich, who were taken with him to the office of the Secret State Police in Berlin - such as Mueller, who later was head of (Dept.) Amt IV; Huber, Fresch, Beck - they were formerly adherents of the Bavarian People's Party, and even the Chief of my small Hessian State Police Office was a former Democrat and Freemason, whom I considered quite suitable for this post.

Q. Why, then, did these officials continue in the police service under National Socialist rule?

A. For a German official it was a matter of course to keep on serving the State, even though the Government changed - as long as he was in a position to do so.

Q. Were these officials removed and later on replaced by National Socialists?

A. No, these gentlemen had mostly a very successful career and obtained good posts.

Q. How did the additional recruiting of personnel for the political police take place in the years that followed?

A. Officials from the German police agencies were transferred to the offices of the political police. In the course of time new candidates were also enlisted and were trained to become officials according to the general rules which were applicable for the appointment and the training of officials.

Q. Were people taken on from the Party, from the SS and the SA?

A. Only in a relatively small way, as service in these police agencies brought in very little in wages and therefore was not very much sought after.

Q. Did the officials volunteer to enter the political police?

A. The officials were transferred from one office to another.

Q. Did the officials have to comply with these transfers?

A. Yes, according to civil service laws they were bound to do so.

Q. What would have been the consequence of a refusal?

A. Disciplinary action, with the result that they would have been dismissed from office, with the loss of their acquired rights; for instance, their right to a pension.

Q. Do you know of any such refusal?

A. No, I have not heard of any.

Q. Was the political police completely separated from the general administrative set-up of the State?

A. No, on all levels there was a close liaison with the general interior administration. The chiefs of the State police agencies were at the same time the political experts of the district presidents. The inspectors of security police were personally responsible to the district presidents or to their Ministers of the Interior and had to comply with their instructions.

Q. Besides the Gestapo authorities were there still other authorities also carrying out political police duties?

A. Yes, the district and local police authorities also carried out police duties.

Q. In what way?

A. The district and local police authorities, the Landraete (the chief magistrates of the district), that is to say the gendarmerie, and the municipal police administration carried out these duties, either on the basis of information which came in to them, or they carried out the orders of the competent political police, that is to say the State police authorities.

Q. What part of the entire political police work did the district and local police agencies carry out?

A. As far as volume is concerned, the district and local police authorities handled the major part of the individual State police cases as the State police offices only sent out their officials for their own information in special cases; above all, in cases of treason and high treason.

Q. Did the district and local police agencies also receive the general decrees issued by the State secret police?

A. Yes, they received these decrees unless they were excluded in some cases by special request.

Q. From what point of view did the officials of the political police take up certain cases?

A. Almost without exception on the basis of reports which were sent in from private persons or other agencies outside the police.

Q. And in what lines did this apply?

A. These reports applied to all spheres which might have interested the political police. The police, therefore, were not in a position to investigate these cases and to check whether they actually existed. A special information service was only created where organised groups were suspected of carrying out their activities such as the illegal Communist Party or for espionage of enemy intelligence. In these cases they tried to find these groups and to expose them through agents or by some other means.

Q. If the Gestapo did not have its own information services, how did arrests and other measures come about against people who had made subversive political statements or the like?

A. It is not the case, as it often has been and still is being asserted, that the Gestapo was a net of spies and information agencies which kept track of the entire people. With the few officials, who were always busy, anything like that could not be carried out. Single reports dealing with subversive political statements came to the police from outside and were not sought for, for ninety per cent. of these cases could not be dealt with anyway.

Q. Please speak a little slower. Was there a special class of Gestapo officials which was completely different from the other classes of officials?

A. No. The officials of the secret police belonged to the same categories as the corresponding officials of other police authorities.

Q. What categories of officials were there in the Gestapo?

A. First of all, a big distinction must be made between administrative officials and executive officials.

Q. How did these categories differ?

A. They were differentiated through their tasks, through their legal status, and through their training.

Q. To what extent did the legal status differ?

A. The administrative officials were subordinate to the Reich civil service laws and to the general civil service law. But for executive officials there was a special law created within the framework of the police civil service law.

Q. How did they differ in training?

A. The administrative officials were trained according to their position as higher or lower or medium administrative officials, in keeping with the procedure set up in the general and internal administrative agencies and in the police administrative agencies, headquarters, directorates and so forth. The executive officials, on the other hand, were trained only in the so-called "Fuehrerschools," of the security police and in the agencies of the Secret State Police and the criminal police.

Q. What tasks did the administrative officials in the Gestapo have?

A. The same tasks as may be found in all other administrative agencies - especially police agencies. That is, dealing with personnel records, with internal economic matters concerning the budget, supplies, and also dealing with legal problems, such as in my department, e.g., German passport laws or the police laws concerning foreigners.

Q. Could the administrative officials look into and control the activities of the executive officials?

A. Only if there was an administrative official appointed to keep a card index of an executive agency. For the rest they were neither concerned with the handling of records nor did they carry out sentences.

Q. Could they receive knowledge about the executive tasks in any other way?

A. No. That was almost impossible, for each official was bound to keep the matters which he dealt with secret, which anyway was an old custom of the police, that individual cases being dealt with were not discussed.

Q. Did the administrative officials join the Gestapo voluntarily?

A. No. Administrative officials were transferred from other internal administrative agencies or from other police agencies to the Secret State Police.

Q. Did all executive officials of the Gestapo carry out the same activities?

A. No. Each one carried out the tasks dealt with by the department to which he had been assigned.

Q. What departments were there?

A. Beside the political police, strictly speaking, there were the defence police and the border police; later the defensive part of the military counter-intelligence (Abwehr) and the Customs Frontier Service were incorporated into the Gestapo so that they became also an integral part of it later on.

Q. Were the special tasks of the various departments dealt with by the Gestapo after 1933 for the first time?

A. No. Even before 1933 this was done. They were mainly carried out by the same officials who were later on taken over into the Gestapo, the officials who had been active in the so-called central police agencies and in the offices of the border police.

Q. You mentioned the counter-intelligence (Abwehr) police as a part of the Gestapo. What were the tasks of the Abwehr police?

A. The criminal investigation of treason cases, and all of these cases, without exception, were handed over to the courts for sentence.

Q. And you mentioned the border police, also. What were their tasks?

A. The border police were active at the border, checking passports. They checked the so-called small border traffic. They gave legal assistance to the neighbouring foreign police, by supervising deportations, repressing international traffic in narcotics and carrying out searches for crirpinals and goods at the border.

Q. What were the tasks of the so-called military counter-intelligence, which was also a part of the Gestapo?

A. As I have already said, the defensive part of the military counterintelligence, which was assigned to the Gestapo during the war, had the task of gaining information about the enemy intelligence service which

Himmler discussing the progress of the investigation into the bombing attack in the Bürgerbräukeller in Munich on November 8, 1939. Left to right: Franz Josef Huber, Arthur Nebe, Heinrich Himmler, Reinhard Heydrich, Heinrich Mueller.

was directed against Germany and of rendering it harmless through their reconnaissance.

Q. A further part of the Gestapo was the so-called "Zollgrenzschutz" (Border and Custom Protection). What were its tasks?

A. The Customs and Border Police, before and after they were assigned and incorporated into the Gestapo, had the task of patrolling the so-called "green border," that is, all the border, where there were no crossings. In these border towns and crossings where no border police were stationed they took over their tasks.

Q. Beyond the executive and the administrative officials, were there other categories of Gestapo members?

A. Yes; there were technical officials, and beyond that there were a large number of people, employees who worked in the offices and on the technical staffs.

Q. What percentage of the entire personnel was made up of these employees?

A. Depending on the particular year, this percentage varied from thirty-five to forty-five per cent.

Q. Did the employees know what tasks were carried out by the executive members?

A. As far as the people, for instance typists and clerical staff, were needed in the preparation of specifications, they only learned of the action affecting their work without being told of the incidents or reasons connected with it.

Q. Did the Gestapo pay especially large salaries to its employees?

A. No; the salaries were in accordance with the various civil service wage laws and tariffs, and they were so small that it was hard to replace officials and employees.

Q. And where did you get your replacements for the Gestapo?

A. According to the law, ninety per cent. of the candidates for the executive and administrative services had to be taken from regular police candidates who wanted to make police work their life work. Only perhaps ten per cent. of the new officials, according to the law, could be taken from other sources, professions, etc.

Q. Did the candidates from the regular police work for the Gestapo of their own will or not?

A. The members of the regular police had their names put down on a list at Potsdam, and without their being asked they were assigned either to the Secret State Police or to the criminal police.

Q. How were the candidates for the executive positions trained?

A. These candidates were trained in the so-called Fuehrer school, which was a school for experts of the Security Police. The training courses, to a large extent, were the same for the criminal police as for the Gestapo, and they received practical training in the various offices and agencies as well.

Q. Were the officials who were in office indoctrinated and influenced politically?

A. No. It may well have been a plan of Himmler in 1939 or so for the Rasse and Siedlungs Hauptamt (The Main office for Race and Settlement of the SS) to undertake a unified political training programme for all the agencies and departments, subordinate to Himmler. As long as I was in office, that is, until 1940, this was not done, however.

Q. Were not the officials of the Gestapo to carry through their tasks according to political views?

A. No; it would have been most undesirable if a minor law official, such as a criminal police assistant, used political judgment in the course of his duty and took his own political decisions. The executive official was to act only according to the general official directives and the orders of the superiors without interfering in politics himself in any way.

Q. And what means the co-ordination of the Gestapo officials with the SS?

A. That meant -

THE PRESIDENT: Dr. Merkel, are you summarising the evidence that has been given before the Commission? I ask that because, you see, we do not want to have it all over again. We have ourselves a written summary. We have the evidence taken before the Commission, and all we want you to do is to bring out the really important points and to call the witnesses before us so that we may see them and form our opinion of their credit and hear them cross-examined in so far as it is necessary. We do not want to go through all the evidence over again that has been given before the Commission.

DR. MERKEL: Yes, indeed, Mr. President; and for that very reason I asked at the outset for only two witnesses. I directed the examination of this witness in such a way that now an essential summary will be given by the witness of those points which he has already been questioned on.

MR. DODD: Mr. President, I think we have gone into much more detail than we went into before the Commission, into matters that have been inquired about here before the Tribunal. I think counsel may be under some kind of a misunderstanding, because before he started his examination I asked him about how long he thought he would be. I thought he was being whimsical when he told me between four and a half and five hours, as he took only two hours or so before the Commission. I fear that if he has in mind a four-and-a-half or five-hour examination when he took only two or two and a half hours before the Commission, then he must be under a misunderstanding as to what is in the minds of the Tribunal.

THE PRESIDENT: I hope, Dr. Merkel, I have made it quite clear what we want. You have only got two witnesses. We shall no doubt read the evidence before the Commission of these two witnesses. We want to see the witnesses in order to see what credit is to be attached to their evidence, and we want to give you the opportunity of bringing out any particularly important points. We do not want you to go through the whole thing over again.

DR. MERKEL: Yes, indeed, Mr. President.

BY DR. MERKEL:

Q. What is meant by the co-ordination of the Gestapo officials with the SS?

A. That meant that the official, because he was an official of the Gestapo, was taken over into the SS and received SS rank commensurate with his position.

Q. Was only the Gestapo to be co-ordinated?

A. No, the officials of the criminal police were to be co-ordinated as well.

Q. When.and how did the Reichsicherheitshauptamt, the Reich Main Security Office, originate?

A. The Reich Main Security Office was first created in September, 1939, when the then chief of the Security Police, Heydrich, in exploiting the situation caused by the war, merged the various departments into one. Up to that time, the Reich Ministry of the Interior and the SS, too, had opposed this unifying move.

Q. Did the concentration camps fall under the jurisdiction of the Gestapo?

A. No.

Q. Were there not any legal directions in this regard?

A. In a Prussian decree, dealing with the execution of the police decree of 1936, concerning the Prussian Gestapo there was a sentence to the effect that the Secret State Police system was to administer the concentration camps. That was one of the aims of the then Chief of the Gestapo office, Heydrich. Himmler, however, never carried out this decree, for he wanted the same situation to prevail as before, that is, that the inspector of the concentration camps remained directly subordinate to him.

Q. Did the officials of the Gestapo have to assume that in the concentration camps the health and life of the inmates were being endangered?

A. I can only speak for the time up to the war, and I remember that during that time the officials of the Secret State Police did not think that..the life and health of the inmates were being endangered in the concentration camps. The officials were constantly occupied both with the inmates' families, who were looked after by the Secret State Police, and with released internees, for whom work was procured, so that they were in a position to obtain an overall picture of the experiences and life of the internees in the concentration camps.

Q. Did the officials of the Gestapo have to assume that a criminal purpose was aimed at in the concentration camps?

A. No; for the Gestapo had no final aim whatever to achieve. Instead it only carried out and fulfilled the orders or regulations and the tasks which were put to it from day to day.

Q. Now, did not the Gestapo also carry out actions which were not demanded of it through the general police directives?

A. As far as the Gestapo had to carry out actions which were not provided for in a general regulation, it was an instrument for the carrying out of matters which were alien to the police sphere. I might say it was misused and abused along these lines. As the first case of this type, I remember the arrest of about 20,000 Jews in November, 1938. This was a measure which was not necessary from the police point of view, and would never have been carried out by the Secret State Police of its own initiative, but it had received this order from the Government for political reasons.

Q. Did the leadership of the Gestapo participate in the decision to arrest 20,000 Jews?

A. No. From my own experience I know that Heydrich, who was then the Chief of the State Police, was completely surprised by these measures, for I was with him when but a few metres from the hotel where we were staying a synagogue went up in flames. We did not know anything about it. Thereupon, Heydrich rushed to Himmler, and received orders there which he transmitted to the agency of the State Police.

Q. And how did the so-called intensified interrogations take place?

A. Concerning the Verschaerfte Vernehmungen (intensified interrogation methods), Heydrich issued a decree in 1937, which I saw for the first time after it had been issued, for I was not called in on such matters, being an administrative official. Thereupon I questioned him about it.

Q. What reason did Heydrich give for this decree?

A. At that time, Heydrich gave me the reason that he had received permission from higher authority to issue this decree. This measure was thought to be necessary to prevent conspiracy activity on the part of organisations hostile to the State and thus prevent actions dangerous to the State; but confessions were in no way to be extorted. He called attention to the fact that foreign police agencies commonly used such measures. He emphasised, however, that he had reserved for himself the right of approval on every individual case in the German Reich; thus he considered any abuse quite out of the question.

Q. From 1933 until 1939, did the Gestapo participate in a conspiracy to plan, prepare and unleash a war of aggression?

A. No. I believe I may be able to say that, for if I, as head of a department in the central office, did not know anything about it, then the minor officials could not have known it, either.

Q. Was the Gestapo prepared for the eventuality of a war?

A. In the first place, it was not armed. It especially lacked arms, vehicles and signal material, etc., for use in occupied territories. There was, in the second place, no possibility of calling in police reserves as was the case with the regular police. The whole system was still in such a state of development with the working out of directives for careers, the construction of office buildings, etc., that in no way can one say that the Secret State Police or the Security Police were ready for a trial of such dimensions.

Q. For what purpose were the task force units set up

A. The task force units were set up on the basis of an agreement with the High Command of the Wehrmacht so that in occupied foreign co fighting units would be protected, and also so that in the occupied countries the most elementary security measures could be taken.

Q. And to whom were they subordinate?

A. During the military operations the task force units were subordinate to the military commanders with whose units they marched. After the operations were concluded, their subordination varied according to the administrative system in operation in the area. That meant, depending upon whether the office of a military chief or of a Reich Commissioner were set up, the Higher SS Leader was subordinate to this superior head, and the task force units were subordinate to the Higher SS Leaders.

Q. And how were these task force units composed?

A. When operations began the task force units were made up of members of the Gestapo, the Security Service and of the criminal police. During the war, however, personnel had to be supplemented in great numbers partly by members of the regular police, partly by emergency drafting by members of the Waffen SS, and employees in the various areas themselves so that finally the officials of the Secret Police made up only ten per cent. of the entire force.

Q. Were the task force units constituent parts of the Gestapo?

A. No, they belonged neither to the central office nor to the Gestapo police offices, but they were Security Police units of a special kind.

Q. From your own experience, do you know about the activities of the task force units?

A. Yes, especially in Denmark, I had the opportunity to watch the activities of one of these task force units and through friendly relations I was also informed about conditions in Norway as well.

Q. What do you know of the activities of these task force units in Denmark and Norway, for instance?

A. I should especially like to emphasise that the forces which were employed there very frequently objected to the measures that they received

Erik Scavenius, Prime Minister of Denmark, with Dr. Werner Best (right), the German plenipotentiary in Denmark.

from central agencies, measures which would have led to severe treatment of the local population. For instance, they were against the use of the "Nacht-und-Nebel" decree against the use of the "Kugel" decree; and against the use of the "Kommando" decree, and they rejected and fought against other measures as well. For instance, the Security Police and I severely protested against the deportation of Danish Jews. In Norway the Commander of the Security Police, as he and the Reich Commissioner Terboven both told me, fought against the severe measures which the Reich Commissioner Terboven ordered time and again, and sometimes with the help of the central office in Berlin even prevented some of these measures. This finally caused a break between Terboven and the Commander of the Security Police.

Q. Did you yourself suggest the deportation of Jews from Denmark as has been mentioned here occasionally?

A. No. In frequent reports in the course of 1943 I strongly rejected these measures. On 29th August, 1943, when the state of military emergency was set up in Denmark against my will, the deportation of Jews was ordered apparently by Hitler himself and then, once more, I objected. But, when the Foreign Office confirmed that the order had definitely gone out, then I demanded that a state of military emergency be maintained as long as the action was going on, for I expected trouble and riots, and this demand of mine that the action was to take place under the state of military emergency was misinterpreted to the effect that I had wanted it. I actually sabotaged it by informing certain Danish politicians of it and when it was going to take place so that the Jews could flee, and in reality 6,000 Jews were able to flee, while only 450 were arrested. The Security Police also helped me in this matter. The Commander of the Security Police could have reported me because he knew about my actions, and this would have cost me my life.

Q. Did the Security Police in the occupied countries participate in the deportation of workers to the Reich?

A. Not a single worker left Denmark, or rather, was deported from Denmark to the Reich. As far as I knew, the Security Police did not assist in this in other areas either.

Q. Who was responsible for the shooting of hostages in France? Was that the police, or who was it?

A. From my own experience I know that the orders for the shooting of hostages in France came regularly from the Fuehrer's Headquarters. The military commander-in-chief who had to carry out these decrees, until 1942, was himself strongly against these measures, and General Otto von Stuelpnagel, because of his conflicts with the Fuehrer's Headquarters, had a nervous breakdown and had to leave the service. Also the new Higher SS and Police Leader, Obert, when taking over office, assured me that he was against these measures too.

Q. From your own experience and observations, can you tell me who ultimately decreed the harsh treatment in the occupied territories?

A. According to my experience, it was Hitler himself who, in each case, issued the decrees.

Q. And what was the characteristic point in Hitler's decrees?

A. I found this to be especially characteristic in Hitler's decrees, that in the most astonishing way he dealt with details which the head of a State and Commander-in-Chief of the Armed Forces would not deal with ordinarily, and that these decrees, so far as they applied to occupied territories, were always intended to have a deterring effect containing intimidations and threats for some purpose or another without taking into consideration that the opposite side also showed a fighting spirit which could not so easily be daunted.

Q. And how did he react to objections of his subordinates?

A. Mostly by outbursts of rage and by a sudden stiffening of his attitude. On the other hand he retained those in office who had asked to resign.

Q. Does your book, The German Police, have an official character?

A. No, it is a purely private piece of work.

Q. Does your book only deal with definite and actual facts?

A. No. In parts the tendencies which were prevalent at the time it was written were pictured as already having attained their fulfilment.

Q. Why did it do that?

A. Partly because I anticipated the tendencies to be realized in a very short time and partly because the book would otherwise have met with difficulties at the time of its publication.

Q. Does not the following fact lead one to believe that certain arbitrary action was taken by the Security Police, namely, that certain measures indicated that the chief of the German police could order measures beyond his ordinary authority?

A. If this was specified in two decrees dealing with the occupation of Austria and the Sudetenland, it meant that the chief of the German police would legally have the authority to issue police decrees in these regions … which might deviate from the laws already existing there. This was a transfer of legal authority, no single acts were to be taken either illegally or arbitrarily.

Q. What was the existing police law according to your theory?

A. In speaking about police law in my book, I started from the National Socialist conception of the State and from the development of State laws at that time in Germany. When after 1933 the legislative power was transferred to the Government, it gradually became the customary law of the State that the will of the head of the State automatically established law. This principle was recognised as law, for one cannot characterise the rules and regulations governing a great power for years on end as anything but customary law. On the same basis, the State's police law developed too. An emergency law issued by the Reich President on 28th February, 1933, removed the barriers of the Weimar Constitution, and thus the police were given much wider scope. The activities and the authority of the police were regulated through numerous Fuehrer decrees, orders, directives, and so forth which, since they were decreed by the highest legislative authority of the State, namely, the head of the State himself, had to be considered as valid police laws.

Q. What would be your judgment concerning the orders to the Gestapo or parts of it, to effect actions, deportations and executions? **A.** I have already said that these were measures quite alien to the police, which had nothing to do with the ordinary activities of the police and which were not necessary from the police point of view. But, if the police received such orders from the head of the State or in the name of the head of the State, then, of course, according to the current conception each individual official had to take it upon himself as an obligation to carry out the decree.

Q. Did you wish to justify these measures when you wrote in your book-

THE PRESIDENT: It is five o'clock now. Can you tell the Tribunal how long you think you are going to be with this witness?

DR. MERKEL: I have just two more questions. minutes, Mr. President.

THE PRESIDENT: Very well.

BY DR. MERKEL:

Q. Did you wish to justify this opinion and this attitude when you said in your book that it was not a question of law but a question of fate that the head of State was setting up the proper law?

A. No. In that passage of my book I meant to give a political warning to the State leadership, i.e., that this tremendous amount of power to set law arbitrarily - at that time we could not foresee an International Military Tribunal - would be subject to the verdict of fate, and that anyone transgressing against the fundamental human rights of the individual and of nations would be punished by fate. I am sorry to say that I was quite right in my warning.

Q. But if the members of the Gestapo recognised the decree which they received to be criminal, how would you judge their actions then?

A. In that case I have to say that they acted in an express state of emergency, for during the war the entire police system was subject to the military penal code and any official who refused to carry out a decree or order would have been sentenced to death in a court martial for reason of military insubordination.

DR. MERKEL: I have no further questions.

THE PRESIDENT:

The Tribunal will adjourn.

(The Tribunal adjourned until 1st August, 1946, at 1000 hours.)

THURSDAY, 1ST AUGUST, 1946

DR. GAWLIK (counsel for SD): Mr. President, may I be permitted to put three questions to the witness Best?

THE PRESIDENT: What special reason is there why you want to put questions to him?

DR. GAWLIK: I wanted to put these questions to Dr. Spengler, a witness who has been granted me but who has not arrived, and for that reason I would like to put the three questions to Dr. Best instead.

THE PRESIDENT: Well, for that special reason we will permit you to put the questions but it is not to be regarded as a general rule.

DR. KARL RUDOLF WERNER BEST - RESUMED

DIRECT EXAMINATION BY DR. GAWLIK:

Q. I should like to show you a copy of the decree of 11th November, 1938. I should like to refer to Page 4 of the German Trial Brief, dealing with the Gestapo and SD. In this decree it says:

"The Security Service of the Reichsfuehrer SS, as information service for Party and State, has to fulfil important tasks, particularly for the support of the Security Police."

Now, I should like to ask you, did you participate in the making of this decree?

A. Yes.

Q. Does this decree correctly represent the actual relationship between the Security Police and the SD?

A. In those years there were experiments constantly going on with the SD so that the scope of the tasks set up for the SD changed frequently. At that time, when the decree mentioned was issued, the chief of both the Security Police and the SD, Heydrich, was interested in having the SD gain an insight into the activity of the offices and agencies of the State. The exact wording of this decree was chosen in order to justify that aim sufficiently. In truth the scope of tasks to be put to the SD, whose model was to be the great foreign Intelligence Service, especially the British Intelligence Service, developed in such a manner that the SD was not to be an auxiliary branch of the police but rather a purely political information organ of the State leadership, for the latter's own control of its political activities.

DR. GAWLIK: I have no further questions, Mr. President.

THE PRESIDENT: Does the prosecution want to cross-examine?

CROSS-EXAMINATION BY LT. COMMANDER HARRIS:

Q. Dr. Best, you realise that you are one of two witnesses who have been called, out of possibly hundreds, to represent the Gestapo before this Tribunal? Do you not?

A. Yes.

Q. And you realize that your credibility is very important, do you not?

A. Yes.

Q. You understand as a jurist of long standing the significance of the oath that you have taken?

A. Yes.

Q. You stated yesterday, I believe, that your publication, the German Police, was a purely private book and had no official status? Is that correct?

A. I said that it was my purely private work which originated without any contact with my superiors and without their knowledge. My chiefs - at that time Heydrich and Himmler - only knew of this work when the completed book was put before them.

Q. The question is whether this book of yours was or was not an official publication in any respect. Was it or was it not?

A. No, it was not an official publication.

Q. I ask that the witness be shown the Ministerial-Blatt of 1941, Page 119.

Now, you will notice that published in the Ministerial-Blatt for 1941 is a circular of the Reich Ministry of the Interior referring to your book and you will note that it states that "the book is for offices and officials of police, State, Party, and municipal administrations. This book represents a reference work which can also serve as an award for worthy officials. It is recommended that this book be acquired especially also by the libraries", and then the distribution is to various supreme Reich authorities. You see that there, do you not, Dr. Best?

A. Yes, indeed, and I can say the following in that connection: This recommendation was published some time after the appearance of the book, without moreover my having prior knowledge of it, and it is not to be considered more valuable than any recommendation of other books which had already been published and which subsequently were recognised as good and usable. I should like to emphasise again that before the publication of this book I had not talked in any way with my superiors, nor with the agency which later published this recommendation.

Q. Now I want to invite your attention to your book, Dr. Best, and particularly Page 86 of it.

You testified yesterday concerning the development of the Gestapo from the pre-existing political police. You say in your book as follows:

"In order to build up an independent and powerful political police force, the like of which had not hitherto existed in Germany, regular officials of the former police force, on the one hand, and members of the SS on the other hand, were brought in. With the uncompromising fighting spirit of the SS the new organisations took up the struggle against enemies of the State for the safeguarding of the National Socialist leadership and order."

That is the correct statement of how the Gestapo came into being, is it not, Dr. Best?

A. To that I should like to say that the number of men newly taken into the SS ... in the political police forces was very small at first. I said yesterday that a certain number of employees were newly employed. Then later, from the candidates who applied for the regular career of the Secret State Police, further members of the SS were added, so that the picture given in my book is completely correct, but the ratio in figures is not mentioned. I can say again today that the number of the regular officials - those old officials previously taken over as well as the candidates from the Protection Police - was greater than the number taken in from the SS.

Q. All right. You said yesterday that you opposed the use of torture by the Gestapo in connection with interrogations and that you called Heydrich to account about that matter, did you not?

A. Yes, indeed.

Q. And you called Heydrich to account, as your superior?

A. Yes.

Q. But you did not prohibit Heydrich from continuing his practice of using torture in interrogations, did you?

A. I was not in a position to prevent my superior from carrying out measures he had ordered or planned. In addition to that, I had nothing to do with the executive side in the Secret, State Police, for I was an administrative official and, consequently, had no authority if Heydrich decreed measures like that or approved of them. I can only say that in the small branch of the Counter-Intelligence which I headed as a Commissioner for some time, I prevented the use of this method.

Q. I want to pass briefly to your experiences in Denmark, Dr. Best, and by way of preliminary I wish to refresh your memory as to the testimony which you gave before the Commission on 8th July, 1946. This appears on Page 2412 of the English transcript:

"**Q.** Have you met Naujocks?

A. Naujocks was in Copenhagen once.

Q. And what was his task in Denmark?

A. He did not give me any details. I only know that he asked me to provide a connection for him with the Research Office in Copenhagen.

Q. Anyway, you have no idea why Naujocks was in Copenhagen, have you?

A. I imagine that he was in Denmark on matters pertaining to intelligence duties.

Q. And if he were to state and even to testify that he discussed the matter with you, you would say it was only a lie?

A. I would say that I could not recall it and that in my memory he remains an intelligence service man."

Now, you were asked those questions and you gave those answers before the Commission, did you not, Dr. Best?

A. Yes.

Q. Yes. And when you gave those answers you knew that you were telling a deliberate falsehood under oath, did you not, Dr. Best?

Now, you can answer that question yes or no, and then explain it if you like.

A. In the meantime - a report from Danish officials -

THE PRESIDENT: One minute. Wait. Answer the question. Do you or do you not know whether you were telling the truth then?

A. My statement was not correct. In the meantime I had seen the Naujocks report and then I was able to recollect exactly that he in a general way had told me about his mission. Even today I do not recall details, however.

LT.-COMMANDER HARRIS:

Q. Well, now, just so that you will remember that interrogation that you had with Dr. Kalki of the Danish Delegation two days later, on 10th July, 1946, I am going to ask that you be shown the written statement which you corrected in your own handwriting and signed with your own signature. Now, I invite your attention to the first paragraph, Dr. Best, in which you state as follows:

"Now that I know that Naujocks has testified as to his connection with the terrorist activities in Denmark, I am ready to testify further on this subject. If I did not testify about this earlier, it was because I did not know whether Naujocks had been captured and had confessed regarding these things. It was contrary to my feelings to drag him into this thing before the facts were known to me."

You gave that statement, did you not, Dr. Best, and that is your signature on there?

A. Yes.

Q. Now, Dr. Best, you know very well when Naujocks came to you in

January of 1944 that there was planned to be carried out by the Gestapo terroristic measures against the people of Denmark, because you attended the conference at Hitler's headquarters on 30th December, 1943, at which that plan was worked out, didn't you?

A. Yes.

Q. At that conference there were present, in addition to yourself, Pancke, the Higher SS and Police Leader for Denmark; General von Hannecken, the military governor for Denmark; Hitler, Himmler, the defendant Kaltenbrunner, the defendant Keitel, the defendant Jodl, and Schmundt. You reported these names in your own diary, did you not?

A. Yes.

Q. And you knew that at that meeting it was agreed that in order to counteract murders and sabotage against German interests in Denmark - that the Gestapo was to go up to Denmark and to carry out ruthless murders and to blow up homes and buildings as a countermeasure, did you not?

A. It is not correct that an agreement was reached, but rather that Hitler gave orders in spite of my opposition and also Pancke's to these plans.

Q. Yes. Hitler gave the order to Himmler, who gave it to Kaltenbrunner, who gave it to Muller, who sent the Gestapo into action, and you knew that those murders and that this wilful destruction of property was carried out in Denmark as a result thereof, did you not?

A. This general fact was known to me, yes.

Q. Yes, and you knew that these were carried out, because you protested about some of them. For example, you remember when these thugs blew up a street car in Odense, killing and injuring the passengers in it, do you not?

A. In the period following, again and again for various reasons I protested against the use of this method; appropriate reports or telegrams -

THE PRESIDENT: You have not answered the question. The question was, did you know that the street car had been blown up.

THE WITNESS: I do not accurately recall the individual cases, and therefore I do not recall for what special reason I made my protests. But I do know that I protested in very many cases.

BY LT.-COMMANDER HARRIS:

Q. Now Dr. Best, I know that you have a very short memory, but I would have thought that you could have remembered some of the events that you recited on 10th July, 1946. If you will look at your statement there that you gave to Dr. Kalki, you will find the following: "I used on such an occasion the blowing up of a street car in Odense, for instance." Do you not see that there, Dr. Best? The statement that you gave on the 10th -

A. Where do I find that, please?

Q. You will find that on - about the middle of the document.

A. Wait just a minute. That is a wrong translation. I said the blowing up of a "Strassenzug" in Odense. That meant that along this street several houses were blown up simultaneously. It was not a car, but a row of houses.

Q. Now, Dr. Best, you also remember the murder of four doctors in Odense, against which you protested because these doctors had been pointed out to you by National Socialist circles as being German sympathisers, do you not?

A. Yes, and apart from that, that was not the only reason. I called attention to the increased senselessness of these measures, for I had found out that some of these physicians were friendly to Germany.

Q. Yes, and that was a terrible thing for the Gestapo to murder German sympathisers in Denmark, was it not? There were so few. Now, to whom did you make your protests against this murderous activity of the Gestapo?

A. My protest always went to the Foreign Office, which was the ministry over me.

Q. Yes, your protests went to the defendant Ribbentrop, did they not?

THE PRESIDENT: Commander Harris, have we got a reference to any document which records the meeting of 30th December, 1943?

LT.-COMMANDER HARRIS:

Yes, Sir. This is in evidence through the official Government report of the, Danish Delegation, Exhibit RF 901.

THE PRESIDENT: RF 921?

LT.-COMMANDER WHITNEY HARRIS: 901, Sir.

THE PRESIDENT: Thank you.

BY LT.-COMMANDER HARRIS:

Q. Now yesterday, Dr. Best, you testified that you learned that the Einsatzkommando of the Security Police and SD in Denmark was opposed to the Kugel Erlass, did you not?

A. Yes.

Q. Who - who in Denmark told you that this Einsatzkommando was opposed to the Kugel Erlass?

A. I was told that by the head of the executive, Dr. Hoffmann.

Q. Yes, Dr: Hoffmann. He was the head of the Gestapo in Denmark, was he not?

A. Of the Gestapo branch with the commander of the Security Police.

Q. Yes, and when, approximately, did Dr. Hoffmann tell you that?

A. I cannot remember exactly, whether through my conversation with Dr. Hoffmann I was reminded of these facts, or whether the individual measures which were turned down at that time were ever reported to me. It may be that this is a new piece of information for me, which confirms to me that this decree never was put into effect. No case of this kind ever occurred.

Q. Now, Dr. Best, you just said in your last answer that Dr. Hoffmann told you that the Gestapo was opposed to the Kugel Erlass in Denmark and that he told you this in Denmark. Now, is that true or is it not true?

A. I did not say when and where I learned of it. I said only that the decree was not put into effect on the initiative of the police. I did not say when and where I was told this.

Q. What was the Kugel Erlass?

A. Today I know, for I have read files and transcripts, that these were measures, I believe, dealing with prisoners of war who had escaped.

Q. Now - when you were asked about your knowledge of the Kugel Erlass before the Commission, you did not say anything about having had a conversation with Dr. Hoffmann about it, did you?

A. According to my memory, I was asked only whether at that time during my time of office I had known of the Kugel Erlass. I did not see the decree at that time. I believe I have mentioned this already. I read if only here.

LT.-COMMANDER HARRIS:

If the Tribunal please, I have two documents which I would like to offer into evidence at this time. These documents have come to our attention and have been made available only in the last two days. Consequently, it has been impossible for us to present them to anyone speaking for the Gestapo before the Commission, and I think that this witness can assist in identifying some of the names. And I would like to ask the permission of the Tribunal merely to show these documents to the witness. They are quite long, and I will then try to summarise them as briefly as possible and develop what I can out of them in the shortest possible time, perhaps fifteen minutes for both documents, sir.

THE PRESIDENT: Yes, go on, Commander Harris.

LT.-COMMANDER HARRIS:

Then at this time I offer into evidence Document R-178, which becomes Exhibit USA 910, and I ask that the document be shown to the witness.

This document was captured by a combined British-American documents exploitation team and sent to the prosecution from the Air Documents Research Centre in London. It contains detailed correspondence concerning a complaint about a certain Major Meinel against the Gestapo officers in Munich, Regensburg, Nuremberg, and Furth over the screening out and murdering of Russian prisoners of war. I ask that the witness turn to Document F, which is Page 7 of the English translation.

BY LT.-COMMANDER HARRIS:

Q. You will note, witness, that this is a report from the Gestapo office in Munich, in which are listed 18 camps screened by the Gestapo, showing a total of 3,088 Soviet prisoners of war screened, of whom 410 are screened out as intolerable. You will note, following Page 8 of the English translation, that the 410 Russians sorted out belong to the following categories: officials and officers, Jews, members of intelligentsia, fanatical Communists, agitators and others, fugitives, and incurably sick. You will note on Page 9 of the English translation that of the 410 Russians so sorted out, 301 had been executed at the concentration camp at Dachau at the date of this report. On Page 10 of the English translation, witness, you will find the following: namely, that these 410 Russians screened out at Munich represent a percentage of 13 per cent, whereas the Gestapo offices at Nuremberg, Furth, and Regensburg screened out an average of 15 to 17 per cent. This report, which is signed by Schuermer, states, quoting at the same place:

> "I wish to refute most emphatically the complaints of the High Command of the Armed Forces that the screening of the Russians had been carried out in a superficial manner."

Now, witness, do you know Schuermer?

A. No, the name is not familiar to me.

Q. All right. Then I want you to turn to Document G. This is a report from the Gestapo office in Munich complaining about the attitude of Major Meinel; and on Page 13 of the English translation you will find a statement that Meinel was thought to have complained to the High Command of the Armed Forces that the Russians had been superficially screened out.

Now, you will note that a report was made against Major Meinel by the SD, in which Meinel was reproached with having shown, to some extent, aversion against the National Socialist creed. For example, he mentioned God but not the Fuehrer in an order of the day.

THE PRESIDENT: Where does that come?

LT.-COMMANDER HARRIS: Sir, you will find that on Page 13 of the English translation, in the middle of the page.

BY LT.-COMMANDER HARRIS:

That was the mark of a bad National Socialist, was it not, Dr. Best - one who would put God before Hitler?

A. I do not know which question you want me to answer. As regards this entire connection, I should like to emphasise that at the end of May, 1940, I left my position in the Security Police Division at the Reich Ministry of the Interior, and therefore I had no knowledge of these things, which transpired in the year 1941.

Q. Then turn to Document G, Page 15 of the English translation. You will find this sentence:

"Experience, however, has shown that the Russians can be compelled to work only by the utmost severity and the use of corporal punishment."

Now, pass to Document H, Dr. Best. There appears on Page 17 of the English translation, this statement:

"Furthermore, I pointed out to Major Meinel that the work of the Gestapo employment detachments was done with the consent of the High Command of the Armed Forces, and according to rules which had been drafted in collaboration with the High Command, Department of Prisoners of War."

Now, this document is signed by Schimmel. Was Schimmel known to you?

A. Schimmel? I cannot remember the name Schimmel, but I do recall that there was a Regierungsrat, I think, of that name, in the Gestapo.

Q. Turn to Document J, then, page 21 of the English translation. At the end of that, you will find that Meinel, in giving his reply to the accusations made against him, stated:

"When I mentioned that it weighed heavily on the officers' conscience to hand over the Russian prisoners, Regierungsrat Schimmel replied that the hearts of some of the SS man who were charged with executing prisoners were all but breaking."

Now, on Document M, witness, which is Page 26, you will find a notice that the Reich Commissioner for Defence was informed about these murders, and approved of them. This was for Defence Area VII. Do you know who the Reich Commissioner for Defence was in Defence Area VII who approved these murders?

A. A Reich Commissioner? You mean the Reich Defence Commissioner?

Q. Yes, the Reich Defence Commissioner. That, is what I said.

A. I do not recall the Reich Defence Commissioner in Area VII, for during that time I was away from the Reich and held a position outside the Reich boundaries.

Q. All right. Let us go on. There are many other cases of the screening of Soviet prisoners of war by the Gestapo for execution; that is, by local Gestapo offices within Germany proper, and I do not wish to take up further time about that. But I wish that you would turn to Document T, witness, because I want to get evidence of the result of this conflict with Major Meinel. Document T is a teletype from the Gestapo office in Berlin, and it states:

"The prisoners of war who have been screened out - "

THE PRESIDENT: What page is that?

LT.-COMMANDER HARRIS: Page 37, sir.

BY LT.-COMMANDER HARRIS:

"The prisoners of war who have been screened out will be transferred to the Buchenwald concentration camp, as the High Command has decided in a conference today. Will you please inform the Higher SS and Police Leader today about this and also that Meinel is getting a different assignment."

Now, this teletype emanated from the RSHA, Office IV A. That was the Gestapo, was it not, Dr. Best?

A. Yes.

Q. And you see it was signed by SS-Obersturmbannfuehrer Panzinger. Now you know who Panzinger was, do you not?

A. Yes. He was the deputy of Muller.

Q. Yes. And he was the head of this Department IV A, which was charged with the handling of opponents and sabotage, assassinations, protective security, and matters of that sort, was he not?

A. He was the head of the Department IV A. Just what was dealt within this department I cannot recall.

Q. Well, you can take my word for that.

LT.-COMMANDER HARRIS: For the Tribunal's information, that appears in Document L-219, and is already in evidence.

Now, I wish to offer the other documents. There are five documents here which are in a group, sir, and I will offer them in order:

4050-PS becomes Exhibit USA 911; 4049-PS becomes 912; 4052-PS becomes 913; 4048-PS becomes 914; and 4051-PS becomes 915.

These documents have just come to us from the Berlin Document Centre, and we have not yet been able to obtain the originals. They sent to us only the photostatic copies. We have requested the originals, and they will be here, we are assured, in a matter of days. As soon as they come, we will, with the permission of the Tribunal and the approval of counsel, substitute the originals for these photostatic copies.

BY LT.-COMMANDER HARRIS:

Now, Dr. Best, turning to Document 4050-PS first, you will see that this refers to the same SS-Oberfuehrer Panzinger. This is apparently a Foreign Office communication, in which it says that Panzinger reports that various changes have been made in the preparation of the matter discussed, and that he has promised a plan for the execution of our proposed action.

Now, if you will turn to the enclosure, which is Document 4049-PS, you will find just what that plan was. You will see there that the plan was to transfer 75 French generals from Koenigstein, in the course of which one general by the name of De Boisse was to have a misfortune - namely, his car was to break down - in order to separate him from the others. This was to provide the opportunity to have the general shot in the back while attempting to escape.

You will find that this document goes on to recite all the details of completing this murder, including this interesting statement, that "a decision has as yet to be reached whether or not the burial of the urn should be carried out with military honours"; and it goes on to say that the question will be looked into once more by the SD.

This is the basic report of November, 1944.

Now, if you will turn to the next document, 4052 -

THE PRESIDENT: Should not you read the last paragraph on Page 2?

LT.-COMMANDER HARRIS: Yes, sir, I will read that.

"Protecting Power investigations: It will be assured, through the selection of the persons concerned, and in the preparation of all documentary evidence, that in the event of the Protecting Power being desirous of an investigation, the necessary documents are available for the dismissal of any complaint."

BY LT.-COMMANDER HARRIS:

Q. Now, turning to the next document, witness, 4052-PS, you will find again the reference to this infamous SS- Oberfuehrer Panzinger. You see, witness, Panzinger had been promoted by this time. He states that the preparations in respect to the French generals had reached the stage where a report concerning the proposed procedure would be submitted to the Reichsfuehrer SS during the next few days. And you will find that he again explains this method of murder, and he says that they will carry it out by one of two methods, either by shooting during escape, or through poisoning by carbon monoxide gas.

Now, you have noticed, witness, that at the end of this document it shows that it was prepared for presentation to the Reich Foreign Minister, Herr von Ribbentrop.

Now, the next document is a particularly interesting one. It is Document 4048-PS. This document is dated 30th December, 1941.

THE PRESIDENT: Was Ambassador Ritter the ambassador in Paris?

BY LT.-COMMANDER HARRIS:

Q. Witness, was Ambassador Ritter the ambassador in Paris?

A. I do not remember exactly. That must have been some time before I knew how the diplomatic posts were filled.

THE PRESIDENT: It does not matter.

LT.-COMMANDER HARRIS: I am informed, sir, that he was a liaison officer between the Foreign Office and the Army. I am not sure of that, however.

Well, passing to Document 4049-PS, here is where the whole plan is laid out in summary form, and I would like to read this briefly. This is addressed to the Reichsfuehrer SS, and it says:

"The discussions about the matter in question with the Chief of Prisoner-of-War Matters and the Foreign Office have taken place as ordered and have led to the following proposals:

1. In the course of a transfer of five persons in three cars with army identifications, the escape incident occurs when the last car has a flat tyre, or

2. Carbon monoxide is released by the driver into the closed back of the car. The apparatus can be installed with the simplest means and can be removed again immediately. After considerable difficulties a suitable vehicle has now become available.

3. Other possibilities, such as poisoning of food or drink, have been considered but have been discarded again as too unsafe.

Provisions for the completion of the subsequent work in accordance with plans, such as report, post-mortem documentation, and burial, have been made.

Convoy leader and drivers are to be supplied by the RSHA and will appear in army uniform and with pay-books delivered to them.

Concerning the notice for the Press, contact has been established with Geheimrat Wagner of the Foreign Office. Wagner reports that the Reich Foreign Minister expects to speak with the Reichsfuehrer about this matter.

In the opinion of the Reich Foreign Minister, this action must be co-ordinated in every respect.

In the meantime, it has been learned that the name of the man in question has been mentioned in the course of various long-distance calls between Fuehrer Headquarters and the Chief of PW Matters; therefore, the Chief of PW Matters now proposes the use of another man with the same qualifications. I agree with this and propose that the choice be left to the Chief of Prisoners-of-War Matters."

BY LT.-COMMANDER HARRIS:

Q. Now, by whom is this letter signed, Dr. Best?

A. At the foot there are the typewritten words: "Signed Dr. Kaltenbrunner."

Q. Signed Dr. Kaltenbrunner. Now, we will pass to the last document, 4051-PS. This is a report on a telephone conversation which carries us to

12th January, 1945, and it says that - repeats that: "A French prisoner-of-war general is going to die an unnatural death by being shot in flight, or by poisoning. Subsequent matters, such as reports, post-mortem examination, documentation and burial have been taken care of as planned." It says that: "The Reich" Foreign Minister's instruction states that 'the matter is to be discussed with Ambassador Albrecht in order to determine exactly what legal rights the protecting power could claim in this matter in order to make our plans accordingly.'"

Now, who is Ambassador Albrecht?

A. He was the head of the juridical department in the Foreign Office.

Q. Now, did you know, Dr. Best, that General Mesne, a Frenchman, was killed on this road at about this time?

A. I knew nothing about this matter, for at that time I was active in Denmark and heard nothing about matters of this kind.

LT.-COMMANDER HARRIS: That concludes my cross-examination, if the Tribunal please. However, I have two documents which the French Delegation ask to be submitted. These are both documents signed by or on behalf of this defendant, Dr. Best, and with your permission, sir, I will offer them in evidence now as on behalf of the French Delegation.

The first is Document F-967. This relates to the deporting of Jews and Communists from France, and states that they have to hold up these deportations for a while because of lack of transportation.

BY LT.-COMMANDER HARRIS:

Q. I ask you to identify your signature on that document if you will, Dr. Best, please?

A. Yes.

LT. COMMANDER HARRIS: That will become Exhibit USA 916.

THE PRESIDENT: I did not hear the number.

LT.-COMMANDER HARRIS: USA 916, Sir.

The next is Document F-972, which is also a document relating to the fight against Communists in France, and I ask that the witness identify that as coming from him and having been signed on his behalf.

A. Yes.

LT.-COMMANDER HARRIS: That becomes Exhibit USA 917.

If the Tribunal please, I am informed that we have just discovered a new document which is of the utmost importance but which has not yet been in any way processed, and we would like the permission of the Tribunal to submit this document later on in the course of the proceedings if and as it is ready for submission.

THE PRESIDENT: Can it not be got ready today?

MR. DODD: Mr. President, I think it may be. It was just handed to me in a hand-written translation. It was discovered in the Document Centre in Berlin and I think it is of such a nature that the Tribunal should know about it. I will try to have it translated before the close of the session today, but I think it is the kind of thing that should not escape the attention of the Tribunal.

THE PRESIDENT: Yes. Well, perhaps you will make further application when you have got the document ready.

LT.-COMMANDER HARRIS: Yes, sir.

THE PRESIDENT: Do you wish to re-examine?

DR. MERKEL: First of all, two brief questions relating to the questions of the defence for the SD.

RE-CROSS-EXAMINATION BY DR. MERKEL:

Q. Who was at the head of the Intelligence Service after Canaris was dismissed?

A. I, as an outsider, learned that at that time the Intelligence Service of the Wehrmacht, which in the past had been led as a whole by Canaris, was divided up into various offices of the Chief of the Security Police. The defensive branch was turned over to Office 4, the so-called Gestapo branch: a further part to Branch 6, Foreign Intelligence Service; and then, finally, the office Mil was set up as something new.

Q. Did Himmler head the entire Security Police, especially after Heydrich's death?

A. Here also I can only state, as an outsider, that I learned that Himmler, after Heydrich's death, took over the leadership of the Security Police.

Q. One question relating to Denmark. What was the organisational difference between the Gestapo in the Reich itself and the Security Police units which were deployed beyond the boundaries of the Reich?

A. Within the Reich there were established State agencies of the Gestapo having a scope of tasks laid down in laws, decrees, orders and regulations. In the occupied areas there were task forces composed of members of the Gestapo, the Criminal Police, the SD, and numerous other auxiliaries, whose scope of activities was not the same and was not already delineated, but varied according to instructions of the Centre Office, in, Berlin and partially according to the directives received from Higher SS and Police Leaders, Reich Commissioners, and so forth.

Q. For how long have you known the witness Naujocks?

A. I believe that I met him some time before I left my job with the Security Police, but I saw him very seldom and had no personal connections with him at all.

Q. Do you know that Naujocks, about six months before the end, of the war, deserted to the Americans?

A. I was told about that here.

Q. The murders, as described by Naujocks, were they murders by the Gestapo?

A. No. The Gestapo proper, that is the Executive Branch of the Commander of the Security Police, did not carry out these deeds. Rather, they were carried out by special forces who were directly responsible to the Higher Police and SS Leader.

Q. Were the executions of Russian prisoners of war in German concentration camps known generally to the public?

A. No. At any rate, I can say that despite my prominent position it is only now, in the course of this trial, that I have learned of these matters.

Q. Does, the recommendation of your book by the Reich Minister of the Interior mean that the book received an official character?

A. I do not believe so, for without doubt, in the same office and in the same way numerous books were recommended, books which in no way were published by a State agency or published on behalf of that agency.

DR. MERKEL: Your Honour, I have no further questions.

DR. LATERNSER: Mr. President, I should like to clarify a question which has arisen during the cross-examination.

THE PRESIDENT: Yes, Dr. Laternser.

BY DR. LATERNSER:

Q. Witness, you were shown Document R-178. On Page 26 of this document, in the centre of the page, you will find that the Reich Commissioner for Defence in the defence areas (Wehrkreis) agreed with the selection of the Russian prisoners of war and their murder. Then the prosecutor asked you just who this Reich Commissioner for Defence was at the time and you said that you did not know. Now I should like to ask you, who usually was the Commissioner for Reich Defence. Was not that the Gauleiter?

A. Sometimes it was the Gauleiter and sometimes, if I remember correctly, it was a senior official, Oberpresident or someone of that kind - the ministers of the various States.

Q. The Commissioners for Reich Defence, therefore, were not military officers, purely military agencies under the OKH, is that right?

A. No. As far as I remember the construction at that time, the answer is no.

DR. LATERNSER: Thank you very much. I have no further questions.

THE PRESIDENT: The witness can retire.

DR. MERKEL: I have another witness, and perhaps, for the sake of a continuous interrogation, it would be better to have our recess now, your Honour.

THE PRESIDENT: Very well.

(A recess was taken.)

DR. MERKEL: With the permission of the Tribunal, I call the witness Karl Heinz Hoffmann.

THE PRESIDENT: Will you state your full name, please?

THE WITNESS: Karl Heinz Hoffmann.

THE PRESIDENT: Will you repeat this oath after me.

I swear by God, the Almighty and Omniscient, that I will speak the pure truth and will withhold and add nothing.

(The witness repeated the oath.)

THE PRESIDENT: You may sit down.

DIRECT EXAMINATION BY DR. MERKEL:

Q. When and how did you come to the Secret State Police?

A. After I passed the senior juridical State examination in the year 1937, I applied to three administrative offices for a job. The first offer of employment

I received was from the State Police, and I accepted it. After one year on trial at the State Police office in Coblenz, I was appointed Deputy of the Chief, and Government Political Adviser. A year later, in 1939, I was transferred, in the same capacity, to Dusseldorf. There I was appointed to the position of Reich Defence Adviser to the Inspector. Then when the Security Police were put to work in Holland I went there as a leading administrative executive. In September, 1940, I was transferred to the Reich Ministry of the Interior, Gestapo office, and there I was put in charge of the Department for Western European occupied territories. In September, 1943, I was sent to the BDS, Denmark, in charge of Department IV.

Q. You say that you were with two State police offices. That was Coblenz and Dusseldorf as Deputy Chief?

A. Yes.

Q. What was the relation of these Gestapo offices to the internal administration?

A. The chief was political expert -

DR. MERKEL: Witness, between my question and your answer, you have to make a short pause.

WITNESS: The chief was political expert to the Regierungspresident (President of the Government) and Leitstelleniter (chief of the office) of the Oberpresident. In towns and districts in which there were no branch offices of the State Police, its lower levels were represented by the Kreis - and the local police officials, and the Gendarmerie. Approximately 80 per cent of all matters came from these police offices.

Q. Could the NSDAP issue any directives to the State Police?

A. According to existing laws they could not. Only in places where the Gauleiter held also the position of Oberpresident or Reichsstatthalter (Governor) it was possible.

Q. How was it in practice? How did it work out?

A. In practice, the medium and lower offices tried to interfere. But the police rejected that, and it occurred mostly when Party members were involved in proceedings.

Q. Was it not the task of the Gestapo to further the ideological aims of the Party?

A. No. The tasks of the State Police were purely counter-intelligence against attacks directed against the State, and that within the legal provisions and regulations.

Q. The basic tendency and work of the Gestapo, therefore, was it aggressive or purely defensive?

A. It was defensive and, not aggressive. That could be seen, first of all, from the following fact: When, in 1944, the duties of the counter-intelligence offices were transferred to police and SD offices, the State Police received only the purely counter-intelligence tasks, whereas active espionage and sabotage were transferred to Amt Mil, or Amt VI (Department VI).

Q. Did officials of the Gestapo generally have any special advantages, for instance, owing to their having had an opportunity to acquire articles which had been confiscated by the Gestapo and put to auction?

A. It had been prohibited by a decree that officials of the State Police could acquire articles which had been confiscated and put to auction. In the same way, the officials had no opportunity to participate in the aryanisation of business establishments in any way, and the immediate acquisition of Jewish property was also prohibited for them.

Q. You took part as a leading administrative official when the Sipo entered Holland, dial you not? Was there any special training of the employees for that purpose?

A. No. There had been no mobilisation measures taken, such as the procurement of interpreters or the increase of the number of officials by any additional assistants. Also, the regulations about pay and other economic regulations were not clear and we were not prepared to cover such tasks.

Q. Did the Gestapo take part in a conspiracy the purpose of which was the planning, preparing and waging of aggressive war?

A. I have to deny that. As adviser for defence to the Inspector of Wehrkreis (district) VI who was the head of six State Police offices, I had no previous knowledge of an aggressive war being prepared. When Norway and Denmark were occupied, I learned the news from the newspapers. As deputy leader of the Gestapo office in Dusseldorf, I did not have any previous knowledge of the date set for the offensive in the West. The morning of that day I heard of it by radio and the newspapers. When the campaign against Russia was started, I was an expert in the Gestapo office. Several days later, it may have been three or four days, we were informed of the beginning of the offensive. Before that we had no idea whatsoever about such plans, that is to say, not any more than any German could have gathered from the political tension.

Q. What was in principle the composition of the personnel of a State Police office in Germany?

A. The Gestapo office at Coblenz, the personnel of which I have reconstructed in my mind, consisted of about forty-five to fifty agents in the criminal department who were mostly taken from the Security Police and Criminal Police, or else from the old I-A; and in addition, about fifteen to twenty administrative and technical officials; apart from that, clerks and assistants, bringing the estimated total for the entire office to about one hundred persons.

Q. Was the employment of all these people on a voluntary basis in general or not?

A. On the whole, they were employees who had entered the police before 1933 and had been detailed or transferred to the State Police. According to my recollection, there were at the most 10 to 15 per cent of them who had entered the organisation voluntarily after 1933.

Q. What were the main tasks of a State Police office in Germany?

A. The main subjects that were dealt with were the combating of high treason, or treason; dealing with Church questions; with questions which arose from the treatment of the Jews; with so-called measures against the Treachery Act (Heimtueckegesetz); with criminal acts within the Party; and with certain important political questions from the whole complex formed by the Press and economy.

Q. How was the question of protective custody dealt with in the course of your activity with the Gestapo?

A. The great majority of the cases were dealt with by means of a warning by the State Police, when the result of the inquiry was negative. In those cases where custody was necessary, we saw to it that the perpetrators were brought before the court. Protective custody was only given for a short time in all those cases where the matter was not ready to be brought to the court. Protective custody by being transferred to a concentration camp was only proposed by the Gestapo if the personality of the perpetrator, judged by his previous behaviour, gave one to expect that he would continue to be an habitual offender against the regulations. To my knowledge, at the beginning of the war there were twenty thousand inmates in the concentration camps, of whom I estimate at the most one-half were held for political reasons.

Q. For what reasons were the other half kept there?

A. They were mostly criminals.

Q. Did the Gestapo take any measures for looking after the members of the political inmates' families?

A. According to a decree of the Gestapo office, the State Police office, when taking people into protective custody, not only had to ask the welfare organisations to take care of the families, but the official who dealt with the particular case had periodically to make sure that they were actually looked after.

Q. Were inmates who were released from protective custody in a concentration camp forbidden to follow certain professions?

A. No, they could go into any profession.

Q. That deals with the period during which you were in charge of the State Police Office? Until what year?

A. That is during the time when I was deputy chief until May, 1940.

Q. The prosecution has said that the Gestapo had fought the churches; what do you know about that from the time when you were in Coblenz and Dusseldorf?

A. Church matters during my period were dealt with on the basis of a separation of Church and State; that is to say, we intervened when a priest violated the so-called "Kanzelparagraph" (pulpit paragraph) which had been put into the penal code in the days of Imperial Germany, or for violating the "Heimtueckegesetz" (treachery act), or if Church organisations were active in worldly matters, which was prohibited by a decree.

Q. What did one mean by "Jewish questions" during the period up to 1938?

A. The emigration of Jews.

Q. What was the number of officials who dealt with Jewish matters, at the two offices of the Gestapo known to you?

A. At the Coblenz Gestapo office, one Criminal Oberassistent, who also dealt with matters pertaining to freemasonry; at the Dusseldorf, Gestapo office, one Oberinspektor with, I believe, two or three assistants.

Q. Was there any change brought about by the order of Heydrich of 10th November, 1938, to arrest an unlimited number of Jews who were able to work?

A. That decree was a complete surprise for us, for the measure could in no way be expected on the basis of the measures which had heretofore been taken. Since to my knowledge the great majority of these Jews were released again later on, one could not recognise that as a basic change of the course pursued by the State leadership.

Q. Did you or the officials in your office have any knowledge that the deportation of Jews to the East, started in 1942 approximately, really meant their destruction, biologically speaking?

A. No. At that time I was an adviser in the Gestapo office. At meetings with the chief of Office IV, nothing was ever mentioned about that. The treatment of the Jewish question was at that time in the hands of Eichmann, who had not risen from the State Police, but had been transferred from the SD to the State Police. He and his personnel were living in a building set aside for that purpose and had no contact with the other officials. He particularly did not bring in the other departments by getting them to countersign, when for instance he ordered the deportation of Jews. To our objections in that regard he always answered that he was carrying out special missions which had been ordered by the highest authorities and that, therefore, it was unnecessary for the other departments to countersign, and thus to be able to state their own opinion.

Q. Were there regulations about secrecy always applied within the individual offices of the State Police?

A. Yes; even within the offices themselves. It was an old police principle as early as 1933 that individual cases should not be talked about. The secrecy was rendered more severe by the well-known Fuehrer decree. The SS and the police courts punished any offenders most severely and all these punishments were regularly made known to the officials.

Q. You were in charge of Office IV-D-4 in the Reich Security Main Office (RSHA) since 1941. What were the duties of that department?

A. To deal with the political and police problems of occupied territories from a uniform point of view and particularly to summarise them in reports to higher and to other offices; later, there was, in addition, the looking after the interned political prisoners and other personalities from these territories.

Q. What was your fundamental attitude, and therefore that of the main Gestapo office, about the origin of the national resistance movement in the occupied territories?

A. After these territories were occupied, the Allies also started to utilise the potential forces in these territories by setting up military organisations. That, in the beginning, was voluntary on the part of the people and whoever wanted to join any such military organisation would do so for patriotic or political reasons. Once he had joined such an organisation, he was subordinate to military orders with all their consequences. The measures which he had to carry out were carried out as part of the Allied strategy as a whole and not in the interests of his own country or on its behalf. As a result, all actions of the resistance movement were military actions which were not carried out spontaneously by the population, and from that it resulted that all measures of a general nature against the population were reactions against the activities of the military organisation, and not only useless but also harmful to German interests, because the members of these military organisations were not deterred by such measures from carrying through their orders. The consequence was that a combating of these forces was only possible on two lines: first, to bring about by means of reports a policy on the part of Germany which would deter people from the political decision to fight against Germany; and secondly, to neutralise the active groups by capturing them.

Q. Why, then, did the State leadership not act in accordance with this fundamental conception of the Gestapo?

A. To begin with, because Himmler had not come from the ranks of the police and his decisions were not usually made according to the reports he received from the police, but primarily on the basis of individual information which he received from other sources, particularly from the Higher SS and Police Leaders. Moreover, the police were not able to report continuously and at the same time give an estimation of the situation. On the other hand, the Higher SS and Police Leaders and the local offices which represented the highest German authorities in the various territories, again and again interfered with the work of the police on the lower level.

Q. You just used the word "interfered." Did not the Gestapo have a well-defined chain of command?

A. No. The offices assigned in the occupied territories were not only subordinate to the Central Secret State Police Office but many other civilian and military authorities had influence and could, for instance, issue directives, especially the Higher SS and Police Leaders, Reich Commissioners, and in part also the military commanders.

Q. Can you give us two very striking examples.

A. First, the policy of Reich Commissioner Terboven, to carry out the shooting of hostages, and other general measures against the population. For three years we fought in order to prevent his measures, and by reports sent to Himmler we repeatedly tried to have him recalled. We took, for instance, prisoners from Norway to Germany in order to get them away from his jurisdiction, and later we were able to release them in Germany. When ship-sabotage in Denmark reached its climax in the autumn of 1944, a directive came from OKW to the military commander, to bring about a decree of the Reich plenipotentiary, so that dockers and their relatives could be arrested if any acts of sabotage occurred in their docks. After hard controversies the measure was revoked because it was evident from our experience that the dockers had nothing to do with those acts at all.

Q. How were Sipo and SD organised in the Western Occupied Territories?

A. The organisation was not uniform. In Norway, and later in Belgium, there were commanders under the Commanders-in- Chief; in Denmark and the Netherlands there were branch offices (Aussenstellen) and in France there were commanders under the Commander-in-Chief. In all cases, the BDS was not only subordinate to Berlin but also to the Higher SS and Police Leader who again was immediately subordinate to Himmler, and who could bring about decisions which did not go through the RSHA.

Q. What was the composition of the personnel of these offices?

A. There was a tremendous shortage of trained Criminal Police officers. Therefore the State Police officers formed only a skeleton staff, which was supplemented by men of the Criminal Police, but primarily by men drafted for that service, who had been transferred with units of the Secret Field Police to Sipo. They represented a good deal more than fifty per cent. of the staff.

Q. Was it a voluntary matter to belong to Sipo in the Western Occupied Territories, or not?

A. No, one was transferred or drafted there. Only the native interpreters had volunteered with the State Police.

Q. Who ordered the deportation of Jews from Denmark?

A. That order came from Adolf Hitler through the Reichsfuehrer SS. The Commander of the Security Police tried in vain to have it deferred, but he was not successful, to my knowledge, as that was also one of the reasons why he was recalled.

Q. What was done on the part of the State Police to mitigate those measures as far as possible?

A. The ordinary police who were charged to carry out these measures in general were informed that doors could not be broken open by force. Secondly, with the help of the Reich plenipotentiary, it was made possible that no confiscation of property should take place, and the keys of the apartments were turned over to the Danish Social Minister.

Q. Was the deportation of Jews known in Denmark beforehand?

A. It had been known to the Danish population and discussed by them for a long time previously.

Q. Why were the Danish Police dissolved and part of them deported to Germany?

A. Because the Danish Police, in their entirety, were in the closest contact with the resistance movement and the British Intelligence Service. For instance, the Chief of the Danish Police turned over information on the composition of German troops on Jutland and Fuhnen to the British Intelligence Service, and was involved in carrying out sabotage work in case of invasion. Other leading officials were involved in a similar manner. Under these circumstances, the armed forces feared the Danish Police might be used to attack them from behind.

Q. Did the State Police suggest and carry through deportations?

A. Deportations were not initiated by the State Police, but the Higher SS and Police Leader had already requested the approval of these measures by Himmler in the Fuehrer headquarters, when he told the State Police about his intentions.

Q. Was there a uniform order to use physical cruelty or torture during interrogations?

A. Brutal treatment and torture were strictly prohibited and were condemned by the courts.

Q. Do you know of any cases in which interrogation officers were sentenced by courts?

A. I remember two Gestapo officials in Dusseldorf who were sentenced for maltreatment of prisoners, by a regular court.

Q. Were third-degree methods used in interrogations in Denmark when you were in office there, and, if so, why?

A. Yes, third degree was carried out during interrogations. To explain this I have to point out that the resistance organisations occupied themselves with the following:

Firstly: Attempts on German soldiers.

Secondly: Attempts on trains, means of transport and Wehrmacht installations in the course of which soldiers were also killed.

Thirdly: Elimination of all so-called informers and people collaborating with the German Police or other German authorities.

In order to forestall those dangers and to save the lives of Germans, the third degree interrogation was ordered and carried out, but only in such cases. There was restriction in practice, in spite of the scope of the decree.

Q. What was discussed at the conference in Brussels in 1943, about the application of third-degree methods?

A. At a conference of officials it was stated, on the basis of experience gained, that it was already decided for the aforementioned reasons that it was advisable to restrict the application of third-degree methods to the extent mentioned.

Q. On whose orders were hostages shot in France, who suggested it?

A. As far as I know, it was a directive from Adolf Hitler. We constantly received reports from the Gestapo office, and we sent reports protesting against these measures, to the same extent as in other occupied territories, for the reason that I have already given.

Q. Why did the Gestapo especially reject the idea of shooting hostages as reprisal for the shooting of German soldiers in Paris?

A. Because we were of the opinion that this had been carried out by a relatively small group of people, and that general measures, therefore, would not only be useless but damaging in view of the considerations which I mentioned before. Facts really proved that in Paris these measures had been carried out by a group of not even one hundred persons.

Q. Who ordered and carried out the deportation of workers from France to Germany?

A. That was a measure of the manpower administration. It was not known to me that the State Police had carried out any deportation of workers. I have to make one limitation concerning France where, upon the orders of the Reichsfuehrer , as far as I remember the so-called Action "Meerschaum" was carried out, in the course of which French nationals, I believe five thousand, who had committed minor political offences were forcibly transferred to Germany in order to be used as workers.

Q. Who was responsible for the evacuation of Jews from France?

A. The evacuation of Jews was carried out by Eichmann's office as I have already explained, without it being possible for the older offices of the State Police to do anything about it.

Q. Upon whose directive was the harbour district of Marseilles demolished?

A. That was a directive by the Reichsfuehrer, sent directly to the Higher SS and Police Leaders who, especially in France, had worked out a close connection with him by-passing the Gestapo. In Berlin we heard about this order only later on.

Q. Did Himmler frequently issue such directives without first telling the police about it?

A. While I was in Berlin that happened rather frequently. He did it on the basis of reports which he received from some other office or as a spontaneous reaction to some act of sabotage or an attempted assassination.

Q. Do you know of any cases of excessive methods during interrogations in the Western occupied territories?

A. In the main, we knew officially at the time only about the Norwegian White Book which caused an investigation in Oslo; and then the basis of our reports to the Reichsfuehrer was to obtain the recall of Terboven.

Q. What do you know about the deportation of French ministers and generals to Germany?

A. This particular deportation was ordered by the Reichsfuehrer evidently after deliberation with only the Higher SS and Police Leaders in France. The Secret State Police office (Gestapo), however, did not know anything beforehand and was confronted with the order that Prime Minister Reynaud and Minister Mandel were to be put into prison cells. The Gestapo office, after much correspondence, succeeded in getting a different kind of quarters for the French statesmen and an understanding that there would be better quarters from the beginning for those people who were later transferred to Germany.

Q. Did you know that one of the French generals at Koenigstein was to be executed upon the orders of Panzinger in November, 1944?

A. No.

Noor Inayat Khan (1914-1944) was a British Special Operations Executive agent, and was the first female radio operator to be sent into occupied France to aid the French Resistance. She was arrested in October 1943 and interrogated at the S.D. Headquarters in 84 Avenue Foch, Paris. She was taken to Germany as a "Nacht und Nebel" prisoner, and on 13th September 1944, was shot in the head with three other agents, at Dachau concentration camp. Their bodies were immediately cremated. She was posthumously awarded the George Cross and the Croix de Guerre with Gold Star.

Q. And that the general was to be taken away from Koenigstein in a car and then shot when allegedly trying to escape?

I put before you the documents which have just been presented by the American Prosecution, 4048-PS to 4052-PS, and I want you to state your opinion as to what you know about this.

DR. MERKEL: I only have an English copy, but the witness understands English very well.

THE PRESIDENT: Is it in your document book?

DR. MERKEL: No, Mr. President, it is not in the document book and I could not put it in because these documents have just been presented by the American prosecution during the session. The numbers are 4048 to 4052-PS. They have just been presented during the cross-examination of Dr. Best.

BY DR. MERKEL:

Q. Witness, I believe it is not necessary for you to read all the documents now. I only want you shortly to refer to these documents and answer my question, that is, if you know anything at all about this incident?

A. The dates of the documents are January, 1945 and December, 1944. At both those times I was in Denmark and I was not in the Secret State Police office.

Q. Generally, was the deportation of foreign workers to Germany carried out by the Gestapo?

A. No. I recall that even the arrests of escaped workers in the Western occupied territories were not carried out by the Gestapo. I remember particularly that in 1940 Reich Commissioner Seyss-Inquart stressed specifically that such things should not be done.

Q. Was the so-called "Nacht und Nebel" decree of the OKW brought before you in order to make it known to the State Police offices and commanders?

A. Yes.

Q. Did you agree with that decree?

A. The "Nacht und Nebel" decree had been issued by the OKW in conjunction with the Reich Ministry of Justice. The Gestapo office had nothing to do with the drafting of it. There were, to begin with, great difficulties in the way of technical and police administration, because the act which had been committed abroad had to be clarified in Germany. If only for these reasons we rejected it as being difficult to carry out.

Furthermore, its effect proved to be negative, for the relatives did not know anything about the person arrested, and this was in contradiction to our fundamental tendencies. The difficulties arose immediately when the first people were arrested and transferred to the State Police offices, which had to clarify the proceedings. They showed that innocent people too were brought to Germany. We then succeeded in spite of the terms of this decree, in getting these people returned to their native country.

Q. Were the so-called "Kugel" decree, the commando order, and the "N.N. decree" applied in Denmark while you were there?

A. No.

Q. What do you know about the application of these decrees in the other. Western occupied territories?

A. All these were decrees which were issued after I left Berlin and therefore I cannot say anything about them.

Q. Do you know whether the Gestapo in the Western occupied territories had special groups in the prisoner-of-war camps so as to select and execute those men who were racially or politically undesirable?

A. I cannot say anything about that because the decree was not known to me before the surrender.

Q. Did the decrees mentioned have the character of State Police decrees?

A. These decrees did not originate as the work of professional police, but they were ordered from above. The normal State Police officials therefore could not expect that such decrees would ever be issued, and besides, owing to the regulations on secrecy, the contents of these decrees were really not known to the great majority of State Police officials.

DR. MERKEL: I have no further questions to put to the witness.

THE PRESIDENT: Does the prosecution wish to cross-examine?

CROSS-EXAMINATION BY MR. MONNERAY:

Q. Dr. Hoffmann, you were a member of the Nazi Party, were you not?

A. Yes.

Q. Since when?

A. Since 1st December, 1932.

Q. And when you became a candidate for Government service, and in particular the police, you indicated too that you were a member of the Party, did you not?

A. I beg your pardon; I did not quite understand the question.

Q. When you became a candidate for Government service, and in particular the police, you indicated that you were a member of the Nazi Party, did you not?

A. Yes, of course.

Q. You said a short while ago that there was no connection between the Gestapo and the Nazi Party, did you not?

A. Yes, that is correct.

Q. Is it correct, though, that police officials were subjected to political screening?

A. I did not quite understand the sense of the question, I am sorry, I did not quite understand the question.

Q. "Political screening" is a special term which you probably know; in German it is called "Politische Beurteilung."

A. Yes.

Q. It is true, is it not, that important officials of the police, before being appointed, were subjected to this political screening by the Party?

A. Yes.

Q. Do you know the circular of the Party Chancellery according to which the authorities of the National Socialist Party were not obliged to consult the USC cards, when it was a question of appointing new police officials, or of giving promotion?

A. Each official who entered was examined regarding his political attitude, and each one who was promoted was screened again.

Q. You were a member of the SS, were you not?

A. Under the assimilation decree I became a member of the SS in November, 1939, after the outbreak of war.

Q. You had to send in an application, did you not?

A. We were directed by the office to make a formal application.

Q. And this application was similarly subjected to a political screening, was it not?

A. I assume so.

Rows of dead inmates fill the yard of Boelcke Barracks in Mittelbau-Dora, a sub-camp of the Buchenwald concentration camp in Nordhausen. Used as an overflow camp for sick and dying inmates from January 1945, numbers rose from a few hundred to over 6000, and the conditions saw up to 100 inmates die every day. Tragically, around 1300 inmates were killed by British bombing raids in April destroyed much of the barracks. Photograph taken on 12 April 1945.

Q. And when you were in Dusseldorf, as delegate of the Chief of the Gestapo services, you had under your orders some Frontier Police offices?

A. Yes.

Q. Is it correct that these offices had exactly the same functions as the branch offices of the Gestapo?

A. No, not at first, they had only the duties of frontier police. In my time, the political tasks of the police were the business of the Landrat.

Q. You are speaking of what period?

A. I am speaking of the period of 1939 to 1940 - until September, 1940.

Q. I remind you of a circular of the Ministry of the Interior for Prussia and the Reich, of 8th May, 1937, published in the bulletin of 1937 of the Ministry of the Interior for the Reich and Prussia, Page 754; which stipulates in its third article that the police tasks at the frontier of the Reich are taken over by the frontier office and posts.

A. Yes, that is correct. You must distinguish between the inner political tasks and counter-intelligence work. Counter-intelligence, of course, was handled by the Frontier Police, but not tasks of inner political nature, because most of the officials of the Frontier Police did not have the necessary training to make criminal investigations independently.

Q. The same paragraph continues that the frontier offices of the police are considered as being Gestapo offices and are assimilated to the "Aussendienststellen."

A. I cannot understand the word. Oh, yes - "Aussendienststelle". The Frontier Police were subordinated to the State Police office, Department III, which dealt with counter-intelligence tasks. As the purpose of counter-intelligence work is to counter aggression coming from abroad, it goes without saying that the Frontier Police had the most urgent task of all police units along the frontier. I have explained that the Frontier Police essentially were not entrusted with the inner political tasks of the police.

Q. You said to us just now that people were sent to concentration camps at the request of the local Gestapo services. Is that true?

A. If an individual was to be sent to a concentration camp, the State Police office in Berlin had to make a request to the Gestapo office. It was only if the Gestapo office or, later on, the Chief of the Security Police, decided for protective custody that the individual could be sent to the concentration camp, because internments were obtained through the usual channels of police administration.

Q. So it is a fact, witness, that internments in concentration camps were made on the initiative of the local offices of the Gestapo?

A. On the demand of the local office of the State Police.

Q. And the local Gestapo services, when making such a request, at the same time arrested the individual?

A. Yes.

Q. Did frontier posts also have the right to make requests for internment in concentration camps?

A. The Frontier Police had only the duty of intervening at the frontier. They did not take any decisions independently. If the Frontier Police arrested a person, all they did was to hand him over with a report to the State Police office, which continued to investigate the matter. The officials of the Frontier Police were mostly beginners who were not yet able to carry out any criminal investigations. The Frontier Police office was not an independent office that could make such requests. The duties of the Frontier Police were in no way different from those before 1933.

Q. I would like to show you, witness, a document which nevertheless dates from 1944 and which comes from the Dusseldorf Gestapo office. That is 1063-PS. Is it a fact that this letter was also sent to the frontier offices to inform them that there was no reason to send arrested Eastern workers to Buchenwald concentration camp?

A. Excuse me; I did not quite understand the question because I was reading.

Q. Is it correct that this letter addressed to the frontier offices informs them -

A. That can be seen from the contents. It is clear, of course, that a State Police office also sends its principal directives to the frontier, for the contents of this letter deal with the treatment of individuals who had been caught and that, of course, happened at the frontier. The letter also states that a police office, having picked up such an individual, has to pass on all information when they hand over the case to the State Police office, that is the principal office.

Q. It is correct, is it, that this document indicates that requests for transfer to concentration camps which would come from frontier offices have to pass via Dusseldorf?

A. Yes, of course. To my knowledge, the Frontier Police office could not have any direct connection with the Gestapo.

Q. So it is also correct that the frontier office could itself file requests for internment in concentration camps?

A. Only to the State Police office at Dusseldorf. But I must add that the document is dated 1944, and that since 1940 I was no longer engaged in State Police work in Germany; and I cannot say whether there were any changes in the directives given for the Frontier Police offices during my absence. This document does not give any cause to suppose there were, because I assume that the same decree was also sent to the Landrate.

THE PRESIDENT: In general, the Tribunal thinks that there is no use cross-examining the witness about documents which are not his own documents and about which he knows nothing. You can put the documents in.

BY MR. MONNERAY:

Q. Do you know the institution of the Secret Field Police?

A. In the country there was only the gendarmerie, and in the smaller towns, the so-called Communal Criminal Police.

Q. I believe there is a mistranslation here. I mean the "Geheime Feldpolizei."

A. That institution is known to me, yes. I did not understand the question at first.

Q. Is it correct that most of the members of Field Police came from the police?

A. The units of the Secret Field Police (Geheime Feldpolizei) were composed of a few police officials, but mostly of soldiers who had been detailed for that purpose. In the groups, of the Secret Field Police which were transferred to Denmark, I estimate that within one unit there were about ten to fifteen per cent. of police officials, and the remainder were soldiers who had been detailed for that duty, and who previously had never had anything to do with the police.

A. The leaders of the detachments (Kommandos) and the staff were mostly police officials, and as far as I can remember, mostly officials from the Criminal Police.

MR. MONNERAY: With the permission of the Tribunal I will hand in two documents, which are Affidavits F 964, and F 965, which become Exhibits

RF 1535 and RF 1536. These documents indicate, for two regions of France, that the great majority of the officers of these military police came from the police originally.

BY MR. MONNERAY:

Q. Is it correct that hostages in the occupied territories were handed over to Sipo?

A. I did not understand that question.

Q. Is it correct that in the occupied territories hostages were handed over by the Army to Sipo?

A. That varied in the different territories. As far as I know, hostages in France were shot by the armed forces; in Norway, upon order of the Reich, Commissioner Terboven, as far as I know, by Sipo. I could not say of my own knowledge how it was in Belgium.

Q. Did you receive any reports on third-degree interrogations, indicating how rigorous these interrogations were?

A. You mean reports during my term of office?

Q. That was in Berlin.

A. No, I have said that as an official basis of information we only found out what had been printed in the Norwegian White Book. Apart from that nothing was known to me.

MR. MONNERAY: I should like to submit to the Tribunal a report from the Commander of Sipo and SD at Marseilles, of 6th July, 1944, concerning arrests of members of the French resistance, of the interrogation of these members, and of deaths which ensued. This is Document F 979, which becomes Exhibit RF 1537. With the permission of the Tribunal I would like to read an extract of this document.

"The arrested men, Nos. 1 to 16, were killed - "

THE PRESIDENT: What page of the document?

MR. MONNERAY: On Page 2 of the French translation, Mr. President, an extract.

"The arrested men, Nos. 1 to 16, as well as the forty- three prisoners named, were killed while attempting to escape on a large scale on 13th June, 1944. Several others were killed in the neighbourhood of Salon on 15th June, 1944 in an attempted escape. No. 17 is still required by special section AF."

And farther on,

"No. 21 died at our office."

BY MR. MONNERAY:

Q. Concerning the "Nacht und Nebel" decree, you said to us that the Gestapo services in Berlin were opposed to it.

A. Yes.

Q. I would like to submit to you Document PS-668, which has already been submitted as Exhibit USA 504.

A. I have explained that the State Police, for technical reasons, were against that decree. But since it was a decree which had been issued by the German

Government, the decree had of course to be carried out by the State Police as well as by other offices.

Q. And your office, IV-D-4, which signed this document, chose the most rigorous solution?

A. The solution which was indicated by the decree.

Q. The Army had asked your office to suggest the solution, had it not?

A. Do you mean the solution in this special case, or the decree in general?

Q. I ask you; witness, whether it is correct that the Army requested you to give a solution to the problem of knowing whether the relatives of a deceased Frenchman should be advised of his decease or not. Is it true that you chose the most rigorous solution?

A. From this document I can only gather that apparently an inquiry was sent by the OKW, and that the Gestapo office gave the answer, stating what was required by the terms of this decree.

Q. Is it correct that on Page 2 the Army answers you that it agrees with your proposal?

A. Apparently.

Q. Did you yourself give instructions, personal instructions, concerning the application of the "Nacht und Nebel" decree?

A. That was not my task. I had as ministerial agent only to pass on the terms of the decree to the competent offices, and the rest was done by the local offices.

Q. Did you have any connection with the concentration camp services?

A. I only had connection with the concentration camps from the time when I was charged with the care of the French ministers, because Prime Minister Reynaud and M. Mandel first lived in cells at Oranienburg, and I had to see them there frequently in order to find out what they needed. And the same happened later with the concentration camp at Buchenwald where Prime Minister Blum and M. Mandel were quartered in a small house, a cottage, in the settlement where the management was quartered. And concerning the castle of Gitter, the guards posted there were taken from units of the concentration camp at Dachau. Those were the only cases in which I had indirect contact with the administration of concentration camps.

THE PRESIDENT: It is time to adjourn.

(A recess was taken until 1400 hours.)

THE PRESIDENT: It will perhaps be convenient to counsel for the organisations to know that the Tribunal proposes to take all the oral evidence, the witnesses for the organisations, first, and then that they should comment upon their documents afterwards, because some of the documents, namely affidavits, have not yet been got ready. I think that will probably be convenient to counsel for the organisations.

And the Tribunal proposes to sit on Saturday morning in open session until one o'clock.

KARL HEINZ HOFFMANN RESUMED

CROSS-EXAMINATION BY MR. MONNERAY:

Q. You told us a while ago that, except for the protection of certain French political persons, you had nothing to do with the control of the concentration camps?

A. Yes.

Q. Did you establish regulations for the concentration camps?

A. No.

Q. Did you send instructions to the concentration camps?

A. I cannot remember.

MR. MONNERAY: I should like to show the witness, with the permission of the Tribunal, Document PS-2521, which will become Exhibit RF 1538. This document is not in the document book, it is a new item.

BY MR. MONNERAY:

Q. On Page 2 of this document, we find an extract of the "Nacht und Nebel" decree for the use of the concentration camp offices. This document is dated 4th August, 1942, and comes from Office IV-D-4.

A. Yes. That is a factual transmission of the "Nacht und Nebel" decree to the Inspectors of the KL (concentration camps). I can no longer remember from when they started carrying out the "Nacht und Nebel" decree in concentration camps.

Q. The document is signed by yourself, is it not?

A. It says: signed, Dr. Hoffmann, and there is a stamp there, too. I must have signed it at some time.

Q. Is it a document that was drawn up in your office?

A. From its appearance, I must assume so.

Q. Was it your office that gave instructions and explanations about this decree?

A. Yes. That is quite clear, and was never disputed.

Q. You told us this morning that the State and the State leadership did not act according to the ideas of the police?

A. Yes, that was so in many cases.

Q. Do you consider that the subject matter of the "Nacht und Nebel" decree conforms to police conceptions?

A. No.

Q. That is to say, you think that this decree is contrary to police conceptions?

A. Yes. I have stated that this decree was given out without any suggestion by the police, and in my statements concerning our conception of the origin and set-up of the military organisations, I declared that this decree was not in conformance with it. If, however, this decree was issued by the supreme State leadership, then, of course, the police had to act according to these principles and could only try to put through their own views within the framework of this decree.

Q. In other words, whether the Gestapo approved of the measures taken or not, they co-operated in carrying them out?

A. Yes, indeed.

Q. Had the Gestapo the right to proceed to carry out executions?

A. No. However, I did hear that in one sector, which did not come under my jurisdiction, regulations of that sort did exist.

Q. What sector?

A. As far as I know, the branch dealing with Polish questions.

Q. Did your office IV-D receive any information on the right of the Gestapo to carry out executions?

A. I cannot remember whether we received decrees of that sort.

Q. I should like to show you Document PS-1715, which will become Exhibit RF 1539. It is a document signed by Kaltenbrunner which was sent to all the offices of the Gestapo for their information and to your office, IV-D.

A. I should like to call your attention to the fact that my department, IV-D was the group in which all occupied countries were comprised. This document is addressed to the Gruppenleiter IV-D, not to Department 4, Dora IV. This document, therefore, was not sent to my department. Since no executions were carried out in the Western sector, the document was not sent to my department.

Q. But the documents correspond to the reality. The Gestapo could carry out executions.

A. From my own knowledge, I cannot give you any further details about the handling of this problem in practice.

Q. Were you acquainted with Eichmann?

A. I know that Eichmann was in charge of the Jewish branch in the Main Reich Security Office (Reichssicherheitshauptamt).

Q. Your office received no information about anti-Jewish activities in occupied territories, did it?

A. My office received the monthly reports from the commanders in the occupied territories. In these, for example, the deportation of Jews was reported on and I have already explained that I learned the fact of the Jewish deportations for the first time from them, and I talked to Eichmann on this matter and asked why these facts were riot previously made known to the department, and he refused to reply because he said that he acted only on the basis of superior orders.

Q. Did Eichmann have deputies in the occupied territories?

A. I know that he had his special deputies with the various BDS commanders.

Q. Did these deputies have the right to give orders to the Gestapo offices?

A. I cannot give you any information from my own knowledge about the exact position of these deputies of Eichmann's. Eichmann was theoretically a part of the Gestapo office.

Q. A part of Office No. IV, was he not?

A. Theoretically he belonged to Office IV, but conducted ... but he conducted a very intense activity of his own and I also emphasised that this may be traced back largely to the fact that he did not ... that he did not come from the police.

Q. Were you kept constantly posted on Eichmann's deputies in the various occupied territories?

A. Only from the monthly reports of the commanders.

Q. And these reports told you, for instance, the number of deportations?

A. Yes.

Q. Did the forces of the commanders of the Gestapo or the Sipo in the occupied territories assist in these deportations?

A. As far as I know, yes.

Q. What were the functions of Office II of the RSHA?

A. Department II of the Main Reich Security Office dealt with administrative and economic questions as well as, from the beginning until, I believe, 1944, questions of passports and the interning of foreigners, as well as the justiciary [sic].

Q. Were the office officials chiefly officials from the executive or administrative branch of the police?

A. Office II consisted mainly of administrative officials and lawyers.

Q. According to you, this office was very poorly informed as to what happened in the executive branch?

A. Yes, because essentially they dealt with legal and administrative questions.

Q. Do you know what were the functions of Office II?

A. If I am not mistaken, it was questions of jurisdiction.

Q. I should like to show you a document which has already been submitted as PS-501, Exhibit USA 288. According to this document, the gas vans which were intended to exterminate populations in the Eastern territories, especially Jews, were supplied by this Office II, which according to this document was perfectly aware of the extermination. Was it in this way that the separation between these offices and the executive offices was established?

A. As far as I can see from the document, Office B II was the technical section which dealt with motor vehicles, and as far as the contents are concerned, it deals with special motor vehicles, and it is obviously a report on the serviceability of the vehicles to the central office for the management of motor vehicles in Berlin.

Q. You admit that this is a document which speaks of certain special vehicles intended for extermination?

A. So far as I can see from running over the document rapidly, you could draw that conclusion from the contents.

Q. Dr. Hoffmann, one last question -

THE PRESIDENT: M. Monneray, I think the document speaks for itself.

MR. MONNERAY: Yes, Sir.

BY MR. MONNERAY:

Q. Did you often have the impression in the course of your activity in the Gestapo that the State leadership was asking you to carry out tasks which were contrary to what you would call police duties?

[Karl Heinz Hoffmann] A. In connection with certain questions during my activity in Berlin, as well as also in Denmark later, I had the feeling that certain duties were assigned to us which were contrary to our duties as policemen; but in this connection I must remark that I could only judge these questions from the point of view of a police official and could define my attitude to things only on the basis of my knowledge as such, and I did not know what had caused the leadership to make the decisions which were transmitted to us.

Q. You did not consider as criminal, for example, the order intended for certain categories of Soviet prisoners?

A. I must honestly say that I was absolutely unable to understand such an order, particularly since it could not be explained at all by police reasons.

Q. But nevertheless the Gestapo lent itself to the execution of these orders, did it not?

A. I cannot tell you that from my own knowledge.

MR. MONNERAY: I have no further questions.

DR. MERKEL: Just a few questions, Mr. President.

SECOND DIRECT EXAMINATION BY DR. MERKEL:

Q. Did the members of the Gestapo who had been assimilated into the SS by the assimilation decree come under the orders of the SS or the SD and perform their service there?

A. No. The registration in the SS was merely an outside measure, and after my formal entry into the SS in the year 1939 I did not perform any service with either the SS or the SD.

Q. In the order of protective arrest issued by the RSHA was the concentration camp already designated to which the prisoner was to be delivered?

A. I think I remember that it was, but I cannot tell you exactly.

Q. Who carried out the arrests of those people against whom an order of protective arrest had been issued, in case these people were still at liberty?

A. Either the officials of the Gestapo directly, or possibly also the constabulary and local police authorities.

Q. Who accompanied the trainloads of prisoners to the concentration camps?

A. As far as I remember, this transportation was handled by the general police administration in regular prisoner transport cars which traversed the entire Reich area according to a regular schedule.

Q. Did you or your office know anything about the true conditions existing in the concentration camps?

A. No.

THE PRESIDENT: What do you mean by "regular schedules"? Do you mean special transports or do you mean ordinary trains?

THE WITNESS: They were special cars for prisoners which were used by the general police administration between the individual prisons and which also carried ordinary prisoners. These cars were attached to the regular express and passenger trains, and these prisoners were also transported in these trains. And so there were no special transports.

BY DR. MERKEL:

Q. Were the concentration camps under the Gestapo?

A. No. Concentration camps were under the Inspector of Concentration Camps at Oranienburg, and as far as I know this Inspectorate was under the Administrative and Economic Office in the SS Main Office.

Q. The very document just submitted by the prosecution, 2521-PS, also speaks for this fact, does it not, since the return address is the SS Economic Administrative Main Office in Oranienburg and it is addressed to all the camp commandants of all the concentration camps?

A. Yes.

Q. Did you know about the annihilation of Jews at Auschwitz?

A. No. I only heard about these things after the ... after the surrender.

Q. Did you know that Eichmann's activity was directly connected with the biological extermination of the Jews at Auschwitz?

A. As long as I was in office ... as long as I was in office, and before the surrender, I heard nothing about problems of that kind.

Q. When was the first time that you received reliable knowledge about these things?

A. After the surrender.

DR. MERKEL: I have no further questions for the witness.

BY JUSTICE BIDDLE:

Q. Witness, you spoke of a decree under which the Gestapo were permitted to use third-degree methods in Denmark, is that right?

A. Yes, indeed.

Q. Was that decree in writing?

A. That was a written decree by the head of the Security Police and the SD.

Q. And was it signed?

A. Yes.

Q. Who signed it?

A. As far as I recall, the first decree was signed by Heydrich and the second one on behalf of Muller, but I cannot say for certain about the latter -

Q. What was the date of the first decree?

A. I believe it was 1937.

Q. What month?

A. That I cannot tell you at this date.

Q. What was the date of the second decree?

A. 1942.

Q. Did you see both decrees yourself?

A. Yes.

Q. What was in the first decree?

A. The contents of the first decree provided that for the purpose of uncovering organisations hostile to the Reich, if no other means were available, the person involved could receive a certain number of blows with a stick. After a specified number, a physician had to be called in. This order could only ... could be used for extracting a confession for the conviction of one individual. Approval for this had to be obtained in every case from the chief of the Security Police and SD.

Q. Wait a minute. Was the decree limited to any particular territory, or did it cover all the occupied territories?

A. The decree of 1937 applied to the Reich territory, but I believe it later applied automatically to the activities of the Sipo in those regions where it was stationed. I cannot remember any limitations.

Q. Were there any other methods of third degree which were allowed as well as the beating in this first decree?

A. No. According to the second decree only ... the only measures approved were those which were milder than blows with a stick. Standing at interrogations, or fatiguing exercises. They are enumerated in the decree, but I do not remember them all.

Q. You remembered one of them - standing up, for instance. What was the provision of the decree with respect to standing up during interrogations?

A. I personally never attended such an interrogation.

Q. I did not ask you that. I said, what was the provision with respect to standing up?

A. It only said that the order could be given that the person involved must not sit down during the interrogation but had to stand.

Q. And how long were the interrogations? How long were they actually?

A. The decree did not mention that, but -

Q. I said, how long were the interrogations? How long were they actually?

A. Well, under the circumstances, they naturally lasted very long. It was only in that way that standing up was a severe measure.

Q. Was the number of strokes that could be used mentioned in the decree? Did it say how many times a man could be struck with a stick?

A. As far as I recall, this measure could be applied only once to the same individual; that is, it could not be repeated. And the number of blows, in my opinion, was specified in the decree.

Q. And then the doctor was called?

A. No, I believe it was this way. If a fairly large number of blows was prescribed in advance, then the physician had to be present immediately.

Q. And what was the number of blows that was to be permitted, do you remember that?

A. As far as I recall, twenty, but I cannot tell you that exactly.

Q. And both decrees covered all of the German Reich, including the occupied territories, is that true?

A. Yes.

Q. And the decrees were effective in France, as well as in Denmark, is that not true?

A. Yes, later. In the second decree, the power of approval of the Chief of the Security Police was delegated to the commanders - that was in 1942.

Q. So that after that the commanders could order beatings without going to the head of the Security Police?

A. Yes, after 1942.

THE PRESIDENT: The witness can retire.

DR. MERKEL: Mr. President, I should like to make one small correction ... a little misunderstanding which I think I can clear up. While examining the witness, the Tribunal has just mentioned a commandant in the occupied territories. I should like permission to ask the witness whether he meant the commandant of the Security Police or the commander of the Security Police. They are two entirely different persons.

THE WITNESS: As far as I recall, the commander.

THE PRESIDENT: That is all. Thank you very much.

LT.-COMMANDER HARRIS: If the Tribunal please, I would like to put one question to this witness, following the questioning of the Tribunal. I believe that the witness testified that in this second decree there was no provision for beatings.

CROSS-EXAMINATION BY LT.-COMMANDER HARRIS:

Q. Did I understand you to say that, witness?

A. No, I said beatings and ... but from now on still further measures which, however, were milder in nature than actual blows.

THE PRESIDENT: I thought, when I took it down, that he said there were milder methods in the second decree, standing up and tiring methods.

LT.-COMMANDER HARRIS: Yes, Sir; that is what I understood, but I now gather that the witness admits that under both decrees beatings were authorised, and that is all that I wish to establish.

DR. MERKEL: I have no further questions to the witness.

THE PRESIDENT: What is it you want, Colonel Karev?

COLONEL KAREV: The Soviet prosecution will request the permission of the Tribunal to present new documents concerning the criminal activity of the Gestapo.

THE PRESIDENT: Yes, certainly.

COLONEL KAREV: First of all, I want to submit to the Tribunal Exhibit USSR 258, containing excerpts from a list of hostages shot by the German police in Yugoslavia. If the Tribunal considers it necessary I shall quote just two sentences out of this document: At the end of Paragraph 1 of this document it says: "The executions were effected according to the decisions and by order of the chiefs of the Gestapo or the SD." Then I shall draw the attention of the Tribunal to item "B" at the end of the second page, which states as follows: "According to different informations, lists, death records, etc., the following number of victims has been established up till the present time ...." I omit here a detailed enumeration of the victims and merely draw the attention of the Tribunal to the fact that 337 persons were shot or hanged in the year 1942, and at the very least 1,575 persons by the SD.

Then I submit here Exhibit USSR 465, which is the notification issued by the German police about destroying a number of villages in Slovenia and of shooting all the men of those villages for helping the partisans. I draw the

Tribunal's attention just to these sentences again at the beginning of which it is said:

"On the 20th of July, 1942, the village of Krosnik and three other villages were destroyed and the male population shot. The remainder were deported, because they had helped the partisans and had carried out hostile activities against the German Reich."

One more sentence of the document:

"In addition to all the measures taken here by the Gestapo, a number of civilians had to be shot as hostages."

The third document is Exhibit USSR 416. I shall not read it. It is a list of citizens of Yugoslavia, compiled in the year 1938. The persons listed were to be arrested without any charges of crime being made against them. Near every 4,000 names listed there was a note - whether the arrested people were to be directed to the Gestapo or to the chief administration of SD of the Reich. However, this document was found in the archives of the Gestapo in Yugoslavia.

The fourth document is Exhibit USSR 418, captured from the Germans. It contains a copy of an order to the State Police in Yugoslavia with a decree of Himmler to arrest all persons who had expressed their joy in connection with the defeat of the Germans at Stalingrad.

I think, Mr. President, there is no need to read it all.

Finally there is Exhibit USSR 71. It is very brief and consists of a wire sent by the German State Police to arrest employees of the diplomatic service, attaches, diplomatic couriers, consuls, etc. The wire was sent one day prior to the German invasion of Yugoslavia, an act which was a violation of International Law.

This telegraphic message to arrest couriers, consuls, etc., is also mentioned in Exhibit USSR 316.

The last document is Exhibit USSR 518. It is the testimony of the former Lt.-General Kappe of the German Army, which states that the Gestapo killed their own collaborator, in order to conceal the fact that a special secret installation was made to overhear what was spoken by the chief. This is all that I wanted to submit.

COLONEL KAREV: If it is possible, I would like to request the Tribunal to permit me also to quote several other USSR exhibits referring to the activity of the Gestapo. These documents have been submitted in connection with other questions; later they were taken into consideration in connection with the Gestapo. May I read them to the Tribunal?

THE PRESIDENT: These are not documents which have already been put in evidence, are they?

COLONEL KAREV: No, Mr. President; these documents have been presented and accepted by the Tribunal, not in connection with the activity of the Gestapo but with regard to other questions; therefore, excerpts contained in these documents which have been read before may be omitted, as it seems to me.

THE PRESIDENT: The Tribunal thinks that the appropriate time for you to deal with these documents will be when the case is argued on behalf of the prosecution, if they are documents which have already been put in evidence.

COLONEL KAREV: They will; thank you, your Honour.

THE PRESIDENT: Now, the witness may retire. Have you had all your witnesses?

DR. MERKEL: Yes, Mr. President. If I understood your Lordship correctly, the presentation of documentary evidence is to take place after all the witnesses of all the organisations have been heard.

THE PRESIDENT: Yes, the object of that being that all the documents can then be dealt with together, as some of the documents are not yet available; so we will go on with the next organisation.

DR. MERKEL: I should like to ask just one more thing. In my submission of documents, may I refer to the documents which have only now been brought forth by the prosecution and possibly introduce evidence to refute them. This concerns the documents which have been introduced today for the first time.

THE PRESIDENT: When you say "refute" you mean criticise the documents and argue upon them, I suppose.

DR. MERKEL: To argue upon them and possibly introduce contradictory evidence against the new documents which were submitted today by means of new affidavits of one kind or another.

THE PRESIDENT: The time for you to "refute," as you say, or to argue upon the documents which have been put in today by the prosecution will be when you make your final argument. At the end of the oral evidence for all the commissions, all the organisations will offer their documentary evidence and comment upon it shortly, and then they will have time within which they may argue the whole case and at that time you will be able to argue and "refute," as you put it, the documents which have been put in today.

DR. MERKEL: Thank you.

THE PRESIDENT: Now I call upon counsel for the SD. Will you please call your witnesses now?

DR. GAWLIK: I have interrogated seven witnesses before the Commission. I have not the complete transcript yet and will hand it in later. With the approval of the Tribunal I shall call the witness Hoeppner.

(ROLF-HEINZ HOEPPNER, a witness, took the stand and testified as follows):

BY THE PRESIDENT:

Q. Will you state your full name?

A. Rolf-Heinz Hoeppner.

Q. Will you repeat this oath after me:

I swear by God, the Almighty and Omniscient, that I will speak the pure truth and will withhold and add nothing.

(The witness repeated the oath.)

THE PRESIDENT: You may sit down.

DIRECT EXAMINATION BY DR. GAWLIK:

Q. First, I shall put a few preliminary questions in order to prove that the witness has the necessary knowledge to answer questions on the subject. When were you born?

A. On 24th February, 1910.

Q. Since when have you been a member of the SD?

A. Since the beginning of 1934.

Q. What activity did you carry on before then?

A. Before that I studied and performed pre-legal service.

Q. What law examination did you pass?

A. I passed the first and second State legal examinations.

Q. What ... what was your position in the SD?

A. First I was an honorary assistant and adviser in an Oberabschnitt, later Stabsfuehrer in a Leitabschnitt, then Abschnittsfuehrer and finally Gruppenleiter in the Reich Main Security Office.

Q. Of what group were you the head?

A. I directed Group III-A, law administration and communal life.

Q. In what other spheres of duty did you work in the SD?

A. In the beginning, during my honorary activity, I worked on Press matters. Later on personnel and organisational questions, and as Stabsfuehrer and Abschnittsfuehrer I was responsible for the entire sphere of duty of the Security Service in my area.

Q. Now I shall turn to my first topic. I want to prove that the SD as an intelligence organisation and the SS formation as SD were completely different organisations. What does the abbreviation SD mean?

A. The SD means Sicherheitsdienst, Security Service.

Q. What different meanings did the word have?

A. The word Sicherheitsdienst has two completely different meanings. First, it means the special SS formation, SD, and second, the Security Service as an intelligence service.

Q. Was the Foreign Intelligence Service also characterised as SD?

A. Yes, it was also characterised as SD, and, indeed, as Foreign SD.

Q. Was Office VII known as SD also?

A. Yes.

Q. What was the activity of Office VII?

A. Office VII occupied itself with questions on archives and library matters, and as far as I know it had a number of special scientific duties.

Q. Was the SD as an SS formation completely different from the SD Domestic Intelligence Service, and the SD Foreign Intelligence Service?

A. Yes.

Q. To whom was the special SD formation of the SS subordinate?

A. The special SD formation of the SS was subordinate to the chief of the Security Police and the SD.

Q. Who belonged to this special formation?

A. This special formation consisted of, first, the members of the

Intelligence Branch of the Security Service, who came from the general SS. Secondly, there belonged to this special formation those who after they worked in this intelligence service were taken into Office VII, and thirdly, there belonged to this special formation the SS members of the Security Police, i.e. the State Police and the Criminal Police, and fourthly and finally, the members of formations who had a certain working connection with the Security Police.

Q. Were there other persons as well who belonged to this special formation and were not active with the Security Police or the SD?

A. Yes, by that I meant the fourth group which I just spoke of, who were taken into the SS as customs frontier guards.

Q. Did this combination of persons have any kind of common task?

A. No. The situation with respect to this combination of persons was merely that they were first registered in the SD Main Office and later, after the Main Reich Security Office was founded in September, 1939, in Office I of this Main Reich Security Office.

THE PRESIDENT: The light keeps coming on. Will you try to pause between question and answer?

Q. Now, I come to the second topic: the relationship of the Domestic Intelligence Service, Office III, to the Foreign Intelligence Service, Office. VI, and to Office VII. Did Offices III, VI and VII represent different organisations, or one unified organisation of the SD?

A. They represented different organisations. I might give the reasons for that in a few words. First, the spheres of duty of these three offices were completely different. Office III was concerned with the Domestic Intelligence Service, Office VI with the Intelligence Service abroad, and Office VII with questions regarding libraries and archives. Secondly, the organisation was completely different. In Office III, Domestic Intelligence Service, the chief value of the organisation lay primarily in the regional office (Aussenstelle) and in the sector (Abschnitt). The method of work was therefore decentralised. Perhaps I might give the reasons for that in a few words: Office VI, Foreign Intelligence Service, involved a strong centralisation of duties. Office VII had nothing but a central office.

Q. Was there any discernible connection between these Offices III, VI, and VII, with a general common purpose?

A. No. The aims of these offices were far too varied for that. The members of these offices had hardly any connection with each other.

Q. Now I come to the third topic, the development of the SD until the establishment of the Main Reich Security Office, particularly dealing with the questions as to whether during this time it was one of the duties of the SD to work with others on a Common Plan or Conspiracy. When was the SD Domestic Intelligence Service established?

A. The SD was established in 1931-1932.

Q. During the period after its formation up to the end of the war did the SD have the same duties, the same purpose and the same activities?

A. One could not say that by any means. The duties and objectives varied even - varied very much according to the political alignment. While the Security Service had the task of helping the general SS up to about 1933 or the beginning of 1934, there was no longer any reason for this task after the parties with which the National Socialist Party had competed were dissolved, and therefore there was no longer a legal opposition party, and the combating, that is, observation, or repelling of an illegal opponent became the task of the Gestapo.

Q. What different periods of time are there to be distinguished, from its formation until the end of the war?

A. I just mentioned one period of time, the one from 1931 to about 1933-34. The second period of time began in 1934. As an event, or perhaps better, as a document of particular importance, I should like to begin with the order of the Fuehrer's deputy which the Security Service -

Q. Witness, first of all just give us the various periods of time; I will then question you briefly about specific periods.

A. The first period of time was from 1931 to 1934, the second was from the middle of 1934 to the formation of the Main Reich Security Office, and the third comprises the period from the establishment of the Main Reich Security Office to the end of the war.

What was the purpose ... what were the purpose, the duties and the activity of the SD in the period from 1931 to 1934?

A. The task of the Security Service from 1931 to 1934 was that of a semi-military formation (Gliederung) of the Party, namely, that of assisting the SS in its task of guarding the Fuehrer and protecting public meetings, by supplying the SS with as much information as possible from its intelligence service in rival, opposition parties as to what measures were being planned by other parties, and so whether speakers were going to be attacked, whether any meetings might be in danger, and so forth.

Q. At this time had the SD already been built up into a powerful, professionally well-trained espionage system by its leader Heydrich?

Mr. President, in this connection I should like to refer to the trial brief against the SS, Page 8b of the English text - 8b at the top, lines 1 and 2.

Please answer the question.

A. I have to base my answer to this question on what I myself saw along these lines when I entered the Security Service in the beginning of 1934 and on what I learned from my comrades then and later about the preceding period. Before 30th January, 1933, the Security Service represented a very small establishment which had hardly more than 20 or 30 regular members and not many more honorary members.

Q. You spoke of 20-30 regular members - for what area?

A. For the area of the entire German Reich.

Q. Were there other members - honorary members?

A. The number of honorary members was not much greater.

Q. Did the members of the SD make a general agreement among themselves to participate in crimes against peace, war crimes and crimes against humanity?

A. No. If you can speak of any agreement at all - since they hardly knew each other - they merely had the intention to help the Party which was legally contending for power by defending it against rival, opposition parties.

Q. During the years 1933 and 1934 did the members of the Security Service pursue the aim of supporting any persons whatsoever who had undertaken a general and common plan to commit crimes against peace, war crimes, or crimes against humanity?

A. No.

Q. During the years 1931 to 1934, did the members of the SD know anything at all about such a plan?

A. I believe the case of the members of the SD was not very different from that of the overwhelming majority of the German people. Nothing was known.

Q. Now I come to the second phase.

What were the aim and task of the SD during the period of time from 1934 until the creation of the Main Reich Security Office in the year 1939?

A. After a legal opposition party was no longer in existence, so that there were merely illegal political opponents, the combating of whom, as I have already mentioned, was the task of the State Police which had been evolved from the political police division, the task of the Security Service had to change. First, it changed in this way, that other ideological and political forms and other ideological groups -

Q. Witness, can you perhaps state the tasks and aims more briefly?

A. Well, to name a few examples, Freemasons; Marxists, Jews, so that these groups would be classified in a more scientific and statistical way and so that the Party would have material for training and other tasks.

That was the ultimate meaning of the Party's order for it to become the sole political intelligence and counter-intelligence service, on about July, 1934; something which, by the way; never did happen, since there continued to be an enormous number of information services and sources of information up to the end.

This task to work in more of an investigatory way with the political groups on other ideological forms was not permanent either, for after a short time it became obvious that this investigatory work too belonged to the sphere of activity of the Secret State Police, because in the long run such an investigation of opponents could not remain separated from the executive branch, from the information acquired in the daily interrogations, and so forth. Therefore, these tasks were changed when a very clear division of tasks was made between the Security Service and the State Police, a division which started in the middle of 1938 and was especially carried through in the year 1939, and which was substantially ended with the creation of the Main Reich Security Office in September of 1939. After this division of tasks the task of the Security Service would have been completely eliminated if it had not been for the fact that out of this Security Service, beginning with the so-called intellectual SD in 1933 and 1934, through a special advisory section for culture and a central department for spheres of life, intelligence service ... out of this Security Service there developed the quite special task for the domestic intelligence service, namely, the task of investigating the spheres of life of the German people according to developments and informing the executive offices about the development as a whole.

THE PRESIDENT: As I said to the other counsel, we do not want these witnesses to go over exactly the same ground that they have gone through before the Commission.

We have got that evidence. We only want you to present them here in order that we may see what credibility is to be attached to their evidence and to deal with any particularly important or new subject which has not been dealt with before the Commission.

Now this witness seems to be going over exactly the same ground which he has gone over before the Commission and at great length. It is simply doing the same thing twice over.

DR. GAWLIK: As I understood it, Mr. President, I was to summarise briefly once more the results of everything which had been taken up in the Commission for longer than two days, and that is what I am doing. I am now bringing ... the witness has been examined before the Commission for two days and now perhaps I shall present that material in one to one and a half or two hours. But I thought that it was precisely these various objectives of the Security Service for each year that would be of interest to the High Tribunal.

THE PRESIDENT: Well, will you try to present the summary within reasonable limits?

DR. GAWLIK: Yes, indeed, Mr. President.

BY DR. GAWLIK:

Q. What can you say about the significance of the work of the SD during this period?

A. The work of the SD during this period was of almost no importance. It was primarily concerned with finding its own proper task, with establishing an intelligence network, and with locating the necessary; basic material. Particularly important is the fact that during this time the Security Service hardly appeared in public.

Q. The prosecution has declared that the SS and likewise the SD were elite groups of the Party, the most fanatical adherents of the Nazi cause, who assumed the obligation of blind loyalty to the Nazi principles and were ready to carry them out unquestioningly, at any cost. In this connection I should like to refer to the trial brief against the SS, Page 7b.

I ask you, witness, were the regular and honorary workers in the SD selected according to those principles?

A. The regular and honorary workers were selected on the basis of being capable in some professional capacity and were men of decent character.

Q. Please answer the question first of all with yes or no.

A. No.

Q. And now please give your reasons.

A. I have already said that the regular and honorary members were selected because they were capable in some professional capacity and were of good character. It was not a prerequisite for either regular or honorary co-operation that anyone had to be a Party member or belong to the SS.

Q. Did the SD do things for which no Government office or political party, not even the Nazi Party, was willing to bear the full responsibility in public?

I should like to call the attention of the High Tribunal to the trial brief against the SS, Page 7, second paragraph.

A. No.

Q. Did the SD work secretly behind the scenes in the period which you described, from its formation until 1939?

A. No. One could give a whole list of examples. First of all, the regular members wore uniforms. They had the SD insignia on their sleeves. The offices had signs and were listed in the telephone directory, etc.

Q. During the period from 1934 to 1939 did the members of the SD make a common and general agreement to participate in crimes against peace, war crimes, or crimes against humanity?

A. No.

THE PRESIDENT: Would that be a convenient time to break off?

(A recess was taken.)

BY DR. GAWLIK:

Q. During the period from 1934 until 1939 did the members of the SD pursue the aim and task of supporting any individuals who had made a general and common plan for committing crimes against peace, war crimes, and crimes against humanity?

A. No.

Q. Did not the SD also support this sort of thing by obtaining information on actual possible opponents of the Nazi leaders and so contributing to the destruction and neutralisation of the opposition?

A. No.

Q. Can you give reasons for your answer to the question?

A. Yes.

Q. But please be brief.

A. It was the task of the Security Service to investigate wrong developments in all spheres of life. Individual cases were examples. It was not its task to instigate proceedings against individuals with any other offices.

Q. Should not the members of the SD have been convinced by the reports on public opinion and the reports on the different spheres of life, especially after the occupation of the Rhineland until the beginning of the Second World War, that everybody in Germany was expecting war?

A. On the contrary -

Q. Please, will you first answer the question with yes or no?

A. No.

Q. Now give the reasons, please.

A. I already said, quite to the contrary. During that period there was hardly anybody in Germany who expected a war, and it was these very reports on the situation in different spheres of life, in the spheres, perhaps, of food production, economy and industry, which showed that we were going to have armament to a limited extent, but not to an extent ... but in no way gave any indications that we were working towards a war of aggression.

Q. Now I come to the relation between the SD and the SS.

Was the SD always an inseparable and important part of the SS?

I refer in this connection to the German transcript of 9th December, Page 1596 of the German transcript, Page 1798 of the English transcript, where this has been alleged by the prosecution.

Please answer my question.

A. No. I should like to give the following reasons for that: After the duty of the SS to help guard the speakers at meetings and the Fuehrer was eliminated, the new task was formed and further developed from the staff of the SD, completely independent of the SS and the Reichsfuehrer SS.

Q. The prosecution has furthermore stated on Page 1759 of the English transcript, "the general SS was the basis, the root from which the various branches grew."

Will you comment on that with regard to the Domestic Intelligence Service?

A. That could not be true for the Domestic Intelligence Service because only about ten per cent of the regular workers had come from the General SS, and because at least 90 per cent. of all the honorary workers and confidential agents of the SD were neither members of the SS nor wanted to be members of the SS, nor, viewed from the standpoint of the organisation, should they have belonged to the SS.

Q. Was there in the SS a uniform headquarters under which the individual main offices operated jointly, or worked together automatically in such a way that each branch of the SS fulfilled a special task within the scope of the whole?

I refer to the transcript of 19th December, 1945, Page 1749. That is the English transcript. State your opinion on this.

A. No.

Q. Give me your reasons.

A. The Reichsfuehrer SS was alone the Supreme Head of the SS. The main offices which were under him were in no way headquarters. Outwardly they represented various points of view on the same questions. They competed with each other, they were frequently jealous of each other. It was not even true that each of these main offices represented a branch which was necessary for the whole, because their duties, their jurisdictions overlapped. For instance, four or five offices shared the responsibility in questions of National Folkways (Volkstum), and it was not possible, although this very suggestion was made by the Main Reich Security Office, to grant jurisdiction to one office. Among these different main offices there was no directing office. The so-called main directing office had only to perform the functions of the Waffen-SS. If any office had claimed that leadership, all the others would have rebelled against it immediately.

Q. What was the influence of Himmler on the development of the tasks of the Domestic Intelligence Service?

A. Himmler did not have a positive influence on the development of the tasks proper of the Domestic Intelligence Service with regard to spheres of life. That task grew out of the work of the office, and it could equally well have developed in some other office. There were even a large number of cases in which the task suffered because ft was connected with one individual who was one leader among several, because it was not always possible to send reports to the office for which they were intended, via the Reichsfuehrer.

Q. In order to prove a uniform will and a planned connection between the SD and SS the prosecution referred particularly to the book by Dr. Best, The German Police, and the speech by Himmler about the organisation and objectives of the SS and police. This concerns Documents PS 1852 and PS 1992. Do you know the book by Dr. Best and do you know that speech by Himmler concerning the organisation and objectives of the SS and police?

A. In a general way, yes.

Q. Please give your opinion as to whether the relation between the SS and SD is described correctly in that book by Dr. Best and in the speech by Himmler?

A. This question essentially involves the clarification of the concept which in many speeches and publications was designated as "Staatsschutzkorps" (Corps for the Protection of the State), and this idea of a Staatsschutzkorps was expressed by Himmler and Heydrich very early, a little after 1936. Its description changed, but although it appeared again and again in speeches, it was never really carried out. The individual parts of this so-called "Staatsschutzkorps" of Himmler's grew independently, developed independently; they were not a unit, so that we can say here, although it was indeed Himmler's wish to create this Staatsschutzkorps, this idea never materialised.

Q. Did the Higher SS and Police Leaders also have authority to issue orders to the SD, and did they have to supervise the activity of the SD? In this connection I refer to the trial brief against the Gestapo and SD, Page 12 of the English edition, and the trial brief of the SS, Page 12 of the English edition also.

A. The Higher SS and Police Leaders had neither authority to issue orders nor did they have to supervise the SD. They were merely representatives of the Reichsfuehrer within their territories without having any actual or disciplinary jurisdiction over the Security Service. Attempts were made in that direction in connection with the above-mentioned Staatsschutzkorps, but it was the Domestic Intelligence Service itself which averted them.

Q. Now I come to the relation between the SD and the Party. What was the organisational relationship between the Domestic Intelligence Service and the political leadership of the NSDAP?

The interior of the Gestapo Headquarters in Prinz-Albrecht-Str, Berlin, 1934.

A. The Domestic Intelligence Service was an institution of the Party, but it did not belong to the organisation of the political leadership. Therefore, no organisational connection existed. The proper and final task of the Domestic Intelligence Service was not given to it by the Party either. The task assigned it by the Party, as I have already mentioned, had already been essentially completed in the years 1938-39.

Q. Did the SD have the task of maintaining the Nazi leaders in power?

A. The Security Service had the task of -

Q. Can you first answer the question yes or no?

A. No.

Q. Now please give me your reasons.

A. The Security Service had a different task. It had the assignment to observe the effects of the measures taken by the leaders of the State, Party, economy and of autonomous bodies, to determine what the people were saying about them, whether the results were positive or negative, and then to inform the leaders about what it had found out.

Q. Was the Domestic Intelligence Service the espionage system of the NSDAP? Here I refer to the trial brief against the SS, Pages 8a and 8b of the English edition.

A. No. Firstly, the Security Service was not an espionage service at all. Secondly, it sent its reports to all executive offices, not only to those of the Party, but also to the executive offices of the State.

Q. Now I come to the next topic of evidence, the relation between the SD and the Gestapo. Were the Gestapo and the SD a uniform police system which became constantly more closely connected?

I refer to the trial brief against the Gestapo and SD, Page 12, Pages 1, 4, 13, 18, 21 of the English edition. What was the connection between the Gestapo and SD organisations with respect to aims, tasks, activities and methods?

A. First, in answer to the first question: it was not a question of a uniform police system, since a Security Service and a police system have absolutely nothing to do with each other. The Security Service and the Secret State Police were two entirely different organisations. While the Security Service had developed from a semi-military formation (Gliederung) of the Party, the Secret State Police was a continuation of an already existing institution of the State.

While the Security Service saw its aim and its task in gaining a general view of the various spheres of life or the specific forms of activity of other ideological groups, and regarded the individual cases as a system and an example, it was the task of the Secret State Police, on the basis of existing laws, ordinances, decrees, and so on, to deal with that individual case itself and to take preventive or subsequent measures in an executive police capacity, the continuation of an already existing state institution. While the Secret State Police worked with executive means, such as interrogations, confiscations, and so on, the Security Service never had executive powers.

Q. Was it the task of the SD to support the Security Police as has been stated in decree and other announcements, particularly the circular letter released on 11th November, 1938; in this connection I refer to Document 1638 PS.

A. No, that was incorrectly expressed. Perhaps I may comment briefly on that circular letter of 11th November, 1938.

We are concerned here with the fact that for the first time an agreement had been made between the Security Service and an office of the State. The chief result of this agreement was that the Security Service was thereby officially and publicly recognised by an office of the State -

Q. More slowly.

A. ... and that officials who worked in it could not, because of that work, be prosecuted for breaking their oath of silence, as had happened repeatedly up to then. At that time the agreement was made dependent on the fact that any State task could be mentioned. As, first of all, the Security Service hardly appeared in the public eye at that time, 1938, and then because work in the field of public life had not yet been officially recognised by the Party and so could not be mentioned in the decree, Heydrich quoted the support of the Security Police, because no one outside could check that.

Q. Did the SD have the task of watching the members of the Gestapo?

A. No.

Q. Can we conclude from the fact that inspectors of the Security Police and SD were established that there was a connection between these two organisations?

A. No, the inspectors only had a certain power of supervision over the organisation in particular cases. All directives, task assignments and so forth came from Berlin.

Q. What was the relation between the Departments III and the offices of the commanders, that is, the commanders of the Security Police and the SD?

A. I do not quite understand that question. Relation to whom?

Q. To the Security Police.

A. The Departments III of the offices of the commanders were departments just as Departments IV. They worked on Security Service tasks, whereas Departments IV worked on State Police tasks. They were departments of the offices of the commanders and not parts or establishments of Office III of the Main Reich Security Office any more than the Departments IV were establishments of Office IV of the Main Reich Security Office.

Q. Now I come to a short discussion of the individual war crimes with which the SD is charged. First, the Einsatzgruppen.

I refer to VI-A among the facts offered in evidence in the trial brief.

Were the Einsatzgruppen and Einsatzkommandos which were used in the East a part of the SD?

A. No, these Einsatzgruppen and Einsatzkommandos were establishments of an entirely original kind.

Q. Was the organisation of the domestic SD used for the activities of the Einsatzgruppen and Einsatzkommandos? That is something important.

A. That question, in the way it has been put, must be answered by No. It is not true that any parts of that organisation were transferred to the Einsatzgruppen. If individual members of the SD entered the Einsatzgruppen or Einsatzkommandos, then it is comparable to military induction. Just as a civil servant who is drafted is assigned different tasks, or at least can be assigned them, this was likewise the case with the SD. If the Einsatzgruppen had to perform Security Service tasks, such as making reports, the directives came to the Einsatzgruppen from Office III (Amt 3).

Q. Did the members of the SD and its subordinate offices obtain any knowledge about mass shootings and other crimes - war crimes or crimes against humanity through the reports from the East, or reports from the Einsatzgruppen?

A. Such reports from Einsatzgruppen were never forwarded to the subordinate offices in the Reich, so that the members of these offices could not have any knowledge of these incidents, either.

Q. Was the SD responsible for the establishment, arrangement, guarding and administration of concentration camps?

A. No.

Q. Could you give me any reasons for that answer?

A. There are no reasons for it. The Security Service never had anything to do with these matters because it lacked jurisdiction there.

Q. Did the SD establish any concentration camps?

A. No.

Q. Did the SD organise any concentration camps?

A. No.

Q. Was the organisation of the SD used for the guarding of concentration camps?

A. No.

Q. Did the SD have authority over the transfer and treatment of concentration camp inmates?

A. No.

Q. Did the Domestic Intelligence Service receive an order from Himmler not to intervene in the case of clashes between Germans and English and American flyers?

A. No, the Security Service could not have had any order, because it had no police functions and there could have been absolutely no question of any intervention.

Q. Did the Domestic Intelligence Service set up summary courts martial in order to pass judgement on persons in special and shortened proceedings? This question refers to Item VI-H of the trial brief.

A. Holding summary courts martial was not one of the functions of the SD at all, and so neither were courts martial of this kind because drat again would have been an executive measure which had nothing to do with the Security Service.

Q. Did the Domestic Intelligence Service Office III only execute people in concentration camps or keep them prisoners because of crimes which allegedly had been committed by their relatives? This question refers to Item VI-J of the trial brief.

A. The Security Service had nothing to do with that.

Q. Did the SD hold any "third-degree" interrogations? This question refers to Item VI-L.

A. The Security Service did not carry out any interrogations at all, consequently not any with the third degree.

Q. Will you briefly describe the aims, tasks, activities, and methods of the Group III-A of the Main Reich Security Office of which you were in charge at times?

A. It was the task of Group III-A to observe the effects of legislation, administration of justice, and administrative measures on the German people, and compile these observations in the form of reports and make them accessible to executive offices. It was furthermore the tasks of Group III-A, and in particular Department III-A-4, to give the executive offices a continuous picture of the general mood and attitude of the German population in regular reports.

Q. Was membership in the SD voluntary, or the result of some legal decree?

A. That question cannot be answered by yes or no. I might take my own group as an example. In my group, at the end, I had rather over 60 employees. About 75 per cent. of these worked there on the basis of legal decrees. For instance, all my four chiefs of departments had been transferred to the Security Service, ordered there on emergency service or detailed there. I believe that for the entire Security Service one could estimate that about 50 to 60 per cent. were working there on the basis of a legal decree. That comparatively high number results from the fact that, firstly, at the beginning of the war a large number of regular workers had been inducted; secondly, that the scope of the work had been increased in extent, and that therefore men and in part women auxiliary workers had to be sent for service in the occupied territories, and that thirdly, the entire work of the Security Service grew during the war, and the personnel had to render compulsory emergency service and so on, according to the legal measures that had been passed for this purpose.

DR. GAWLIK: Mr. President, I have no further questions.

THE PRESIDENT: Does the prosecution wish to cross-examine?

CROSS-EXAMINATION

MAJOR MURRAY: If the Tribunal please, Major Murray cross-examining for the United States Chief Prosecutor.

BY **MAJOR MURRAY:**

Q. Witness, when did you become chief of Office III-A in the RSHA?

A. In July, 1944.

Q. Who was the chief at that time and for some time prior thereto?

A. Office III had only one chief, and that was the then Gruppenfuehrer Ohlendorf.

Q. At times you substituted for Ohlendorf, did you not?

A. I believe the entire question did not come through. I heard only "at times you substitute."

Q. At various times during your career, you took Ohlendorf's place as chief, did you not?

A. No. When I was in that office, Ohlendorf was always there. Moreover, there was no general deputy for him. When he was away on business the chiefs of the various groups represented him for their own territories. But during the period while h was in Berlin, that happened very rarely.

Q. Do you know Dr. Wilhelm Hoettl; who was a member of Office 6, RSHA?

A. May I ask for the name again, please? I did not understand the name.

Q. Perhaps I do not pronounce it properly. Dr. Wilhelm Hoettl, spelled H-o-e-t-t-l.

A. Hoettl? I met him here for absolutely the first time.

Q. You do know that he held a responsible position in the SD, now that you have met him here?

A. No, I have not spoken to Hoettl here, either.

MAJOR MURRAY: With the permission of the Tribunal, I should like to read briefly from the affidavit of Dr. Wilhelm Hoettl, Document 2614 PS, dealing with the activities of the SD. This will be Exhibit USA 918. Dr. Hoettl executed this affidavit on 5th November, 1945. I quote:

> "It was the task of the SD to inform its chief, Himmler, and through him the Nazi regime about all matters within Germany, the occupied territories, and the other foreign countries. This task was carried out in Germany, by Department III - Information Service for Germany proper - and abroad by Department VI - Foreign Information Service."

Omitting a few lines:

> "For the task in Germany proper Department III had organised a large net of informers who operated from the various regional offices of the SD. This organisation consisted of many hundreds of professional SD members who were assisted by thousands of honorary SD members and informers. These informers and honorary collaborators of the SD were placed in all fields of business, education, State and party administration. Frequently they performed their duties secretly in their organisations. This information service reported on the morale of the German people, on all the important events in the State, as well as an individuals."

BY MAJOR MURRAY:

Q. Do you consider that a fair statement of the task of the SD?

THE PRESIDENT: Answer the question, please. Witness, answer the question:

Do you consider it a fair statement of the work of the SD? No, you need not go on reading the rest of the document. Answer the question.

A. It is a mixture of truths and untruths. I feel that the way and manner in which the Court ... in which this report judges the Security Service is somewhat superficial. It does not give the impression, according to this document, that Hoettl worked in the Domestic Security Service very long.

Q. You know, do you not, witness, that your chief, Ohlendorf, was in 1941 and 1942 the head of Einsatzgruppe D in Southern Russia? You were informed of that, were you not?

A. Yes, indeed.

Q. You knew also, did you not, that these Einsatzgruppen were made up from members of the SD and of the Gestapo and of the Criminal Police?

A. I knew that members of these organisations were detailed there for special service.

Q. You knew that they were commanded by SD members, did you not?

A. The Einsatzgruppen and Kommandos were commanded by members of widely different organisations, by members of the State Police, Criminal Police, and also the Security Police. I myself, moreover, was never on special service.

MAJOR MURRAY: I would like to refer, if the Tribunal please, to the affidavit of Ohlendorf. This is Document 2620-PS, to become Exhibit USA 919. This affidavit has not been used in evidence before. This affidavit of Ohlendorf which is very brief states:

"The Einsatzgruppen and the Einsatzkommandos were commanded by personnel of the Gestapo, the SD, and the Criminal Police. Additional men were detailed from the regular police."

And dropping down a few lines:

"Usually the smaller units were led by members - "

THE WITNESS: May I interrupt you? Excuse me, please.

It does not say here in the document that they were led by members of the regular police. It says only that "additional personnel was provided by the regular police."

BY MAJOR MURRAY:

Q. Yes, I omitted that. A few lines farther on: "Usually the smaller units were led by members of the SD, the Gestapo, or the Criminal Police." So that actually members of the SD were leading these Einsatzgruppen in the East, were they not?

A. The affidavit states that members of the Security Service as well as the State Police and the Criminal Police were in charge of units of this kind.

Q. Now, as a matter of fact, the Einsatzgruppen officers wore SD uniforms in the performance of their tasks, did they not?

A. Excuse me. I only understood a few words. The Einsatzgruppen wore these uniforms?

Q. The Einsatzgruppen officers wore the uniform of the SD while performing their duties in the East, is that true?

A. All members of the Einsatzgruppen wore field-grey uniforms and wore the SD insignia on the sleeve. That was one of the main reasons for the many misunderstandings which occurred, because members of the Security Police also wore this SD insignia. That was the case with the special SS formation of the SD which was mentioned right at the beginning of today's examination. And because beyond that even those members of the Einsatzgruppen and Einsatzkommandos wore uniforms who were not SS members at all and so who, in peace time, had never worn a uniform in Germany proper. They were sent into special service as so-called uniformed personnel and received a service rank corresponding to their civil service grade.

Q. In any event, many members of the Einsatzgruppen were members of the SD and many of those officers wore the uniform of the SD while killing these people in the Eastern territories; is that not true?

A. I do not quite understand the meaning of the question. There were very few people from the SD detailed to these Einsatzgruppen or Einsatzkommandos, at least from the three branches mentioned, and during their entire period of service these men and leaders wore the uniform with the SD on the sleeve.

MAJOR MURRAY: If the Tribunal please, I should like to bring into evidence another brief document, Document 2992-PS, Exhibit USA 494. This is a portion of that affidavit which has not previously been read into evidence. It is the affidavit of Hermann Friedrich Rabe. I am sure the Tribunal will recall that affidavit where this German citizen recounted the SS-SD men shooting large numbers of helpless individuals, the document which was referred to by the Attorney-General of Great Britain a few days ago.

In the first part of that affidavit Rabe states:

"SS man acting as a guard on the edge of the pit during the shooting of Jewish men - "

THE PRESIDENT: Wait a minute. This document is in evidence already, is it not?

MAJOR MURRAY: It is, my Lord, but not this particular portion of it referring to the SD. I did not intend to repeat the other portions, but this portion refers specifically to the SD and it is only those two sentences that I intend to read.

Paragraph 1:

"The SS man acting as the guard on the edge of the pit during the shooting of Jewish men, women and children, at the airport near Dubno, wore an SS uniform with a grey armband about three centimetres wide on the lower part of his sleeve, with the letters 'SD' in black on it, woven in or embroidered."

And dropping down to the last portion of the second paragraph:

"On the morning of 314th July I recognised three or four SS men in the ghetto whom I knew personally and who were all members of the Security Service in Ravno. These persons also wore the armband mentioned above."

It is a fact, is it not, witness, that many, of the members of these Einsatzkommandos were members of your SD organisation?

[Rolf-Heinz Hoeppner] A. I already said before that few members of these Einsatzgruppen and Einsatzkommandos were members of the Security Service. It is not said here in any way that these people to whom reference is made in this document had anything to do with the Domestic Intelligence Service; and if there was one there who belonged to that body - which is certainly not seen from the document, because it only says that he wore a uniform with the SD insignia - then he had been detailed for that special service just as anyone else may be inducted into the armed forces. That is precisely the chief reason for a large number of mistakes which were made with that term SD, that even the members who were on special service all wore the same uniform.

Q. In any event, Ohlendorf was a member of the SD, was he not?

A. Ohlendorf was chief of Office III, but that had nothing to do with the fact that he also commanded an Einsatzgruppe. That Einsatzgruppe could just as well have been commanded by the chief of Office IV or V, or by an inspector or anybody else. That had nothing to do with the activity of Ohlendorf as chief of Office III.

Q. Now, Ohlendorf has testified that frequent reports were compiled by the Einsatzgruppen and sent back to the headquarters. Did you see any of these reports while you were in the headquarters of RSHA?

A. No. That was not possible because during the period when I came to Berlin most of the Einsatzgruppen from the East had been recalled. At any rate, no further reports were coming in, and I am entirely of the opinion that in Office III, the Domestic Intelligence Service, only a very few men saw the reports from the Einsatzgruppen.

Q. I would like to have shown to you a series of fifty-five weekly reports of the activities of the Einsatzgruppen, and, incidentally, the Einsatzgruppen are known as the Einsatzgruppen of the Security Police and the SD.

A. No, no, there were no Einsatzgruppen of the Security Police and the Security Service, but rather there were only the Einsatzgruppen A, B, C and D in the East; and, indeed, there were good reasons for that.

Q. Before submitting that document to you, witness, I would like to have you examine Document 3876-PS, which has already been admitted in evidence as Exhibit USA 808; I call your attention to the title page of that document, signed by Heydrich, which reads as follows:

"I herewith enclose the 9th summary report concerning the activity of the Einsatzgruppen of the Security Police and the SD in the U.S.S.R.

This report will be sent out periodically in the future." Signed Heydrich.
Are you not mistaken, witness, in saying that these were not known as Einsatzgruppen of the Security Police and SD?

A. No. These Einsatzgruppen figured as Einsatzgruppen A, B, C and D. They were commanded by a deputy of the chief of the Security Police and the SD with the Army groups in question, or with the army.

The designation "Einsatzgruppen of the Security Police and the SD" is unfortunately wrong.

Q. So Heydrich is wrong again, is he, and all the documents are wrong?

A. No, I do not want to say that the document is false, but I merely maintain that the expression is not correct. I ask you to look at the distribution list; it says there: "To the chiefs of Einsatzgruppen A, B, C arid D." Besides, the Einsatzkommandos were not called Kommandos and Security Police of the SD, but, as far as I know, they had Arabic numerals from one to twelve.

Q. This, of course, is a report of your chief, Heydrich, and I will not enlarge on the point. Turn now to Pages 331 and 32. It is at the bottom of Page 32 in Heydrich's -

A. One moment, please. There is no Page 31 or 32 in my document.

Q. It is a very short passage. I will read it to you:

"In White Ruthenia the purge of Jews is under way. The number of Jews in the part up to now handed over to the civil administration amounts to 139,000."

A. Yes.

Q. "In the meantime ..." in the last sentence. "In the meantime, 33,210 Jews were shot by the Einsatzgruppen of the Security Police and the Security Service SD." It does not say anything there about groups A, B, C or D, does it?

A. No, it says Security Police and SD. I only do not understand what that is supposed to have to do with the Domestic Intelligence Service, Security Service.

Q. Except that Ohlendorf was the head of your service, was he not?

A. When he functioned as chief of Office III - in Berlin, but during the time when he directed Einsatzgruppe D, he was on special service, and the period of special service is treated exactly like a period of compulsory military service.

Q. Witness, are you informed of the fact that the SD was carrying on espionage activities in the United States prior to Germany's declaration of war against the United States?

A. I cannot imagine that the Domestic Intelligence Service would have worked in the United States.

Q. I would like to offer in evidence, if the Tribunal please, Document 5043-PS, which becomes Exhibit USA 920. This document is a teletype message of the Foreign Office, dated 11th July, 1941. I will read just one sentence from it, "Reference teletype No. 2110 of 5.7 from Washington. Herr Reich Foreign Minister (RAM)." That was Ribbentrop, was it not?

"Herr Reich Foreign Minister requests you submit immediately a written report as to who, amongst those in New York arrested on suspicion of espionage, worked with the Abwehr and who with the SD."

Witness, does not that look as though the SD was carrying on espionage activities in New York long prior to the declaration of war on the United States?

A. One of the first questions which Herr Gawlik presented to me was whether one could designate the Foreign Intelligence Service as SD. I said, "Yes," and further clarification was that the Domestic Intelligence Service and the Foreign Intelligence Service were different organisations. Whether the Foreign Intelligence Service, the foreign SD, Office VI, had anything to do with this matter I cannot judge, because I never worked in Office VI and understand nothing about these things.

MAJOR MURRAY: Of course, when they were all part of the SD I mean they were all members of the SD. I have no more questions.

THE PRESIDENT: Would you re-examine if you, want to? Did the Soviet Prosecutor want to ask any questions?

COLONEL SMIRNOV: Mr. President, I did want to put a few questions to the witness, but these questions are in connection with one new document - quite an interesting document - which we only received today, and for this reason, we have not had the translation into English made up. Therefore, I do not know whether it would be appropriate for me to put this question now when I do not have an English translation to present to the Tribunal.

THE PRESIDENT: Perhaps we could do it in the morning. It would be translated by then. Perhaps you could do it in the morning?

COLONEL SMIRNOV: Thank you very much, Mr. President, yes.

THE PRESIDENT: Dr. Gawlik, would you re-examine him now?

DR. GAWLIK: Mr. President, I do not know whether I will not also have more questions after the new document is presented. That, of course, I could not judge now.

THE PRESIDENT: Well, if there is anything that arises from the new document, you could put the questions later on. You will have a further opportunity if necessary.

DR. GAWLIK: Yes.

RE-DIRECT EXAMINATION BY DR. GAWLIK:

Q. Were the SS uniforms with the SD sign also worn by persons who had nothing to do with the SD?

A. Yes, I have explained that repeatedly.

Q. Were the SS uniforms with the SD flash, also worn by persons who had nothing to do with the SS?

A. Yes. I have already explained that repeatedly.

Q. Can you make any explanation as to why individuals who had nothing to do with the SD wore the SD flash?

A. First, because all members of the Security Police also wore that uniform; secondly, because any man at all who served with an Einsatzkommando or an Einsatzgruppe wore a uniform and the only uniform was the field-grey SS uniform with the SD-flash.

Q. Why did they wear the SD flash?

A. Because it belonged to the uniform.

DR. GAWLIK: I have no more questions.

EXAMINATION BY THE TRIBUNAL

BY THE PRESIDENT:

Q. Have you got this document before you, 3867-PS?

A. 3867-PS?

Q. Yes. You see what it says there. "I herewith enclose the 9th summary report concerning the activities of the Einsatzgruppen of the Security Police and the SD in the U.S.S.R." That is the second paragraph, you see that - describing the report?

A. In my document book there are several loose documents. Is it the one of 27th February?

Q. 27th February, 1942, Page 17. Have you got it?

A. Yes, I have it.

Q. First of all you see it says "regarding report No. 9 concerning the activity of the Einsatzgruppen of the Security Police and the SD in the U.S.S.R." And then the first enclosure. Heydrich encloses the 9th summary report concerning the activity of the Einsatzgruppen of the Security Police and the SD in the U.S.S.R.

A. Yes.

Q. And you said, as I understood it, these were not the Einsatzgruppen of the SD but were called Einsatzgruppen A, B, C and D?

A. Yes.

Q. That is what you meant, was it not, that you could not explain why they were "called of the SD"?

A. Yes.

Q. Well, will you explain why when distribution is set out it is to be distributed to the chiefs of the Einsatzgruppen A, B, C and D, and also to the commanders of the Security Police and the SD?

A. May I make a statement concerning this report?

If Einsatzgruppen and Einsatzkommandos of the Security Police and the SD are mentioned, then this designation is not accurate in this report, because that designation did not exist in the East. There were only Einsatzgruppen A, B, C and D and Einsatzkommandos numbers 1, 2, 3, and so on.

Q. Assuming that that is so, why then should the report be sent to the commanders of the Security Police in the SD in a separate distribution to them as well as the distribution to the chiefs of the Einsatzgruppen unless the SD had something to do with it?

A. I believe I was misunderstood somehow. It is a report about the activities of all the Einsatzgruppen which was summarised by the chief of the Security Police of the SD and which then went to the individual Einsatzgruppen, as I assume, so that they would know what had happened in other Einsatzgruppen, and so Einsatzgruppe D would know what had happened in Einsatzgruppen A, B and C.

Q. Yes, it was not only sent to the Einsatzgruppen A, B, C and D; it was also sent to the commanders of the Security Police and SD. What I am asking you is: Why was it sent to the commanders of the Security Police and the SD if they had nothing to do with it?

A. Probably Heydrich wanted the commanders of the Security Police and SD in Cracow, and the Higher SS and Police Leaders to be informed of what was done in these Einsatzgruppen, because it was also sent to the Higher Police Leaders in Breslau, Dresden, etc., who certainly had nothing to do with the activity of the Einsatzgruppen - to the Reich Defence Commissioners in Konigsberg, Stettin, Breslau.

Q. Well, then, your answer is that Heydrich made a mistake when he described it as the activity of the Einsatzgruppen of the Security Police and the SD, and when they sent out and distributed it to the commanders of the Security Police and SD, it was merely a matter of information; is that it?

A. Yes.

Q. Do you see the final distribution on Pages 46 and 47 or is that the distribution of a different report; it is a report on the 23rd of April, 1942.

A. Yes, 23rd April, 1942.

Q. And will you look at Pages 46 and 47?

A. Yes.

Q. About eight lines down, you see, it was distributed to Major-General Kaltenbrunner, Vienna.

A. Yes.

Q. And the last line but two, it was distributed to Governor- General Reich Minister Dr. Frank.

A. I cannot find Reich Minister Dr. Frick.

Q. Frank - Frank, I said.

A. Yes, for the attention of Oberregierungsrat Dr. Shepers.

Q. And the same is true on Page 18 of the report of the 27th of February, 1942.

A. 27th February?

Q. Yes, on 27th February, 1942, it was also distributed to the same people?

A. Yes.

THE PRESIDENT: The Tribunal will adjourn.

(The Tribunal adjourned until 2nd August, 1946, at 1000 hours.)

FRIDAY, 2ND AUGUST, 1946

CROSS-EXAMINATION BY COLONEL SMIRNOV:

Q. Witness, I request that you explain some of the testimony which you gave yesterday. Please give me very brief answers. First, you said yesterday that SD had nothing to do with the working out of the plans of aggression and was not even aware of such plans.

A. Yes.

Q. You further stated that the SD since 1934 and up to 1939, in other words during the period of the organisation of the RSHA, was engaged in activities which were very far removed from carrying out any police functions and actually had the nature of a scientific research; is that correct?

A. I did not talk of scientific problems.

Q. No, I said of a scientific research nature.

A. I explained that the SD had two tasks, one was the work of ascertaining living conditions in Germany and the other was more of a statistical and research nature directed against other philosophies of life.

Q. You further stated that the SD had no relations whatsoever with crimes against peace and crimes against humanity; is that correct?

A. Yes.

Q. Mr. President, I would like the permission of the Tribunal to submit the original of a German document from the archives of the Central SD, which is a document captured by the Red Army in the Berlin district and refers to plans concerning the invasion of Czechoslovakia.

Will you kindly follow me, witness, while I quote from the document in the Russian translation?

"Communication. June, 1938. Berlin. Secret. Subject: employment of SD in Czechoslovakia." Text follows:

"The SD should prepare to start its activity in case of complications between the German Reich and Czechoslovakia ... The manifold planning and the preparation of the operational staff for mobilisation should be effected on the basis of approval ..."

THE PRESIDENT: Stop - you read out a date of June, 1938. I cannot see that at the head of the document.

COLONEL SMIRNOV: June, 1938, yes.

THE PRESIDENT: It does not appear in the copy at the head of the document. Does it appear somewhere else?

COLONEL SMIRNOV: Your translation probably does not have it, Mr. President. The original has it. We submitted copies of two different documents and I am afraid the mistake might have been caused by the fact that your translation is not the translation of the document which I am submitting now. We submitted copies of two different documents, two different translations.

THE PRESIDENT: Either it is an entirely different document or else some parts are omitted. The date is not on the document. Go on. Go on.

BY COLONEL SMIRNOV:

"Dividing functions, the SD follows, wherever possible, directly behind the advancing troops and fulfils duties similar to those in the Reich which are the security of the political life, and at the same time, the security in as much as possible of all enterprises necessary to the national economy and so, also, to the war economy. In order to achieve this purpose, we suggest the division of the country into larger territorial units - Oberabschnitt, and smaller territorial units - Unterabschnitt. The latter are to be sub-divided into Aussenstellen so that the co-workers of the SD" (I draw your attention to the words "co-workers of the SD,") "intended for employment in Czechoslovakia can be immediately assigned to their tasks."

This document shows, therefore, that the SD was not only well informed of the plans but had also actively taken part in the elaboration of these plans of aggression. I am asking you, witness, this excerpt shows that the SD was not only aware of the plans of invasion and aggression, but also that it took an active part in working out the plans. Does it not?

A. May I first say something about the document?

Q. I would like you to answer briefly, first. Answer yes or no. Explain later, please.

A. From the document, it is obvious that it is only a draft -

Q. We will talk about that a little later. You will see, then, what the main point is. I refer to the excerpt which I read. Do you not see evidence there that the SD was both informed and took an active part in the plans of aggression?

A. I said yesterday that the interior and foreign information services are two different organisations. The interior -

THE PRESIDENT: Witness, we do not care what you said yesterday. We want to get your answer today. You were asked a question which can be answered by yes or no. You can explain afterwards.

A. The document has nothing to do with the interior information service.

Q. In that case, I would like you to look on Page 3 of the document. You testified yesterday that the SD had nothing to do with the staffing of the Einsatzkommandos. I am going to read an excerpt here. It is Item 2. Please pay attention to what I am reading now. "The staffing of the planned organisations of SD" (I draw your attention to the "organisations of SD") "should be effected with the following considerations: 1. According to the demands of the SD ... Does that not prove ..."

THE PRESIDENT: It is being read too fast. You know the translators do not have time.

COLONEL SMIRNOV: Thank you, Mr. President.

BY COLONEL, SMIRNOV:

Q. Does not the excerpt that was just read testify that the Einsatzkommandos were staffed according to the demands of the SD? It says here: "The staffing is effected according to the demands of the SD."

A. Excuse me. It was apparently translated incorrectly. Your question does not make sense to me.

Q. It seems to me the question is quite clear. It says here "The staffing of the agencies of SD should be effected with the following considerations." Please look at the text of the document.

A. In my text there is absolutely nothing concerning this.

Q. 202 (a), Page 3?

THE PRESIDENT: To which words are you referring now?

COLONEL SMIRNOV: I am referring to Section II, Mr. President.

THE PRESIDENT: You must go slowly. You simply say Page 3. It happens not to be on Page 3, on our Page 3. It is on Page 2. How do you expect us to find it when you refer to it in that way? It is Paragraph 2, then, at the start.

COLONEL SMIRNOV: It is Section II, Mr. President; there is the Roman numeral II in front of the section.

BY COLONEL SMIRNOV:

Q. What answer will you give then, witness? What answer will you give me, with regard to manning the staffs? Were they not to be staffed according to the demands of the SD?

A. From the paragraph, it is only evident that it was requested that the SD should keep men in readiness, but not that the SD asked to have men kept in readiness.

Q. In that case, I should like to ask you to turn to Section III.

COLONEL SMIRNOV: Mr. President, please turn to Section III. It is

Prisoners of Montelupich Prison, Krakow in 1939. This notorious prison was used by the Gestapo throughout World War II, and its inmates included political prisoners, British and Soviet spies and parachutists, Waffen-SS deserters, convicted members of the SS and SD. After the war, 21 Nazi war criminals were hanged here.

Page 4 of the Russian text. I refer to Roman III, Item 1. Special "Einsatz" groups from the Reich (pay attention to the words "Einsatz groups" which appear for the first time in this document) will be collected with a view to their prospective work in distributing centres, etc., where they will receive equipment and instructions. Then I refer to the next page of the Russian text which follows right after the list of cities. It is Page 4 of the English Text.

"As soon as any district is free from the enemy, that is when it is occupied, the allocated groups are immediately sent to the District Administration following the advancing troops. At the same time, the groups which are intended for the next district still in enemy hands will follow along."

Will you deny after this that it was precisely the SD which staffed the first Einsatz groups?

A. From this document it can only be seen that the head office at that time of the SD had prepared this group.

Q. If this does not convince you, then I would like you to turn -

THE PRESIDENT: You must go more slowly. We will not hear what the witness says, if you interrupt him during the time it takes for the translation to come through. It is impossible for us to understand it.

COLONEL SMIRNOV: I beg your pardon, Mr. President. I stated that if this does not convince the witness, that it was precisely the SD that helped to staff these operational groups, then I would be obliged -

THE PRESIDENT: Wait a minute. Then the witness said something about Einsatz groups. What did you say about Einsatz groups?

THE WITNESS: The question was whether I am now convinced that the Einsatz groups were being prepared beforehand, and I answered that -

THE PRESIDENT: No, you were not asked about Einsatz groups at all. You were asked about the SD.

THE WITNESS: I was asked whether the SD was preparing the Einsatz groups beforehand, and I said that from the document it is evident that the head office of the SD had prepared these groups.

BY COLONEL SMIRNOV:

Q. Please look at Paragraph V - Section V - entitled "Preparatory Measures." Page 5 of the English text.

A. Yes.

COLONEL SMIRNOV: Mr. President, I want to quote Section V, "Preparatory Measures."

"Preparatory Measures; Demarcation of the spheres of activity of the SD under the Gestapo

(a) in Germany

(b) in occupied territory.

Suggestion: Measures in Germany are carried out under the guidance of the Gestapo and with the assistance of the SD. Measures in the occupied regions are carried out under the leadership of the senior officer of the SD. Gestapo officials are assigned to certain operations staffs. It is important that, as far as possible, similar preparations, training and the use of materials, should be conducted in the Gestapo as in the SD."

BY COLONEL SMIRNOV:

Q. Would you not say that this shows that it was precisely the SD that took the leading part in preparing Einsatz kommandos and that the Einsatz groups carried on their criminal activity under the guidance of SD officials?

A. I read nothing here about criminal activity. And as far as the SD is concerned I would like to refer to the first answer that it had nothing to do with the Domestic Information Service.

THE PRESIDENT: The man had not yet finished his answer. We do not know what his answer is. Now repeat your answer.

THE WITNESS: I said that I read nothing about criminal measures in the document, and I said previously that the document had nothing to do with domestic information services.

BY COLONEL SMIRNOV:

Q. It says there SD. Can you argue about the term used by the document? Can you deny that?

A. The word "SD" means many things.

Q. But it seems to me that in this connection the term is used in precisely the sense in which the authorities in Germany had used it. The German officials understood the terms they used, did they not?

A. Yes, but it is about the Foreign Information Service.

Q. I would like you to look at the continuation of the same quotation, Number 2, entitled, "Establishment of Files in Section III, 225 of the Central Administration of the SD

(a) Collection and utilisation of all available materials of the SD Oberabschnitt is concentrated in Section III, 225.

(b) In establishing duplicate local files for each region, one copy remains with the central department while the second is sent to the operations staff appointed to the region."

I am stopping there and would like you to pay special attention to Item (c):

"Files must have notations such as these: 'to arrest,' 'to liquidate,' 'to remove from work,' 'to place under observation,' 'to confiscate,' 'police surveillance,' 'deprivation of passport,' etc."

Do you not think that when the filing department of the SD made a note like these on the cards of specific persons, such as to liquidate, to arrest, that the SD was participating in crimes against humanity?

A. I can only repeat that the document has nothing to do with the Domestic Information Service of the SD.

Q. Did I understand you correctly yesterday to say that you deny that there was any liaison or relationship between the SD and the SS units?

A. Yes.

Q. I would like you to look at the end of this plan, the last paragraph, Number VII:

"It is necessary that an SS unit or Totenkopf unit be ready for disposal for special purposes."

After seeing that, do you still deny that there was any direct relation between the SD and the SS units and the organisation of the activity of the Einsatz groups?

A. From this paragraph, in any case, it is not evident.

Q. In that case, how should we interpret the sentence which I just read?

A. From this paragraph one can only deduce that if such an Einsatz group was put to use and a special SS troop was to be present whenever a unit of some other civilian agency marches into a civilian territory, then from that one cannot conclude that there was some sort of a liaison between this military unit and the civilian agency. But I should like to repeat once more that this document shows only that it is a draft project of an expert - of an assistant expert who did not even ... I stress that this is a draft of an assistant expert (Hilfsreferent) which was not even countersigned by the expert, not to mention the department head, the central department head, office head or main office head.

Q. In that case, it appears that you claim that the document just shown you is merely a plan?

A. It is only the plan of the assistant expert chief of Department III, 225, and the head of Department III, 22, did not countersign it, nor did the head of Division III, 2 do so, nor did the chief of Office III countersign it.

COLONEL SMIRNOV: Mr. President, to show that the witness's testimony is not correct, I would like you to turn to a document signed by Schellenberger, Chief of the Central Division I, and to the chart which you will find in the original.

It shows that even the chiefs of the Einsatz commands were appointed -

Q. May I say something?

THE PRESIDENT: Just wait a minute. Just wait a minute.

Colonel Smirnov, the Tribunal would like you to read on from the place you had got to in Paragraph V, so that the document may be translated and translated now at once. You had got just to the place where it speaks of files, and at the end of "Files," Paragraph 2 -

COLONEL SMIRNOV: That is right, Mr. President. Do you want me to start reading from point (b) or from point (c)?

THE PRESIDENT: Paragraph 3.

COLONEL SMIRNOV: "Yes. Establishing of duplicate local files for each region -"

THE PRESIDENT: That is not what I meant. You had read Paragraph V, Roman V, down to the end of (2), the last words of which are "- deprived of passports," etc. The next paragraph is (3), small (3), Arabic (3) - "It is imperative to speed up -"

COLONEL SMIRNOV: That is right, Mr. President.

THE PRESIDENT: We want the whole of the document from there.

COLONEL SMIRNOV: Yes, Mr. President.

"It is imperative to speed up the obtaining of necessary economic and political materials, such as maps, dictionaries, stationery and office supplies.

5. Allocated members and agents of SD have to undergo a training course in order to get acquainted with the language and with the general conditions of life in Czechoslovakia. However, it might be advisable to train only persons appointed for the subsections as heads of foreign branches and managers of enterprises in order not to allow the number of persons becoming acquainted with the preparations to be too great.

6. Release from military conscription of the appointed persons.

7. Elaboration of plans, (a) for carrying out the task mentioned in Paragraph III; (b) for notification in due time, of the persons mentioned in Paragraph III5, II, I d and II c before invasion in order to give them the possibility to hide themselves to avoid arrest and deportation and to enable them to fulfil their missions.

8. Providing necessary passes in due time for entering zones of operation in order to secure a free passage and first-class living and working accommodations."

Shall I read Paragraph VI, Section VI, Mr. President?

THE PRESIDENT: Yes.

COLONEL SMIRNOV: VI. "Miscellaneous. It is suggested that wherever possible only militarily trained people be employed, as:

1. In the initial stages guerrilla and partisan warfare will probably have to be reckoned with.

2. For that reason the following weapons will be necessary: carbines, pistols, hand grenades, gas-masks, and if possible sub-machine guns.

3. Relations in the zone of military operation demand appropriate conduct.

VII -

THE PRESIDENT: You have read VII already. But you had better go back now to III, Paragraph 5, which I think you have not read and which has just been referred to.

COLONEL SMIRNOV: Yes, Mr. President. "Training of special agents (beforehand) from (mentioned in Item II - Id) persons of German extraction living in Czechoslovakia who are to take over the duties of secretaries of the most important enterprises for the purpose of preventing sabotage on the part of Czech organisations and offices."

THE PRESIDENT: Now I think you had better go back to II, Paragraph 2a, "training of suitable persons."

THE PRESIDENT: Wait a minute. Is the interpreting division ready?

INTERPRETER: Yes.

THE PRESIDENT: The interpreting division had better have the original documents in German and read the passages which I will indicate to them. I think you can go on, Colonel Smirnov, because this would be checked over in the translating division. The transcripts will be checked over against the original document ....

Now, you were reading II, Paragraph 2a, beginning with the words, "Training of suitable persons," were you not?

COLONEL SMIRNOV: That is right, Mr. President. May I continue?

THE PRESIDENT: Yes.

COLONEL SMIRNOV: "Besides" - interpreting verbatim from the Russian text - "besides staff members of the SD we should also try to employ honorary workers, because German agencies should not be deprived of proper personnel, and other frontier regions should take similar measures to provide for the necessary personnel.

b. Measures concerning Item II is are necessary for it may be found inexpedient to take people from the frontier regions for these new organisations, as an increase of work in these regions is expected anyhow."

THE PRESIDENT: I do not think you need read that. The Tribunal directs that the original documents as read into the transcripts, the shorthand notes; shall be checked over by the translating division against the original German text.

COLONEL SMIRNOV: Yes, Mr. President, we shall do it today.

THE PRESIDENT: The Tribunal directs that the original German document shall be re-translated into the other languages, namely, into English, into French, into Russian.

COLONEL SMIRNOV: Yes, Mr. President.

THE PRESIDENT: Now will you turn to the document which follows the document you have been reading and which appears to be some sort of letter from an Oberfuehrer of the SS. It is addressed to Dr. Best.

COLONEL SMIRNOV: Yes, Mr. President. Shall I read the whole document or just the first paragraph?

THE PRESIDENT: You had better read the first paragraph, anyhow.

COLONEL SMIRNOV: 2253. To SS Oberfuehrer, Dr. Best, Berlin. The contents follows:

"Introduction of the Einsatz of Gestapo and of the SD, Reichsfuehrer SS on the territory of Czechoslovakia. Text: "The suggestion to introduce the Gestapo and SD of which 12 detachments were provided for along the Czechoslovakian frontier will be subject to some modification as a result of the new situation arising from the fact that the Czechs may concede the Sudeten territory. Since some of the detachments will not be employed in the districts which will become German, we offer the following changes."

Shall I continue the quotation, Mr. President?

THE PRESIDENT: You do not need to read the rest. But is that document dated?

COLONEL SMIRNOV: No, Mr. President, there is no date on the document.

THE PRESIDENT: What you stated then did not come through.

COLONEL SMIRNOV: There is no date here, but there is another date on another document, which I would like the Tribunal's permission to submit. The document which is addressed to Dr. Best has no date, but the next document has a date, and it is this document that I consider extremely important. I would like the Tribunal's permission to submit it. It is a very short document, signed by Schellenberg.

"Berlin-1, 13th September, 1938, State Chancellery 1-113, to the Departmental Chief, III, SS Oberfuehrer Jost or his deputy.

Contents: Organisational Chart of the Einsatzkommandos, Operational Command."

Omitting the next sentence.

"According to the regulations of the above-mentioned letter, I enclose herewith a photostatic copy of the Einsatzkommandos Organisational Chart. The Chart has been prepared by Department C according to the enclosed form.

(Signed) The Chief of the Central Department I, 1aB

SS Hauptsturmfuehrer Schellenberg."

Mr. President, I should like you at this point to look at the chart which is attached, and which at that time already reproduced very correctly the organisation of the Einsatzkommandos. You have all the details of the organisation there showing eleven different units. Among those who are the leading collaborators of the Central Headquarters, in the second column, you can find that at that time the proposed chief of the gas chambers was included, the man to whom later all the reports about the activity of the gas chambers and the special death wagons were directed. They have been read here before.

THE PRESIDENT: I do not see that on the chart.

COLONEL SMIRNOV: It is in the second column.

THE PRESIDENT: Show me where. Where is it?

COLONEL SMIRNOV: (indicates.)

THE PRESIDENT: Yes. But cannot you show me where it is?

COLONEL SMIRNOV: Yes, Mr. President. There it is. (Indicating.)

(A document was handed to the President.)

THE PRESIDENT: But, Colonel Smirnov, there must be some words on the document which indicate what you are saying.

COLONEL SMIRNOV: I think, Mr. President, that what happened is to be explained by the inaccuracies of the translation; that is, by misunderstandings here. You see, I just drew your attention to the name Herr Rauff, the man who was mentioned there, to whom the reports about gas chambers and other methods of killing people were directed. And there he is. That post had been prepared and foreseen in that chart.

THE PRESIDENT: What is his name?

COLONEL SMIRNOV: Rauff, Mr. President. As early as 1939 we see his name and the post which he was to occupy. This is why I want to draw your attention to that.

May I continue the interrogation?

THE PRESIDENT: Colonel Smirnov, the Tribunal would like to have photostatic copies of this document.

COLONEL SMIRNOV: Yes, Mr. President; we have ten copies.

THE PRESIDENT: We anticipate that you are going to give the document to the witness and examine him upon it.

COLONEL SMIRNOV: Yes, Mr. President. The witness has it before him already.

THE WITNESS: Yes; I have a photostatic copy here.

COLONEL SMIRNOV: Mr. President, I should like to ask the witness the following question

BY COLONEL SMIRNOV:

Q. Witness, tell me this. Did not the confidential agents of the SD make and keep a list of persons who were to be annihilated, or exhausted by hard labour?

[Rolf-Heinz Hoeppner] A. Is the question being asked with reference to this document?

Q. In connection both with the document and with your knowledge of the situation.

A. I do not know whether lists were compiled.

COLONEL SMIRNOV: Mr. President, I am asking your permission to submit

THE PRESIDENT: The witness has not answered.

Will you answer the question?

THE WITNESS: I said that I did not know whether such lists were made.

COLONEL SMIRNOV: Mr. President, I request your permission to submit the second German document which does not concern the leading man of the SD.

THE PRESIDENT: Colonel Smirnov, we wanted you to ask the witness some questions so as to explain the chart. We have only just seen the chart. Have you no questions to ask on the chart?

COLONEL SMIRNOV: Yes, Mr. President, I will ask these questions.

BY COLONEL SMIRNOV:

Q. Do you have the chart before you, witness?

A. I have the photostatic copy of the manuscript chart.

(A document was handed to the witness.)

BY COLONEL SMIRNOV:

Q. You will now have the original of the chart.

Do you recognise the names of the collaborators mentioned in the chart?

A. Yes.

Q. Who was Jost?

A. Jost was the chief of Office III of the Foreign Information Service in the former SD Head Office, and he had been the first chief in Division VI of the Foreign Intelligence Service.

Q. Anyway, in 1938 he was a member of the SD?

A. Yes, he was a member of the SS Special Department, SD, and was chief of the Central Department III of the SD Head Office.

THE PRESIDENT: Wait a minute, I thought you told us the SS had got no connection with the SD. You are now telling us that this man was head of the SS Department, SD, are you not?

THE WITNESS: There must have been a false interpretation. Mr. President, may I repeat my answer?

THE PRESIDENT: Yes, repeat your answer.

THE WITNESS: Jost was the head of Central Department III, Foreign Intelligence Service, in the former SD Head Office. He was later the first Division Head of Office VI of the Foreign Intelligence Service, the predecessor of Gruppenfuehrer Schellenberg, who has already been heard by this Tribunal.

BY COLONEL SMIRNOV:

Q. Are you acquainted with the name of Ehrlinger?

A. Yes.

Q. Who was he?

A. I know Ehrlinger only from a later period. He was the last No. 1 Division Head of the Reichsicherheitshauptamt.

Q. He was also a member of the SD, was he not?

A. He also belonged to the SS Sonderformation SD.

Q. Do you know the name of Rauff? Do you recognise that?

THE PRESIDENT: The translation came through then to us that he was a member of the SS-SD.

THE WITNESS: He belonged to the SS Special SD Formation, about which we spoke in detail yesterday; that is to say, the merger of SS members who were in the Security Service, in the Gestapo and in the Criminal Police; that is to say, not all members of these, but only those who belonged to the SS, and also those who were honorary co-workers belonging to the SS, and also some other officers who worked with the Sicherheitspolizei - for instance, the border police and customs investigations officials arid later a number of Landrate, too.

COLONEL SMIRNOV: May I continue, Mr. President?

THE PRESIDENT: Go on.

COLONEL SMIRNOV: Thank you.

BY COLONEL SMIRNOV:

Q. Do you know the name of Rauff?

[Rolf-Heinz Hoeppner] A. Yes.

Q. What was he at that time

A. Rauff at that time was in charge of the motor cars belonging to the Security Service, as far as I remember today. I should like to say that at that time I had no direct connection with the Central Office in Berlin, as the Hauptamt of the SD was so organised at that time that between the lower divisions and the Head Office there was an organisational set-up, Oberabschnitt, which was abolished in September, 1939.

COLONEL SMIRNOV: Mr. President, the American prosecution kindly gave me the text of a document already submitted to the Tribunal which shows that orders concerning death vans were addressed specifically to Herr Rauff. These are the documents which I am now passing on to the Tribunal. These documents have been. submitted already. I am merely reminding you of them.

BY COLONEL SMIRNOV:

Q. And now, witness, I should also like you to look at the circle showing "Einsatzkommando" in the chart. Do you recognise the names mentioned there?

A. I do not know yet which names you mean.

Q. I am talking about the last circle, Einsatzkommando 2, 3, 8, 9, and others. Have you found the place?

A. Is that another document?

Q. No; that is precisely the same document.

A. On the manuscript document which I have, I can see no such circles. It must be another document attached to another letter.

Q. Please look at the circles around "Einsatzkommando." Do you recognise any of the names within those circles?

A. On the document which is appended to the one signed by Obersturmfuehrer Seitl.

Q. Do you recognise the names there? Particularly, did you know Gottschalk?

A. No.

Q. Dr. Lehmann?

A. No.

Q. Schultze?

A. I gather that there must be a confusion of names there, and it should be "Schultz."

Q. That is right, "Schultz."

A. Yes, I know. Here we have "Schultze."

Q. That is a mistake. I have it as "Schultz."

A. I know Schultz, but not Schultze.

Q. Was he a collaborator of the SD?

A. I think that he was at that time Stabspolizei Chief somewhere in Northern Germany.

Q. Do you know Biermann?

A. I do not know him personally, but I have heard his name.

Q. Who was he?

A. I beg your pardon. I think that he was then a chief of the Secret State Police. Later he became Inspector of the Security Police and the SD.

Q. Do you know Heinrich?

A. I do not know Dr. Heinrich.

Q. You do not know him?

A. Was he the commander of Einsatzkommando 10?

Q. No, Einsatzkommando 4, Hoehnscheid.

A. I did not know him.

Q. Hoffmann?

A. No.

Q. I do suppose that you knew Stahlecker, though?

A. I knew him by name but I did not know him personally.

Q. You are acquainted with the post he held, though?

A. I think he was then inspector of the Security Police, or Stabspolizeileiter or Oberabschnittsfuehrer, but I cannot quite remember what he was.

Q. And do you know Guenther?

A. Guenther, if I remember right, was at that time inspector in Berlin.

Q. Inspector of SD, was he not?

A. There were no SD inspectors at that time; there were only inspectors of the Security Police.

COLONEL SMIRNOV: I have no more questions about the chart, Mr. President. May I ask some other questions?

THE PRESIDENT: Wait a minute - These letters "EK" in the circle at the bottom mean Einsatzkommando, I suppose, do they? And will you tell the Tribunal What the purpose of the chart is? What is the organisation which it is supposed to define?

THE WITNESS: The translation did not come through. Could you repeat your question, Mr. President?

THE PRESIDENT: What is the organisation which the chart is supposed to define?

THE WITNESS: I suppose that it is the preparation of some plan of Gruppenfuehrer Heydrich to employ the offices of the Security Police and the SD, which were under his jurisdiction in case of possible complications with Czechoslovakia. The abbreviation "EGA" will mean Einsatzkommando (task force unit). Actually, later, when the German troops marched into Czechoslovakia units of the Security Police and of the SD went along which, just like the Einsatzkommandos and the Einsatzgruppen in the East, were mobile units of a very special nature which had been newly set up and had entirely new tasks, and which were dissolved later when the State Police office in Prague and the SD Department Prague were organised.

THE PRESIDENT: Well, I am not concerned with whether they were later dissolved. Heydrich, I suppose, was in command of the whole of the SD, was he not?

THE WITNESS: Yes, Heydrich was head of the SD Main Office and at the same time head of the Security Police, both offices personally united in him.

THE PRESIDENT: Was Stahlecker a member of the Information Branch of the SD that you are speaking of?

THE WITNESS: I cannot state that for certain. If I remember correctly, Stahlecker had at that time some function in East Prussia.

THE PRESIDENT: You said just now, I thought, that Stahlecker was in Berlin?

THE WITNESS: In East Prussia at that time. In my opinion, Guenther was in Berlin. His name was also mentioned previously.

THE PRESIDENT: Yes. Well, was he a member of the SD Information Service?

THE WITNESS: Yes, I think that he was then head of the SD, Berlin Oberabschnitt (Oberabschnittsfuehrer). I cannot say it with certainty.

THE PRESIDENT: Ehrlanger, was Ehrlanger also a member of the SD Information Service?

THE WITNESS: I do not know in what office Ehrlanger was then employed. I heard his name only later when he became head of Office I.

THE PRESIDENT: What about Rauff?

THE WITNESS: Rauff was then in charge of the motor transportation corps of the SD head office, but here, too, I cannot state for certain whether

THE PRESIDENT: What about the Information Service of the SD, was he a member? Was Rauff a member of the SD Information Services?

THE WITNESS: He was head of a technical department in the SD head office. In the SD head office at that time, which handled foreign information and domestic information, there were several technical offices in the central head office No. I which were at the disposal of the entire Amt.

THE PRESIDENT: Well, what about his functions? One of his functions was to work in the Information Service of the SD, in the Domestic Information Service of the SD?

THE WITNESS: He was also in charge of the motor cars for the Domestic Information Service.

THE PRESIDENT: Yes, but you can answer the question yes or no. Was it part of his function to work in the Domestic Information Service of the SD?

THE WITNESS: Not in the Information Service as such, as far as I know. No, he only -

THE PRESIDENT: Well, he had no competence, as you call it, in the Domestic Information Service of the SD?

THE WITNESS: As far as I can remember, he was only in charge of the motor transportation of the SD Head Office; also for the Domestic Information Service.

THE PRESIDENT: Does not that chart show that the SD was working in transport co-ordination with the Gestapo?

THE WITNESS: In my opinion the chart only shows that the head of the organisations was prepared, in case of a march into Czechoslovakia, to employ men of both organisations there.

THE PRESIDENT: And do not these documents show that your comment about the first document was inaccurate and that that document was being used by Schellenberg in September, 1938, for the purpose of organising the SD in Czechoslovakia?

THE WITNESS: I think it is impossible that this document should have been used, because otherwise the date would have been filled in; and the Roman figures at the end of the document would have been indicated. Whether another draft was made later and submitted to Schellenberg, that I do not know.

THE PRESIDENT: Well, you see that the first document is headed Roman III, Arabic 225. The letter to Dr. Best is also headed Roman III, 225, and it refers to the suggestion which is no doubt contained in that document; and the chart itself is also headed III, 225.

THE WITNESS: Yes; I suppose that some other draft was made, for this is months later. This draft was almost certainly not used because then the Roman figures would under all circumstances have been indicated. In any case, the Roman figure III of that time had nothing to do with the later organisation III, because the department from which the accused Office III originated was Central Department II/2.

COLONEL SMIRNOV: Mr. President, in connection with the witness's replies on the fact that he does not know whether the confidential persons of the SD made up lists of persons who were to be annihilated or mobilised forcibly or else arrested and placed in concentration camps, I would like your permission to submit another short document pertaining to another country, to Poland, which contains the instructions of the Blockstellenleiter of the SD in Poland to his trusted collaborators. I ask your permission to read this document into the record.

THE WITNESS: May I say one more word? There is nothing in my document about annihilation or concentration camps.

COLONEL SMIRNOV: You will now have the document before you.

May I quote the document? It is USSR 522. I quote:

"Security Service of the Reichsfuehrer SS, Block Station Mogilno, 24th August, 1944." Translating verbatim. "To Trusted persons. Subtitle The preparation of the lists of Poles." The text follows: "I have repeatedly pointed out to you the necessity of paying special attention to the Poles. For that reason, I am giving below the speech of the Reichsfuehrer of the SS, Himmler, delivered on 15th, March 1940, at the meeting of the concentration camp commanders in former Poland, and according to the directives given in that speech, I ask you to submit to me the list of names of all the Poles concerned." Extract from speech, I quote: "For that reason, all our collaborators, both men and women, should consider it their most important and urgent task to prevent all unscrupulous leaders of the Polish people from exercising their activity. You, as commanders of the concentration camps, will know best how to fulfil this task. All skilled workers of Polish origin are to be utilised in our war industry; later all Poles will disappear from the face of the earth. In fulfilling this very responsible task, you must, within the prescribed limits of time, exterminate the Poles. I give this directive to all the camp commanders. The hour is drawing closer when every German will have to prove himself. For that reason, the great German nation should understand that its most important task now is to exterminate all the Poles. I expect all my trusted collaborators to report to me immediately all Polish grumblers (Miesmacher) and defeatists. For such a task we must also utilise children and aged persons, who can help us considerably, because of their so-called friendly attitude towards the Poles.

Extract from Himmler's speech on 15th March 1940. Heil Hitler.

SS Hauptsturmfuehrer

(Signature illegible)"

BY COLONEL SMIRNOV:

Q. I would like to ask you now, after seeing this document, whether you still deny that the workers of the SD in the occupied territories trained and oriented all persons they could use to make up lists of such persons that were to be annihilated?

A. Yes, I deny that, especially as I cannot state whether this document is a genuine one or not.

Q. This document was captured by the Polish Army in Mogilno in the building of the SD.

A. I take, for example, the words "camp commander meeting" as being absolutely impossible. I do not see what it could refer to and it seems to me impossible to ascertain what "Polish grumblers and defeatists" might mean. It seems to me absolutely self-evident that the Poles hoped that Germany would lose the war.

Q. I am not asking you to make propagandistic speeches on the subject of Poland, I am asking you something quite different. I am asking you this question: Are you still denying the fact that the SD compelled those collaborating with it to make lists of persons to be annihilated?

A. Yes, I deny that.

COLONEL SMIRNOV: I have no more questions.

THE PRESIDENT: What evidence is there that this document was found in the SD Headquarters?

COLONEL SMIRNOV: It was not found in the SD Headquarters. That was not properly translated.

THE PRESIDENT: Your answer did not come through.

COLONEL SMIRNOV: This was not found at the central headquarters, Mr. President. It was not translated to you correctly if that is what was said. The document was found by the Polish Army -

THE PRESIDENT: What was translated to me was that it was captured by the Polish Army at the SD Headquarters. Is that right?

COLONEL SMIRNOV: That is right, but not at the central headquarters of the SD for Poland but at the headquarters in the Block Station of Mogilno.

THE PRESIDENT: I did not say anything about the central headquarters. All I want to know is what evidence there is that it was found at the headquarters of the SD.

COLONEL SMIRNOV: Yes, Mr. President. May I now read the document of the Polish Delegation on the subject which says, "It is hereby certified that the submitted document in the German language dated 24th August, 1943, consists of the instructions of the Security Police of the Reichsfuehrer SS, in the city of Mogilno, containing an extract from Himmler's speech and that it is the exact photostatic copy of the original submitted by the Chief Commission for the Investigation of Nazi Crimes in Poland."

The original was found in an envelope. In the left-hand corner at the top there was stated "Landrat of the Area of Mogilno of the Governmental District Bodenschatz." The rest contains a number and a statement in German, but the date is 28th August, 1943.

THE PRESIDENT: Colonel, I am sorry, I did not hear the beginning of what you said. What are you reading from now?

COLONEL SMIRNOV: I am reading, Mr. President, from the certificate which the Polish delegation submitted on the subject of this document. This was a document which was submitted to us by the Polish Delegation.

THE PRESIDENT: How did you identify this particular document? You see, we have a document produced before us which appears to have nothing on it which connects it with that certificate. I mean, how do you connect it with this certificate?

COLONEL SMIRNOV: Mr. President, I was just handed a note here from our documentary section which says that since the Tribunal has the original, the original does not have the certificate of the Polish Delegation attached to it, whereas I have the certificate attached to my document, and that is why I wanted to read it to you. I am very sorry about the mistake. You will receive the certificate.

THE PRESIDENT: I see - and the certificate you have, identifies the translation in Russian? Is that right?

COLONEL SMIRNOV: Mr. President, yesterday I myself verified the translation which I have with the original, and I have found it to be accurate and correct, and the certificate also states that the Russian translation is correct.

THE PRESIDENT: Colonel Smirnov, you must offer in evidence that certificate in order to make it clear that this is the document which was found at this SD headquarters at Mogilno. That should be attached to this exhibit. Has this got a number, this exhibit? 522, is that it?

COLONEL SMIRNOV: Yes, the number is USSR 522, Mr. President.

THE PRESIDENT: Well, we will have to have the certificate attached to it; then we shall be able to look at it.

COLONEL SMIRNOV: Yes, Mr. President. I have no more questions to ask this witness.

THE PRESIDENT: The Tribunal will adjourn.

(A short recess was taken.)

COLONEL SMIRNOV: Mr. President in connection with one of the points to which my esteemed American colleague has drawn my attention, I request your permission to put another question here to the witness concerning the first document which I submitted.

THE PRESIDENT: Which was the first?

COLONEL SMIRNOV: USSR 509, the chart.

THE PRESIDENT: Yes.

COLONEL SMIRNOV: Thank you.

CROSS-EXAMINATION BY COLONEL SMIRNOV:

Q. Witness, will you kindly tell us-do you deny that Gengenbach, whose name is to be found in this chart as belonging to the Einsatzstab - you will be shown the chart in a minute - was a member of the SD?

(The document is handed to the witness).

[Rolf-Heinz Hoeppner] A. He was on the staff of the SD.

Q. He was a member of the SD?

A. Yes, he was. He was Gruppenleiter of III-A. He was my immediate predecessor.

Q. Tell us then - was it not you who became his deputy later on?

A. I was the successor of Gengenbach but not his deputy. When I came to Berlin he was already dead. Besides Gengenbach, was not in Berlin then for, as far as I can recall today from talks I had with him later on, he was at Munich. I met him only during the war.

Q. But, at any rate, you did afterwards hold the post which had been held before by Gengenbach?

A. The position which Gengenbach held later in Berlin. I took over from him. He was Gruppenleiter III-A just as I was.

COLONEL SMIRNOV: Thank you very much. The American prosecution, Mr. President, has a copy of the documents which have already been submitted under No. USA 175 and USA 174, and it is stated here in the places underlined that the head of the division III-A was Gengenbach, that is the same man whose name is to be found in the chart. I have no further questions to put to the witness, Mr. President.

THE PRESIDENT: Has the speech of Himmler, dated 15th March, 1940, already been put in evidence?

COLONEL SMIRNOV: As far as I know, Mr. President, no. At any rate, I do not know this speech.

THE PRESIDENT: Thank you. Now, Dr. Gawlik.

RE-DIRECT EXAMINATION BY DR. GAWLIK (for the SD):

Q. Witness, do you still have Exhibit USSR 509?

A. I have no documents at all.

(The document is handed to the witness.)

Q. Witness, please look at Page 1. What was the task of these Einsatzgruppen (task force units) which were to be employed in Czechoslovakia?

A. I do not know: I had nothing to do with the preparation of these tasks.

Q. I said please look at Page 1.

A. "To secure political life and to secure national economy," it says on Page 1.

Q. Was this a completely different task from that which later in 1941 was given to Einsatzgruppen A, B, C, and D in the East?

A. I do not know the tasks in the East very well, either because I had nothing to do with them, but as far as I am informed the Einsatzgruppen in the East certainly had nothing to do with safeguarding the national economy. The Einsatzgruppen in the East had to secure the rear army area.

Q. Please look at the chart, the organisation of these Einsatzgruppen.

A. The hand-written one or the printed one?

Q. The second one. With the aid of this chart, can you answer the question whether these Einsatzgruppen belonged to the organisation of the SD?

A. You mean the chart that says "Staff SS Gruppenfuehrer Heydrich" at the top?

Q. Yes, that is the chart I mean.

A. No, that was not an organisation of the Security Service but was something completely new.

Q. Regarding the tasks these Einsatzgruppen or these Einsatzstabe had, were they a part of the duties of the Security Service?

A. I do not know the tasks which were assigned to these Einsatzstabe In any event, the task mentioned on Page 1, "securing the national economy," is not a task of the Security Service; it is not a task related to the Information Service nor does the "safeguarding of political life" have anything to do with the Information Service.

Q. Were parts of the organisation of the SD used by these Einsatzstabe? Can you answer the question with the aid of this chart?

A. As far as the chart shows, parts of the organisation were not used but only individual members of the Security Service, just as in the case of the State Police too. The same will probably have applied later in connection with the Einsatzgruppen in the East, that is, it can be compared with being drafted into the Wehrmacht.

Q. Were the individual members of the Security Service, by being assigned to the Einsatzstabe, no longer active in the Security Service?

A. No, of course not. For they received completely different tasks. Again, I can only make this comparison: If a judge is drafted into the Army, then he no longer carries on his activity as a judge.

Q. Were the activities and tasks of these Einsatzstabe generally known to the members of the Security Service, particularly the members of the subordinate agencies of the Leitabschnitte of the Aussenstellen?

A. Not in the least.

Q. Now, I come to the second document that deals with the letter of the Blockstelle Mogilno.

(The document is handed to the witness.)

Q. What was a "Blockstelle"?

A. In the structure of the Security Service, the term "Blockstelle" did not exist but, nevertheless, it is possible that regional offices (Aussenstellen) organised sub-branches and then used this term; in general, what was subordinate to a regional office was called an "Observer" (Beobachter).

Q. What was the staff of an Aussenstelle in general?

A. According to the period and according to the importance of the Aussenstelle, it differed considerably. On the average, in, say, 1943 or 1944 there were one or two regular officials in a branch and a large number of honorary workers whereby the head of the branch was sometimes an honorary official and sometimes a regular one.

Q. Was the Blockstelle above an Aussenstelle or was it subordinate to it?

A. Above the Aussenstelle was the Abschnitt, not the Blockstelle and, as I said before, the different Aussenstelle sometimes selected terms for subordinate offices which were not really officially organised. "Observers" (Beobachter) were, however, organised.

Q. Did Amt III issue any orders as established in this document?

A. No, under no circumstances.

Q. Then is this the case of the head of the Aussenstelle in Mogilno acting on his own initiative? I mean the head of the Blockstelle?

A. In case Himmler did make this speech, that would be true. I can imagine Himmler saying that he expected something from all his men when talking to camp commanders.

Q. I am not speaking of Himmler. I am speaking of the orders of the head of the Blockstelle.

A. But the instructions are in the speech of Himmler or do you mean the instructions in the first sentence "to give especial attention to Poland"? The head of the Blockstelle in Mogilno will, of course, have cared for the Poles in the same way as he cared for the Germans. He was naturally interested in the general attitude and frame of mind of the Poles, and he reported to the main office, to Group III-d.

Q. Then I show you Document PS-3876.

THE PRESIDENT: How does this arise from the cross-examination?

DR. GAWLIK: Mr. President, I have a few more questions in connection with the questions which your Honour asked yesterday at the end of the session relating to distribution.

THE PRESIDENT: You are putting in some document which has not been referred to before.

DR. GAWLIK: Mr. President, the document was submitted yesterday by the American prosecution.

THE PRESIDENT: Oh, well, it was. I beg your pardon.

THE WITNESS: I have here the English text of the document.

Q. Please look at Page 45 now - the distribution. Did commanders of the Security Police and the SD belong to the Einsatzgruppen A, B, C, and D?

A. No, that is something different. The Einsatzgruppen were mobile units, which advanced together with the Wehrmacht in the rear army area. The offices of the commanders were offices in the civilian administration. When an area was taken into civil administration, the commander's post or office was set up.

Q. How were the Einsatzgruppen A, B, C, and D organised?

A. They were divided into the Einsatzkommandos.

Q. What names did these Einsatzkommandos have?

A. These Einsatzkommandos had no names at all, as I said yesterday, they were numbered from 1 to 10, as far as I can recall, possibly even to 11 or 12.

Q. Please look at the distribution. There it says that the chiefs of the Einsatzgruppen A, B, C, and D received copies for the commanders of the Security Police, and the SD.

A. No, that is wrongly translated. It should be for the Kommandeure of the Security Police and the SD, not for the chiefs, that is the Kommandeure of the Security Police who were subordinate to the chiefs of the Security Police and the SD. To state it more clearly, the Einsatzkommandos were not led by a Kommandeur of the Security Police and the SD, but by the Kommandeure of Einsatzkommandos 1, 2, 3, etc. In the territory which was under civil administration, the situation was the same as in occupied France. There were agencies of the Kommandeure of the Security Police and of the SD. That was something quite different from the Einsatzkommandos.

Q. Who were the officers superior to the Kommandeure?

A. To which Kommandeure?

Q. Of the Security Police and of the SD.

A. The commanders of the Security Police and the SD.

Q. Who were their superiors?

A. The chief of the Security Police and the SD in Berlin.

Q. Who was the superior of Einsatzgruppen A, B, C, and D?

A. That cannot be answered in one word. In reality the chiefs of the Einsatzgruppen had two superiors. In the first place, they were assigned, to the army group in question, and had to take instructions from the chief of the army group. On the other hand, they received instructions from the chief of the Security Police and the SD. That is the very reason why I said yesterday that they were entirely unique and different.

Q. Now I ask you again. If the Kommandeure of the Security Police and the SD did not belong to the Einsatzgruppen. A, B, C, and D -

THE PRESIDENT: Dr. Gawlik, has not all this been thoroughly gone into already? I mean, we have got the document. We have asked the witness a number of questions and he has given his answers: You are now asking him the same questions over again.

DR. GAWLIK: Mr. President, I only have one more question in regard to the copies.

THE PRESIDENT: Ask your one question, then.

Q. Why did the chiefs of the Einsatzgruppen A, B, C, and D receive copies for the commanders of the Security Police and the SD if they were completely separate organisations?

A. Probably there were different organisations but in certain cases the people were the same; or, as I assume, the distribution was misleading. I had a German copy yesterday. Various words were used for "Kommandeur." Sometimes it was commander and sometimes another word, Befehlshaber. Those are completely different functions.

THE PRESIDENT: The witness can retire. Dr. Gawlik, your next witness.

DR. GAWLIK: With the permission of the Tribunal, I call as the next witness Dr. Roessner.

(DR. HANS ROESSNER, a witness, took the stand and testified as follows):
BY THE PRESIDENT:

Q. Will you state your name, please?

A. Hans Roessner.

Q. Will you repeat this oath after me:

I swear by God, the Almighty and Omniscient, that I will speak the pure truth and will withhold and add nothing.

(The witness repeated the oath.)

THE PRESIDENT: You may sit down.

DIRECT EXAMINATION ON THE WITNESS HANS ROESSNER **BY DR. GAWLIK:**

Q. When were you born?

A. 1910, in Dresden.

Q. Please describe briefly your professional career.

A. After the customary schooling, I graduated in 1930, then studied the German language and literature, German history and Protestant theology. From 1936 on I was assistant at the University of Bonn. From 1939 to 1940 military service. In 1940 deferred for the University of Bonn and emergency service in the Reichssicherheitshauptamt, Amt III.

Q. Since when have you been a Party member?

A. Since 1937.

Q. What office did you have in the Reich Security Main Office?

A. I was an expert (Referent), later section chief in Group IIIC, Amt III.

Q. Are you well acquainted with the tasks, methods and aims of Group IIIC?

A. Yes, I am.

Q. Please wait a little before you answer. In addition, do you also know of the tasks, methods and aims of Amt III?

A. Yes, I also know these, because they were fundamentally the same as those of Group IIIC.

Q. What were the tasks and aims of Amt III since 1939?

A. Amt III was a domestic German information service. It had set its aims and tasks to a great extent itself and worked independently in the domestic German sphere of life; that is to say it took up important questions of domestic German life in various fields, such as economics, culture, administration, law and others as far as information service was concerned and in particular attempted to collect and sum up criticism on the part of the population regarding mistakes, faulty developments, measures, etc., and to report on them.

Q. Please give a few examples by way of explanation.

A. For example, every week and sometimes daily, Amt III reported on the opinion of the population on German propaganda to the agencies concerned. Beyond that, in 1943 for example, Amt III, through its reports, prevented the closing of German universities in spite of Germany's total war effort.

Q. The prosecution has submitted, on Page 11 of the English Trial Brief, that Amt III had to carry out police investigations in all phases of German life. Did Amt III have to carry out police investigations?

A. Never did Amt III as long as it existed have any police tasks.

Q. Did the SD, Amt III, have the practical task and the fundamental aim of giving information through its information centre on actual and possible opponents of the Nazi movement? This refers to Page 17 of the Trial Brief.

A. No. Amt III was basically not an information service on opponents, but on the German domestic life.

Q. What was the purpose of the information service reports of Amt III? In particular, was the main object to support the leaders of the Party and State as partners of a conspiracy and to, keep them in power?

A. No. Amt III never had such a task and did not set up such a task for itself. The task of the information service of Amt III was to furnish an extensive and objective picture of the domestic problems of German internal life and to present them in an open and direct manner.

Q. Did the members of Amt III know that the leaders of the Party and the State were participating in a secret plan for the purpose of committing crimes against peace, war crimes and crimes against humanity?

A. To my knowledge, the members of Amt III did not know anything about this. All the material collected by Amt III is evidence to the contrary.

Q. Can you answer this question for the members and honorary members of the subordinate agencies?

A. Yes.

Q. Did the dose collaborators of the chief of Amt III know of such a conspiracy?

A. No. Not even the closest collaborators knew anything about this.

Q. On what is your knowledge based for your answers to the last few questions?

A. I often participated in internal Gruppenleiter conferences with the chief of Amt III.

Q. Were the tasks and aims of the Domestic Information Service known to all workers even in the subordinate agencies?

A. Yes, the tasks and aims were known to the workers and honorary workers of the subordinate agencies. They were continually announced in the individual meetings, lectures, etc.

Q. On what is your knowledge based by reason of which you have answered my last question?

A. On numerous individual conferences and meetings where I myself announced the aims and tasks of Amt III.

Q. In the reports made on a situation, were the, names of the persons mentioned?

A. No, not usually, since the SD was not interested in the names of individual persons, but in typical examples of questions regarding the different spheres of life.

Q. In giving personnel data, was the aim being pursued, to bring persons into influential State positions who would not oppose the execution of a plan for committing war crimes, crimes against peace and crimes against humanity?

A. No, Amt III did not have any such aims. Such data and reports of the SD were kept separate from the reports on the general situation. The SD; Amt III, gave personnel data, but did not have permission to pass judgement on people. That was the sole task of the Hoheitstrager of the Party.

Q. What was the purpose of giving out information on personnel data by the SD?

A. This was to supplement the political judgement and purely specialised judgement of the individual Party offices and departments and present if possible a total picture of the personality, character, professional ability, political attitude and personal way of living independent of any departmental point of view or of any power or political interests.

Q. The prosecution describes the task of the SD as follows: the task consisted in taking necessary steps to destroy the opposition or to make it harmless. Does this correspond with the actual facts and ideological aims of Amt III since 1939?

A. No, by no means. I have already emphasised the fact that Amt III was not an intelligence service for gathering news about opponents.

Q. When did Amt III give up this task?

A. Amt III never had this task.

Q. The prosecution further submitted that the SD had an extensive spy net that would spy on the German people in their daily work, in the streets and even in the sacred precincts of the Church. This is on Page 66 of the English trial brief. Did the SD conduct such an extensive spy network as described?

A. During the whole period of its existence, Amt III never worked with spies or a spy network in the domestic German sphere of life. The spy network would have contradicted all the basic aims of this internal German information service.

Q. Did the SD for its tasks use only regular officials?

A. No, they were by far in the minority. The work of the internal SD was dependent upon the big staff of honorary workers from all parts of the country and all professions.

Q. Can you give any figures?

A. I cannot give accurate figures, but in the last few years we estimated the honorary workers at some 10,000. They worked on a completely voluntary basis and a large part worked on their own initiative for the internal SD.

Q. From what point of view were the confidential agents chosen for the information service for internal German spheres of life?

A. Such confidential agents had to offer proof that, free from selfish interests, they would give clear and objective information on questions relating to their professional spheres or to the population amongst whom they lived and on other concerns and worries and statements of criticism of the population with which they came into contact. In addition, they had to be persons of decent character.

Q. Did these agents have to be members of the Party?

A. No, by no means. It was even desired to have as large as possible a percentage of non-Party members amongst these agents of the SD so as to get a complete and independent picture of the total situation within Germany through them.

Q. Did the agents have to be members of the SS?

A. No, the percentage of members of the SS amongst these agents was, according to my estimate, still less than that of Party members.

Q. What were the tasks of these confidential agents?

A. The tasks varied. In Amt III we had agents who were to give general information on the frame of mind, attitude and opinions of the population on urgent questions during the course of the war years. Then we had another type of agent who gave information on their professional cares and worries and on questions relating to the specialist fields into which they had insight.

Q. What was the task of the SD Arbeitskreise?

A. In the so-called SD Arbeitskreise the agents of the subordinate agencies were called together for free and frank conferences. In these Arbeitskreise questions and problems concerning technical matters and measures of the Party and State agencies were discussed with absolute sincerity and frankness. The results of these discussions and criticism were summarised and then sent to Amt III in Berlin. The main prerequisite was absolute objectivity and absolute frankness and criticism.

Q. Did the agents or the Arbeitskreise work under any special cloak of secrecy? This question refers to the Trial Brief, Page 16.

A. I do not know what you mean by the expression, "cloak of secrecy." I can answer that these agents never acted under any special personal secrecy and these Arbeitskreise, which I just mentioned, had no special obligation for secrecy. They were publicly known as such.

Q. Were there, apart from those employed, other agents of the SD?

A. Yes. In the last few years of our work there were more and more representatives of the various professions and walks of life, who on their own initiative came with some worry, criticism, or some positive suggestion to the SD, in order, on the basis of a personal confidence in the SD, to be able to turn over their worries to it.

Q. Now, I show you prosecution Documents PS-1650, D-569 and PS-1514. They deal with the Kugel decree concerning the treatment of Russian prisoners of war and the turning over of prisoners of war to the Gestapo. It is the first point of the Indictment VI (c) against the SD.

Was the SD Amt III competent for executing this decree?

A. No, the SD was not competent because Amt III, from the beginning, had no executive power.

Q. Can you give any further explanation of the individual documents?

A. The documents all refer to the Secret State Police, the Gestapo. One document merely mentions the chief of Amt III. The document of the Wehrmacht also refers to the Gestapo.

Q. Was the SD, the Domestic Information Service, used to carry out these decrees?

A. No, this would have been in opposition to its tasks.

Q. Did the SD, the Domestic Information Service, participate in the deportation of citizens of the occupied territories for forced labour?

A. No, this was an executive task for which the SD, Amt III, was not competent.

Q. Did the SD have the power to inflict punishment on forced labourers? This question refers to Page 1941 of the English transcript.

A. No, this also would have been an executive task.

Q. Did the SD, through its reports, contribute to deportations?

A. No, quite on the contrary. Amt III repeatedly showed up the negative effects of such measures.

Q. Did the SD have any control over the forced labourers brought into the Reich?

A. No, this control would also have been an executive task which Amt III did not have.

Q. Now, I show you Document PS-205. This is a memorandum on the general principles for the treatment of foreigners employed in the Reich. Did the SD have any part in the drafting of this memorandum?

A. Yes, to my knowledge the SD, Amt III, had a part in the drawing up of this memorandum. It made its material available in setting up directives for a positive treatment of foreign workers. This material, which was used in this memorandum, corresponded moreover to the basic principles of the domestic SD in the treatment of national questions in the European area.

Q. What is your knowledge based on as to the drawing up of this memorandum?

A. Part of the material comes from Group IIIC, in which I myself was section chief.

Q. Did the SD, Amt III, have the right to make confiscations? This question refers to the part of the Indictment VI (k) of the Trial Brief.

A. No, the SD had no right to confiscate. This also would have been an executive task.

Q. Did the SD Domestic Information Service participate in the confiscation and distribution of public and private property?

A. No.

Q. On Page 51 of the Trial Brief it says, referring to Document 071-PS:

"In connection with the planned confiscation of scientific, religious and art archives, an agreement was reached between Rosenberg and Heydrich on the basis of which the SD and Rosenberg were to co-operate closely in the confiscation of public and private collections."

Was there any such close co-operation between the SD and the staff of the defendant Rosenberg, his agencies or any of his deputies?

A. No. In this document we are again confronted by the customary mistake concerning the Security Police and the SD. Such co-operation, if it existed, would have had to be known to me, since Group IIIC would have been competent for it.

DR. GAWLIK: Mr. President, I now come to my last point. Shall I begin it?

THE PRESIDENT: Have you any questions to ask upon it? It looks as if you had, so perhaps we had better adjourn.

DR. GAWLIK: There are 34 questions.

(A recess was taken until 1400 hours.)

HANS ROESSNER RESUMED

DIRECT EXAMINATION BY DR. GAWLIK:

Q. I come now to my last point, the persecution of the Church, Trial Brief, Paragraph VII b. I should like to call the attention of the Tribunal to the fact that the SD is charged with its activities only until the 12th of May, 1941. Page 60 of the English text of the Trial Brief. My taking of testimony limits itself to the time since the creation of the RSHA in 1939 up to 12th May, 1941.

THE PRESIDENT: Wait a minute. Which does that mean, May, 1940, or May, 1941?

DR. GAWLIK: The 12th of May, 1941, Page 64, the last section but one of the Trial Brief, where it states that the political treatment of the Church was divided between the Gestapo and the SD and from that point on was taken over entirely by the Gestapo.

BY DR. GAWLIK:

Q. Did Division IIIC handle Church questions?

A. No.

Q. Did any other office in Division III handle Church questions?

A. No. Since the foundation of Amt III, no Church matters were handled in that office at all.

Q. What was handled in Amt III?

A. In Amt III, Group IIIC, only general religious matters were handled in various spheres of life.

Q. In what manner were the matters regarding religious life handled?

A. The principles of the handling were the same as for any other sphere of life. It was the task of Amt III to observe all the religious wishes, cares, proposals and movements of the German population and the influence of the German religious movements and the Christian creeds on the opinion, spirit and attitude of the German people in the Reich and to report on them.

Q. The prosecution has stated that the persecution of the Churches was one of the fundamental purposes of the SD and Sicherheitspolizei.

That is Page 1999 of the English transcript.

Did the SD have this basic purpose in common with the Security Police?

A. To my knowledge as responsible head of a department, no such common purpose existed.

Q. Did the SD on its own initiative have and realize any such programme?

A. No. That would have been against all the principles of our work.

Q. Did the SD, Amt III, practically engage in the persecution of the Churches?

A. No.

Q. Was the SD, Amt III, in any way involved by the Gestapo in an alleged persecution of the Church?

A. No. Between the Gestapo and Amt III there was a complete separation of material, personnel, and organisation.

Q. Was the SD involved in the persecution of the Church by any other office of the Party and State?

A. No. The SD worked quite independently in this sphere. No offices of the Party or of the State were entitled to give direct assignments to the SD.

Q. Were the regular and honorary members of the SD under control in the matter of their attitude toward the Church, and induced to leave the Church by means of threats?

A. No. I know nothing about that, and it would also have been contrary to our fundamental conceptions. Until the end, a large number of regular and honorary officials were and remained members of the Christian Churches. I might mention that the head of Amt III himself left the Protestant Church as late as 1942.

Q. Did the SD, Amt III, undertake any secret proceedings in the fight against the Church? This question is relevant to Page 58 of the Trial Brief.

A. Neither in this sphere nor in any other sphere of activity of Amt III were there any concealed aims or secret proceedings. As head of a department, I would have had to know of them.

Q. I submit to you prosecution Document PS-1815. Will you look at Page 59 of this, please?

A. May I ask ... the document does not go up to Page 59; is it Page 29 or 39?

Q. It must be 29 or 39.

A. I have both pages here.

Q. Will you look at Page 1?

A. I have Page 1 here.

Q. There it says that the former workers should be detailed to the Gestapo for the time being.

Was this order given on the ground that organisation, tasks, aims and activities in the sphere of Church affairs were the same in Amt III of the SD and Amt IV of the Gestapo?

A. This order was given for an entirely different reason. Since Amt III and Amt IV were entirely different offices, the transfer of the former SD employees to Amt IV would have taken too long, and for that reason this planned transfer was undertaken in the form of an order so as to save time for the work.

Q. Will you now comment on Page 29 of the prosecution document? That is Number 18. Will you look at the first two sentences. Can it not be seen from that that the SD handled Church matters in collaboration with the State Police and the Criminal Police?

A. The document before me shows that SD, Amt III, did not at all participate in this connection. At the time of this conversation in 1942, Amt III, according to the order of separation which was previously mentioned, was not allowed, on principle, to handle Church matters.

Q. Will you now look at Page 1 and Page 2. On the basis of these two pages, the prosecution has suggested - I refer to Page 58 of the Trial Brief - that the handling of Church matters had until then been divided between the Gestapo and the SD, and that the SD files on Church opposition were then to be transferred to the Gestapo, but the SD was to retain material concerning Church influence on public life. Will you make a statement on this?

A. I have said that SD, Amt III, ever since its foundation, had never handled Church matters. The old material that was to be given on the basis of this order to Amt IV was general informational material which was not suitable for the executive police tasks assigned to Amt IV. In general, the order submitted to me was formulated by Amt IV and consequently took into consideration the point of view of Amt IV.

Q. Now will you look again at Page 19, please, where it says, in summarising, that in Church matters the struggle against opposition and the work in everyday life must go hand in hand. Does this not indicate a collaboration of the SD and State Police with the common aim of a struggle against the Church?

A. No, because Amt IV, to my knowledge, never had the fundamental task of a struggle against the Church. What is formulated here, in this page, is the personal desire of an inspector, who had no factual right to give orders either to the Gestapo or to the SD.

Q. Now look at Page 24. Especially note Paragraphs r and 4, where it says, "For the reasons stated, I request the 'Information service on opponents' immediately to extend and intensify work in the field of Church policy." Also note the half-sentence immediately afterwards,

" ... as soon as informational connections have been made in this manner."

Does it not seem from that that the SD had an "Information service on opponents" in the sphere of the Church?

A. No. It indicates exactly the opposite. The decree in front of me is dated August, 1941, that is to say, after the order separating the two services. If the SD, on the basis of this order of separation, had transferred to Amt IV its information service apparatus as "Information service on opponents," then this decree of August, 1941, need not have given the order finally to begin the establishment of an information service in Amt IV. In general, the order was given to a large number of State Police offices and it cannot be simply a matter of one local case.

Q. I refer you now to Page 27, which discusses the transfer of Amt "V" men (agents) to the Gestapo, and a common leadership for these Amt "V" men. What have you to say as to this order of the inspector in Dusseldorf?

A. I must first again point out that this can be only a personal desire of the inspector, since he had no factual power to give orders. Practically, such a desire could never have been realised because, owing to the variety of the tasks, it was completely impossible to provide common confidential agents between Amt III and Amt IV with practical assignments on specific questions. Each agent of the SD would have refused to undertake police tasks as well.

Q. On the basis of your activity, what can you say on the scope of the files which, as a result of the separation order of 12th May, 1941, were handed over to the Gestapo by the SD.

A. That will have varied considerably according to the way in which cases were handled in the various offices. Divisions with good information services would have had correspondingly more material which would then have been given to the State Police.

Q. On the basis of your knowledge, were the documents handed over by the SD of any use for the police tasks of the State Police against individuals?

A. No, they certainly were not, as the Information Service's attitude toward the problems of Church and creeds on the part of the SD was entirely different. Particularly, it was never organised on the basis of individual cases.

Q. According to your knowledge, were the files that were then handed over actually worked on by the State Police?

A. I cannot make any statement in detail on this, but for the reasons I have just given, a large part of the material was never utilised any further, as it was completely useless for police tasks.

Q. Did Amt III of the SD have the fundamental task and aim of persecuting the Churches, or preparing a general persecution of the Church, and did it work at all for the persecution of the Church? That is to say, in the period between 1939 and the order of separation of 12th May, 1941?

A. No, Amt III never did at any time receive such a practical assignment, nor did it ever set itself such a goal.

THE PRESIDENT: Dr. Gawlik, you remember that you told us before the adjournment that you had come to your last point.

DR. GAWLIK: Yes. I have only about six questions.

THE PRESIDENT: Then you can compress them into a short time.

BY DR. GAWLIK:

Q. Did Amt III regularly inform leading offices of the Party and the State on the questions pertaining to religious matters, with a view to a common persecution of the Church?

A. No, the reports about religious matters in everyday life, in the last period, came in very slowly and incompletely because the department in Amt III had for years only one man to work on these matters.

Q. What was the aim of the SD in informing other offices about these matters?

A. Amt III in addition to its ordinary reports also pointed out in public reports that according to its opinion it was not a matter of a struggle for political power with the Church but, in fact, of the vital questions of religion affecting the German people, in conjunction with other cultural questions.

Q. Did the reports of the SD lead to the preparation or institution of measures g inimical to the Church?

A. No. On the basis of Amt III's reports, on several occasions, strong criticism was directed against individual measures against the Church on the part of individuals or particular offices.

DR. GAWLIK: I have no further questions to ask.

CROSS-EXAMINATION BY MR. MONNERAY:

Q. Witness, you said that you were mobilised in the SD in 1940?

A. I did not say that I was called up but that I was detailed to the Reichssicherheitshauptamt on emergency duty.

Q. You forgot to state that you were already a member of the SD before that?

A. I was asked by defence counsel, as far as I know, since when I had been in the SD.

Q. Were you a member of the SD before 1940?

A. I did not understand the question exactly.

Q. Were you a member of the SD before 1940?

A. Yes. From 1934.

Q. You forgot that, did you not?

A. Not as far as I know. Besides, I said it all in detail before the Commission.

Q. Is it a fact, witness, that before the seizure of power by the Nazi Party the SD was a secret and illegal organisation?

A. May I ask again? Did you say before the seizure of power?

Q. Yes, before the seizure of power.

A. I cannot say anything about that, as I was not a member of the SD.

Q. After the seizure of power, was the SD utilised by the Party? And on the other hand by the State, along with the Gestapo, in order to fight opposition groups?

A. As far as I know, the SD always had an entirely different information service task from that of the Gestapo.

Q. During the war, in the occupied territories, did the SD appear at the same time as the Sipo (Security Police) within the Einsatzkommandos (Operational detachments)?

A. I can unfortunately give no testimony about the organisation and activity of the Einsatzkommandos, as I was never in occupied territory as a member of the SD.

Q. Do you know Streckenbach?

A. Yes.

Q. What were his functions?

A. As far as I know, he was for some years head of Amt 1.

Q. And Amt No. 1 was in charge of organisational questions as much for the Sipo as for the SD, is that right?

A. Yes.

Q. Therefore, he should know sufficiently the respective functions of the Sipo and the SD?

A. May I ask again who knew the functions exactly?

Q. Witness, the question was quite clear. I was referring to Streckenbach.

A. No, one cannot assume that, since under him the duties and organisational problems were worked on entirely separately, even in his Amt I. I cannot judge to what extent Streckenbach knew and supervised the tasks of the SD.

Q. I should like to read to you Document F-984. It is an appeal by Streckenbach, published in the bulletin of the chief of the SD and Sipo.

THE PRESIDENT: Has this already been offered in evidence or not?

MR. MONNERAY: This document will be Exhibit RF 1540. It has not yet been offered in evidence, Mr. President.It is an appeal by Streckenbach to all members of the Sipo and the SD, dated the 7th of September, 1942. Extracts from this appeal read as follows:

"Even before the seizure of power, the SD had done its share in contributing to the success of the National Socialist revolution.After the seizure of power the Sipo and SD assumed the responsibility for the internal security of our Reich and opened up the way for the forceful realisation of National Socialism in the face of all opposition.

Since the beginning of the war our Einsatzkommandos are everywhere

where you find the German Army and are carrying on, each in its own sector, the fight against the enemies of the Reich and of the people."

Farther on, this appeal requests material and information about the activities of the Sipo and the SD. "For instance, in particular, articles, reports or pictures are to be sent in on the following subjects: the history of the SD, its inception, the fight for its acknowledgement as the sole information agency of the SS and later on of the Party. Difficulties and experiences when first setting up offices, development of the SD from its beginning (illegal camouflage) until its full expansion after the seizure of power, particularly important instances of its activity in supplying information before and after the seizure of power (illegal mission), etc." And farther on, "Common action of the Gestapo and, of the SD for the destruction of antagonistic groups."

BY MR. MONNERAY:

Q. Witness, this appeal by Streckenbach is contrary to your declarations, is it not?

A. No, because there is no word in this appeal about the actual tasks of Amt III of Inland SD. Besides, the excerpt submitted to me does not indicate who actually drafted this appeal and formulated it. The name "Streckenbach" only means that he had signed it.

Amt III can hardly have participated in it, because otherwise the tasks of this Amt III would have had to be described more or less accurately in this appeal.

Q. What were the offices of the SD apart from Amt III?

A. For the Inland SD there was only Amt III.

Q. Witness, I would be grateful to you if you would answer my question.

A. I thought I had just answered your question, Mr. Prosecutor.

Q. I asked you what the offices of the SD were, and not what the offices of the Inland SD were.

A. Under the general concept of SD, which had nothing to do with the concept of "Inland SD," there were also Amt VI and Amt VII.

Q. What were the functions of Amt VI?

A. That was the Foreign Information Service.

Q. When one speaks of the struggle against opposition groups, in conjunction with the Gestapo, you no doubt think it means a struggle in foreign countries, do you not?

A. That cannot be deduced in detail from the document which I have before me.

Q. Again you are not answering my question, witness. Can you imagine the Gestapo fighting against antagonistic groups situated outside the Reich?

A. No. To my knowledge the Gestapo had a police task within the frontiers of the Reich.

Q. Good. So when this appeal mentions a fight carried out against opposition groups and led by the SD on the one hand and the Gestapo on the other hand and jointly, reference is really being made to a fight which is going on inside the country, is that right?

A. Yes, although nothing is said there about the task of the Inland SD.

Q. You told us several times, witness, that the duties of the Inland SD, and no doubt with greater reason those of the SD outside the Reich, were very different from the task of the Gestapo and that of the police in general, is that not so?

A. I have said absolutely nothing today about the "foreign" division of the SD (SD Ausland), except in mentioning the existence of Amt VI.

Q. Please, witness, can you answer for the Inland SD?

A. Yes.

Q. According to you, the police were imbued with a "police spirit"?

A. May I ask the Prosecutor what he means by this statement?

Q. As opposed to the spirit of the SD, which was objective, is that right?

A. I cannot say with what spirit the police were imbued, because I was never a member of the police.

Q. But you told us the SD had an objective, impartial, scientific spirit. That is right, is it not?

A. I never said a scientific spirit, but always an objective, critical spirit, and I would like to stress this formulation expressly.

Q. That was also the spirit of the police?

A. I cannot judge that, as I said, I never belonged to the police.

THE PRESIDENT: Put the question again, would you, M. Monneray.

BY MR. MONNERAY:

Q. This impartial and objective spirit was also the spirit of the police?

A. I cannot state an opinion on this, as I was never a member of the police, but only of the Inland SD, Amt III.

Q. Let us be clear about this, witness. You gave us long explanations as to the differences between the SD and the police, did you not? If you can give us evidence about this difference, you must at least know what the police is.

A. I have for certain spheres explained the difference between the SD tasks and the police tasks, but I am not in a position to define all the duties of the police, because I do not know them. I spoke only of the principles of the work of Amt III and of concrete examples that I know from the departments in which I worked.

Q. Is it correct to say, witness, that the young candidates who had to, or wished to, enter the SD received exactly the same training that the young candidates did who wished to enter the Gestapo or the Kripo?

A. The education of candidates for the SD was not known to me in detail. I know only that the head of Amt III repeatedly, from year to year, raised positive objections to a certain planned similarity in the form of training. How far his objections achieved a practical result, I cannot say from my own knowledge.

Q. Well, I shall put to you a paper which will improve your knowledge of matters with which you were always concerned. It is a circular published in the official bulletin of the chief of the Sipo and the SD, dated the 18th May, 1940, which states that young candidates, young students of the police and

SD, in spite of its character, which was so objective and impartial, would have to be attached for a period of four months to the Criminal Police: for three months to the Gestapo and three months to the SD. You were unaware of this, were you not?

A. No.

Q. Now you have told us also that the SD had very little to do with the official policy of the personnel and the Nazi Party. Is that right, witness? Perhaps you now recall the fact that the political leaders of the Party had to give the German Government their opinion of the political outlook of candidates for Government posts. You know that, do you not?

A. May I ask the Prosecutor to repeat his question? I did not quite follow it.

Q. When it was a question of promoting a civil servant of a certain grade, or of appointing a civil servant, the political leader, the Gauleiter or the Kreisleiter, for, instance, would have to furnish to the Government a sort of political appreciation of the sound outlook of the candidate, is that right?

A. Yes, I said this morning that this was the duty of the Hoheitstrager of the Party.

Q. And it was the chief who had to supply the political appraisal?

A. No.

Q. Very well. I shall read to the witness an extract of Document F-989, which becomes Exhibit RF 1541 (Page 2 of the extract). It is a circular of the Chancellery of the National Socialist Party concerning political reports supplied by political leaders. First of all, this political report is defined as follows. It is an opinion of the political and ideological point of view and the moral attitude, and of competence of the candidate.

> "It has no value except if it reflects the moral and political outlook of the candidate."

And afterwards there is a short paragraph saying who will have to supply this opinion:

> "The people who are competent to give this opinion are the political chiefs of the technical office of the SD and the SS. Political information can be given by all offices of the Party and particularly by the SD offices."

That is not right, is it?

A. I said clearly this morning that the SD could give information but never political judgements, and that the SD itself put special value on giving as complete a personal picture as possible in this information which was supplied along with other reports. In the extract which is before me, moreover, there is no mention that I can see of personal information but only of information on the general situation of which I spoke this morning.

Q. In this document there is no mention of the political appreciation as a useful judgement of the political and ideological attitude?

A. Not in this document, no. It only mentions generally situation reports.

Q. Very well.

MR. MONNERAY: I would ask that the witness be shown the original letter in a little while.

I continue.

Q. There was close collaboration between the SD and the Party, was there not?

A. One cannot in any way speak of close co-operation. The relations between the SD and the Party, specially between Amt III and the Party Chancellery, were to a great extent strained to the utmost in the last years. I would be very glad to illustrate this with concrete examples.

Q. I would like to read you another extract from the same circular, dated 21st August, 1943. It says:

A. That is the same extract as I have already had before me.

Q. "The SD is directed by the RSHA to keep the leaders concerned currently informed as to the political events which take place in their sector and further the attention of the political chiefs must be directed constantly to particularly urgent affairs in order to enable them to undertake the necessary political steps." Is that right?

A. Here, unfortunately, theory and practice are completely at variance. Amt III would, contrary to the usual practice, have been very glad in many cases to be heard by the Hoheitstrager of the Party so that all the critical material could have been submitted. But, in many cases, this did not take place for years since the local representative of the SD was not received by the Hoheitstrager.

Q. Very well, we will see by a few practical examples if there was a difference or an inconsistency between practice and theory. Before the Commission you were shown Document R- 142, Exhibit USA 481, concerning the control by the SD of the 1938 plebiscite, when the collaborators of the SD, who were so honourable and so disinterested, had even falsified the ballot papers. As this was a practical instance, you told us that this was an isolated instance, is that not so?

A. I would like again to repeat most emphatically before the High Tribunal that this document does not refer to the SD but to one single subsidiary office among many hundreds of branch offices of the SD. The document makes absolutely no mention of the fact that the RSHA, Amt III -

THE PRESIDENT: Do not raise your voice, please.

A. ... that Amt III in Berlin had ever given any order to make these reports.

Q. Well, I will show you another document which, no doubt, is another isolated case. This time reference is made to the city of Erfurt. It is Document D-897, already offered by the British Delegation when they were submitting evidence against the political leaders, Exhibit GB-541. This is a secret circular of 4th April, 1938, coming from the Erfurt SD office and addressed to all subsections, requesting all outside agents to send in reports urgently on all those persons who, they were sure, were going to vote "No." This document makes you smile, witness. However, if you look a little farther down you will see that the matter was a serious one, for the head of the SD, a conscientious man, as you call him, says as follows:

"The tremendous responsibility of the operational point leaders is stressed once more particularly in regard to this report, as they must be fully aware of the possible consequences to those persons named in their reports."

Witness, you call that objective reporting, do you not?

A. I am sorry, Mr. Prosecutor. You spoke just now of the head of the SD, and the document is signed by a local Scharfuehrer, which is approximately the same as a private, first class, in the Army; I do not think you can speak of the chief of the SD. I am also sorry to have to state that this is certainly an exaggerated, isolated case since to my knowledge it was never one of the assignments of the "Inland SD" to supervise elections.

THE PRESIDENT: M. Monneray, I think a good many leaders have already been examined on this document.

MR. MONNERAY: Yes, Mr. President.

I will also draw the attention of the Tribunal to Document D- 902, already offered in evidence as Exhibit GB 542, on the same subject.

THE PRESIDENT: Does the witness know anything about this document? - because if it is already in evidence there is no use putting it to him unless he knows something about it.

MR. MONNERAY: Yes. It has already been submitted in evidence and I understand, Mr. President, that you do not wish me to interrogate on that document.

THE PRESIDENT: Well, if there is any particular reason for asking this witness questions upon this document, you may ask them, but there is no use putting a document to him if he has never seen it before, if it is already in evidence. I do not know what the document is.

MR. MONNERAY: Mr. President, I wanted to ask this witness questions on both documents to show how little faith one can attach to his depositions, since he declared before the Commission that it concerned a very exceptional case; whereas, as a matter of fact, it seems that it was a general measure of the SD, which was in force in many different parts of Germany.

THE PRESIDENT: If you want to cross-examine the witness as to the document, you can put questions from the document to him, but you cannot - at least the Tribunal does not want you to put the document to him.

BY MR. MONNERAY:

Q. Witness, you told us, concerning wireless, that the SD furnished also very objective reports without any political intentions behind them, is that right?

[Hans Roessner] A. Yes. Every week we sent in reports about the reception of radio programmes by the German population, as objectively as possible, including all critical opinion.

MR. MONNERAY: I have submitted to the Tribunal a Document PS- 3575, already produced in evidence as Exhibit USA 158, which established that in this domain also the SD had a mission which was not merely objective reporting.

BY MR. MONNERAY:

Q. Witness, what was the work of Office III-B-3?

A. I cannot answer from memory as I no longer have the individual department in my head; in any case, certainly not with radio as that was the task of Amt III-C-4.

Q. Is it right to say that they looked after questions concerning race and health?

A. I answered just now that I no longer remember the duties of that office.

Q. Did you have anything to do with or did you receive reports through your colleagues about general situation reports concerning foreign workers in Germany?

A. No. I, personally, had nothing to do with these matters. The question was quite beyond the scope of my duties.

MR. MONNERAY: I should like to show to the Tribunal Document 1753-PS, which becomes Exhibit RF 1542, and which contains a report from one of the departments of the SD concerning the possibility given by the RSHA to German doctors to practise abortion on female workers from the East, if they requested it.

This report establishes that the statements of the SD in this matter are in no way objective statements, but that they definitely take a favourable view of the official policy of the Nazi State.

I submit another Document, PS-1298, which becomes Exhibit RF 1543, concerning slave labour by workers in Germany. In this document the person who wrote the report, who was an agent of the SD, after having mentioned the numerous desertions of foreign workers, recommends practical measures, such as reprisals against relatives by withdrawal of ration cards, and so forth.

Q. Witness, you call those objective reports which do not of themselves support the policy of the police, do you not?

A. Yes, for this is a report of one of the many subsidiary offices which existed under the Reichssicherheitshauptamt in order to obtain a cross-section of public opinion in which, of course, the opinions of members of the Party would also be represented.

Moreover, I would like definitely to refute the assertion of the Prosecutor that it involved any agent of the SD. Amt III was never concerned with this matter, nor had any agents in the home information department, as I already stated this morning. I must again state that concerning the technical questions which are contained in these documents, I can only take a subjective attitude because they did not belong to my department. I still maintain my fundamental declaration concerning the duties of the SD, even in the face of these documents.

Q. But, witness, this document was not addressed to the RSHA to be centralised; it was addressed to the office for the utilisation of manpower.

It is therefore a report in view of the execution of those treasures which are suggested, is that not so?

A. From the document which I have before me, it is not evident from what SD office it came.

Q. I am going to show you a photostatic copy of this report.

A. This also does not indicate in any way from which SD office the document was sent.

Q. Do you admit that the report is addressed to the Manpower Commitment Office?

A. Yes; but at the same time I would like to point out that under the signature it says, "Secretary": and the SD, as far as I know, never had any secretaries. There should be a SD or a SS rank shown there.

Q. And there is also written in the same document: "I am sending you herewith a copy of the report from the Inland SD."

A. Yes.

Q. In the occupied territories, the SD was represented by organisations under Amt III and Amt VI, is that not so?

A. No, Amt III - here again I can speak only of Amt III - had no organisations which were directly subordinate to it, but only individual SD agents of Amt III who carried out the specific SD tasks in the occupied territories.

Q. Amt VI of the RSHA looked after the SD abroad, did it not?

A. Yes.

Q. And it had its representatives within the German police organisations operating abroad, did it not?

A. About this I can say nothing because I never worked in that office.

MR. MONNERAY: I offer to the Tribunal in evidence Documents F- 973 and F-974. Those are information sheets addressed to Section 6-ST-2. The two documents will become Exhibits RF 1544 and 1545. Those are information sheets and agents' reports addressed by the office.

THE PRESIDENT: Go on. Have they been translated? Have copies been given to the German counsel?

MR. MONNERAY: It has not been given to the interpreters because I am not going to read the whole document. The original is in German.

It is a report made out on a printed information form, sent out by the SD agents to the competent services of the Gestapo, concerning the Jewish question; and thereby the relations existing between the two offices can be established, contrary to the statements of the witness.

THE PRESIDENT: Have these documents been translated into the various languages?

MR. MONNERAY: Only into French, Mr. President.

THE PRESIDENT: Well, you know the rule is that they must be translated into four languages. You must read it then, if that is so.

MR. MONNERAY: With the permission of the Tribunal, I shall read only one of the two documents, Section 6-N-I.

THE PRESIDENT: M. Monneray, we have been a long time, and we have

1939 map showing the origin of German colonisers in the annexed Polish territories.

now apparently got to the stage that we have got to read this document, all these documents, which are of very remote importance. We have got to read them through because they have not been translated. It is taking up a long time; and it does not seem to be achieving any great result.

MR. MONNERAY: Mr. President, I shall pass directly to the last point, concerning the transplanting of population.

Q. Do you know, witness, if the SD participated with the Gestapo in sending people into concentration camps?

A. I cannot say. From my personal knowledge, I can only say in general that Amt III had no executive duties at all. Also, therefore, it was not empowered to send any people into a concentration camp.

Q. Do you know that the SD collaborated with the Gestapo to check which Poles were capable of being Germanised and which of them, on the other hand, should be sent to concentration camps?

A. No, I have no factual knowledge of any of these questions.

MR. MONNERAY: I would ask permission merely to read an extract of document R-112.

THE PRESIDENT: Is this new?

MR. MONNERAY: It is a document which has already been offered in evidence, Exhibit USA 309.

THE PRESIDENT: Then you must not refer to it because the witness says he does not know anything about it.

MR. MONNERAY: I would like merely to read the passage from this document which establishes, contrary to the statements of the witness, who does not know these facts, that the SD did in fact collaborate with the Gestapo in selecting Poles to be Germanised.

THE PRESIDENT: If there is anything in the document which shows that the witness is not telling the truth you can put that part of the document to the witness.

MR. MONNERAY: The document refers to Amt III B of the SD and does not indicate any element which directly affects the witness. Therefore, it bears only on the general question of the activity of the SD and does not affect the witness personally.

THE PRESIDENT: M. Monneray, the witness has just said that Amt III did not have anything to do with deportation of populations. If this document shows that he did, then you can put that fact to him.

MR. MONNERAY: That is why, Mr. President, I was asking permission to read a passage of this document.

THE PRESIDENT: You can put the document to him.

MR. MONNERAY: It is a letter of the 1st July, signed by Streckenbach. It emanates from Amt III B (1) and it is addressed to the Gestapo, office of the SD, in the newly occupied territories of the East. This document says, on Page 2, first point:

"The Gestapo Services must immediately ask the branch offices of the DVL, the SD departments and the Kripo departments for all available material on persons belonging to Group 4."

Third point:

"The office chiefs of the State Police offices and the leaders of the SD offices, or their permanent representatives (B-agents in SD III) must participate in the racial examinations in order to see for themselves the people involved."

On Page 3, fourth point:

"After the selection, from the racial point of view, the chiefs of the State Police offices and the leaders of the SD departments, or their permanent representatives (B- agents in SD III) will verify in common (this is underlined in the document) the material available, and will if necessary ask the RSHA, Amt IV C2, for arrest and consignment to a concentration camp. In particularly difficult cases the documentary files will first of all have to be sent to the RSHA; Amt III B."

On Page 4, the last paragraph of this order, signed by Streckenbach:

"In execution of the current control of Germanisation, the SD services in the old Reich territory -"

THE PRESIDENT: One moment. As far as I understand the document it clearly applies to Amt III. Well, why do you not put it to him?

MR. MONNERAY: I should like to ask the witness afterwards if he still maintains that Amt III had nothing to do with the Gestapo and had no authority to carry out arrests and send people to concentration camps.

First of all, I would like to finish reading the last paragraph.

The Sudeten Germans destroying the Czech name of the city of Šumperk after the German annexation of Czechoslovakia in 1938.

THE PRESIDENT: All right, go on.

Q. "... the SD services in Reich territory proper will carry on in a similar manner with the supervision of and reporting on Poles capable of being Germanised; they should afford all assistance to the 'advisers' on Germanisation."

The report is signed Streckenbach.

BY MR. MONNERAY:

Q. Witness, this order really emanates from Amt III of the RSHA, does it not?

A. Apparently some mistake has occurred, Mr. Prosecutor, because according to the document before me, the document does not come from the RSHA at all, but from the Reich Commissioner for Germanisation. After the date of 1st July, 1942, there is III B (I), it is true, but it has the letterhead "Reich Commissioner for the Establishment of Germanisation," an office which is completely separated from the RSHA.

Q. Well, then, witness, is it correct to say that according to this order signed by Streckenbach, the services of the SD, in common with those of the Gestapo, were to check their files and to request, if necessary, the arrest of people concerned and have them sent to concentration camps? Will you please answer yes or no?

A. Unfortunately from my own experience I can give no information about that. In any case it is clear that the Reich Commissioner for Germanisation could give no orders to the SD, Amt III. Therefore, one remains quite vague, from this document, as to what the SD did in practice in this matter, and the specialist concerned should be questioned here.

Q. You did not answer the question. According to this text, is it correct to state that the SD actively collaborated with the Gestapo in these matters.

A. I believe -

Q. Yes or no?

A. I cannot answer the question with yes or no, but I think I have already answered it when I said that the Reich Commissioner for Germanisation could give no orders to the SD. I cannot judge therefore what the SD actually did, as these are two entirely different offices. As far as I know the competent Gruppenleiter has already been heard before the Commission.

Q. You are still not answering the question. Is it true, yes or no, that according to this text the SD collaborated with the Gestapo in examining people and, if necessary, had them arrested and sent to concentration camps?

A. Unfortunately I must again repeat my answer to your second question. Since the Reich Commissioner could give no direct orders to the SD I cannot answer by yes or no as to whether the SD, on the basis of this order by the Reich Commissioner, actually collaborated with the Gestapo. And that is the question.

THE PRESIDENT: I think the document speaks for itself and now I think the Tribunal had better adjourn.

(A recess was taken.)

BY MR. MONNERAY:

Q. One last question, witness, concerning this document. Who helped the "Reich Commissioner for the Consolidation of Germanism"?

A. I did not quite understand the question.

(Question repeated.)

A. That was a supreme office.

Q. Which was under the authority of the chief of the SS, and the chief of the German Police, is that not true?

A. Himmler.

Q. You maintain that this letter of 1st July, which came from Himmler's offices and was addressed at the same time to the Gestapo office, the SD office, and the Criminal Police office, does not correspond with the real state of affairs.

A. From my own knowledge I can only point out once more that there are two completely different agencies concerned. To what extent the formulation of the document coincides with the actual work of the SD, I cannot, I repeat, judge from my own knowledge.

MR. MONNERAY: I have no more questions to ask.

THE PRESIDENT: Dr. Gawlik - wait a minute.

LT.-COMMANDER HARRIS: May it please the Tribunal, we would like to offer, merely as a supplement to our last exhibit, a new document which has just come to our hands, which is Document 4054-PS and becomes Exhibit USA 921. The only significance of this document is that it shows that the SD was running agents in Los Angeles, California, shortly before the outbreak of war between the United States and Germany.

THE PRESIDENT: You have got a copy of this, Dr. Gawlik? Have you got a copy of it?

DR. GAWLIK: Yes.

THE PRESIDENT: Do you wish to re-examine?

DR. GAWLIK: I have no questions.

THE PRESIDENT: The witness can retire. And I think that finishes your evidence, Dr. Gawlik - that is all of your evidence, is it not? That is all of your evidence, is it not? Wait a minute. You have no more witnesses, have you?

DR. GAWLIK: I have no more witnesses, Mr. President.

Submission of Documents

MONDAY, 19TH AUGUST, 1946

THE PRESIDENT: Now we will deal with the Gestapo.

DR. MERKEL (counsel for the Gestapo): Mr. President, first of all I should like to have permission to discuss my document book. I have already introduced the various documents with the exception of Gestapo Exhibit No. 31, which I submit at this point.

Gestapo Exhibits 1 and 2 deal with the concept and the aims of a political police system in general. I ask the Tribunal to take judicial notice of both these documents and I ask the same with reference to Gestapo Exhibits Nos. 3 to 8. They contain the basic laws and directives dealing with the origin, the development and the aims and purposes of the Gestapo, first taking into account Prussia and finally the entire Reich.

Gestapo Exhibit No. 9 is a copy in extract of the law dealing with German police officials dated 24th June, 1937. I shall read paragraph I from it. This is found on Page 28 of Document Book 1.

"This law affects the executive officials of the Civil Police, the Criminal Police of the Reich and of the communities, the Military Police, and the Gestapo, as well as other executive officials of the Security Police."

From this we can see that police executive officials had a special position in that they alone were subordinate to the law affecting police officials, which was not the case with regard to the other branches, such as, for instance, the administrative officials.

Gestapo Exhibit No. 10 contains the temporary provision for execution of this law which we have just mentioned. It gives a definition of the executive police officials. I quote from Part I, concerning paragraph 1 of the law; and this may be found on Page 33 of the document:

"Police executive officials are, in the Reich Criminal Police, the Gestapo, and also in other branches of the Security Police: Criminal Assistants (Kriminalassistenten), Criminal Senior Assistants (Kriminaloberassistenten), Criminal Secretaries (Kriminalsekretaere)"

and so forth.

By the law of 19th March, 1937, the officials of the Gestapo became direct Reich officials. I quote from Gestapo Exhibit No. 11, Page 36 of the document book, paragraph 1:

"The following become direct officials of the Reich:

(2) Officials of the Security Police (Gestapo and Criminal Police), but not the administrative police officials serving the Criminal Police in the State police administrations."

I ask that judicial notice be taken of Gestapo Exhibit 12. It is a copy of the law of 17th June, 1936, dealing with the assignment of the Chief of the German police to the Reich Ministry of the Interior.

I also ask that judicial notice be taken of Gestapo Exhibit 13, which concerns the employment of inspectors of the Security Police.

Gestapo Exhibit 14 has already been submitted as Exhibit USA 266 as evidence that the Party was prohibited from taking action in matters which were a concern of the Gestapo. I quote from Figure 1, second paragraph, which is at Page 42 of the first document book:

> "I forbid all offices of the Party, its branches and affiliated associations to undertake investigations and interrogations in matters which are the concern of the Gestapo. All occurrences of a political-police character, without prejudice to their being further reported along Party channels, are to be brought immediately to the knowledge of the competent offices of the Gestapo, now as before."

From Page 2 of the same document, Page 43 of my document book, I quote the third paragraph:

> "I particularly emphasise that all treasonable activities against the State coming to the knowledge of the Party are to be reported to the Gestapo without delay. It is in no way a task of the Party to make investigations or inquiries of any kind in these matters on its own initiative."

THE PRESIDENT: From which page was it that you were reading then?

DR. MERKEL: Page 43, Mr. President, of the German document book.

THE PRESIDENT: May I have the heading?

DR. MERKEL: Yes, the heading is "Reporting of Treasonable Activities to the Gestapo," and from that I read the third paragraph, starting with the words:

> "I particularly emphasise that - "

THE PRESIDENT: Yes, I see.

DR. MERKEL: That the assumption of political offices by officials and employees of the Gestapo was not desired, may be seen from Page 3 of this document, which is Page 44 of the document book, the last paragraph:

> "Since it," that is, the Gestapo, "is still in the process of organisation and the available officials and employees are very much in demand, they are only to take over positions in the Party to the extent that this is compatible with their official duties in the Gestapo."

From Gestapo Exhibit I5, which is an excerpt from the Reich administrative gazette Of 1935, I quote evidence of the fact that it was possible to enter a complaint against measures of the Gestapo through inspection channels. This is the first paragraph, Page 46 of the document book:

> "Since the Law on the Gestapo of 30th November, 1933, became effective, orders of the Gestapo office can no longer be contested according to the provisions of the Law on Police Administration. The only remedy against them is a complaint through investigation channels."

Further, to clarify the legal status of the Gestapo and of the Gestapo office, I should like to quote Page 3 of this same document, which is Page 48 of the document book. I shall quote paragraph 2:

"In accordance with all this, the legal status of the office of the Gestapo, since the law of 30th November, 1933, became effective, is the following: The office is part of a special governmental organisation, the 'Secret State Police,' which forms an independent branch of the Administration of the Prussian State. It has, like the Secret State Police as a whole, a special field of duties: the management of affairs of the political police."

Of Gestapo Exhibits 16 and 17, I ask that judicial notice be taken. They deal with the introduction of the laws establishing the Gestapo in non-German areas. Gestapo Exhibit 18 deals with the Border Police as a part of the Gestapo. It is the copy of a circular by the Reich and Prussian Ministry of the Interior dated 8th May, 1937. I shall quote from No. III. This is Page 53 of the document book.

"The execution of police tasks at the Reich frontier is entrusted to the Border Police offices."

I shall omit the next sentence.

"The Border Police Commissioners' offices, including the Border Police posts established by them, are, as previously, the border stations in Prussia and Baden, branch offices of the State Police offices competent for their district."

Gestapo Exhibit 19 is a copy of a circular issued by the Chief of the Security Police and the Security Service, dated 30th June, 1944, in which the unification of the military and political police counter intelligence machinery is ordered. I quote from the text, the first three paragraphs, at Page 56 of the document book:

"The result of the transfer of the special department 'Economy III' existing within the former counterintelligence agencies to the agencies of the State Police, is the union of the military and political police counterespionage in industry and economy.

The responsibility for intelligence protection of the armament industry as well as of all other war plants and vital industries is henceforth the responsibility of the Chief of the Security Police and of the SD and the offices of the Gestapo subordinate to him.

The carrying out of intelligence protection as well as the direction and employment of the counter-intelligence organs within the plants are now exclusively the task of the Gestapo offices, in keeping with the instructions given by the Reich Security Main Office."

I ask that judicial notice be taken of Gestapo Exhibit 20. It contains a directive issued by Himmler on 25th October, 1938, dealing with the erection of a central office for registration for police service. Through the setting up of this office it was possible to order candidates to do service in the Gestapo against their will.

I also ask that judicial notice be taken of Gestapo Exhibit 21. It concerns directives for qualification tests for applicants for service in the Security

Police. I make the same request with reference to Gestapo Exhibit No. 22, which is a directive of 14th December, 1936. It says that candidates for Criminal Police service will have to meet the same tests as candidates for the regular Criminal Police.

Then I ask that Gestapo Exhibit 23 should be given judicial notice, which is a decree of 2nd June, 1937, which says that civil police and military police officials were detailed for service in the Gestapo, and therefore, they did not come to the Gestapo voluntarily.

THE PRESIDENT: What you are doing now is not assisting the Tribunal in the very least. Would it not be better to submit all these documents, that is to say, to put them in, and ask us to take judicial notice of them, which we shall do, because they are decrees, and then to refer to any particular paragraphs in them when you come to make your argument? I say that because this 1s meaningless to us to read excerpts; and it is confusing to read a number of them without making any submissions at all about them. When you come to make your argument, you can draw our attention to any particular passage you want to in order to explain the arguments, but this is not doing you any good at all.

DR. MERKEL: Yes, Mr. President, I have made provisions for that in my final summary. However, there I have naturally tried to be very brief, and only to refer to these documents, on the assumption that I might read them during the submission of documents. However, it will suffice if the High Tribunal wishes merely to take judicial notice of these documents.

THE PRESIDENT: It is much more informative to our minds than to have it separated between the reading of the documents now and your final argument. If we have to listen to the same sort of thing from all other organisations, it is beyond human ability to carry all these things in our minds.

Dr. Merkel, if there are any special passages in these decrees or documents which you wish to draw our attention to now, in order that we may read them carefully before you make your speech, well and good; but it is no good going through one after the other like this without making any comment at all. Do you follow what I mean?

DR. MERKEL: For that reason I only read brief sentences from the most important of these documents and asked that judicial notice be taken of the rest.

THE PRESIDENT: I do not know what you call a very few brief ones, but we have had about fifteen or twenty already. That does not seem to me to be very few.

DR. MERKEL: Of course we must take into consideration that we have only three hours at our disposal for the final speech. For that reason it seemed suitable, first of all, to submit my documentary evidence in such a way that the documents could, as far as possible, be read to the Tribunal, and then, m the final speech, be referred to in a brief way. For this documentary material must at some time be submitted to the High Tribunal in some form or another, and we considered it more suitable to separate the two, to submit the documentary material now, briefly, and in our final speech to restrict ourselves to an evaluation only of the evidence which had been submitted.

Apart from that, I have almost concluded my submission of these individual documents. In the second volume of my document book there are but a few documents from which I wish to quote a few brief passages -

THE PRESIDENT: Go on, then.

DR. MERKEL: Gestapo Exhibit 32, the first one in Document Book 2, shows that the combating of partisan bands was not the concern of the Party or of Himmler, but of the Army. I refer in this connection to an affidavit deposed by a certain Rode, which has already been submitted as Exhibit USA 562.

Gestapo Exhibit 33 shows that the orders regarding the execution of Russian prisoners of war in the concentration camps came from the Inspector of Concentration Camps and not from Department IV of the RSHA.

Gestapo Exhibits 35, 36 and 37 deal with protective custody, and I ask that judicial notice be taken of them.

Gestapo Exhibit 38 is a copy of a letter of the Inspector of Concentration Camps dated I 5th October, 1936. I quote from paragraph 2, on Page 101 of the document book:

"Besides the Chief of the German Police, the following are authorised to enter concentration camps:

(a) The Chiefs of the three SS main offices,

(b) The administrative Chief of the SS,

(c) The Chief of Personnel of the Reichsfuehrer SS,

(d) The SS Gruppenfuehrer."

Then also 4:

"All other SS members, representatives of offices, and civilians, desiring to enter premises in which prisoners are lodged or engaged in work, for the purpose of visiting, require my express written authorisation."

Gestapo Exhibit 39 deals with the same topic.

I submit Gestapo Exhibits 40, 41, 42, 43, 44 and 45, as proof of the fact that concentration camps were not under the Gestapo but under the SS Economic and Administrative Main Office.

Gestapo Exhibits 46 and 47 run along a similar vein. Number 46 is a questionnaire addressed to August Eigruber of 27th March, 1946; and No. 47 is a questionnaire addressed to Friedrich Karl von Eberstein, dated 26th March, 1946. Both have already been submitted by the defence counsel for the defendant Kaltenbrunner.

Numbers 48 and 52 deal with the recruitment of foreign workers for the Reich area, and show that this was the sole responsibility of the General Plenipotentiary for Labour Mobilisation.

The setting up of labour training camps may be seen from Gestapo Exhibits 54 to 57.

The seizing and securing of cultural articles in the occupied territories are matters contained in 58 and 59.

Gestapo Exhibit 60 is the well-known decree about intensified interrogations.

Number 61 is a copy, in excerpt form, of a letter from Heydrich to Goering dated 11th November, 1938, and shows that the Gestapo took steps against the excesses of the night of 9th to 10th November, 1938.

Gestapo Exhibit 62 is a copy, in excerpt form, of testimony given by Dr. Mildner on 22nd June, 1945. It refers to the deportation of the Jews, and the subordination of the concentration camps under the SS Administrative and Economic Main Office.

This concludes my documentary evidence.

As far as the affidavits are concerned, I submit to the Tribunal first of all the German copies of the transcripts taken before the Commission, which I did not have till now. They are copies of the transcript of 9th, 19th and 27th July and 3rd August. They are contained, in summary form, in Gestapo Affidavits 1 to 91.

THE PRESIDENT: Dr. Merkel, it is not necessary for you to submit copies of the transcript of the Commission's evidence; it comes to us directly from the Commission, so you need not trouble about that.

DR. MERKEL: Very well, Mr. President.

THE PRESIDENT: It is suggested to me that perhaps it would be better for you to offer it in evidence and give it a number in your list of numbers.

DR. MERKEL: Then I shall give the transcript of 9th July the member Gestapo Exhibit 63; 19th July shall be Gestapo Exhibit 64; 27th July, Exhibit 65, and 3rd August, Gestapo Exhibit 66.

I should like to suggest that the submission of these affidavits be effected in the following way so that time can be saved. Twenty-two out of the 91 have been translated. I shall now summarise the most important of these 91 affidavits according to subject matter, and I shall also read some few brief passages from the affidavits which have been translated, which seem of especial importance to me, into the record. Of the remaining affidavits, I ask that the Tribunal take judicial notice.

Besides these 91 individual affidavits, a collective affidavit is at hand composed of 1265 individual affidavits. This summary, in line with the resolution of the Tribunal of 5th July, 1946, was prepared by former members of the Gestapo who are now imprisoned, and the authenticity of this summary was certified by me. I ask your permission to read also this brief summary into the record.

I turn to the first group, and I shall summarise Affidavits Nos. 1, 2, 3, 4, 9, 13, 71 and 90. They deal with the occupied countries. Jewish questions here were handled by a special detachment under the leadership of Dannecker. From 1940 to 1942 they were carried out by the French Government, in agreement with the military commander and the German Embassy. Detention camps in France were supervised by the military commander.

The recruitment of French labourers for the Reich area was done by the Field Commanders. In May of 1942 the Secret Field Police were arbitrarily taken into the Security Police. Police executive power, until April of 1942, lay in the hands of the French Police and of the German military police units.

From Affidavit 2, which has been translated, I ask permission to read the following: Page 1, paragraph 2:

"From October, 1940, until October, 1941, I was chief of the branch office of the Security Police and of the Security Service in Dijon, and from December, 1943, up to the retreat from France, I was Commander of the Security Police and of the Security Service in Dijon.

Composition of the Security Police Command Dijon:

There were about 10 Gestapo members; 13 criminal police (Kripo) members, and 69 men for emergency service (Notdienstverpflichtete). As can be seen from the list, of the 92 male members of my command at the time, only ten belonged to the Gestapo. In this connection it must be taken into account that of these ten Gestapo members, the larger part did not volunteer for the Gestapo, but were transferred or ordered to it, or came to it for some other reason, without those concerned having been able to have any influence on the decision, or to resist it."

I pass the next sentence:

"The Security Police Command Dijon must be regarded as an average command in France in respect to its strength as well as to its composition."

On Page 3 of this affidavit, after the heading "Jewish Questions," I shall read the brief paragraph which follows. It reads:

"Recaptured prisoners of war were in no case brought to a concentration camp or shot by the Dijon office, but immediately turned over to the nearest competent Army office."

THE PRESIDENT: Where are you reading now?

DR. MERKEL: The second passage in Affidavit 2, at Page 3 of the German original; it follows directly after the brief heading, "Jewish Questions." It is the next paragraph.

THE PRESIDENT: Yes.

DR. MERKEL: I shall omit the next four paragraphs and read on:

"There were no special Security Police or Security Service prisons in the Dijon area. Furthermore, never were arrestees in any prisons executed by order of the Security Police (Sipo) or Security Service (SD), to prevent their liberation by Allied troops."

Dealing with Affidavit 3, I read the beginning of the second paragraph:

"In September, 1941, I was transferred from the infantry to the Secret Field Police, and without my having anything to do with it, in June, 1942, I was assigned to the office of the Commander of the Sipo and the SD in Poitiers."

Next paragraph:

"The Security Police Command at Poitiers was composed of about five officials of the State Police and about five officials of the Criminal Police, about 80 former members of the Secret Field Police, who, like myself, were discharged from the Wehrmacht and engaged in compulsory war emergency service in the Security Police."

On Page 2 of this affidavit, under the heading "Commando Order," I should like to read the following:

"This order is known to me only in its basic substance through Wehrmacht reports, the Press, etc." I shall omit the next sentence. "This order was not carried out in the Poitiers region. I can mention two examples: In June, 1842, in a joint operation by the Security Police and the Wehrmacht, a camp of 40 English parachute troops was raided, and during the short fight, three Englishmen were killed, the rest being taken prisoner and handed over to the Wehrmacht, although it was established that the group had carried out sabotage on a railroad three kilometres from Poitiers, more than 200 kilometres behind the invasion line, and had organised French partisans and provided them with arms."

And the next paragraph as well:

THE PRESIDENT: What does that mean, "200 kilometres behind the invasion line" in reference to June, 1942?

DR. MERKEL: That is the town of Poitiers, which is about 200 kilometres behind the invasion line.

THE PRESIDENT: There was no invasion in 1942.

DR. MERKEL: In June, 1944. That is a typographical error.

THE PRESIDENT: Go on.

DR. MERKEL: "Likewise, in March, 1944, in the same territory, five American airmen, who were met wearing civilian clothes and in company of forty armed partisans, were taken prisoner and turned over to the Luftwaffe."

Next I should like to summarise those affidavits numbered 5, 6, 7, 8 and 14. Mr. President, I beg your pardon that the numbers are not in consecutive order, but this can be explained through the fact that these affidavits, in so far as they came from camps, were received at very great intervals. Also the witnesses who deposed affidavits here in the Nuremberg prison arrived one at a time, therefore it is unavoidable that these affidavits are not numbered consecutively. I should like to repeat the numbers: 5, 6, 7, 8 and 14. They prove that the Gestapo not only did not take part in the excesses of 9th and 10th November, 1938, but took steps against them and in numerous cases it undertook arrests of members of the SA, the Party, and the SD. The 20,000 Jews who were arrested were largely released again after their emigration papers had been procured.

Numbers 15 to 27, 29 to 34, 72, 73, 76, 84, and 85 deal with the following: The offices of the Security Police and the Security Service in occupied countries were not made up of voluntary members. Administrative officials or technical officials of the Gestapo had nothing to do with carrying out orders, and in view of the strictest secrecy which was preserved, they could not know anything about details. Employees and persons in compulsory emergency service cannot be considered as accomplices in, or as having knowledge of, the possibly criminal nature of the organisation. New members were not brought in by voluntary recruitment, but rather as a result of assignment, orders and transfers.

I shall read the following into the record from Affidavit No. 15, the second paragraph:

"In May, 1919, I was assigned to the Political Police, newly established as Dept. VI with Police Headquarters in Munich."

THE PRESIDENT: Wait a minute. Are you reading affidavit No. 15?

DR. MERKEL: Yes.

THE PRESIDENT: You say the second page, the second paragraph, and you begin something about 1919. I do not see that.

DR. MERKEL: No, Mr. President, it is the first page, second paragraph, right at the beginning of the affidavit.

THE PRESIDENT: On the first page, it begins "On 1st January, 1913."

DR. MERKEL: "On 1st January, 1913." I had only omitted this first sentence and the third sentence begins with:

"In 1933 I, with almost all other members of this office, was transferred to the Bavarian Political Police which, with almost the same personnel set-up, was in turn transferred to the Secret State Police in Munich. The entire personnel was screened politically by the SD, resulting in a large part of the civil servants and employees of the former political department of Police Headquarters being judged negatively."

Then I shall read from Page 2 of the German text, under No. 2:

"While I was in charge of the office from 1933 to 1939 I always pointed out to the officials under me that it was forbidden to ill-treat prisoners. I did not hear of any of my officials laying violent hands upon a prisoner."

From No. 4 I shall read the next to the last sentence of the first paragraph:

"I learned that persons frequently pretended to be Gestapo officials. These persons also committed criminal acts. Because of the increase of such incidents, Himmler issued a decree according to which all persons who impersonated Gestapo officials were to be put into a concentration camp."

From Affidavit 16 I should like to read the following on Page 1, the fourth paragraph:

"On the basis of my activity with the Gestapo office in Berlin I can confirm that the Gestapo office was made up almost exclusively of officials of the former General Criminal Police as well as of the Berlin Police Administration, who were without exception ordered to duty in the State Police."

THE PRESIDENT: You are reading 16, are you? Which page?

DR. MERKEL: The paragraph from which I was reading is on Page 1. It begins with "In 1935," and the fourth sentence, "On the basis of my activity - "

THE PRESIDENT: "In 1935 without being consulted I was ordered and transferred -."

DR. MERKEL: Yes, yes, Mr. President, that is the paragraph. And in this paragraph the fourth sentence, "On the basis of my activity with the Gestapo office in Berlin." Then I shall read the following paragraph:

"As in the Gestapo office in Berlin, so too did the great majority of the police personnel of the State Police offices throughout the Reich consist of old professional police officials who had been transferred from the old 1- A section of the Criminal Police and from the remaining branches of the police to the State Police, or were ordered there, without their wishes being taken into consideration in this connection."

Then I omit a paragraph:

"Transfers back were entirely out of the question because an order existed which absolutely prohibited them. If, in spite of this, requests were handed in for transfer back or transfer from the Gestapo to another branch of the police, such requests were usually answered with penal transfer. Such requests were not made because the Gestapo was considered a criminal organisation, but mostly for purely personal reasons."

From Affidavit No. 18 I should like to read the following, on Page 3 of the German original:

"1. Officers: There were about 50 to 60 officers' positions in the whole Security Police Force.

2. Administrative officials: The administrative officials were engaged exclusively in office work for the entire police administration. They were strictly separated from the executive officials by different regulations concerning their career, by different titles, and different duty passes. Above all they had nothing to do with executive work. A change in their position and activity never took place.

3. Executive Officials: They executed the real tasks of the Gestapo which were laid down by law. In this connection it should be noted, however, that a number of these officials also were engaged in pure office work as is the case in every office.

4. Civilian Employees: The civilian employees were mainly clerks and other office personnel and personnel for subordinate work.

5. Emergency Service Conscripts."

Here I shall read only the end of this paragraph:

"No right whatsoever to complain existed if an emergency service conscript was sent to the Gestapo and not to any other governmental office or to some private enterprise."

I shall omit two paragraphs and shall read the third one which follows:

"I estimate that the Gestapo had about 10,000 emergency service conscripts by the end of 1944."

"6. Men detailed from the Waffen SS: In order to guarantee the personnel requirements of the Gestapo, members of the Waffen SS who, due to wounds and other physical handicaps, could not be utilised at the front any more were detailed to the Gestapo in increasing numbers during the war."

THE PRESIDENT: I think we had better break off now.

(A short recess was taken.)

DR. MERKEL: From Affidavit No. 18, I should like permission to read Section 7, relative to the members of the former Secret Field Police:

"With the transfer of the tasks of the Secret Field Police to the Security Police, at first in the occupied territories in the West, the members of the Secret Field Police were also taken over into the Sipo, respectively into the Gestapo. This transfer was done by order, so that none of the transferred men could have done anything against it."

And then the final sentence of that:

"Altogether approximately 5,500 men were taken over."

And the first sentence of the following paragraph:

"Particular importance was attached to secrecy in the Gestapo."

I pass the following sentence, and continue:

"Particularly by means of the Fuehrer order of 1940, which was extended immediately by the Reichsfuehrer SS to include the Security Police, keeping of secrecy was pronounced the supreme duty of all members of the Security Police, and thereby of the Gestapo. This secrecy rule was circulated at certain intervals to all members of the individual offices, receipt being acknowledged by their certified signatures. In that connection it was pointed out time and again that any offences against the secrecy regulations would be severely dealt with, and, in important cases, even be punishable by death."

From Affidavit 20, I beg permission to read from Page 1, second paragraph:

"The members of the administrative service in the lower, middle and higher grades were, by order of the Gestapo, and after 1937 of the Main Office of the Security Police, taken out of their positions as civil servants in all offices, mainly, however, from the police administration, and were transferred to the Security Police and/or to the Gestapo."

From number 30 I shall read the following, on the first page under the heading "Organisation and Composition of the Gestapo in Bielefeld," second sentence:

"When this Gestapo office was founded, in 1934, about eight criminal investigation officials and two police administration officials of the Bielefeld State Police, and about five criminal investigation officials from branch offices were transferred to the Bielefeld Gestapo. The transfer was made without previously obtaining the consent of the officials."

Then, from Page 3 of the same affidavit, I beg to be allowed to quote one example of the composition of a fairly large Gestapo office.

"Organisation and composition of the Gestapo in Bruenn. In the spring of 1944 the personnel comprised about 800 persons, distributed approximately as follows: administrative officials, about 35; executive officials, about 280; drivers, employees, about 110; frontier police officials, about 65; criminal investigation employees, for instance interpreters, about 90; prison supervision personnel, about 80; female office personnel, about 90; other auxiliaries, about 50."

And then the second paragraph after that:

"When the Gestapo office in Bruenn was created, about 400 officials were transferred from offices in the Reich proper, without their consent having been secured, to Bruenn or to the branch offices connected with Bruenn. More than half of the personnel consisted of emergency service conscripts or was doing compulsory service."

From Affidavit 31, I shall read on Page 2, at the beginning:

"At the end of 1944 the Gestapo consisted of approximately the following: Administrative officials, 3,000; executive officials, 15,500; employees and workmen, including 9,000 called up for emergency service, 13,500. Grand total, 32,000. These members of the Gestapo may be considered to be the permanent ones in so far as they made up the normal staff. In addition to these persons, there were the following groups: Detached from the Waffen SS, 3,500; taken over from the Secret Field Police, 5,500; taken over from the military counter-intelligence of the OKW, 5,000; personnel of the former military mail censorship, 7,500; members of the customs- frontier guard, 45,000."

Then I come to Affidavit 34, where I shall read from the first page, under the heading "Professional career," the last quotation:

"1st April, 1933, transfer, that is, order to join the Gestapo Department of Berlin. I received at that time a letter reading as follows:

'By virtue of the authority vested in me by the Reich Minister of the Interior, you are hereby transferred as of to the Gestapo office.'

I had nothing to say in the matter of this transfer. The attempt of my superior in the Police Presidency to save me from this transfer failed."

I now beg to be permitted, in connection with the relationship of the Gestapo to the Frontier Police, to read the following from Affidavit 22; this is on Page 2 of the German original:

"The members of the Frontier Police were taken over from the Frontier Police, which already existed in Bavaria before 1933, into the Frontier Police of the Gestapo. Later on, after the annexation of Austria, the Austrian Frontier Police were added as well. The incorporation of the Frontier Police officials in the Gestapo was not voluntary either in Bavaria or in Austria. On the contrary, the officials were transferred as a group when Control of the Gestapo was transferred to the Reich or when the annexation of Austria took place."

I omit the following sentence.

"The officials could not object against their transfer to the Gestapo on grounds of the, instructions concerning the rights of officials. They had to agree to this transfer."

The transportation of Polish Jews, September 1939.

Then the second paragraph farther on:

"The tasks of the Frontier Police consisted mainly in the supervision of the traffic of persons across the frontier, the carrying out of police instructions with regard to passports, and in the supervision of the traffic of goods in connection with the customs authorities. Political tasks, like those of the Gestapo in a stricter sense, were not the business of the Frontier Police."

I omit the next sentence and go on to quote:

"I know from my own experience that the tasks of the Frontier Police and also its activity did not change after 1933."

Then the last paragraph:

"I must also draw attention to the fact that the same tasks as those of the Frontier Police were performed at many small frontier passages by members of the Reich finance administration and the customs administration. In this the customs officials were bound by exactly the same instructions as members of the Frontier Police."

Numbers 23, 24, 35 and 39 deal with the question of secrecy.

"No department within the State Police knew anything about orders issued by any other department. Even private conversation was forbidden. Considering the strict secrecy, only the few persons of the Reich Security Main Office who were immediately concerned therewith knew of the individual measures."

From 35 I read the following; and this is on Page 8 of the original, the second paragraph:

"The centre of gravity of the factual discussions lay in the personal conferences between the department chief and group chief or their deputies on the one hand, and, as until now, between the department chief and his department heads on the other."

Then the beginning of the following paragraph:

"In view of this form of personal collaboration it follows that only the persons actually and directly taking part in a matter were informed about it, the more so as, due to the directives which had been issued, the principles of secrecy were strictly observed in Department IV."

Then the beginning of the next paragraph:

"Still a further fact must be given decisive consideration in this connection. In the course of the war up to September, 1944 - but particularly in the course of the air raids - Department IV in Berlin was decentralised to an increasing degree and spread to various quarters of the city."

Then also on Page 12 of the affidavit, the second paragraph in the German text:

"In view of the practice of absolute secrecy and isolation of information prevailing in all fields, it should be clear of itself that a problem which had as little to do with general tasks and activities as the physical extermination of Jews was, if that is possible, kept even more strictly secret. All plans and measures in connection therewith must of necessity have been discussed only in the closest circle of persons directly involved, for all other members of Department IV never received knowledge of it."

And then the beginning of the next paragraph:

"The same must have been the case with regard to knowledge about the reports concerning mass shootings in the East, as quoted by the prosecution. It is not known in detail who could have had knowledge of such reports besides the Reichsfuehrer SS and some individual department chiefs. If this knowledge should, at the most, have extended even to the immediately competent group chiefs and specialists, it is still far from being the case, as asserted by the prosecution, that the bulk of the personnel in Department IV, or even in the Reich Security Main Office or in the offices throughout the Reich, were informed."

From Affidavit 39 I read the following from Page 3 of the original:

"Upon my assuming office in the Reich Security Main Office in August, 1941, Muller declared to me that in his sphere of activity he placed great value upon observing the stipulations for secrecy and that he would proceed without pity, with the severest measures, against violations thereof."

And then the last sentence of the same paragraph -

THE PRESIDENT: We have heard about this secrecy over and over again, not only in your affidavits but throughout the trial. Surely it is not necessary to read the paragraphs of these affidavits about secrecy.

We quite understand that everybody alleges that.

DR. MERKEL: Gestapo Affidavit 25 contains an opinion about Exhibit USA 219. It deals with the transfer of 35,000 prisoners capable of work into armament plants attached to concentration camps.

The affidavit originates from a sub-department chief (Stellenleiter) of the Gestapo and I shall quote from the third sentence of the third paragraph:

"In another case, the order by the Chief of the Security Police and the SD of 17th December, 1942, according to which at least 35,000 persons capable of working were to be transported to concentration camps to work in the armament plants there, was not carried out by many Gestapo offices. These persons were to be recruited from the prisoners of the labour training camps of the Gestapo offices. This was incompatible with the customs followed until then, and by many office chiefs known to me was interpreted as an arbitrary measure. At conferences in the Reich Security Main Office I learnt that the office was unable to fulfil the request of the Reichsfuehrer SS to provide prisoners, because the Gestapo leaders did not provide prisoners from their labour training camps, avoiding doing so by means of pretexts."

The summary of Affidavit 36 states that in the spring of 1944 the bulk of the members of the department of foreign intelligence (Amt Ausland Abwehr) in the OKW were forcibly transferred into the Security Police.

Affidavit 40 states that the order for the evacuation of Jews from Hessen in 1942 came directly from the Chief of the Security Police and not from Department IV of the Reich Security Main Office. Commitment for work in the East was given as the reason for the evacuation.

Affidavits 42, and to some extent 91, deal with the decree that the crucifixes should be removed from schools. From Affidavit 42 I shall read the second sentence on the first page:

"Approximately in 1942, as I remember, Gauleiter Adolf Wagner, in his capacity of Bavarian Minister of Culture, ordered that the crucifixes were to be removed from all Bavarian schools."

I omit the following sentence:

"Enforcement (of this ruling) met with the greatest difficulties due to the attitude of the population, so that the departments of the Party which were dealing with the carrying out of that order called upon the district officials (Landrate) and the district police offices for assistance. Since the affair had a political character, the district officials approached the State Police department in Nuremberg with the request for advice or assistance. As an expert for Church matters, I stated to the first district official approaching me that the Gestapo in Nuremberg would not help with this decree unless they were forced to it directly and that he would not receive any assistance from the State Police for the carrying out of the order. Even in the case of further instructions to the political officials, the State Police would not take any action."

I omit the following sentence.

"I then reported the matter to the police chief, who entirely and without reserve shared my point of view. In agreement with him, I then informed the remaining district officials concerned, by telephone, to the effect that they should act accordingly."

Affidavit 43 says that, upon objections raised by the competent commander of the Security Police, the intention of the district official to turn the Protestant church in Welum into a cinema was thwarted.

THE PRESIDENT: Dr. Merkel, you heard what I said to Dr. Servatius, did you not?

DR. MERKEL: Yes, Mr. President.

THE PRESIDENT: Is not the state of affairs exactly the same in your case, that all these affidavits have been summarised in the transcript before the Commission, which we have got before us in writing, and therefore what you are doing is simply cumulative?

DR. MERKEL: I had merely thought that in order to support these summaries in the record, short extracts from these affidavits -

THE PRESIDENT: It is no use telling me what you merely thought. You heard what I said to Dr. Servatius, that the Tribunal did not want to hear the same thing over again which appears in the transcript of the proceedings before the Commissioners. It was all gone into perfectly clearly with Dr. Servatius, and it was explained to him, in your hearing, that we cannot carry all these things in our minds and that it is useless to go over them twice unless there is some matter of very great importance. which you want to draw our attention to before you make your final speech; and I said that before and I do not want to have to say it again.

DR. MERKEL: In that case, if I may, I shall refer to the summaries of the transcripts of the Commission, that is to the following numbers up to 91, and then I shall assume that the Tribunal will take cognizance of the contents of these summaries. I then have left only a collective affidavit. If the Tribunal wishes me to do so, I can read the summary contained in that affidavit; as far as I know, that has not been translated. There are six pages of this summary of 1,276 individual affidavits which do not appear in the Commission report.

THE PRESIDENT: Yes, go on.

DR. MERKEL: Regarding the question of membership being compulsory, 665 affidavits are available. They state that when the Gestapo was created, the requirements for personnel were for the most part met from the existing Political Police. Regarding forced membership of persons doing compulsory service, there are 127 affidavits which deal with the same subject.

Seven hundred and eighty-five affidavits state that they had no knowledge of the crimes of which the Gestapo is being accused.

Thirty-nine affidavits treat with the difference in organisation between the Gestapo in the Reich and the Security Police in occupied territories.

One hundred and ninety-five affidavits state that the writers had no knowledge of inhuman treatment and atrocities in the concentration camps. A few officials who had visited concentration camps on conducted tours could not notice any irregularities there. Also released detainees did not speak about concentration camps in a critical manner.

One hundred and thirty-three affidavits state that no participation or supervision of the excesses of 9th and 10th November had taken place.

Sixty-seven affidavits state that the looting of private or State property was expressly forbidden to members of the Gestapo.

One hundred and thirty-five affidavits state that a large number of Gestapo members knew nothing about the existence of the Special Purpose Groups or of atrocities committed by them.

Two hundred and eighteen affidavits state that the "Kugel" (Bullet) decree was unknown to the majority of the Gestapo officials and that recaptured prisoners of war were turned over to Wehrmacht offices.

One hundred and sixty-eight affidavits state that enemy parachutists were turned over to the Air Force by the of evidence by means of documents and affidavits.

LT.-COMMANDER HARRIS: May it please the Tribunal, I have just two short comments to make concerning documents which were presented here as to which I think he was in error, and I respectfully request the Tribunal to turn to his Gestapo Exhibit No. 33.

THE PRESIDENT: Yes.

LT.-COMMANDER HARRIS: Dr. Merkel has cited this document as evidence that the executions in concentration camps were ordered by the WVHA, but I would respectfully invite the attention of the Tribunal to the sentence in the centre on the first page and I quote: "For this measure, permission of the Chief of the Security Police must be obtained."

THE PRESIDENT: Commander Harris, the Tribunal thinks that this is a matter which can be dealt with in argument and not at this stage.

LT.-COMMANDER HARRIS: Very well.

THE PRESIDENT: Now, the Tribunal will hear the case of the SD. Is counsel for the SD not present?

DR. STAHMER: He is being fetched and will be here any moment.

THE PRESIDENT: Marshal, have you made any effort to get - to obtain the presence of this counsel? Have you communicated with him?

THE MARSHAL: We got in touch with his office, and we are looking for the defence counsel now.

THE PRESIDENT: The Tribunal will adjourn now until tomorrow morning at ten o'clock.

(The Tribunal adjourned until 20th August, 1946, at 1000 hours.)

TUESDAY, 20TH AUGUST, 1946

THE PRESIDENT: Dr. Gawlik.

DR. GAWLIK (for the SD): Your Lordship, may I first of all apologise for my failure to be ready for the submission of my documents yesterday. I regret that this resulted in a delay of the proceedings, but the defence counsel of the organisations were informed that the sequence for the submission of documents would be different from that of the examination of witnesses, and the sequence of which we were informed was the following: Political Leaders, Gestapo, SS, and SD. I therefore assumed that I would follow the SS with the submission of documents. I ask the Tribunal to take into consideration that I am at present preparing my final speech and that I am therefore not able to participate in all the sessions.

THE PRESIDENT: Are you saying that you are not able now to participate in the session?

DR. GAWLIK: Now I am ready, your Lordship.

THE PRESIDENT: I do not know how any such misunderstanding as you indicate can have occurred, because no order was given by the Tribunal that there would be any alteration of the order, and counsel for the defendants and the defendant organisations must understand that they must be here when their case is called on, and the Tribunal cannot be kept waiting as it was yesterday. This is the first occasion on which it has happened, and the Tribunal hopes it will not happen again.

DR. GAWLIK: Your Lordship, it is a notice dated 1st August which is posted on the blackboard in the counsel's room.

THE PRESIDENT: Just what does it say?

DR. GAWLIK: It says that for the examination of witnesses, the sequence was altered and the SD witnesses were heard before the SS witnesses, but that for the submission of documents and the final speeches the old sequence will be followed, and then the sequence is quoted: Political Leaders, Gestapo, SS and SD.

THE PRESIDENT: The Tribunal will inquire into that matter.

DR. GAWLIK: First of all, may I submit the records with regard to the witnesses I have examined. I shall now begin with the submission of affidavits. On account of the pressure of work in the Translating Division, only some of the affidavits have so far been translated. I request that those affidavits -

THE PRESIDENT: Dr. Gawlik, as you were not present the other day, perhaps I had better tell you what the Tribunal's wishes were and are with reference to these affidavits.

A large number of these affidavits, if not all, have been summarised and the summaries set out in the transcript before the Commissioners, and, therefore, for you to give a summary again of these affidavits merely creates on the transcript of the Tribunal a repetition of the summary which is already in the transcript before the Commissioners. The Tribunal does not desire that. Therefore, if you will confine yourself to commenting on or summarising the affidavits which have not been summarised before the Commissioners, that is all that is necessary, subject, of course, to offering them in evidence.

Is that clear? I was not suggesting that you should bring before us affidavits which have not been brought before the Commissioners, but I was merely telling you that we do not want to have a repetition of summaries, which were put before the Commissioners and which are set out in the transcript before the Commissioners.

DR. GAWLIK: That was not my intention, your Lordship. I have only asked for some of these affidavits to be translated, and I was going to submit only those completely translated; but of those which I wanted to submit I have received only a part fully translated. Therefore I cannot at this moment submit the translation of all the affidavits I propose to use, and so I request that I may submit some of them later.

THE PRESIDENT: Very well. Before you begin, this will be a convenient time to break off.

DR. GAWLIK: Very well.

(A recess was taken.)

DR. GAWLIK: I shall present my affidavits in order of the points of the Indictment, as they appear in the Trial Brief against the Gestapo and SD; that, I believe, would be of aid to the Tribunal. This order will not agree with the sequence of the numbers, but I believe that can be taken into account, because this method will enable the Tribunal to see that I have endeavoured not to present cumulative evidence.

First, I come to the point of conspiracy, to the tasks, aims and activities of the SD from its foundation to the establishment of the RSHA. On this point I submitted Affidavit SD-27 by Dr. Albert; a summary appears in the transcript of 23rd July, 1946.

The next affidavit refers to the assertion of the prosecution that it was a task of the SD to obtain secret information on actual and possible opponents of the Nazis. The reference is the Trial Brief against the Gestapo and SD, statement of evidence IIIb, Page 77 of the English version. In this connection I submitted Affidavit SD-28 by Dr. Albert; the summary of the contents is also shown in the records of the Commission, on the 23rd July, 1946.

Then on this point also I now submit Affidavit SD No. 1, by Ferdinand Sackmann.

THE PRESIDENT: Go on.

DR. GAWLIK: The next affidavit will prove that the reports, of the SD to the Party Chancellery were not made for the purpose of supporting a conspiracy. On this topic I have submitted Affidavit SD No. 27. The short summary appears in the transcript of 3rd August, 1946.

The next affidavit was submitted to prove the aims, tasks and activities of Group III-D of the RSHA and in connection with the fact that Group III-D did not support a conspiracy. For this point, I have submitted Affidavit SD No. 40, by Ohlendorf, from the protocol of 23rd July, 1946.

My next affidavits refer to the aims, tasks and activities of the branch offices and the confidential agents and to the fact that the tasks, aims and activities of the branch offices and confidential agents were not to support a conspiracy. In this connection, I submit Affidavit SD-65, by Professor Dr. Ritter. I asked for the complete translation of this affidavit but I have not yet received it, since the Translating Division is overloaded with work. I call the especial attention of the Court to this affidavit. It was deposed by one of the best-known German historians, and I should like to quote the following from it:

Question one: "Please give details of your profession." Answer: "Since 1925 I have been Professor of Modern History at the University oaf Freiburg."

I omit one sentence.

Second question: "Were you a member of the NSDAP or any of its branches?" Answer: "No."

Third question: "Were you a member of a resistance group against the Hitler regime and were you persecuted by it?" Answer: "Yes. I belonged to the circle of friends of Dr. Goerdeler who selected me as Minister of Education in his new cabinet. In November, 1944, I was arrested in connection with the events of the 20th of July, and was placed before the People's Court in Berlin. On the 25th of April, 1945, I was liberated by the Russian Army."

THE PRESIDENT: The translation came through to us as "November 1934." Was it 1944?

DR. GAWLIK: Yes, November, 1944.

THE PRESIDENT: Very well.

DR. GAWLIK: Fourth question: "Do you know the activities of the SD Arbeitsgemeinschaft and where did you obtain your knowledge?" Answer: "Yes. My knowledge originates from my activity as Chairman of the Purification Committee of the University at Freiburg."

Fifth question: "What were the tasks of the SD Arbeitsgemeinschaft?" Answer: "Firstly, to keep the supreme SD command - I do not know the exact term - informed of feelings among the population and the criticism expressed on Party measures."

To save time, I should like to omit the rest of this answer; I also omit the next question and come to question No. 7: "What were the aims, tasks and activities of the confidential agents (Vertrauensmanner)?" Answer: "The aims and tasks were essentially the same as in the case of the Arbeitsgemeinschaften, to which the confidential agents belonged; but while the other members of the Arbeitsgemeinschaften were asked for information and requested to attend conferences with the SD only occasionally, the confidential agents were in constant contact with the SD." Now, I come to the eighth question: "Was it the task of the confidential agents to collect and pass on remarks hostile to the State and to watch persons hostile to the State?" Answer: "I do not know of a task of this sort." I leave out a few lines and come to the ninth question: "What was the purpose and what was the aim of the SD reports within Germany?" Answer: "In contrast to the frequently 'rosy' official Party reports, the SD reports were to give a picture corresponding to the actual conditions and feelings of the people. In the field of cultural policy, in addition, inadequacies and failings were to be pointed out."

Tenth question: "Did the SD in Germany watch and report on your lectures and addresses?" Answer: "Yes, I know that in the branch of the SD in Karlsruhe or in Strassburg a number of reports and stenographic notes on my lectures and addresses were found. I can also say that several scientists and high officials corresponded with me on the SD's activity - "

THE PRESIDENT: Dr. Gawlik, I think it would be more convenient to the Tribunal or more easy for them to follow if you can summarise the affidavit rather than read it.

DR. GAWLIK: I have only a few more brief questions to read from this affidavit. I ask the Tribunal to take into consideration that this is the only affidavit which I want to read. I attach special importance to this affidavit because its author is not an SD member but a man who was himself watched by the SD.

THE PRESIDENT: Very well.

DR. GAWLIK:

"I can also say that several scientists and high officials corresponded with me on the activity of the SD, and confirmed that my presentation of the facts agreed in all points with the experience of these men."

Eleventh question: "Did the SD cause Gestapo measures to be taken against you as a result of watching your lectures?" Answer: "I know of none."

I leave out one question.

Thirteenth question: "Did the Gestapo arrest or warn you because of your lectures?" Answer: "No. I was warned once by the Gestapo but on the basis of a denunciation of which I knew and which did not come from the SD."

Fourteenth question: "For what reason were you arrested?" Answer: "On account of my connections with some leading men of the 20th of July."

Fifteenth question: "Did the examining officials in the case against you know the contents of your lectures?" Answer: "No, apparently not. They accepted without contradiction that as part of my defence I referred to the proper 'patriotic attitude of my lectures.' I consider it out of the question that the Gestapo officials knew my lectures and the SD reports based on them."

Sixteenth question: "What was the attitude of the Political Science Faculty in Freiburg toward the Hitler Reich?" Answer: "Not only the Political Science Faculty of the University but the majority at least of the Arts professors were opponents of National Socialism. This was well known to Dr. Scheel, the head of the Reich organisation of university teachers, and he had announced that after the war the whole University would be dissolved."

Seventeenth question: "Did the SD know of this attitude?" Answer: "There can be no doubt of that."

Eighteenth question: "Did the SD cause Gestapo measures to be taken against the Faculty of Political Science or any other members of the teaching staff?" Answer, "I know of none."

I also submitted on this point an affidavit by Hans Timmermann, SD No. 29, which is in the transcript of the Commission of 23rd July, 1946. Then by Dr. Horst Laube, SD- 31, also recorded in the transcript of 23rd July, 1946. Furthermore, SD-26 by Dr. Zirnbauer. Of that there is no summary in the transcript; therefore, may I make a brief statement about it?

Zirnbauer submitted two original reports which as honorary associate he had sent to the SD, and he testified on oath that these were reports which he had prepared as confidential agent of the SD. I should like to state that these are the only two original reports which I was able to obtain.

Supplement One is a report stating that the edition of the Alsace-Lorraine catalogue of the geographical economic section of the Saarbrucken Municipal Library was absolutely necessary.

Supplement Two is a report on Salzburg concert life.

I further submitted SD No. 30 of Zellem, also in the transcript of the 23rd July, 1946.

The next affidavit refers to the assertion of the prosecution that the SD was f all the time a part of the SS; the reference is the introduction to the Trial Brief against the Gestapo and the SD, Page 12 of the German version, and Page 67 of the English version.

In this connection I submitted SD No. 32; the short summary is in the transcript of 23rd July, 1946.

The next affidavit refers to the assertion of the prosecution that the SD played a role in the execution of one or more tasks, the reference is the Indictment against the SS, No. II, Page 8 of the German translation. In this connection I submitted affidavit by Otto Ohlendorf, and the short summary is in the Commission transcript of 23rd July, 1946.

The next affidavits -

THE PRESIDENT: You did not give the number of that affidavit, I think.

DR. GAWLIK: SD No. 23, your Lordship. No, I beg your pardon, it is No. 33.

The next affidavits refer to the assertion of the prosecution that the SD and Gestapo together formed a unified police system; these are statements of evidence No. II B, and No. III B of the Trial Brief against the Gestapo and the SD, Pages 9 and 17 of the English version. In this connection I have submitted SD No. 2 by Otto Ohlendorf, the short summary is in the transcript of 9th July, 1946.

Furthermore, SD No. 34, a short summary of the contents is in the transcript of 23rd July, 1946. SD No. 35 by Dr. Hoffmann, and the short summary is in the transcript of 23rd July, 1946, and SD No. 36 by Otto Ohlendorf, and the short summary of the contents is in the transcript of 23rd July, 1946.

With the next affidavit, I want to prove that the SD had no executive power.

In this connection I have submitted the affidavit SD No. 20 by Alfred Kutter, and the short summary of the contents is in the transcript of 9th July, 1946.

The next two affidavits supplement the affidavit of Dr. Wilhelm Hoettl, prosecution Document PS-2614. I submit in this connection a supplementary Affidavit SD No. 37 by Dr. Wilhelm Hoettl.

THE PRESIDENT: That has been submitted to the Commissioner, has it?

DR. GAWLIK: Yes, your Lordship. The summary is in the transcript of 23rd July, 1946. I have asked that this affidavit be translated completely; and I am submitting the complete translations.

I further submitted on this point SD No. 38 by Theo Gahmann, the short summary of this affidavit is in the transcript of 23rd July, 1946.

With the next affidavit I want to prove that the SD had no influence on the selection of SA leaders. The reference is statement of evidence, No. III B, Page 18 of the Trial Brief against the Gestapo and SD. On this point I submit

Affidavit SD-4 by Max Juettner. The short summary of the affidavit is in the transcript of 9th July, 1946.

With the next seven affidavits I want to prove that the SD had no influence on the selection of Party leaders. The reference is statement of evidence, No. III B, Page 18 of the English Trial Brief. On this topic I submit SD No. 5 by Otto Frehrer, for the former Gau Mainfranken, SD No. 6 by Otto Biedermann for the former Gau Thuringia, SD No. 7 by Siegfried Uiberreither for the former Gau Styria, SD No. 8 by Karl Wahl for the former Gau Schwaben, SD No. 9 by Paul Wegener for the former Gaue Mark Brandenburg and Weser-Ems, SD No. 10 by Albert Hoffmann for the former Gaue of Upper Silesia and Westphalia-South.

Furthermore, SD-39 by Adam Foertsch for the former Gau of Upper Bavaria. I have not yet received the translation of this, and I shall hand it in later.

The next affidavit refers to the assertion of the prosecution that the SD scrutinised the loyalty and reliability of state officials. The reference is statement of evidence III B of the Trial Brief, Page 18 of the English version. In this connection I have submitted Affidavit SD-3 by Dr. Werner May. The short summary of the contents is in the transcript of 9th July, 1946.

I now come to crimes against peace. With the next affidavit I want to prove that the SD was not used in the border incidents of August, 1939, and that the members of the SD had no knowledge of the statement of evidence V, Page 23 of the English version.

In this connection I submitted Affidavit SD-11, by Dr. Marx. The short summary of the contents is in the transcript of 9th July, 1946.

I now come to war crimes, first of all to statement of evidence VI A of the Trial Brief against the Gestapo and SD, Page 25 of the English version. In this connection I submit Affidavit SD-,41 by Karl Heinz Bent. The summary of the contents is in the transcript of 23rd July, 1946.

I have also submitted on this point SD-42 by Walter Schellenberg. The summary of the contents is in the transcript of 23rd July, 1946.

I shall also later submit the complete Affidavit SD-43 by Heinz Wanninger and SD-44 by Otto Ohlendorf. The summary of the contents is in the transcript of 23rd July, 1946.

I have also submitted on this point Affidavit SD-45 by Erwin Schutz, the summary of the contents is in the transcript of 23rd July, 1946, and SD-46 by Otto Ohlendorf, the summary of the contents is also in the transcript of 23rd July, 1946.

With the next three affidavits I want to prove that the members of the Leitabschnitte (the central regional authority), the Aussenstelle (branch offices) and the Vertrauensmanner (confidential agents) had no knowledge of the activities of the Einsatzgruppen employed in the East.

In this connection I have submitted SD-47 by Wilhelm Duerhof, which refers to the former Gaue South-Hanover and Braunschweig. SD-48 by Karl Heinz Bent refers to the former Oberabschnitt Neu-Stettin, Breslau, Dusseldorf.

SD-49 by Adolf Rott refers to the former SD regional authority at Neustadt-Weinstrasse and at Saarbrucken.

These three affidavits were submitted on 23rd July, 1946.

The next affidavit refers to the assertion of the prosecution that the SD Abschnitt Tilsit participated in the liquidation of Jews and Communists in the border areas, statement of evidence VI A of the Trial Brief. I shall submit a complete translation of my Affidavit SD-12 by Wilhelm Sieps later. The summary of the affidavit is in the transcript of 9th July, 1946.

The next affidavit refers to prosecution Document PS-1475 and statement of evidence VIA of the Trial Brief, Pager 25 of the English version. In this connection T submit the affidavit of Gerti Breiter, SD-69.

With the next affidavit I want to prove that the SS Major Puetz, mentioned on Page 26 of the English Trial Brief against the Gestapo and SD, did not belong to the SD but to the Gestapo.

In this connection I have submitted Affidavit SD-50 by Heinz Wanninger. The summary is in the transcript of 23rd July, 1946.

The next affidavits refer to statement of evidence VI F of the Trial Brief, Page 54 of the English text.

The first subject of evidence is this: in prosecution Documents PS-553, PS-498, and PS-532, SD does not mean Home Intelligence, Amt III, or Foreign Intelligence, Amt VI, or Amt VII, but the Security Police. In this connection I submit Affidavit SD-52 by Wilhelm Keitel. The summary of the contents is in the transcript of 23rd July, 1946.

The next subject of evidence: that the SD did not participate in lynchings. In this connection I have submitted SD-51 by Walter Schellenberg, summary of the contents is in the transcript of 23rd July, 1946.

Furthermore SD-68 by Hans Steiner. The summary of the contents. is in the transcript of 3rd August, 1946.

The next two affidavits refer to the. assertion of the prosecution that the SD murdered prisoners in the prisons in order to prevent their being liberated by Allied troops, statement of evidence VI J, Page 56 of the English version of the Trial Brief.

On this subject I have submitted SD-13 by Horst Laube. The summary of the contents is in the transcript of 9th July, 1946. SD-14, by Fritz Wolfbrandt, is in the same transcript.

The next affidavit refers to the assertion of the prosecution that the SD participated in the forcible confiscation and partitioning of public and private property; statement of evidence VI K, Page 67 of the English version. In this connection I have submitted SD-15 by Kurt Klauke. The summary of the contents is in the transcript of 9th July, 1946.

The next affidavits refer to the assertion of the prosecution that the SD persecuted Jews, statement of evidence VII A, of the English text of the Trial Brief. I have submitted in this connection SD-16, by Walter Keinz. The summary of the contents is in the transcript of 9th July, 1946. SD-17, by Emil Hausmann, is in the same transcript. Also SD-53, by Emil Froeschel, in the transcript of 23rd July, 1946, and SD-54 by Dr. Laube in the same transcript.

The next affidavits refer to the charge that the SD persecuted the Church statement of evidence VII B, Page 63 of the English text of the Trial Brief.

I have submitted in this connection SD-55, summary of the contents being in the transcript of 23rd July, 1946. Walter Keinz, SD-18, in the transcript of 9th July, 1946.

I shall submit later a complete translation of SD-19 by Helmut Fromm, summary of the contents being in the transcript of 9th July, 1946.

With the next affidavit I want to prove the methods, aims, activities and tasks of the SD in the Government General. On this topic I shall later submit a complete translation of SD- 56 by Helmut Fromm, summary of contents is in the transcript of 23rd July, 1946.

With the next affidavit I want to prove that the police in France was called SD. I have submitted in this connection an affidavit by Dr. Laube, SD-23, summary of contents is in the transcript of 9th July, 1946.

The next affidavit is submitted as proof that the members of the Gestapo and Kripo in Belgium and Northern France wore the SS uniform with the SD insignia. I have submitted SD-24 by Walter Hofmeister, summary of contents is in the transcript of 9th July, 1946.

With the next affidavit I want to prove that the members of the SD employed in Belgium and Northern France did not belong to Amt III. For this point I have submitted SD-25 by Walter Hofmeister, summary of contents is in the transcript of 9th July, 1946.

With the next affidavit I want to prove that membership of the SD Amt III during the war was in general not voluntary but was based on a legal order. In this connection I have submitted SD-57 by Bernhard Dilger in the transcript of 23rd July, 1946; SD-58 by Dr. Ehlich in the same transcript; SD- 59 by Karl Heinz Bent in the same transcript: SD-60 in the same transcript, and I shall submit later SD-21 by Oskar Eisele, summary of the contents is in the transcript of 9th July, 1946.

With the next affidavit I want to prove that withdrawal from the SD was not possible for full-time and salaried members. I submit SD-22 by Werner May, summary of contents in the transcript of 9th July, 1946.

The next three affidavits refer to the tasks, aims, and activities of Amt VI. On this subject I shall submit later SD-61 by Walter Schellenberg; the summary of the contents is in the transcript of 23rd July, 1946. Furthermore, SD-62 by Walter Schellenberg, summary of contents is in the same transcript. Furthermore, on the tasks and activities of Amt VI, I submit SD-66, by Otto Skorzeny.

The next affidavit refers to the aims, tasks, and activities of Amt VII. I submit this affidavit provisionally as the Commission did not decide whether Amt VII falls under the Indictment. The chairman of the Commission told me that the Tribunal would decide this question. The affidavit is SD-63 by Dr. Dietl, which I shall submit later.

The next affidavit refers to the assertion of the prosecution that the immigration offices had the purpose of carrying out evacuations with the aim of permanent colonisation of the occupied territories, destruction of the national life of these territories, and thus constant expansion of the German borders. (Trial Brief against the SS, III G, Pages 33 and 35 of the German translation.) I have submitted in this connection SD-64 by Martin Sandberger, summary of the contents is in the transcript of 23rd July, 1946.

Now I have an affidavit to refute the Affidavit F-964 which was submitted by the prosecution during the examination of the witness Dr. Hoffmann. I was notable to submit this affidavit to the Commission because the Commission had already concluded its sessions when I received it. May I therefore submit it now under SD-65.

THE PRESIDENT: You have one 65 already, have you not? It came through the translation.

DR. GAWLIK: That should be SD-71, your Lordship. From this affidavit I shall read the following, briefly:

> "(1) To prove my knowledge of the facts given, I, Georg Schebel, state the following: From 1930 to 1939 I was Government Councillor in Brunswick. In 1939 I was temporarily in the Reich Criminal Police Office in Berlin, and from 1941 to 1945 I was Section Chief of Personnel in the Main Office of the Security Police of the Reich Ministry of the Interior. From January, 1944, on, I was also in charge of the Personnel Department of the Secret State Police, Gestapo. My last rank was Regierungsdirektor and SS Standartenfuehrer."

Now the facts:

> "At no time in the existence of the Gestapo and the SD were instructions or decrees issued by the Chief of the Security Police and the SD, or by the Reich Ministry of the Interior, ordering that the activities of the Gestapo, either at its headquarters or at its agencies throughout the Reich, were to be influenced or supervised by the SD. The agencies of the Gestapo were at all times completely independent. The independence and the special position of the State Police made all general influence of the SD impossible; supervision would not have been tolerated either by the Chief of Amt IV or the Chief of the Security Police, because such supervision would not have been respected and would have been quite incompatible with the actual responsibility of the State Police itself."

I ask that I may be allowed to submit this affidavit later when I have the translation.

Now I have a collective statement on 6,123 affidavits. I have not yet received the translations. I beg your pardon, I have the French translations, may I be allowed to submit those? I also submit the list of these affidavits. From my collective statement I ask only to be allowed to read subject 18, concerning participation of SD members in executions in the areas of the Einsatzgruppen. On this subject I have 140 affidavits from agencies of the SD in all parts of Germany for the period 1939 to 1945, which state the following:

"The agencies and members of the SD Amt III had no knowledge of the participation of SD members in executions carried out by the Einsatzkommandos in the East."

I now come to the presentation of my documents, which are also numbered according to the Trial Brief against the Gestapo and SD. The first document refers to the charge of conspiracy.

I submitted as Document SD-1 an agreement between Himmler and Ribbentrop for the establishment of a uniform German Secret Intelligence Service. The document has already been submitted under USSR 120. I quote from this document the following: "The Secret Intelligence Service has the task, as far as foreign countries are concerned, of gathering for the Reich information in the political, military, economic and technical spheres." And the following paragraph: "Information received by the Secret Intelligence Service from foreign countries will be put at the disposal of the Foreign Office by the Reichssicherheitshauptamt."

SD-2 is an excerpt from the special plan for searches of the Security Police and the SD. I shall not read this document, but I would like to call the attention of the Tribunal to the fact that although Amt III and Amt VI were united with Amt IV and Amt V in the Reichssicherheitshauptamt, Amt III and Amt VI had no police tasks, and there was a strict division between the offices of the Security Police and those of the SD; Amt III and VI were not entitled to order any searches.

The next six documents, SD-3, SD-4, SD-5, SD-6, SD-7 and SD- 8, belong together. They are excerpts from decrees of the Reich Minister of Justice, SD-3; of the Reich Traffic Authority, SD-4; of the Office of the Reich Food Estate, SD- 5; of the Reich Forestry, SD-6; of the Reich Ministry for Armament and War Production, SD-7; and of the Reich Ministry for Food and Agriculture, SD-8; decrees concerning the co-operation of these agencies with the Security Service, SD.

I call the special attention of the Tribunal to the tasks of the SD as shown in these documents: to inform the leading Reich authorities of the effect of official measures on the population. I submit these documents also as evidence that it was the task of the SD to co-operate not only with the State Police but with all agencies of the State.

The next document is SD-12. With this I want to prove that the SD, in the years around 1936, did not have the significance ascribed to it by the prosecution.

The next document is SD-13. It is an excerpt from the circular decree of the chief of the Sipo and the SD of 16th October, 1941. This document shows that the SS and police jurisdiction applied only to full-time and salaried members of the SD, but not to honorary members and not to those who were carrying out single tasks. The majority of the members of the SD were honorary members, and were therefore not under the SS and police jurisdiction.

The next document is SD-14. It is an excerpt from a decree of the Party

Chancellery, from which I quote the following: "Only the Hoheitstrager of the movement, from Kreisleiter up, are entitled to issue political testimonials or certifications of political reliability." This document refers to the Trial Brief against the Gestapo and the SD, statement of evidence, III and IV. The next document, SD-15, deals with the same subject of evidence. It is an excerpt from the circular decree of the RSHA, dated 12th June, 1940. This decree shows that from 1st July, 1940, the information bureau of the Amt I, SD, was to be transferred to Division IV, C 1, and thus for political information of all kinds the Gestapo Amt became competent, and the Gestapo had no more support from the SD.

The next document is SD-15A, which refutes PS-3385 submitted by the prosecution and shows that the SD was neither the only information service of the Party nor the information service of the Party at all. Within its political organisation, the Party had its own political situation reports, and from the Kreisleiter up it had specific reports from all offices.

Document SD-16 is an excerpt from the memorandum by Hitler about the problems of a four-year plan.

With SD-17 I want to prove that the activity of members of the SD in the occupied territories was not a voluntary one, but was based on a legal order. I quote from this document the following: "Refusal of departmental personnel to undertake employment in occupied territories."

"The order ..." - I omit the details - "has approved on principle that personnel in public service can be compelled to undertake work in places other than the regular place of service. Since it is not intended to limit this order to apply only to Reich territory, a staff member - provided the terms of the special service order have been complied with, especially now in time of war - may also be called upon and detached to fulfil a mission in the occupied territories."

With the next documents, SD-18 to SD-22, I want to refute the assertion of the prosecution that the SD had special units in prisoner-of-war camps with the task of segregating and executing racially undesirable persons; the reference is the Trial Brief against the Gestapo and the SD, statement of evidence, IIIB.

Document SD-18 is an excerpt from the circular decree of the Chief of the Security Police and the SD. I call the attention of the Tribunal to the file note "IVA," which shows that the Gestapo was competent in this matter. Moreover, the decree is addressed to all State Police authorities and to the commander of the Security Police in Lublin.

I should also like to call the attention of the Tribunal to the file note "IVA," of the next document, SD-19. I quote the following from this document. "The State Police directorates are again requested to speed up the current examinations still incomplete."

Document SD-20 concerns employment of Russian prisoners of war -

THE PRESIDENT: Dr. Gawlik, what is the meaning of SD-19, paragraph 2? The writing refers especially to various figures and then "No. 92/42 Top

Secret," according to which the selection of all prisoners of war is to be made in the future in the Government General only. How do you select prisoners of war? What does that mean?

DR. GAWLIK: That is the charge which the prosecution has made, and I want to prove that this was done by the Gestapo alone. This decree orders that in future these selections are to be carried out only in the Government General. But that is not relevant in this connection, your Lordship. I am only concerned with paragraph 3.

THE PRESIDENT: But it is a document of the SD, is it not?

DR. GAWLIK: Yes.

THE PRESIDENT: It is an administrative ruling, is it not?

DR. GAWLIK: Your Lordship, the Chief of the Security Police and the SD had seven offices (Amt). It is, therefore, important which of his offices acted. Amt IV was the Secret Police, Gestapo, Amt III was the Inland SD, Amt VI was the Foreign News Service. Each of these offices had its own chief, and Amt IV was an organisation different from that of Amt III and that of Amt VI. Above these seven offices was the Chief of the Security Police and of the SD. This title does not in itself show that the SD had anything to do with any matter, but one must examine which of the offices acted, Amt IV, III or VI. And for that reason I called your Lordship's attention to the file note, IVA, that is Amt IV, the Secret State Police, Gestapo. This shows that Amt III and Amt VI had nothing to do with this matter, but that it concerned Amt IV only. This is also shown by the numeral III which expressly lists only the State Police directorates.

THE PRESIDENT: Very well, we will adjourn now.

(A recess was taken until 1400 hours.)

DR. GAWLIK: In answer to the last question of your Lordship, I think it would assist the Tribunal if I were to indicate briefly the drift of my evidence and what I propose to establish by means of these documents.

It is assumed by the prosecution that the Gestapo, the Security Police and SD are independent organisations. The Gestapo is indicted separately, the Kripo (Criminal Police) is not indicted and the SD is indicted as a part of the SS. Over all of them stood the Chief of the Security Police and the SD, so that in a small way it can be compared with the position of the defendant Goering, who was the Commander-in- Chief of the Air Force, Prussian Minister President, and Reich Hunting Master.

Thus, one cannot conclude from that which office it was, and that becomes apparent from the file numbers and the people who dealt with these files, and I am trying to establish that by means of my documents.

I now come to Document SD-20, which deals with the employment of Soviet Russian prisoners of war. One paragraph deals with the very questions which your Lordship addressed to me with reference to the previous document, and I shall, therefore, read this paragraph.

"In order to avoid any delay in moving fresh arrivals of prisoners of war
into the Reich, the singling out of political commissars and 'politruks'

by the Einsatzkommandos of the Security Police will in future be carried out in the Government General only.

In the Government General the singling out will continue to be carried out by the Security Police."

By this by wish to establish that we are here purely concerned with a measure of the Security Police and not of the SD.

It then goes on to say:

"In order to ensure a more rapid execution, the Security Police will reinforce its Einsatzkommandos in the Government General."

I then pass on to Document SD-21. In this connection I beg to draw the Tribunal's attention to where it expressly says:

"If occasion arises the request by the Kommandantura to examine certain Arbeitskommandos through the Security Police is to be complied with," and I beg to draw the attention of the Tribunal to the file references IV, that is: measures of Amt IV. Amt IV was the Secret State Police, the Gestapo. Had it been the SD, then the file reference would have had to be III or VI. I now come to -

THE PRESIDENT: In the document you have just been dealing with you have got 2A III E at the top, and you have III B a little bit farther down.

DR. GAWLIK: Your Lordship, the one at the top is the general collection of decrees of which there are several volumes and which I got from the library here, and "A III" refers to this general collection of decrees. The fact that it was Amt IV can be seen from the file reference "IV A (1 c) 2468 A/B 42 G."

THE PRESIDENT: Just by 1st April, 1942, there is III B. What does that mean - OKW File No. 2F 2417B, prisoner-of-war organisation 3 B?

DR. GAWLIK: I have not got that. Your Lordship, I have not got that here; I do not know -

THE PRESIDENT: Immediately under the words: "re: labour detachments for agricultural work."

DR. GAWLIK: May I ask your Lordship, did you refer to SD-21? That is a military file reference, your Lordship. It says OKW, High Command of the Armed Forces, file reference of the armed forces, chief of prisoner-of-war organisation III B, and that III B has nothing to do with Department III.

THE PRESIDENT: All right, go on.

DR. GAWLIK: I now come to Document SD-22. Here we are concerned with an extract from the directives for the Kommandos of the Chief of the Security Police and of the SD to be assigned to the prisoner-of-war camps. The date is 17th July, 1947.

I beg to draw the Tribunal's attention to the fact that the leaders of the Einsatzkommandos are ordered to get in touch with the chief of the nearest State Police office or the Commander of the Security Police and the SD.

The commander can be compared on a small scale with the office of the Chief of the Security Police and the SD; he too had several sub-departments, III was SD, IV was State Police, V was Criminal Police; so that even the title of commander does not show which department issued it.

I should like to draw the attention of the Tribunal to the following sentence:

"As a matter of principle, such communications are to be passed to the RSHA IV A 1 by way of information."

From that it becomes evident that the measures were only dealt with in Amt IV, that is the State Police, and that the Amt III had nothing to do with it.

The following documents, SD-23 to SD-28 inclusive, refer to the allegation on the part of the prosecution, according to which the SD had carried out the "Kugel" (bullet) decree (Trial Brief against the Gestapo and SD, statement of evidence VI c).

I shall first of all deal with Document SD 23. The document has already been presented by the prosecution under the number PS-1650. It concerns the teleprint letter from the Gestapo, the Aussendienststelle Aachen, to all main State Police offices. I quote in order to prove that here, too, we are merely concerned with measures of the Secret State Police, the Gestapo.

"In this connection, I order the following:

1. The main offices of the State Police are to take over the recaptured prisoner-of-war officers from the Stalag commandants and transfer them to the Mauthausen concentration camp according to the procedure customary up to now, unless circumstances make special transport necessary.

2. The OKW has been requested to instruct the prisoner-of-war camps that, for the purposes of camouflage, the recaptured persons should not be delivered directly to Mauthausen but to the competent local office of the State Police."

I come to Document SD-24.

THE PRESIDENT: Why do you leave out the fact that those documents were addressed to inspectors of the Sipo and the SD?

DR. GAWLIK: Your Lordship, the case of the inspectors is the same as that of the Chief of the Security Police and SD and the commanders. The inspector was over the Criminal Police, over the State Police, and over the SD, and, therefore, he was exercising all three functions.

THE PRESIDENT: According to this he was an inspector of the SD.

DR. GAWLIK: He was inspector of the SD; but it does not follow that because the inspector of the Sipo was the same person, that when carrying out that activity he was acting in the capacity of the inspector of the Sipo. We are here concerned with several offices under one person. But the contents show that prisoners of war were only to be taken over by the main offices of the State Police, and that the SD offices had nothing to do with it. It says expressly under No. 1:

"The main offices of the State Police are to take over ... "

The inspector of the Security Police and of the SD also had jurisdiction over these police offices. He had control of these measures of the State Police in his capacity as inspector of the Security Police. The fact that he also simultaneously was inspector of the SD does not mean that these things were to be carried out also by the SD offices.

THE PRESIDENT: Please continue, Dr. Gawlik.

DR. GAWLIK: I come to Document SD-24. It has already been presented under PS-1165 and in this connection I beg to draw the attention of the Tribunal, to the fact that this is signed by Muller, who, as is known to the Tribunal, was the chief of Department IV. This again shows that the Gestapo alone were competent.

Document SD-25 is a circular decree from the Chief of the Security Police and the SD, dated 20th October, 1942, which deals with the treatment of escaped Soviet prisoners of war, and again I beg to draw the attention of the Tribunal to the file reference, which is IV.

I will now quote: "I request that the main offices of the State Police instruct all the police offices of the area, even if it has already been done, according to Article 3 of the decree of the High Command of the Armed Forces of 5th May, 1942.

May I inform your Lordship in this connection that if this had been one of the tasks of the SD offices, then the SD offices would also have had to be informed.

THE PRESIDENT: Dr. Gawlik, I do not think it is doing any good at all to argue upon each document. You must make your final speech at some time; and unless there is anything really very important in particular documents which you want to draw our attention to, so that we can really consider it before you make your final speech, you had much better leave the argument upon the documents until you get to your final speech. This is simply wasting our time without serving any useful purpose at all.

DR. GAWLIK: Your Lordship, I only did -

THE PRESIDENT: Well, up to the present you have commented upon each document as far as I can see, SD-22, SD-23, SD-24, SD-25, each one of them; and you are going through the book like that. Why do you not offer them all in evidence in bulk; and then if you want to draw our attention to any particular document for some particular purpose, as I said, because you think it is important and we should consider it before you come to make your final speech, do so. But do not spend time in just explaining what each document is. We have to hear all the other organisations before we come to hear your speech.

DR. GAWLIK: I only did it because I gathered from the question that there was some confusion with regard to the positions of the Chief of the Security Police and the SD, and that of the commanders and of the inspectors.

THE PRESIDENT: I only put a question to you because you were going through each document in turn and I could not understand what the documents were about.

DR. GAWLIK: Documents 27 and 28 also deal with the allegation on the part of the prosecution regarding the "Kugel" decree. May I perhaps quote from Document No. 28:

"In so far as escaped Soviet prisoners of war are brought back to the camp according to this order, they are in every case to be turned over to the nearest office of the Gestapo."

The following documents, SD-29 to SD-42, deal with the accusation raised against the SD by the prosecution, according to which the SD is to be held responsible for the setting up of concentration camps and determining their purpose, and for the transfer of political and racial undesirables to concentration and extermination camps for the purpose of forced labour and mass extermination (Page 43 of the British Trial Brief). These documents show that the SD did not in any way participate in these measures; and, if I may, I should like to read one sentence of Document SD-29:

"In the future, restrictions of personal liberty" - I leave out some lines- "may be ordered only by the Secret State Police office, and this applies to the entire State territory, by the administrative heads of provinces (Regierungsprasidenten), by the police commissioner in Berlin and by the State Police branch offices for the local sphere of their authority."

From Document SD-31 I quote:

"Protective custody can be ordered for any person as a coercive measure of the Secret State Police in order to combat any activities hostile to the State and the people. Only the Secret State Police is entitled to decree protective custody."

Document 37 deals with the allegation by the prosecution according to which the SD also administered concentration camps. I shall, therefore, quote one sentence from the document:

"The camp commandant is in charge of the administration of a concentration camp and of all economic industries of the SS within its sphere of organisation."

The administration of camps is also shown in Document SD-38.

THE PRESIDENT: I cannot see any point in drawing our attention to that document at the present time.

DR. GAWLIK: I do so because in the Trial Brief the accusation has been raised against the SD that it also administered concentration camps.

THE PRESIDENT: But this document does not show that they did not.

DR. GAWLIK: Document SD-37 is a decree from the Chief of the SS Economic Administration Main Office. That was a completely different office, which had nothing to do with the RSHA.

THE PRESIDENT: It seems to me to be quite vague as to who the camp commandants of concentration camps are. As I say, it does not seem to me to be a document which it is necessary to refer to at this stage.

DR. GAWLIK: I then refer to Document SD-39. There it says:

"The transfer of the Inspectorate of the Concentration Camps to the Economic Administration Main Office has been carried out with the full agreement of all the main offices concerned."

From this it becomes apparent that, first of all, concentration camps were under the jurisdiction of the Inspectorate of the Concentration Camps, and that this was then transferred to the SS Economic Administration Main Office. However, the SD belonged to the RSHA. The fact that concentration camps were under the jurisdiction of the Inspectorate of Concentration Camps also becomes apparent from the previous Document SD-38.

I beg to refer you to Document No. 40, in which it is explicitly stated -

THE PRESIDENT (Interposing): You are not taking the slightest notice of what I said to you. You are going through every document, or practically every document. You began this by saying that 29 to 42 dealt with concentration camps. Then you went to 37; then you went to 38; then you went to 39. They really do not help the Tribunal at all: You have told us that 29 to 42 referred to transfer to concentration camps. Well, that is quite enough. Unless there is a document which is really important, which we should study before we hear you make your speech, the summary that 29 to 42 deal with transfer to concentration camps is quite enough.

DR. GAWLIK: I thought that I could assist the Tribunal by drawing their attention to the fact that concentration camps came under the SS Economic Administration Main Office and not the RSHA. Only for that reason did I discuss these further documents.

Documents SD-43 to 49 deal with the accusation that the SD had participated in the deportation of citizens of the occupied territories for the purpose of forced labour, and that it had the task of supervising this forced labour.

SD-43 shows the jurisdiction of the State Police.

I quote from these documents only the following. From Document SD-43, under figure "2".

"The tasks arising from the employment of Soviet Russians are to be comprised in a section attached to the State Police Main Office. This section will be in charge of a criminal police official, who in turn will be under the constant personal supervision of the Chief of the State Police Main Offices."

I now quote one sentence from Appendix I to Document SD-43:

"The recruitment of labour from the former Soviet Russian territory will be carried out by recruitment commissions from the Reich Ministry of Labour." And:

"The recruitment commissions of the Reich Labour Ministry will set up reception camps."

Document SD-50, deals with the Commando Order. I beg to draw the Tribunal's attention to the words "are to be handed over to the Security Police."

Documents SD-51 to 53 deal with the allegation on the part of the prosecution that the SD had the task of protecting civilians if they had lynched airmen belonging to the United Nations.

Document SD-54 is already in evidence under USA 504 and PS-668. It deals with the carrying out of the "Nacht and Nebel" (Night and Fog) decree.

Documents SD-55 to 57 deal with the assertion on the part of the prosecution that the SD, in summary proceedings, had arrested citizens of occupied territories and sentenced them before the Courts.

I beg to draw the attention of the Tribunal to Document SD- 55, which is also L-316, and from that I shall quote one sentence:

"These foreign nationals are in the future to be turned over to the police."

I quote one regulation, one sentence, from Document SD-56:

"Penal actions of Jews will be punished by the police."

Documents 58, 58A, 58B and c deal with the assertion on the part of the prosecution that the SD had participated in the confiscation by force and partitioning of public and private property.

I shall quote one sentence from Document SD-58:

"The confiscation will be declared by the main offices of the State Police for the benefit of the Greater German Reich."

SD-59 and SD-60 deal with the third-degree methods during interrogations. In this connection I beg to draw the Tribunal's attention to filing reference Roman numeral IV which deals with the jurisdiction of Amt IV, Secret State Police.

In Document SD-60 the existing regulations applicable to the Security Police in the Government General are expressly specified.

Documents 60A to SD-64 deal with the charge against the SD according to which Crimes Against Humanity were committed. SD-60A to 63 deal with the persecution of Jews. In connection with Document SD-62 I beg to draw the attention of the Tribunal again to IVB and also to the signature "Muller, Chief of the Secret State Police."

Document SD-64 refers to the charge against the SD in reference to the persecution of the Churches (statement of evidence VIIB, Page 57). Documents SD-65 to 69 set forth the legal regulations on the strength of which during the war a large portion of members of the SD Amt III and VI were called up for compulsory and emergency service; I should like to draw the attention of the Tribunal to the following sentence in Document SD-65:

"As employers of labour" - and I shall omit a few words - "the SD sections can request the labour offices to place at their disposal replacement and supplementary manpower in accordance with the principles of allotment and use of the population during war time."

SD-60 contains the punishment decreed for those who have not complied with such regulations.

I now come to Document SD-70, regarding which I have been unable to agree with the prosecution. I ask, therefore, that first a decision be made as to whether or not I may introduce this document.

THE PRESIDENT: I have only got one document book.

DR. GAWLIK: It is in the appendix, your Lordship. May. I send up the original, your Lordship?

THE PRESIDENT: Yes. Will you tell the Tribunal what it is about?

DR. GAWLIK: With this document I want first of all to prove that the SD did not belong to the police and did not belong to the SS. Furthermore, I wish to establish that the SD in the Reich and the organisation of the Security Police and the SD outside the Reich wore separate organisations, and I want to establish the tasks of Department III. I beg to draw the Tribunal's attention to the fact that in Section 4 the SD is mentioned under German Intelligence Service.

THE PRESIDENT: This is a book produced by the Allied Command, is it not? Supreme Headquarters, Allied Expeditionary Forces, and you are offering that, is that it?

DR. GAWLIK: The General Secretary

THE PRESIDENT: Has there been any formal application for this document?

DR. GAWLIK: Oh, yes. The document is contained in the appendix to the document book. But I have not been able to reach an agreement with the prosecution regarding the appendix of this book.

THE PRESIDENT: We will hear the prosecution about it.

LT.-COMMANDER HARRIS: May it please the Tribunal, we have no strong objection to this document. It is simply one of several which we discussed and we did not agree upon it. Our objection is primarily to its value in so far as evidence is concerned. It is an intelligence book and therefore what is said in that book relates exclusively to matters of intelligence. It is dated April, 1945, That is the date of its publication and quite obviously, as of that date, the information could not be available such as is now available to the Tribunal in a competent form.

DR. GAWLIK: Your Lordship -

THE PRESIDENT: The Tribunal will admit the book for what it is worth.

DR. GAWLIK: First of all, I beg to draw the Tribunal's attention to the fact that in this book the organisation of the State and the Party is subdivided into four parts and the Intelligence Service is given a section of its own - Roman numeral IV. Roman numeral I is the State and Party; Roman numeral II is Para-Military Units; Roman numeral III is the German Police, and Roman numeral IV is the German Intelligence Service; the organisation of Offices 3 and 6.

I then beg to draw the attention of the Tribunal to the fact that in the case of the SS it states that the SS consists of (1) Waffen SS, (2) the General SS, and (3) the Germanic SS. The SD is not listed there. And I further beg to draw the Tribunal's attention to the fact that the Intelligence Service mentioned under Roman numeral IV is subdivided into SD III, the organisation of the Security Police, and the SD outside the Reich, and thirdly into Offices 6 and 7.

And then I beg to draw the attention of the Tribunal particularly to the following statements regarding the activities of Office 3. There it says:

"The information supplied by intelligence agents is digested into situation reports and ..." it goes on to say ... "these reports are extraordinarily frank and sincere" - I translated that myself - "and contain a complete and unvarnished picture of the attitude and frame of mind in Germany."

I now pass on to my last document. That is a letter from an assistant master (Studienassessor) Wolfarts, and I submitted the letter because I had only just received it and I could not get an affidavit. The letter refers to Document 142. It is the well-known document from Koehem, where the SD is supposed to have supervised the voting ... and this letter mentions the evangelical clergyman Alferich Wolfarts, who voted "no," and the vote is attached to the report. The daughter's letter shows that no measures were taken either by the Gestapo or the SD against the father, who has since died.

I have finished.

Your Lordship, should I read to the Tribunal a list of the documents or should I submit a written statement as to where the documents are to be found? Most of the documents have already been submitted.

THE PRESIDENT: I think we have got that. Have we not got it at the beginning of your document book? We have an index.

DR. GAWLIK: Yes.

THE PRESIDENT: You mean to make a separate document of it?

DR. GAWLIK: I only have part of the documents, some of them are documents of the prosecution, of course.

THE PRESIDENT: If you think it would serve a useful purpose, by all means submit your index under a separate number and deposit it with the Tribunal.

DR. GAWLIK: Very well.

Concluding Speech from the Defense

FRIDAY, 23RD AUGUST, 1946

THE PRESIDENT: We call on Dr. Merkel.

DR. MERKEL (defense counsel for the Gestapo): Mr. President, may it please the Tribunal, in the proceedings against the individual defendants the deeds of individuals were examined. During the proceedings against the organisations the question we are concerned with is whether a new basic principle is to be introduced into the legal structure of this world. The trial of the Gestapo is given its significance by the conception of the prosecution that the Gestapo had been the most important instrument of power of the Hitler regime.

If I am to defend the Gestapo, it is with the knowledge that a terrible reputation is associated with that name, yes, even that horror and fear are radiated by it, and that waves of hatred beat against this name.

The words I am about to speak will be spoken without regard for the opinions of the day because I hope to be able to present factual and legal evidence which will place this High Tribunal in a position:

1. To examine whether by sentencing the organisations a legal development will be introduced which will serve humanity;

2. To establish the truth regarding the Gestapo and by this:

3. To spare the innocent amongst the former members of the Gestapo from an unfortunate fate.

The first two tasks necessitate the answering of a question which represents a preliminary problem connected with the problem of the Gestapo as a whole.

No allegation made by the prosecution has shaken me more than the assertion of the British Chief Prosecutor that the Germans, after six years of Nazi domination and through replacing the Christian ethical teachings by idolatry of the Fuehrer, and by the cult of blood, had become a degenerate nation. If this assertion is just, then, apart from the circumstances just mentioned, this is due to yet another extraordinary factor - a factor of a character so unusual that history hardly knows it: the symptoms of the demon, the demon in Hitler, and the infiltration of the demon's spirit into his regime and into the institutions which he created and employed.

How far Hitler was a demoniac has been illustrated by Goethe's words already quoted from Dichtung and Wahrheit by my colleague Dr. Dix:

" ... he (the demoniac) radiates an enormous force ... all united ethnic forces cannot defeat it ... it attracts the masses ... and it is from such remarks that the strange yet dynamic slogan may have arisen: Nemo contra deum, nisi deus ipse (No one can do anything against God except God himself)."

The effect of demonocracy in the wide world has become clear to you in some of the cases of the individual defendants. The case of the Gestapo will demonstrate to you how an institution of the State was repeatedly misused by the demoniac leaders of that State. Here, during the discussion of this preliminary question, yet another interest arises, the interest of the legal significance of demonocracy for this trial. In order to satisfy that interest I shall give another short quotation from Goethe:

"Demonocracy is a power which, though it does not oppose the moral world order, nullifies it."

According to this verdict the crucial point is that two powers determine the history of the world, "the conflict of which," as Mr. Justice Jackson said agreement with Goethe, "forms much of the history of humanity: the moral world order and the demoniac." The juridical value of this judgment for our set of circumstances becomes clear from the following considerations:

The moral world order was represented by the traditional order. Opposed to this, Hitler represented the power which, while it did not oppose it, nevertheless rendered it ineffective. In this trial the aim must be to exterminate the remains of this demoniac power. Can this and should this be done in accordance with the traditional principle of the victorious moral world order, or should it be done by other methods?

Here we have the first juridical alternative of this trial clearly before us, deriving from the greatest of possible perspectives, i.e., consideration of the differences between the moral world order and the demoniac.

Controversial points of view dominate the present attitude toward these matters. The Charter on one hand has chosen the traditional specific principles of the moral world order. It wishes to see judgment passed against the representatives of demonocracy, the individual defendants and organisations, by means of an orderly trial, a proper indictment, with appointed defense counsel and resulting in a sound verdict. On the other hand, the "law of the Charter" itself, according to the words of Mr. Jackson, is "a new law" with principles which contradict the age-old traditional legal conception. As examples I quote the assumption of collective guilt and the introduction of laws with retroactive effects.

In this way it becomes apparent that the leading ideas directing this trial are in opposition to each other. It is our common task to recognise this fact and also, through joint efforts on the part of the prosecution, the defense, and the Tribunal, to arrive at a concordantia discordantium, a balance of conflicting opinions.

My leading argument as defense counsel for the Gestapo will have to be devoted, therefore, to the question of how the rules of the Charter are to be understood, according to which the Tribunal can declare, from the trial of Goering, Kaltenbrunner or Frick, that the Gestapo was a criminal organisation.

Once again I must come back to the principal consideration. If two powers of historic importance to this world decide the moral world order and the demoniac, then, if this world is to be cleansed, moral order must be victorious. But is the moral world order empowered to conduct the fight against its opponent with exceptional rules which differ, themselves, from the basic principles of the moral order? For the sake of the purity of its character and of its victory, the moral world order must only fight with the weapon of its own categoric imperative, without any compromise. Because it is thus that the opponents of Hitler fought during six years of war, starting with the principles of the Atlantic Charter. But is it right that they, the declared representatives of the moral order, should now, with the battle of arms at an end, conduct the final struggle against demonism with such exceptional rules? Surely that is impossible! Would it not create the impression that the victorious powers, particularly in the realm of ethics, do not have sufficient confidence in their inmost being?

As a result, for coming generations this maxim would develop: "That which is useful to the victor is right." The pitiless vae victis would have been enthroned, although the victors had especially emphasised that they entered the lists for justice, and because of justice. With the word "Justice" the signatory powers have called the Tribunal into existence by stating in Article 1 of the Charter that an International Military Tribunal shall be established for a just trial ....

They gave the word "Justice" emphasis by having Article 16 of the Charter headed "Fair Trial for Defendants," and then they took the precaution of specifying that the regulations contained in Articles 9 and 10 are such as may be applied.

That the victors should wish to have organisations with such a reputation as the Gestapo declared criminal - who would not understand that? But they guarded against making Articles 9 and 10 compulsory regulations. In that way justice became the first remise of the Tribunal. Within its limits, therefore, the regulations that may be applied under Articles 9 and 10 are to be handled as if the entire stipulation had the following wording: "If the Court considers it just, it may declare the organisations criminal." In this way the entire decision rests on the concept of justice.

Justice in its truest form is an attribute of God - "God is just." This sentence has penetrated our consciousness in the sense that God will call to account only him who is really guilty according to the word of Josiah: "I have called you by name."

This confirms the principle which should guide all the deliberations according to which the organisations and their members must be dealt with. In the main, two elements are involved: the members of the organisations and their families, who comprise at least fifteen million people; now we have to see that the remarkable but terrible proverb - "No one can do anything against the moral order of the world except that moral order itself" - does not prove itself true because of the judgment.

From this, the following conclusion arises for my final pleas regarding the question put by the Charter to the prosecution, to the defense, and to the Tribunal, whether rules of exception are admissible, whether, above all, the organisations are to be considered collectively capable of guilt, whether laws with retroactive power may be applied - that these questions must be answered in the negative.

The counter-question, whether the world in the future can, on the basis of the system of individuality, be protected from demoniac catastrophes, and whether the Hitler catastrophe did not prove the opposite, I should like to answer to this effect: The protection of the world against such catastrophes is not a question of a system, but rather a question of determined men who rest secure in the moral order of the world.

The significance and the consequences of the demand voiced by the prosecution to have the organisations declared criminal are of tremendous scope. That is reason enough for the defense counsel to examine with the utmost conscientiousness and thoroughness, and in every possible direction, whether the foundations are present which can carry an indictment of such consequence in terms of justice, under the moral world order.

First of all, I should like to establish with all emphasis the first and most important result of my examination: A group (Gemeinschaft) cannot be declared guilty. For criminal guilt means the embodiment of conditions which are punishable not only in an objective but also in a subjective form. In other words, a crime can only be committed in terms of guilt, that is, only intentionally. According to natural concepts, we can speak of intent only in the case of a single individual but not in the case of a group, and if foreign laws are referred to in this connection, this, in the final analysis, is a case of confusing the coinciding will of numerous individual persons directed toward a fixed aim.

However, the problem of collective guilt lies in a sense much deeper. The thought of rejecting collective guilt goes back to the most ancient times. It originated in the Old Testament and through Hellenic culture and Christianity it spread over the entire world. In this way it has become the guiding legal principle of the entire moral order of the world. In Roman law this sentence was expressed clearly Societas delequere non potest. In modern times we have retained the thought of individual guilt.

On 20th February, 1946, the Pope said in his radio speech that it was a mistake to assert that one could treat a person as guilty and responsible merely because he had belonged to a certain organisation, without taking the trouble to investigate in the individual case whether the person in question had made himself personally guilty through his actions or his failure to act. That would be an infringement on the Rights of God.

In the same sense the Hague Rules on Land Warfare of 1907 in Article 50 expressly prohibit the infliction of punitive fines because of the actions of individuals for which the population cannot be considered co-responsible.

Finally, the former State Secretary K. H. Frank was condemned to death and executed because he had, among other things, wiped out the village of Lidice because of the conduct of individual inhabitants thereof. That is to say, the fact that he had assumed the collective guilt of the community and inflicted a collective punishment on the village was counted as a crime. Thus, in our case, it cannot be proper to punish an organisation as a whole, collectively, because of the crimes of individuals.

With these brief references I believe I have made clear that the basis of the accusation against the organisations is not firmly established. I agree with the legal statements of Mr. Jackson only in so far as he concludes his observations the statement that: "It is quite intolerable to let such a legalism become the basis of personal immunity." The personal immunity of the individual members of an organisation in connection with the punishable actions committed within the organisation cannot be derived from the denial of collective guilt; rather, the culpability of the individual for the punishable actions committed by him can be emphasised more strongly.

The legal basis of the whole trial against the individuals and organisations here accused is the Charter created by the United Nations.

The defense has already taken the opportunity to express its misgivings about the Charter. To this I make reference.

I want to bring out only one point of view once more. If, in case an organisation is declared criminal, the former members are to be punished because of their mere membership, then they must do penance for something which was legally permitted at the time of the action. Thus the Charter establishes standards with retroactive force. The legal principle, however, which prohibits laws with retroactive force is firmly established in the law of all civilised States.

Thus the French Constitutional Assembly on 14th March, 1946, decided to give the Constitution of the French Republic, as a preamble, a new formulation of the "Declaration of Human Rights." Article 10 reads:

"No one can be condemned or punished unless on the strength of a law passed and published before the deed."

In accordance with this general international legal concept, the American Military Government in Germany ordered, through. Law No. 1, in Article 4:

"A charge can only be pressed, sentence passed, and punishment executed if the act at the time of its commission was expressly legally declared punishable."

The same law prohibits the use of analogy or so-called sound public opinion as a legal basis. Yes, the American Military Government considers the principle mentioned so important that it punishes its violation with the death penalty.

Finally, may I be permitted in this connection to mention Article 43 of the Hague Convention of the year 1899, according to which the United States of America, as well as England and France, undertook the obligation toward the other States, including Germany, in occupying a foreign country, to observe the laws of this country unless a compelling obstacle existed.

The United Nations have proclaimed that the goal of this trial is to restore justice and respect for International Law, and thus to promote world peace. They have acknowledged fundamental human rights and the recognised principles of International Law. Stamping as criminal formerly held legal political convictions, however, could be considered a limitation of this acknowledgment and could shake confidence in fundamental human rights. As a precedent, such a judgment could have disastrous consequences for the idea of justice and personal freedom.

My previous statements concerned the admissibility of the charge against all organisations. For the Gestapo there are two further factors.

The Gestapo was a State institution, an aggregation of State agencies. An agency, in contrast to a society or other private organisation, pursues not self-chosen but State- ordered aims, not with its own but with State means. It fulfils its function in the framework of the total activity of the State. Its actions and measures are State administrative acts. In the case of a State agency one cannot speak of submission to a common will of the agency nor of an association, more or less by agreement, for a common purpose. Thus there is lacking here the prerequisite for the concept of an organisation or group and of membership in the sense of the Charter. If private organisations cannot be considered responsible and subject to punishment, then State agencies and administrative offices certainly cannot. Only the State itself could be held responsible for its institutions if that were at all possible, never the institution itself.

The institution of the police - the political police too - belongs to the internal affairs of a State. A recognised international legal maxim, however, prohibits the interference of a State in the internal legal affairs of a foreign country. And so from this viewpoint as well, there are objections to the charge against the Gestapo, which I consider it my duty, as defense counsel, to point out.

Finally, there is a further question to be examined: If the Gestapo is to be declared criminal one of the principal defendants should have been an official of the Gestapo. But was any one of the principal defendants ever an official and thus a member of the Gestapo? That this prerequisite for trial exists seems very doubtful, for Goering, as Prussian Prime Minister, was Chairman of the Prussian Secret State Police and could give orders to it, but he did not belong to it. His position as Chief of the Secret State Police was, moreover, eliminated with the appointment of the Chief of the German Police and with the Nationalization (Verreichlichung) of the Prussian Secret State Police in the years 1936 and 1937. Frick, as Reich Minister of the Interior, was the competent minister for the police, but he was never an official of any particular branch of the police. Kaltenbrunner, finally, testified that with his appointment as Chief of the Security Police and the SD he was not made Chief of the Gestapo, and in fact he was not - as Heydrich had been since 1934 - the head of the Secret State Police Office. Nor was the Chief of the Security Police and the SD on the budget of the Secret State Police but was carried on the budget of the Reich Ministry of the Interior.

In case indictment and condemnation of the Gestapo should nevertheless be judged admissible, I now turn to the question of whether the substantive legal prerequisites are given for declaring it criminal. In other words, it must be examined whether the Gestapo as a whole was a criminal organisation or group in the sense of the Charter. In the examination of this question I shall follow the conditions laid down and designated as relevant in the decision of the Tribunal of 13th March, 1946.

But before I go into this question I must point out a general error regarding the type and extent of the activity of the Gestapo. Among the German people, and perhaps even more so abroad, it was customary to ascribe to the Gestapo all police measures, terror acts, deprivations of freedom, and killings, as long as they had any police tinge at all. It became the scapegoat for all misdeeds in Germany and in the occupied territories, and today it is to bear the responsibility for all evil. Yet nothing is more mistaken than that. The error arises from the fact that the whole police system, whether Criminal Police, Wehrmacht Police, Political Police, or SD, without distinction of the branches, were considered Gestapo. When Heydrich said at the German Police Rally in 1941: "Secret State Police, Criminal Police and Security Service are enveloped in the mysterious aura of the political detective story," this characterised the almost legendary atmosphere by which the Gestapo in particular is surrounded, even up to the present day. It was apparently in keeping with Heydrich's tactics to let the Gestapo appear in the opinion of people at home and abroad as an instrument of terror, to spread fear and horror of it, in order to create fear of engaging in activity hostile to the State.

That the Gestapo was unjustly accused of many crimes may be shown by a few examples. One of the most disgraceful individual crimes during the war was the murder of the French General de Boisse at the end of 1944 or the beginning of 1945. The French prosecution charges it to the Gestapo on the basis of Documents 4048 to 4052-PS. According to 4050-PS, however, Panzinger, who was entrusted with the execution of the plan, was at the time head of Amt V, of the RSHA, that is head of the Reich Criminal Police Office. Schulze, who is mentioned in 4052-PS, also belonged to the Reich Criminal Police Office. Document 4048-PS, according to the file note V, was also drawn up by the Reich Criminal Police Office as Amt V of the RSHA. Amt IV of the RHSA - Gestapo Office - was thus not involved, but only the Reich Criminal Police Office which included the section charged with searching for prisoners of war. Himmler, who as Chief of the Replacement Army was also in charge of the prisoner-of-war system, contacted Panzinger directly in this matter; Amt IV did not have knowledge of this occurrence at any stage. Whether Kaltenbrunner knew anything, he must make clear.

These facts are proved by the Gestapo Affidavit 88.

In the report on the condemnation of participants in German war crimes in the Russian city of Krasnodar (USSR 55), which was submitted by the Russian prosecution, the commission of these terrible crimes is charged against the Gestapo without further proof. In reality, this was the activity of an Einsatzkommando, not of the Gestapo. (See Gestapo Affidavit 45.)

I would like to refer to the testimony of the witnesses Dr. Knochen and Franz Straub. It proves that in Belgium and France, as everywhere, the Gestapo was frequently unjustly accused of crimes.

Through several witnesses (Dr. Knochen, Straub, Kaltenbrunner) it has been established that frequently, both in the occupied territories and in the home area, swindlers and other shady characters appeared who falsely passed themselves off as Gestapo officials. Himmler himself demanded that such false Gestapo officials should be handed over to the concentration camps. (See Gestapo Exhibit 34 and Gestapo Affidavit 68.)

As indicated, the Supreme Commander of the Security Police, Heydrich, was not entirely without responsibility for the false opinion about the Gestapo. Thus he deliberately furthered the rumour that the Gestapo knew everything politically suspicious because it spied on the population. That this could not be true is proved by the fact that the approximately 15,000 to 16,000 Gestapo officials in question, even if they had watched and spied on the people, would have been far from adequate for this purpose (see statement of Dr. Best).

The crimes which Gestapo members actually committed are not to be excused in any way. But it is equally certain that many things occurred for which the Gestapo officials are not responsible, and that customarily no effort was made to examine and differentiate whether certain deeds or misdeeds were carried out by members of the Gestapo or the Kripo, the SS or the SD, or even by native criminals. If, in the interest of combating crimes, it is judged proper in passing sentence at a trial to establish a form of selection as regards the deed, in the sense that punishment is to be inflicted according to whether the deed comes under this or that penal law, such a selection can never be practised as regards the person of the perpetrator. In other words, it would not be just to ascribe a deed to the Gestapo if the guilt of its members is not absolutely established.

As already stated the Gestapo is no union of persons in the technical sense of the word and probably also not in the sense of the Charter. Its constitution, its aims and tasks and the methods employed by it, cannot fundamentally be designated as 28 criminal. The position of the political police, its special tasks and the measures to be taken by it, of course demanded the form of organisation especially adapted to these purposes. In this connection I consider a brief but still comprehensive presentation of the organisational and personnel structure of the Gestapo all the more important since the Tribunal in its decisions of 14th January and 13th March, 1946, showed that it might possibly ascribe decisive importance, to the clarification of this question.

Your Lordship, in order not to tire the Tribunal with the presentation of the organisational structure and the personnel structure, I shall not read the next nine pages, but shall ask the Tribunal to take judicial notice of them.

I draw the special attention of the Tribunal to Pages 20 to 24. They deal with the fundamental difference between administrative and executive officials, the technical personnel, the employees, the emergency service workers, and the groups of persons who were taken over as units into the Gestapo - the Secret Field Police, the Customs Border Guards the Military Counter-Intelligence, and affiliated units.

I now continue on Page 24 at the top.

The above-mentioned State organism of the Political Police with its character as a branch of the state administration was outside the structure of the NSDAP and its organisations. The Gestapo was not dominated by the Party; on the contrary, its independence within the State and outside the structure of the Party was in particular intended to enable it to combat misdeeds of Party members with governmental measures. If Himmler, as Reichsfuehrer SS, became the chief of the Political Police in all States in 1933, and later in the Reich, then the State police agencies were without influence in that connection. Nothing important changed at first with regard to their activities. The Political Police offices in the German States, when they were reconstituted in 1933, were mostly staffed with officials from the previous police agencies; not even the directing officials were Party members in every case. Even later these officials who had been taken over were not replaced by Party members. Only to a small extent, and only as employees and workmen for technical duties, such as drivers, teleprint operators and office help, were persons from the Party, the SS and the SA taken over.

This independence of the Party and its affiliated organisations appears to be contradicted by the so-called assimilation of the Gestapo into the SS. This assimilation merely meant a nominal affiliation with the SS. The reason for this assimilation was the following:

The system of professional civil servants had been introduced and maintained in the Gestapo. But civil servants were, in part, not particularly respected by the Party because of their political or non-political past. In order to strengthen their authority during the carrying out of their duties, in particular when acting against National Socialists, they were to appear in uniform, as the witness Dr. Best has testified - who has described himself as the "motor" of this assimilation. With this assimilation the Gestapo officials - as, incidentally, also Criminal Police officials who were also to be assimilated - were formally listed among the SD formations of the SS, though they remained solely under the jurisdiction of their own superiors without doing any SS or SD duties. Besides, the assimilation was only carried out slowly and to an inconsiderable degree. At the outbreak of war in 1939 only approximately 3,000 members of the Gestapo out of a total of 20,000 had been assimilated. It is significant that Himmler by no means liked to see members of the Gestapo appearing in public wearing SS uniforms, as becomes evident from Document USA 447.

During the war even non-assimilated persons had to wear the SS uniform on certain assignments, even without being members of the SS. Apart from that the SS did not control the police or exert any type of influence upon its activities; it was only in Himmler's person that there was personal union in the leadership of the two.

With reference to this statement I refer you to the testimony of Dr. Best.

The Gestapo as a whole had nothing to do with the SD, which, as is known, was purely an organisation of the Party. Personal union only existed in the person of the chief of the Sipo and the SD (Heydrich, later Kaltenbrunner), which were accidental, however, and did not signify an organisational or function inter-connection. In no case was the SD centralised with the Gestapo in order to form a police system. The SD did not have to support the Gestapo in its tasks; it had no police tasks whatever.

The officials of the Gestapo did not, by any means, consider themselves members of a uniform organisation with the SS and the SD. Everyone in any of the three organisations knew that he belonged to an independent institution serving independent purposes.

Although the Gestapo was, therefore, in no way organisationally or, from the point of view of duties, connected with the Party, it was, nevertheless, not altogether detached from the administrative tasks of the State, being a State authority. To the contrary, on every level interconnections existed with the general and interior administration. The higher administrative organisations, the Ministers of the Interior of the States, the Presidents (Oberprasidenten) and Government Presidents (Regierungsprasidenten) were entitled to receive reports and issue instructions. Evidence has, indeed, shown that the majority of all State Police actions were carried out by the district and local police organisations and the Gendarmerie. This fact in particular furnishes an indication of how serious and questionable it is to indict the Gestapo as an institution of the State. Because, thinking consistently, the officials of the aforementioned administrative organisations, to the extent that they worked in a State Police capacity, would have to be indicted together with the Gestapo.

If it is impossible for these reasons to speak of a union of persons in the case of the Gestapo, that is of membership in the sense of the Indictment, the requirement of voluntariness was even less fulfilled. Not one of the witnesses examined was able to uphold the prosecutions allegation in any way; on the contrary, all witnesses had to testify that, as a matter of principle, membership of the Gestapo, was generally not on a voluntary basis.

The assignment of officials to the Gestapo took place, to a large extent, in that they were transferred to an agency of the Gestapo from a previous organisation. The order for transfer had to be obeyed on the strength of the civil service law. Severe disadvantages in one's profession would without a doubt have been the result of a refusal and very probably the loss of the position held; and had such a refusal been based on the statement that for conscientious reasons the official did not approve of the activities of the Gestapo, then he, as any civil servant in a similar case, would have become subject to disciplinary proceedings or even regular penal proceedings, resulting in the loss of his position and hard-earned privileges and, apart from that, he would even have gone to a concentration camp.

Replacements of civil servants in the Gestapo were regulated in such a way that, in accordance with the police civil service law, 90 per cent were drawn from former regular police officials who wished to become criminal police officials, whereas only 10 per cent could be taken from other professions.

Aspirants from the regular police could not, however, freely decide whether to join the Gestapo or Kripo; they were allotted by the "assignment department of the police," at Potsdam, to the Gestapo or the Kripo, according to requirements and even against their will. Incidentally, we are here concerned with regular police officials with eight to twelve years' service; that is, old police officials who had been in the police service before 1933.

It was almost impossible for an official to break loose from the Gestapo, apart from general reasons such as death, sickness and dismissal because of malfeasance. During war the Gestapo, just like the entire police, was considered as being on active service and was subject to military discipline, so that resignation was totally impossible. It was even prohibited to volunteer for military service at the front.

The same principles of assignment and retirement also applied to the institutions under the jurisdiction of the Gestapo, such as Border Police, Military Counter-Intelligence, and Customs Police, not to forget those drafted to the numerous emergency services during the war who, at times, represented nearly one-half the total personnel strength.

From these statements mostly based on the testimony and affidavits, particularly of the witnesses Best, Knoehen and Hoffmann, the following becomes apparent: The Gestapo consisted of a multitude of State agencies. But in the case of an agency, one cannot speak of members of that agency in the same way as of members of a private organisation. For that reason there was no "membership" in the Gestapo, much less a voluntary one; there was only the official position of a civil servant.

The question, also, whether the aim and task of the Gestapo were criminal must be answered in the negative. The aim of the Gestapo - just like that of any political police - was the protection of the people and the State against attacks of hostile elements upon its existence and its unhampered development. Accordingly, the task of the Gestapo is defined in Article 1 of the Law of 10th February, 1936 (Gestapo Exhibit 7), as follows. I quote:

> "The Secret State Police has the task of investigating all tendencies dangerous to the State and combating them, of collecting and exploiting the result of such investigations, of informing the national government and other authorities of findings important to them, keeping them informed and supplying them with suggestions."

These tasks of the Gestapo had the same character as those of the Political Police before 1933, and as those of any other Political Police forces in foreign countries. What is to be understood by "tendencies hostile to the State" depends upon the respective political structure of a State. A change in the political leadership cannot retroactively render illegal the activities of a political police force which had been directed against other forces regarded as hostile to the State. The activities of the Gestapo had been regulated by legal instructions issued by the State. Its tasks consisted, in the first place and mainly, of the investigation of politically illegal activity in accordance with the general penal code, in which connection the officials of the Gestapo became active as auxiliary officials of the Public Prosecutor's Department, and it further consisted of warding off such activity through preventive measures.

Now, of course, the methods of the Gestapo are made the basis of serious accusations against it in three ways, even held against it as crimes. One method is the protective custody and transfer of persons to concentration camps. I know that when I merely mention that name it radiates the cold breath of the grave. Nevertheless, even the imposition of protective custody was governed by exact regulations. Protective custody, which, by the way, is not a specifically German or specifically National Socialist invention, was recognised as legal in several findings of the Reich Courts, the Prussian Supreme Administrative Court; that is, constitutional courts.

A second method - that of the so-called third degree interrogation - must, to put it mildly, give rise to serious misgivings. On the other hand, this method was only rarely used (see particularly witness Dr. Best), and then only by order from the highest authorities and never to force a confession. This method as well, which we shall consider further in connection with the discussion of the individual crimes, was regulated by law, even during the time of the war (compare Gestapo Exhibit 60).

And, finally, the prosecution accuses the Gestapo particularly of the fact that it was not bound by law but rather that it acted purely arbitrarily. In reply to this I should like to say that if it is established in two laws (dealing with the Anschluss of Austria and the annexation of the Sudetenland) that the Chief of the German Police could take measures going beyond the existing laws, arbitrary police action is not legalised thereby; rather, we are concerned with a typical legal transfer of the authority to establish police law. The measures in the sense of this law did not mean individual action but orders of a general sort which could be issued even if in the annexed countries no law existed as yet in this regard, but which were nevertheless, binding on the population and the executive power of the police, because the necessary authority had been granted by the head of the State.

The principle that no individual action could be carried out arbitrarily, but rather that exact regulations were to exist and be observed in all executive actions, was strictly adhered to. (The witness Dr. Best.)

It never even occurred to Gestapo officials, at least not before the war, that they might be accused by the world of arbitrary actions. The tasks and methods, which were well known and legally limited not only for the members of the Gestapo but for all the world, cannot be considered criminal by the world, a world which not only formally recognised the German Reich Government, which bore the sole responsibility in this matter, but a world which repeatedly gave visible evidence of its recognition to the German people.

If foreign countries had objected to the aims pursued by the Gestapo, it would not have been conceivable for numerous foreign police systems to work in close collaboration with the German Gestapo, a collaboration which was not negotiated through diplomatic circles, obviously with the intention of learning from it (compare Gestapo Affidavits 26 and 89). In any event, because of this the individual Gestapo official must have considered his activity internationally recognised.

The aims, tasks and methods of the Gestapo remained basically constant even during the war. In so far as acts other than the ones described were intended for it, they must be evaluated as acts foreign to the police and outside the organisation. Later we shall deal particularly with the Einsatzgruppen, their composition, their activity and their relation to the Gestapo.

Following the structure of the Indictment, I shall now turn to the question of whether the Gestapo participated in a joint plan for the commission of crimes and whether it participated as a deliberate part of the whole so-called Nazi conspiracy in the sense of the Indictment. In order to deal with this question, however, it appears necessary to examine, first of all, just which crimes can be proved to have been committed by the Gestapo.

In order to characterise an organisation as criminal, just as in characterising an individual, only typical aspects may be considered, that is, only such actions and characteristics as are in accord with the peculiar nature of the respective organisation.

Therefore, incidents cannot be used which, even though they took place within the organisation, must be considered as foreign to the organisation, in this case foreign to the police; and furthermore, actions may not be cited which were committed by individual members.

In order to determine whether these actions are to be considered criminal, German law, which does not deviate from the views held by other civilised countries in the designation of general criminality, should be consulted.

In line with the method followed in the Indictment, I shall subdivide the crimes of which the Gestapo is accused, into Crimes Against Peace, War Crimes and Crimes Against Humanity.

(a) CRIMES AGAINST PEACE.

In this connection the Indictment makes the charge that the Gestapo, together with the SD, had artificially created frontier incidents in order to give Hitler a pretext for a war with Poland. Two frontier incidents are cited, the attack on the radio station Gleiwitz and a feigned attack by a Polish group at Hohenlinden.

The attack on the radio station at Gleiwitz was not carried out with the participation of Gestapo officials. The witness Naujocks, who was the leader of this undertaking but who did not belong to the Gestapo, has confirmed unequivocally that no member of the Gestapo participated in this action. Instructions for this undertaking emanated directly from Heydrich and were transmitted orally by him directly to Naujocks.

Instructions concerning the feigned attack at Holienlinden were transmitted by Muller, the Chief of Amt IV of the RSHA, to Naujocks; however, Naujocks, who directed this action, has expressly denied any participation by Amt IV.

THE PRESIDENT: Dr. Merkel, would that be a convenient time to break off?

(A recess was taken until 1400 hours.)

DR. MERKEL: Mr. President, I have heard that the French translation of my final plea is not yet available to the interpreters. For that reason I shall have to speak more slowly in the interest of the interpreters.

I have already deleted another sixteen pages from my plea in order to comply with the rule that I should finish in a certain period of time.

THE PRESIDENT: No doubt your speech will subsequently be translated and we shall have those pages before us.

DR. MERKEL: I had gone as far as the testimony of the witness Naujocks, regarding the attack on the radio station at Gleiwitz and the attack of that group near Hohenlinden. He stated that, quite naturally, it was not one of the tasks of Amt IV of the RSHA to engineer frontier incidents. Nor did Muller select members of Amt IV for the purpose of staging the last-named frontier incident but only individuals who were in his confidence; for Heydrich did not trust the Gestapo with respect to secrecy and reliability.

Naujocks stated literally: "I cannot identify Muller with the organisation of the Gestapo."

These frontier incidents were therefore not a concern of the Gestapo, but rather a personal concern of Heydrich, even to the extent to which Muller participated in them.

The Gestapo has not been accused of other Crimes Against Peace.

(b) WAR CRIMES.

One of the gravest accusations raised against the Gestapo deals with the mass murder of the civilian population of the occupied countries through the so-called "Einsatzgruppen." Not only the defense but the entire German people condemn the inhuman cruelties committed by the Einsatzgruppen. Those who committed cruelties like that and thereby defiled the name of Germany must be called to account.

Members of the Gestapo participated in the actions of the Einsatzgruppen. However, I should like to examine the extent to which the organisation of the Gestapo in toto can be held responsible for the criminal deeds of the Einsatzgruppen.

The Einsatzgruppen had to fulfil the tasks of the Chief of the Sipo and of the SD in rear echelon areas, which meant that they had to maintain law and order along the rear of the fighting units. They were subordinate to the armies, to whom liaison officers were detailed.

The Einsatzgruppen were units which had been established for certain purposes. They were composed of members of the SD, of the SS, of the Kripo, of the Gestapo, the Public Order Police, of those who had to render emergency service, and of indigenous forces. The members of the SD, of the

Rudolf Diels (1900-1957), head of the Gestapo during 1933-1934, addressing inmates at the Esterwegen concentration camp which was under control of the Prussian Interior Ministry. December 1933.

Kripo, and of the Gestapo were used without consideration for their former membership in their own branch.

Looking at it from the point of view of personnel, we are concerned here with the duties of the entire police and of the SD, not with the duties of the Gestapo alone. The actual participation of the Gestapo in the Einsatzgruppen amounted to approximately ten per cent. This, of course, was a very small number in comparison with the total figure of Gestapo officials. Their selection for the Einsatzgruppen took place without any application on their part, very frequently against their will, but on the strength of orders from the RSHA. Upon being detailed to the Einsatzgruppen, they were eliminated from the organisation of the Gestapo. They were exclusively subordinate to the leadership of the Einsatzgruppe which received its orders in part from the Higher SS and Police Leader, in part from the High Command of the Army and in part from the RSHA directly. Any connection to their home office and thereby to the organisation of the Gestapo was almost completely severed through their being used by the Einsatzgruppe. They could not receive orders of any kind from the Gestapo, and they were removed from the sphere of influence of the Gestapo.

These principles governing the Einsatzgruppen applied particularly to the Einsatzgruppen in the East, which are the ones that have been accused of the most crimes and the most serious crimes. To them also applies the fact that the Osteinsatz was not a Gestapo Einsatz either in personnel or in the tasks given, but an Einsatz of various units which had been set up especially for this purpose.

The witness Ohlendorf testified to the same effect.

The fact that the Gestapo also supplied men for this does not justify the conclusion that it was responsible for deeds committed by the Einsatzgruppen. Nor is this changed by the fact that the Chief of Amt IV, i.e., Muller, the Director of the Gestapo within the RSHA, had an important part in passing on all orders. He was acting here directly on behalf of Himmler and Heydrich. The activity of Muller cannot be decisive in view of the fact that the overwhelming majority of the agents under him had no knowledge of the events. If that had been the case, the Kripo or the Public Order Police (Ordnungspolizei) would have had to be held equally responsible for the events as a unit. But the Gestapo cannot be declared criminal because of Muller's position with regard to the Einsatzgruppen any more than the Kripo - whose chief, Nebe, by the way, was himself the leader of an Einsatzgruppe in the East - can be held responsible, on the basis of the participation of its chief and individual members, for the mass executions undertaken by the Einsatzgruppen. Therefore, mass murders of the civilian population, like all other atrocities committed by the Einsatzgruppen, cannot be charged against the Gestapo as such.

The next charge refers to the execution of politically and racially undesirable prisoners in camps.

I beg the Tribunal to take judicial notice of it, as well as of the third charge, according to which the Gestapo together with the SD sent prisoners of war who had escaped, and who had been recaptured, to concentration camps.

I continue on Page 38 of the original, in order to deal further with the concentration camps.

The American prosecution says that the Gestapo and the SD bear the responsibility for the establishment and distribution of the concentration camps and for the assignment of racially and politically undesirable persons to these and to extermination camps for forced labour and mass murder; that the Gestapo was legally entrusted with the responsibility of administering the concentration camps; that it alone had the power to take persons into protective custody and to execute the protective custody orders in the State concentration camps and that the Gestapo issued the orders to establish such camps, to convert prisoner-of-war camps to concentration camps, and to establish labour training camps.

In the treatment of this point of the Indictment the widespread error must be corrected that the concentration camps were an institution of the Gestapo.

In reality the concentration camps were at no time established and administered by the Gestapo. It is true that Paragraph 2 of the order for the execution of the law concerning the Secret State Police of 10th February, 1936 - Gestapo Exhibit 8 - that the Secret State Police Office administers the State concentration camps, but this regulation was only on paper and was never carried out in practice. It was rather the Reichsfuhrung SS which was responsible for the concentration camps, and appointed an inspector of concentration camps whose duties were later transferred to Amtsgruppe inspector (Dept. D) of the WVHA of the SS.

This is clearly confirmed among other facts by the witnesses Ohlendorf and Best and a large number of documents. (Compare among other material Gestapo Exhibits 40 and up to and including 45.)

After Hitler's seizure of power in 1933 the SA and SS had independently established numerous camps for political prisoners. The Gestapo on its own initiative took steps against these unauthorised concentration camps, eliminated them, and released the inmates. Gestapo Chief Dr. Diels even brought upon himself the accusation that he was supporting the Communists and sabotaging the Revolution. (See affidavit 41, testimony of the witnesses Vitzdamm and Grauert.)

Thus the concentration camps were never under the Gestapo. The Inspectorate of Concentration Camps and the Economic and Administrative Departments of the WVHA remained independent agencies and their chiefs were directly subordinate to Himmler.

The order contained in Document USA 492 does not affect the administration of concentration camps, but it regulates the assignment of prisoners to the various camps, so that political prisoners would not be sent to camps which, according to their structure and their form of work, were meant for hardened criminals.

Of the large number of documents which prove the non-participation of the Gestapo in the administration of the concentration camps, I should like to mention only one more: Gestapo Exhibit 38. This shows that all persons not mentioned there - and thus all Gestapo officials regardless of their rank or position - needed the written permission of the Inspector of Concentration Camps to enter a camp. If the concentration camps had been subordinate to the Gestapo, there would not have existed a necessity to obtain this written permission to enter.

In each concentration camp there existed a so-called political department, the position of which in the camp and its relationship to the Gestapo is a matter of conflicting views. In this political department were employed one to three officials of the criminal department of the Gestapo. These officials did not form an office of the Gestapo or of the Kripo; rather they were attached to the commandant of the camp as experts to fulfil police tasks in regard to individual prisoners. Above all, they had to conduct the interrogations of those prisoners against whom a case before the ordinary court was pending. This was done upon the request of the ordinary courts or of the Secret State Police, or Criminal Police. With regard to the power to issue orders they were exclusively subordinate to the commandant of the concentration camp. They had no influence whatsoever on the administration and conduct of the camp or on the transfer, discharge, punishment and/or execution of the prisoners.

As it can be seen, the concentration camps were not institutions of the Gestapo, but rather institutions which served the Gestapo requirements in the transaction of its police tasks. For the Gestapo they were the same as the regular prisons were for the courts or for the Public Prosecutor, namely, executive institutions to carry out the protective custody ordered by the Gestapo.

In my plea I shall not deal with the matter of protective custody and beg the Tribunal to take judicial notice of it.

I pass to Page 43, the second sentence of the last paragraph. If one takes the trouble to analyse the numerical relationship of the cases to the various measures available to the Gestapo, such as instructions, warning, security fee and protective custody, one will find that when the latter was chosen the transfer to a concentration camp was the least practised measure. At the beginning of the war approximately 20,000 people were kept in protective custody in the concentration approximately half of them were professional criminals, the other half political prisoners. At the same time there were kept in the regular prisons about 300,000 prisoners, of whom approximately one-tenth were sentenced for political crimes.

THE PRESIDENT: What evidence is there of those figures, of the proportions?

DR. MERKEL: Dr. Best made this statement before the Commission on 6th July, 1946. Larger use of the concentration camps was made by transferring to them the professional criminals and the anti-social elements, particularly those who had been sentenced by the court to protective custody, a measure which was not ordered and executed by the Gestapo (compare witness Hoffmann).

On the basis of Gestapo Affidavit 86 the maximum numbers of prisoners sent to the concentration camps by the Gestapo at the beginning of 1945 were about 30,000 Germans, 60,000 Poles, and 50,000 subjects of other States. All other prisoners - on 19th December, 1945, the prosecution claimed that there were in the concentration camps on 1st August, 1944, 524,277 prisoners - had been sent there not by the Gestapo but by the criminal police, the courts, and various authorities in the occupied territories.

The following parts of my brief which deal in detail with the question of concentration camps will also be omitted by me; and I again beg the Tribunal to take judicial notice of them. I shall continue on Page 50, approximately in the middle of the page.

It is correct that the Gestapo established and maintained labour training camps and that it was responsible for any commitment to them.

The purpose of a labour training camp is described by the periodical The German Police (Gestapo Exhibit 59):

"The purpose of the labour training camps is to educate in a spirit of workers' discipline those who have broken their work contracts and those who shirk their duty, and to bring them back to their old jobs after that aim has been accomplished. Any commitment is handled exclusively by offices of the State Police. To stay there is not to be considered a penalty, but an educational measure."

It is incorrect to say, as the prosecution has done, that only foreign labourers were sent to the training camps. They had been established equally for

Germans and for foreign labourers, and also for employers who had abused the rights of their employees.

The maximum length of stay stipulated (which was established after thorough investigation in each individual case) was originally twenty-one days, later fifty-six days, in contrast to the sentences of courts for breach of contract which ran from three months up to one year of imprisonment. Those who broke a contract and were committed to a labour training camp in every respect found themselves in better conditions than those who were sent to prison. The commitment was not included in the individual's court register of penalties, and in general, shelter, feeding and treatment in the labour training camps were better than in the prisons. The food consisted of the regular prisoners' rations supplemented by the additional rations for heavy work; these rations were continuously submitted to inspection as to quantity, quality, and taste, as is shown by Gestapo Exhibit 58.

On the basis of these facts, it is not possible to characterise the supervision of the foreign labourers and particularly the establishment of and commitment to labour training camps by the Gestapo as a crime.

6. Execution of Commandos and Paratroopers.

The next link in the chain of major crimes of which the Gestapo is accused is the charge that the Gestapo and the SD executed commandos and parachutists who had been captured and protected civilians who had lynched airmen. What can be said in this connection?

In Exhibit USA 500 - it is a secret order of the OKW of 4th August, 1942, concerning countermeasures against parachutists - the treatment of captured paratroopers is characterised as the exclusive concern of the Army, while that of single parachutists was transferred to the Chief of the Security Police and the SD. The latter task did not include their execution, but was to serve only the purpose of discovering possible sabotage orders on these parachutists and obtaining news about the intentions of the enemy.

On 18th October, 1942, Hitler ordered the destruction of all commando groups (Exhibit USA 501). This order was directed not to the German Police but to the German Army. Article 4 of that order stated that all members of such commandos falling into the hands of the Army should be transferred to the SD. Nothing can be learned about any part played by the Gestapo in these measures against the sabotage commandos. If, however, the Gestapo had played a part in it, a task not in the character of a police task would have been transferred to it, for the execution of which the Gestapo as an organisation cannot be accounted responsible since doubtless under any circumstances only a small number of individuals participated in it.

Besides, the following should be pointed out: As Rudolf Mildner stated in his affidavit of 16th November, 1945 - Document PS-2374 - an order was issued in the summer of 1944 to the Commanders and Inspectors of the Sipo and the SD to the effect that all members of the American and English commando troops should be surrendered to the Sipo for interrogation and execution by shooting. This may be taken as a proof that, at least up to that moment, the Sipo had not shot any commando groups, otherwise a need for this order would not have existed. Mildner continues to say that that order had to be destroyed immediately, which means that only the Commanders and Inspectors of the Sipo could gain knowledge of it. On account of the invasion which had started at that time and on account of the relentless advance of the Allies into the interior of France, it was practically impossible to execute these orders, because there were no longer any officers of the Sipo left in the field of operations, which was being pushed back continuously. Equally it is unlikely that that order, which presumably was issued by Himmler, ever became known to the mass of Gestapo members.

Above all, the prosecution rests its case on an order of Himmler of 10th August, 1943 (Document USA 333), stating that it was not the task of the police to interfere in controversies between Germans and bailed-out English and American terror flyers, and from this the prosecution concludes that the Gestapo approved of lynch law. However, it is of significance that this order of Himmler's was addressed to all the German Police, above all to the uniformed regular police. For in case of the bailing out of Allied airmen, as a rule it was not Gestapo officials who made an appearance, but members of the uniformed regular police, the military police, or the local police. Only those branches of the police were in charge of street patrols, and not the Gestapo.

As proved by the numerous affidavits, all the Gestapo members were not informed of this order, but rather learned of it only through the statement Goebbels made over the radio.

The evidence given by the witness Bernd von Brauchitsch, first assistant to the Supreme Commander of the Luftwaffe, shows distinctly that that order was generally sabotaged. He stated: "In the spring of 1944 the civilian losses through air attacks rapidly increased. Apparently this made Hitler issue orders not only for defense but for measures against the airmen themselves. As far as I know, Hitler advocated the most severe measures. Lynchings were to be permitted more liberally. The Supreme Commander and the Chief of the General Staff did, it is true, condemn the attacks on the civilian population in the sharpest terms, yet they did not desire special measures to be taken against the airmen; lynching and the refusal to give shelter to the crews who had bailed out were to be rejected."

And his further statement is of particular importance. I quote:

"The measures ordered by Hitler were not carried out by the Luftwaffe.
The Luftwaffe did not receive any orders to shoot enemy airmen or to transfer them to the SD."

Actually the Gestapo officials, in the few cases when members of the Gestapo were accidentally present after Allied airmen had bailed out, not only did not kill them but protected them against the population - see Gestapo Affidavit 81 - and if they were wounded they saw to it that they were given medical care. As to the few cases in which higher Gestapo officials ordered and executed the shooting of crews who had bailed out, these men have already been justly punished by the courts of the occupying powers. To hold all members of the Gestapo responsible for them is not justifiable.

The next point of the Indictment states: The Gestapo and the SD brought civilians from occupied countries into Germany in order to place them before secret courts and sentence them there.

On 7th December, 1941, Hitler issued the so-called "Nacht and Nebel" decree. According to this decree persons who had transgressed against the Reich or against the occupying power in the occupied areas would, as a measure of intimidation, be taken to the Reich where they were to be put before a special court. If, for any reason whatsoever, this was not possible, the transgressors were to be placed in protective custody in a concentration camp for the duration of the war.

As may be seen from the distribution list in Document 833-PS, this order went only to the offices of the Wehrmacht and not to the offices of the Gestapo - with the exception of Amt IV of the RSHA itself. The execution of this decree was a task of the Wehrmacht, not of the Gestapo. According to directives contained in Document 833-PS, it was for the Counter-Intelligence offices to determine the time of arrests of individuals suspected of espionage and sabotage.

In the Western areas, for they were the only ones concerned here, this order was to be carried out therefore by the Wehrmacht which exercised police power through its own men or those of the Security Police who were directly subordinated to the Wehrmacht commanders-in-chief.

Only to that extent did the Security Police participate in the execution of this order. The Gestapo, which was numerically very weak in the occupied Western areas, was only involved to the extent that the RSHA established a Stapo office which had to take charge of those arrested. Through the Stapo offices, in agreement with the competent Counter-Intelligence offices, the details of the deportation to Germany were determined, particularly in cases where it still remained to be decided whether transport was to be conducted by the Secret Field Police, the Field Gendarmerie, or by the Gestapo. The Gestapo had no other tasks assigned to it by the "Nacht and Nebel" decree.

Just how active Gestapo officials or Gestapo offices actually were in the execution of this decree has not been determined in these proceedings. On the contrary, according to the testimony of witness Hoffman, it has been established that Amt IV rejected this decree and that it was not applied at all in Denmark for instance.

As this decree was to be kept strictly secret, and as it emanated from the highest Wehrmacht offices, we may assume with assurance that only the most intimate circle of individuals, those charged with its actual handling, knew the contents of this decree and its significance. The officials of the Stapo offices charged with the transport received instructions to see that the arrestees were brought to a certain place in Germany without being told for what purpose or on the strength of what decrees the arrest had taken place.

If this were the case - details have not been established - you cannot hold the entire Gestapo responsible for the practice of turning over prisoners to some offices in occupied territory in order to take them under orders to Germany.

The portion of my speech dealing with the deportation of members of foreign States to Germany for the purpose of condemning them under summary proceedings and the arrest of kindred will also not be read by me, but I beg the Tribunal to take judicial notice of it.

I should now like to continue on Page 60, section 10.

The next point of the Indictment concerns the killing of prisoners upon the approach of Allied troops.

As a basis for this charge Exhibit USA 291 of 21st July, 1944, has been submitted. It is an order by the Commander of the Sipo and the SD for the Radom district through which he informs his subordinates of the order of the Chief of the Sipo and the SD in the Government General, that in the case of unforeseen developments which would make the transfer of the prisoners impossible, they should be liquidated.

The question to what extent these or similar orders have existed or were known elsewhere, and to what extent such orders were carried out, is not a matter for consideration. The essential question for me to consider, namely, the participation of the Gestapo, has not been fully determined. On the basis of the affidavits before me, and the statements by the witnesses Straub and Knochen, the Gestapo only in a few places had prisons of its own. As a rule, there existed only one police prison to be used by all local police branches. The administration and supervision of these police prisons were always the tasks of the local police administrator; in the occupied territories it was partly the task of the Army. At any rate, the Gestapo had no right to interfere with the conditions in which the prisoners found themselves. Therefore, it is unlikely that the Gestapo would have carried the killing of prisoners upon the approach of the enemy. On the other hand, it has been established with certainty that in many places the prisoners either were dismissed or were handed over to the Allied troops when they occupied the locality. (Gestapo Affidavits 12, 63, and 64.)

May I be permitted to dwell on two cases which came up during the proceedings: The witness Hartmann Lauterbacher has given evidence concerning an order, in accordance with which the inmates of the prison at Hameln in Westphalia were to be killed upon the approach of the enemy. The person who issued the order however, was not a Gestapo official, but the Kreisleiter of Hameln who, for doing so, was sentenced to seven years' imprisonment by the Fifth British Division, and those who were to execute that order were not Gestapo officials, but prison employees, who, however, refused to carry it out.

The second case concerns the camps Muhldorf, Landsberg, and Dachau, in Bavaria. I refer to the evidence given by Bertus Gerdes, the former Gaustabamtsaleiter under Gauleiter Giessler of Munich (Exhibit USA 291). It states April, 1944, the inmates of the Dachau concentration camp and of the Jewish work camps Muhldorf and Landsberg were to be liquidated; i.e., to be killed by order of Hitler. It is certain that the order was not given to the Gestapo, and, above all, that neither of these actions was carried out, owing to the refusal on the part of the Luftwaffe and the witness Gerdes - for their exoneration this must be stated here. Thus, at least in this case, crimes did not take place the frightful planning of which alone severely shocks our deepest feelings. What is of importance for the organisation of the Gestapo, which I represent, is something which it is my duty as its defense counsel to draw to your attention: The order was given to the competent Gauleiter in Munich, who was to discuss it with the head of the Gau Staff and the competent Kreisleiter. Never was there any mention that the Gestapo should be used for its execution.

Regarding the next point, the confiscation and dividing up of public and private property, I beg the Tribunal to take judicial notice of 1t and I shall continue on Page 63 of the original, section 12.

The prosecution accuses the Gestapo of having employed the third degree method of interrogation. I had already spoken about this when I discussed the question whether the methods employed by the Gestapo were criminal. At this point I have the following to say with reference to this accusation:

The documents submitted by the prosecution made it perfectly clear that it was only permissible to employ third degree methods of interrogation in exceptional cases, only with the observance of certain protective guarantees and only by order of higher authorities. Furthermore, it was not permissible to use these methods in order to force a confession; they could only be employed in the case of a refusal to give information vital to the interests of the State, and finally, only in the event of certain factual evidence.

Entire sections of the Gestapo, such as the counter-intelligence police and frontier police, have never carried out third degree interrogations. In the occupied territories, where occupation personnel were daily threatened by attempts on their lives, more severe methods of interrogation were permitted, if it was thought that in this manner the lives of German soldiers and officials might be protected against such threatened attempts. Torture of any kind was never officially condoned. It can be gathered from the affidavits submitted, for instance, numbers 2, 3, 4, 61, and 63, and from the testimonies of witnesses Knochen, Hermann, Straub, Albath, and Best, that the officials of the Gestapo were continuously instructed during training courses and at regular intervals, to the effect that any ill-treatment during interrogations, in fact any ill-treatment of detainees in general, was prohibited. Violations of these instructions were, in fact, severely punished by the ordinary courts and later by the SS and Police Courts (see Gestapo Affidavit 76.)

Then I beg official notice be taken of the subsequent pages and I shall continue on Page 65. Discussion of the crimes of which the Gestapo is accused leads me now to the third and last group - Crimes Against Humanity.

The prosecution alleges that the Gestapo, together with the SD, had been the foremost instrument for the persecution of the Jews. The Nazi regime

The Warsaw Ghetto, with a child lying on the pavement.

was said to have considered the Jews as the chief obstacle to the "police State" by means of which it had intended to pursue its aim of aggressive war. The persecution and extermination of Jews is supposed to have served this aim too. The National Socialist leaders had regarded anti-Semitism as the psychological spark to inflame the populace. The anti-Jewish actions had led to the murder of an estimated six million human beings.

Truly a shattering accusation. What has been unveiled during this trial, and confirmed by the witnesses Hoess and Ohlendorf, forms the basis of a guilt which, unfortunately, will for ever adhere to Germany's name. Yet what must still be examined after these sad facts have been ascertained is the question as to the extent to which the Gestapo has participated in the persecution and extermination of Jews.

An examination which will lead to correct results is only possible if a differentiation as regards time is made concerning the activity of the Gestapo.

After the seizure of power, the Hitler Government had published a number of penal laws concerning the Jews. As far as these legal regulations contained penal clauses, possibly necessitating the employment of force by the police, the Gestapo may, under certain circumstances, have been connected with them. Infringements of such penal laws by Jews were comparatively few, and only the Nuremberg laws announced in 1935 caused increasing police activity, in which, however, during the first period, every case was handed to the proper courts for the passing of sentences. A change only occurred in the last years of the war. That the Gestapo began to act in these cases cannot be held against it because it, too, had to comply with the existing laws of the State, that is to say, it had to obey the orders of the State just as the soldier must obey orders.

Apart from that, other administrations, such as the Administration of the Interior of the Reich, the Finance Administration, and the Municipal Administration had, to a much greater extent than the Gestapo, become active against the Jews, that is to say, regarding their personal legal status as well as their property, houses, etc., those administrations are not being accused here.

Through the excesses of November, 1938, the Jewish problem became considerably more acute. It has been ascertained beyond doubt that this revolting action did not originate from the Gestapo. In fact, the prosecution implicates the Gestapo only to the extent that it did not intervene. Information on this point is contained in the testimony of the witness Vitzdamm, according to which during the conference on the 9th November, 1938, in the evening, in Munich, with Gestapo chiefs present, Heydrich declared quite openly that this action did not have its origin in the Gestapo. Over and above this, he explicitly forbade the Gestapo to participate in the action, and gave instructions to the Gestapo chiefs present to return to their departments at once and take all steps to stop the action. The contradiction contained in this testimony and the contents of Heydrich's teleprint letter, sent to all Gestapo departments during that night (Exhibit USA 240), can be explained by the fact that between this conference of Heydrich's with the Gestapo chiefs and the issuing of the order, a development had taken place which could only be limited but no longer stopped. When the Gestapo offices received Heydrich's circular, the holocaust of senseless destruction had already swept over Germany. Nothing remained to be done but the prevention of further excesses; that was done.

In this connection I refer also to Affidavit 5, which has been submitted by the defense counsel for the SS, stating that Himmler himself had dictated the order to the Gestapo offices and revealed his conversation with Hitler, from which one learned that Hitler had ordered the safe keeping of Jewish property and the protection of the Jews. As shown by the evidence given by the witness Vitzdamm and as proved by numerous other affidavits, this order was carried out generally. I refer to the Gestapo Affidavits 6, 7 and 8.

The arrest of 20,000 Jews which followed the excesses was caused by Himmler (Exhibit USA 240) and was carried out by the Kreis and local police authorities. The overwhelming majority of the Jews, however, were not transferred into concentration camps and were released gradually. This is proved by Gestapo Affidavit 8.

For the first time, the Gestapo was burdened with a task foreign to its nature by the arrest of the Jews in November, 1938. The Gestapo - as shown by the evidence given by the witnesses Best and Hoffmann - would never have carried out or suggested these arrests, which were considered unnecessary from a police point of view. The fact that the arrested Jews were soon discharged justified the assumption of the Gestapo officials that it was but a solitary gesture and not the forerunner of worse things to come.

The Jewish question, which the National Socialist administration had raised to a major feature of its programme, was originally to have been solved by the emigration of the Jews. For this reason, in 1938, there had been founded in Vienna the Central Office for Jewish Emigration which resulted in the emigration of a large number of Jews. During the war, too, the emigration was continued according to plan as shown by Exhibits USA 304 and 410. In addition to that, evacuations of Jews started which were carried out in accordance with a detailed decree of the Chief of the German Police. On the basis of that decree, the local Gestapo offices had to prepare the evacuation and to co-operate with the Jewish communities. To their task belonged particularly the equipment of these evacuees with clothing, shoes, tools, etc. In most cases the transports were not accompanied by Gestapo officials; the personnel was composed of members of the Security Police, the Criminal Police, and the Gendarmerie. The destination was not announced in most cases. The evacuations were carried out without friction or unnecessary harshness.

From a humanitarian point of view one might well regret those evacuations of Jews most profoundly; yet the part played by the Gestapo in them consisted in the carrying out of the decrees and orders originating from higher authorities. Actually, the competency of the Gestapo in regard to the Jewish question had not at all the importance generally attributed to it. In the Jewish department of the Gestapo, both in the RSHA and in the individual Gestapo offices, only a very few officials were employed.

In 1941 Himmler decreed that the Jews in Germany should be isolated in ghettoes in Poland. This resettlement of the Jews was the task of the Higher SS and Police Leaders and was carried out by the regular police.

Hitler's policy regarding Jewry up to 1941 aimed only at the elimination of the Jews from Germany by emigration and later by evacuation, but became increasingly harsh after America's entering the war. In April, 1942, Hitler ordered the final solution of the Jewish question, i.e., the physical extermination, the murder of the Jews. The proceedings have shown in how terrible a manner this order was carried out. The tool which was used by Hitler and Himmler for the carrying out of that order was SS Obersturmbannfuehrer Adolf Eichmann, who, however, though his department was attached to the organisation of Amt IV of the RSHA, had actually an entirely independent and autonomous position, which above all was wholly independent of the Gestapo. The preparation and carrying out of the order for the murder of the Jews was kept strictly secret. Only a few persons knew the order to its full extent. Even the members of Eichmann's office were left ignorant of the order and learned of it only gradually. The evacuation and the transfer into the extermination camps were carried through by Eichmann's Sonderkommandos. They were composed of local police, almost exclusively regular police. The police were not permitted to enter the camps but were replaced immediately upon arrival at the station of their destination. In the camps themselves the circle of persons carrying out the murder orders was kept small. Everything was done to conceal the crimes.

This description, based essentially on the evidence of the witnesses Knochen, Wisliceny and Dr. Hoffmann, is supplemented in a surprising fashion by the evidence of Dr. Morgen. He declared that three persons were charged with the extermination of the Jews, Wirth, Hoess and Eichmann.

Wirth, the former Criminal Commissioner of the Criminal Police in Stuttgart, known as "Murder Commissioner for terroristic investigation methods," had, for his special task, his headquarters with his staff in Hitler's Chancellery. His task was at first the mass extermination of insane persons in Germany, then, secondly, the extermination of Jews in the Eastern countries. The Kommando which was set up by Wirth himself for the purpose of exterminating Jews was known as "Action Reinhard," and was extremely small. Before the beginning of the action Himmler personally received the oath of the members and declared explicitly that anyone who said anything about the action would be put to death. This Kommando Reinhard was independent of any police office. It did not belong to the Gestapo and it wore the uniform and carried the credentials of the Security Police only in order to allow its members free circulation in the rear of the armed forces. The Kommando started its activities with the extermination of Jews in Poland and later extended its diabolical work over the further Eastern territories, by setting up special extermination camps in inconspicuous places, and by a hitherto unknown system of deception allowed these camps to be run by the Jews themselves. The fact must be stressed that it was the Security Police of Lublin who reported Wirth's misdeeds to the RKPA and thus brought these hideous crimes to light. This fact corrects the testimony of Hoess, who declared that the extermination camps of Maidanek and Treblinka had been operating under the orders of the Security Police. In fact, they had been operating under Wirth.

According to Dr. Morgen's testimony, Auschwitz was made a centre of mass extermination of Jews by Hoess at a later date. Because of his methods, he is said to have been called by Wirth "an untalented pupil."

According to Dr. Morgen's testimony, the Organisation Eichmann was separated from these two Kommandos. Its task consisted of deporting the other European Jews to the concentration camps. According to witness Wisliceny, Eichmann, by reason of the full powers accorded to him, was also personally responsible for the carrying out of the extermination order. He established special Kommandos in the occupied countries. Though economically under the Chief of the Security Police, they could not receive any instruction or orders from them.

The organisations of Eichmann and Wirth were now amalgamated, but this was done in such a way that only very few people in Eichmann's circle knew about it. In this way, and by the use of Jewish collaborators, the knowledge of these killings was restricted to very few Germans and thus the secret was maintained.

The declarations of witnesses and affidavits might differ as to the details in the organisation of the extermination programme, but one thing is clear beyond any doubt, the Gestapo as a whole did not participate in this horrible mass murder and, with very few exceptions, could and did not know anything about it. The few leading persons who knew about it, such as Eichmann, Muller, Himmler, kept strictest silence about their tasks and intentions and in death they took their secret with them. This is confirmed most clearly by Dr. Morgen's testimony. For how could the limitation of knowledge to the above-mentioned group of persons be made more evident than by the fact that the Criminal Police itself started investigations and discovered the crimes, and that even the Chief of the Security Police and Nebe were astonished, while Muller seemed to have known, as his behaviour indicated. This being the case, how can it be assumed that the minor Gestapo official knew about the secret?

With regard to the persecution of the Church and the shooting of hostages by the Gestapo, I ask you to take note of the statements in the pleading. I continue on Page 73, Number IV of the original.

I have now dealt broadly with the individual crimes of which the Gestapo as a collective organisation has been accused by the prosecution. As to the question whether the crimes, as far as they were committed by members of the Gestapo, have to be imputed to the Gestapo as a whole, I finally come to the following conclusion so far as it has not been arrived at before when dealing with the individual crimes:

The Gestapo was a public Reich authority bound in its aims and activity to the existing laws. The fact that the Gestapo officials, during the twelve years of the existence of that institution, essentially carried out quite normal police work is not sufficiently taken into consideration. The working day of most of the Gestapo officials was occupied with official business which had no connection with the crimes alleged here. Third degree interrogations were only carried out by a small fraction of the officials; the decree concerning that was in the safe of the departmental chief marked "Secret." However, sections of the Gestapo officials, by the exploitation of the traditional duty of obedience, were used by the highest government offices for measures which went beyond the actual duties of the Gestapo. And here it is of decisive importance that only a small part of the Gestapo officials participated in these tasks which were alien to their police duties. As the most serious charges against the Gestapo are in connection with its activity in the occupied territories, it follows that only a comparatively small percentage, at most 15 per cent, of the executive officials can be accused, and not the Gestapo as a whole.

Regarding this question, it is of special importance to know whether the aims, tasks and methods of the organisation or group were generally known. Publicity, or, in other words, general knowledge: must include two things: knowledge of the objective facts of the criminal action and knowledge of the illegal, criminal character. Judgment as to whether this dual knowledge existed must be based on common sense. What can be assumed, if the individual members of the organisation were told nothing of the criminal incidents?

May I make a few fundamental additions to what I have already said about the individual crimes?

The reason why the Gestapo as a whole had no knowledge of the capital crimes committed lies in the following: Hitler from the beginning knew how to surround himself with a veil of secrecy, to conceal his true intentions, to see to it that no minister and no department and no official learned too much from any other. The well-known Fuehrer Order No. 1, which was submitted as Gestapo Exhibit 25, is only the actual confirmation of a long-established practice.

Taking into consideration the demoniacal influence which emanated from Hitler, the feeling of inviolability of all his orders (explainable only through the demoniacal aspect of his character) and the fear of the serious consequences to life and limb in the event of failure to carry out a so- called Fuehrer Order, is there any wonder that this secrecy order was scrupulously observed? So, it is really not incredible that almost all defendants and witnesses examined here have actually only now learnt of all these heinous crimes. It is significant that, for example, the driver of a special vehicle was condemned to death by the SS and Police Court in Minsk because, in an intoxicated condition, he had spoken, contrary to orders, about the purpose of the vehicle. (Gestapo Affidavit 47.) Even Dr. Gisevius had to admit that Heydrich endeavoured to keep his actions secret, and the defendant Jodl characterised the system of secrecy in the most striking manner when he said that secrecy was a masterpiece of Hitler's art of concealment and a masterpiece of deception by Himmler.

It is a recognised legal principle that ignorance through negligence is not sufficient in case of crime; therefore, in order to declare an organisation criminal, it is necessary for the members of the organisation actually to have known of and approved of the criminal aims and methods. That, however, is not proved in our case, and cannot be assumed from all the facts established during the trial, no matter how strange the contrary assumption may seem in retrospect today to one who cannot appreciate conditions in Germany.

With regard to the question of whether the terrible crimes which actually were committed are to be imputed to the Gestapo as a whole, the further fact must not be disregarded that the members of this organisation did not act on their own initiative but on orders.

Those concerned contend, and can prove by witnesses, that if they had refused to carry out orders received, they would have been threatened not only with disciplinary proceedings, loss of civil service rights, and so forth, but also with concentration camps, and, in case of war assignments, with court martial and execution. Do they thereby invoke a reason for exemption from guilt?

This question must be examined with regard to the so-called "duress induced by official duties" (beruflicher Notstand) which is not recognised in written law. It represents far more a concept which cannot be dispensed with in legal life. Where the written law is not adequate, as when a state of emergency exists, sensible and practical considerations must fill up the gaps. Public opinion approves this, and legal administration and jurisprudence have recognised the so- called extra legal state of emergency as a reason for exemption from guilt. It is true cowardice is not a virtue; but it is equally true that heroism and martyrdom in the world of human beings are the exception. Should the Gestapo members form this exception? Could one, from a purely human point of view, really expect them to take upon themselves loss of livelihood, family suffering, concentration camp, and perhaps even a shameful death? Besides, the members of the resistance movement in the occupied territories, in their killing of members of the German occupation forces, again and again referred to orders from their superiors and to the duress imposed on the terrorists who came under these orders.

Therefore, in our case as well, I would consider without hesitation that there was actual danger to life and limb for the perpetrator in the sense of Paragraph 54 of the German Penal Code. Here there existed what Judge Jackson called "physical compulsion."

Moreover, in Germany every official was and is trained in the conception of the strictest obedience to orders and instructions from higher authority. Perhaps as nowhere else in the world the official in Germany is dominated by the thought of authority. He was trained in the attitude, correct in itself, that a State breaks down if the orders issued by it are no longer obeyed and that the denial of governmental authority has its logical result in anarchy.

Added to this deep-rooted attitude was the devilish atmosphere which, with hypnotic power, made the small officials particularly tools without a will of their own. All of these motives were added to the threat emanating from the very nature of the occupation and they all together created a duress so oppressive that the Gestapo official no longer retained the freedom of will to examine a criminal order as to its legal and moral value, and to refuse obedience. Taking all these considerations into account, these proved crimes cannot be charged to the whole of the Gestapo so as to declare the Gestapo criminal.

The Prosecutors state - and this is just the very basis and aim of the Indictment - that the crimes were not isolated acts committed independently of each other, but rather parts or aspects of a criminal policy, either as part of a common plan or as a means of carrying out that common plan. The contention is that this very plan was directed towards the unloosing and waging of an aggressive war which, in its beginning, had no definite aim, but that later the aim of that war became the enslavement of Europe and the peoples of Europe in order to gain living-space. Everything important that was carried on within that conspiracy, characterised as such by the Indictment, is described as having had only one aim and purpose, to secure for the Nazi State a place in the sun and to push all internal and external adversaries into the darkness. The essential point of the individual crimes was the intentional participation in the planning and carrying out of the plan. The crime of the individual consisted in his having joined the common plan of the conspiracy. It is claimed that the purpose of the conspiracy was generally known and that, therefore, no one can claim that he acted without knowledge of it.

These contentions of the Indictment aim above all at the individual defendants, but presumably they are also valid for the indicted organisations. It is claimed that the role played by the Gestapo within the conspiracy consisted in aiding the Nazi conspirators to create a police State, set up to break every resistance, to exterminate Jews and faithful Christians, as well as politically undesirable persons, as the main elements of the resistance movement; furthermore, to enslave the employable inhabitants of foreign countries and to eliminate and suppress by cruelty and horror all of those who might resist the German lust of conquest within the Reich or in the conquered territories.

If we examine again the individual crimes, as to whether they are to be considered as of assistance to the crime of conspiracy against world peace, it is recommendable that the activity of the Gestapo before the war and during the war be studied concerning the characteristics mentioned. Without repeating myself unnecessarily, I believe I can state that the duties and methods of the Gestapo before war were a manifestation of a State institution existing in all civilized countries, which cannot be imagined apart from the State; its existence, therefore, in no way infers the planning of an aggressive war or any other conspiracy against world peace. The individual Gestapo official fulfilled his duty as he as an official had learned it. Equally, in the upper strata of the Political Police it is unlikely that any other thought would have prevailed than to guarantee peace and security within the State. One must not identify the Gestapo with such superiors as Himmler and Heydrich, whose knowledge and action were alien to the police. If these men acted only from the political point of view their subordinates cannot be blamed for it. Taking into account the well-known system of secrecy, the individual Gestapo official and the overwhelming majority of all Gestapo members could not have bad the least idea that their work was aimed at preparing a war of aggression and helping to create the basis for it. I believe that no Gestapo official, hearing that contention, or asked whether he had knowledge of the attack on world peace, would have even understood the question.

The Gestapo as a whole can only be charged with responsibility for the crimes committed by members of the Gestapo during the war when those crimes - apart from the general knowledge of them - were committed with the knowledge that they formed part of a plan to bring the war of aggression to a victorious ending at all costs, and by using means which were criminal in themselves and conflicted with International Law. That cannot be proved either. The preliminary condition would again be that the Gestapo officials who participated in the crimes knew that the war which we waged was a war of aggression. Now we all know that a perfectly organised propaganda, which reached even the remotest hamlets, never spoke of the war except as something forced upon us criminally and that Hitler himself always spoke of the war which others wanted and not ourselves. It may have happened that some thinking individuals, who had not entirely lost their soundness of judgment, had their doubts and may have thought vaguely that our Government was not altogether blameless in regard to this war which had been forced upon us; but as the opposite case is the more likely, it is impossible to establish the existence of this suspicion or certainty to any great degree in the minds of all the members of the Gestapo.

The prosecution assumes, and quite unjustly, in my opinion, that every activity of the Party, but, above all, its fight against the Jews, against its political opponents and against the Churches, arose out of the intention and plan to eliminate all tendencies standing in the way of the war of aggression it proposed. The National Socialist struggle against Jewry sprang from the doctrine of anti-Semitism which had become part of the Party programme and which saw in all Jews an element destructive to the State. Because this fight was an immoral one, the Christian Churches rightly protested against it. This explains to a great extent the fight between Party and Church. The steps taken by the Party against its political opponents - especially against the Communists - were, in all probability, taken in the first place for the purpose of maintaining and protecting the State; in any case, that was the way in which the German people-and therefore the Gestapo officials- regarded the measures taken. It did not occur to anyone to see in them evidence of a conspiracy against world peace.

One last point, however - perhaps the most profound - must not be overlooked in this connection. The German soldier, the German official, the German working man, and indeed every German knew that the war had placed us in a situation which meant a struggle to the death. In the course of the war it gradually became terrifyingly clear that it was a question of existence or extermination. Indeed, you would be misjudging the soul of the German people if you overlooked the fact that every decent German, when he realised this horrible truth, felt himself under an obligation to do everything which was expected of him in order to save his country. And when we judge the behaviour of the German people and its political police we must take these factors into consideration in order to be fair and just.

The prosecution has stated that the Tribunal is in a position to restrict its decision with regard to the collective guilt of the organisations - whether in regard to certain sub-groups or in regard to time. The organisational structure, the variety of the groups of individuals active within the Gestapo, and the results of the evidence presented in reply to the prosecution's assertions concerning the criminal activities of the Gestapo, form the basis for a possible limitation in regard either to persons or to time - which I should like to have taken into account should the High Tribunal arrive at a verdict of guilty. Criminal participation in the crimes listed under Article 6 of the Charter can certainly not be imputed to the following groups of persons, for they neither committed crimes themselves nor did they plan to commit them, much less actually commit them collectively; nor could they have had knowledge of criminal plans and activities; and, in fact, they did not have such knowledge.

(1) Administrative officials. They did not receive their instructions from the office of the Secret State Police or from Amt IV of the RSHA, but from Amter I and II of the RSHA whose members are not covered by the charges raised against the Gestapo. The rooms occupied by the administrative offices were never in the same place as those of the executive officials. Administrative officials had no insight into the activities of executive officials, partly because of the secrecy obligation which has been mentioned many times and which was observed particularly strictly in the Gestapo, partly because the administrative officials were looked upon by the executive officials as merely nominal members of the Gestapo, and were treated with marked reserve.

The difference in the designations of duties, such as Police Inspector for police administrative officials and Criminal Inspector in the case of the executive service, must be pointed out in order to stress the fundamental difference between these two categories of officials.

When the prosecution argues that the activities of the executive constituted the pre-condition for the activities of the administrative officials, this argument is as ineffective as my arguing that the activities of the officials of the Reich Finance Ministry, which secured funds for the salaries and other expenses of the Gestapo, was the cause of the activities of the executive officials.

(2) Employees and wage-earners. Chief Justice Jackson, in his speech of 1st March, 1946, excepted two groups of persons from the Indictment against the organisations, firstly, the SA Reserve and, secondly, the office employees, stenographers, and general labourers of the Gestapo. A part of the groups of persons which I have dealt with are thereby already excepted from the Indictment, but I deem it nevertheless my duty to point out that this group of persons, both on account of their subordinate positions and the consequent impossibility of their acquiring detailed knowledge of the Gestapo's activities, has been very justly excepted in its entirety from the Indictment. It is my opinion that all employees and wage-earners, including, for instance, drivers, as far as they were not officials, teletypists, telephonists, draftsmen and interpreters, are to be included in this excepted group, no matter whether their membership of the Gestapo was based on a free labour contract, or whether the labour office directives allowed them the choice of a different place of work.

(3) The witness Hedel has made a detailed statement on the activities of the staff who dealt with technical communications. This statement makes it clear that they had nothing at all to do with executive work; that they were not in a position to have any knowledge of the activities of the executive staff, and that on the basis of their own activities they were not bound to realize that they belonged to an organisation whose activities might be criminal. This group of persons; too, may justly be treated as exceptions.

(4) The same applies to groups of persons who in the years 1942 to 1945 were collectively transferred to the Secret State Police on orders from higher quarters; They are the fifty-one groups of the Secret Field Police and the Military Counter-Intelligence Service, including Foreign Censorship and Telegraph Censorship Offices, who were subordinated to the Gestapo by the Wehrmacht, and the Customs Frontier Service, which was subordinated to the Gestapo by the Reich Ministry of Finance.

THE PRESIDENT: Dr. Merkel, were you referring just now to fifty-one groups? Can you tell the Tribunal where those fifty-one groups are specified? In what document?

DR. MERKEL: The testimony of Krichbaum, who was examined before the Commission. Even with reference to these groups there cannot be the slightest doubt that neither the fact of voluntary membership nor the knowledge of criminal aims, as alleged by the prosecution, nor the fact of an alliance applies. The individual, no matter what rank or office he held, was powerless when he was collectively transferred on the basis of an order emanating from the highest office of the Wehrmacht and the State. Disobedience to this order would have been punished by death, on the charge of desertion or military disobedience.

(5) There still remains the group constituted by the executive officials. The executive officials originated in the political department staffs of the police commissioners' offices prior to 1933. These officials, who had been employed in part even before 1914 and currently up to the year 1933 in combating the various political opponents of the various governmental systems and the governments which came into power through them, were almost without exception absorbed by the political police of the new regime. The only exceptions were those officials who had been particularly active as opponents of National Socialism. But even these were only dismissed in rare cases. For the most part they were transferred to the Criminal Police.

The staff of the Secret State Police was filled up by transferring officials and candidates from other police departments to the Gestapo without consulting them beforehand. In the same way municipal police officials with a long record of efficiency, who wished to remain in the police service, were transferred after nine years' service to the Criminal or State Police. They had no control as to which department they were to be employed in.

With reference to the Counter-Intelligence and Frontier Police, I can demonstrate that the members of these bodies, who were included as officials of the Secret State Police executive, could have nothing whatsoever to do with the crimes of which the prosecution accuses the Gestapo. The Counter-Intelligence Police exercised their police activities in a manner common to every civilized State, as one of the most noble tasks of the police or their affiliated institutions. It is clearly established through the testimony of Best and through Gestapo Affidavits 39, 56. and 89, that the staff of the Counter-Intelligence Police did not change very much; and in view of the special obligation to secrecy and for the sake of the defense of the country, a transfer to other Gestapo or police departments was not permissible as a rule. The Counter-Intelligence Police were mostly isolated within the Gestapo offices and had no official contact with other departments. The cases handled by the Counter-Intelligence Police were always submitted to the regular courts for decision.

The functions of the Frontier Police from 1933 to 1945 were the same as in the preceding period and the same as those carried out today by the officers of the new Frontier Police. The officers of the Frontier Police did not carry out third degree interrogation, nor did they submit applications for commitment to a concentration camp, nor did they - and most of them had served for a long period in the Frontier Police - participate in any persecution of the Jews, nor could they on account of the nature of their employment participate in any other crime with which the Gestapo is charged.

These two groups of the Gestapo numbered five to six thousand individuals. On the basis of the figures which I have previously submitted for the strength of the separate groups of the Gestapo, I estimate the number of its staff, during the period when it was numerically strongest, at approximately 75,000. The executive officials, numbering approximately 15,000 men, therefore constituted only 20 per cent of the total strength. If we deduct from that the five to six thousand men belonging to the Counter-Intelligence and Frontier Police, there remain nine to ten thousand executives, or 12 to 13 per cent of the total strength.

I believe I have already advanced sufficient reasons as to why the Gestapo, as a subordinate part of the State organism, cannot be sentenced at all, for reasons which are based both on natural law and on the common State law of all countries. But even if those legal objections did not exist, no sentence could be pronounced, as the characteristics of criminality as defined by Chief Justice Jackson, on 28th February, 1946, do not appear in the case of the Gestapo. And even if this argument is not valid, I ask: Is it possible that - simply because some of its members may perhaps be held responsible for the commission of crimes - an organisation as such can be declared criminal, including also those members who certainly did not act in a criminal manner and had no knowledge of the criminal acts of others?

I am referring to the summary of affidavits given by a large number of former members of the Gestapo who are at present in internment camps. I must also draw your attention to the numerous acts sworn to in those affidavits and which aimed at sabotaging certain evil orders issued by the head of the State.

I turn now by way of precaution to an argument dealing with the question of time limitations. I may be more brief. The Gestapo cannot be described as being under unified leadership throughout the Reich, and hence of having a unified will - at least up to the time of Himmler's appointment as deputy chief of the Prussian Secret State Police, that is up to the spring of 1934.

In Prussia, Ministerialrat Diels had acted with one short interruption as deputy head of the Secret State Police under Goering. It is impossible to connect Diels with the illegal tendencies which became apparent after the outbreak of the National Socialist Revolution. I may refrain - and owing to pressure of time I must refrain - from pointing to those who were really guilty of those excesses; compare Affidavit Number 41.

As a State institution, the Gestapo had no part in the events of 30th June, 1934. In the following period up to 9th November, 1938, the Gestapo did not play any role which could justify the charge of criminality. The arrest of 20,000 Jews which the Gestapo was ordered to carry out was, as witness Best testified, a matter outside the competence of the police. It is therefore impossible to fix that date as the beginning of the criminal activity of the Gestapo. It must be stated that, at least up to the beginning of the war, the criminal character of the Gestapo cannot be proven.

Does the basis of judgment change for the period covered by the war? I have already stated that the activities of the Einsatzgruppen and Sipo offices in the occupied territories cannot be charged to the Gestapo, since leadership, organisation, personnel and order of command of those offices do not permit discrimination against the Gestapo.

There is not the slightest doubt that if the Gestapo is sentenced considerable time limitations must be made. I have indicated briefly the insurmountable nature of the difficulties in the way of a time limitation.

CONCLUSION

And with this, gentlemen of the High Tribunal, I end my remarks on the Indictment of the Gestapo. I did not consider it my duty to excuse crimes and evil deeds or to whitewash those who disregarded the laws of humanity. But I desire to save those who are innocent, I desire to clear the way for a sentence which will dethrone the powers of darkness and reconstitute the moral order the world.

If we glance through the annals of European history in recent decades and centuries, we read again and again how might conquered right among the nations and how the spirit of revenge beclouded the perceptions of mankind.

Peace was only concluded on paper; it was not accepted by the human heart. Solemn pacts were made - only to be broken. Promises were given and not kept. We read in this narrative of revolutions among the nations, of economic need and of unspeakable sorrow. The last pages, however, are written in blood - the blood of millions of innocent people. They speak of unimaginable cruelties, of utter disregard of the sacred laws of humanity and of mass murders which brought suffering to the peoples of Europe.

With your judgment, gentlemen of the High Tribunal, you will write the last chapter of this narrative - a chapter which must be the end and the beginning - the end because it closes the gruesome battle fought by the powers of darkness against the moral order of the world - the beginning because it is to lead us to a new world of liberty and justice.

This justice, I hope, will inspire the judgment which is engraved in golden letters on the floor of the Palace of Peace in The Hague: Sol justitiae illustra nos. Do not, therefore, make your judgment merely with the cold logic of your keen mind, but also with the warm love of a seeing heart. This applies especially to the judgment against the organisations; for a condemnation must be unjust, since among the millions whom it affects there are also millions who are guiltless. They would all become victims of desperation; they would all be despised and damned, and would perhaps even deem those happy who now rest in their graves as victims of National Socialism.

The present world needs peace, nothing but peace. To extend the consequences of a judgment to a large, guiltless section of the German people would be to work against world peace, which, in any event, rests on an unsure basis, and would thereby mutatis mutandis repeat Hitler's idea of punishing a people - the Jewish people - collectively and of exterminating them.

Out of this injustice against the laws of God and of Nature was born the indignation of the creatures tortured - and the right to have the evildoers called to account. Hitler and his regime proved the truth of the words: "Hodie mihi, cras tibi." From the history of the Jews in the Old Testament we know that God would not have destroyed the City of Sodom if even one just man had lived there. Is not God's truth contained in these words - that a group may not be punished if even one member of the group is not deserving of punishment?

Then, gentlemen of the High Tribunal, place your signatures under a judgment which will bear the test of History and the Court of the World: Place your signatures under a verdict which will be praised as the beginning of a new Era of Justice and of Peace, and which will form a golden bridge leading to a better and a happier future.

(The Tribunal adjourned until Monday, 26th August, 1946, at 1000 hours.)

Concluding Speeches from the Prosecution

THURSDAY, 29TH AUGUST, 1946

MR. DODD: It is not our contention that the institutions themselves were basically criminal, but rather that they became criminal under Nazi domination, although, by its very nature as a secret political police system, the Gestapo was the most easily adapted to criminal purposes and became one of the most effective of all instruments of Nazi criminality.

From its earliest days, the Nazis always regarded that portion of the police forces called the "Gestapo," or Secret State Police, as a separate group, a clearly identifiable aggregate performing a common function. The very purpose of Goering's decree of 26th April, 1933, establishing the Gestapo in Prussia, was to create in that province a single body of secret political police, separated from the other Prussian police forces, an independent force having its own particular task, on which he could entirely rely. The same motives led to the establishment of similar identifiable groups of secret political police in other German provinces. The steps by which these groups were all consolidated into a single secret political police force for the whole Reich are fully detailed in the decrees and laws which have been cited to the Tribunal. When the RSHA, the Reich Main Security Office, was created in 1939, the Gestapo was not dispersed, but became a distinct department of that central office, as shown by the chart of RSHA introduced in evidence, and by the testimony of the witnesses Ohlendorf and Schellenberg. They easily estimated the number of persons in the Gestapo at from 30,000 to 40,000.

Throughout these proceedings, the Gestapo and the SD have been considered together, due to the fact that the criminal enterprises with which each is chargeable were supported, to a greater or lesser degree, by both. The Indictment charges the Gestapo with criminality as a separate and independent group or organisation. The Indictment includes the SD, by special reference, as a part of the SS, since it originated as part of the SS and always retained its character as a Party organisation, as distinguished from the Gestapo which was a State organisation. The SD, of course, had its own organisation, an independent Headquarters with posts established throughout the Reich and in occupied territories and with agents in every country abroad. It had a membership of from 3,000 to 4,000 professionals assisted by thousands of honorary informers, known as V-men, and by spies in other lands, but we do not include honorary informers who were not members of the SS, nor do we include members of the Abwehr who were transferred to the SD toward the end of the war, excepting in so far as such Abwehr members also belonged to the SS.

If we ask where the ubiquitous SD man is to be found, the answer is not at all difficult, although some of the testimony and arguments may have been confusing to the Tribunal. Until 1939, the SD man was always to be found in the head office of the SD of the Reichsfuehrer SS or in the various regional offices of the SD throughout the Reich. During that period, the SD was repeatedly identified as a department of the SS in SS organisation charts and plans, and by laws and decrees issued by the Government. During this period the SD was the political intelligence agency of the SS, the Party, and the State, and it provided secret political information to the executive departments of the State and Party, particularly to the Gestapo. After 1939, the SD man is to be found in Offices III and VI of the RSHA and in the various regional SD offices within Germany, in the occupied territories, and in the Einsatz Groups of the Security Police and the SD in areas close behind the front.

In the course of the argument, some confusion has also arisen over the characterization of the RSHA, WVHA, Department Eichmann and Einsatz Groups. The RSHA was a department of the SS, and substantially all of its personnel belonged to the SS. It was under the command of the SS Obergruppenfuehrer Kaltenbrunner. In addition to the SD, which was always an SS formation, it included the Gestapo and the Reich Criminal Police, both of which were State agencies. For this reason the RSHA was also carried as a department of the Reich Minister of the Interior. The WVHA was another strictly SS department. The WVHA was under the leadership of SS Obergruppenfuehrer Pohl, who was charged with the administration of concentration camps and the exploitation of the labour of the inmates. There was no Department Eichmann as such. Eichmann was simply the head of the department of the Gestapo which was charged with matters pertaining to the Churches and to the Jews. It was this department of the Gestapo which had primary executive responsibility for the rounding up of the Jews of Europe and the committing of them to concentration camps. The Eichmann department within the Gestapo was no more independent of the Gestapo than any other department under Muller. The Einsatz Groups of the Security Police and SD - and it is very important that the full title be held in mind at all times - were the offices of the Security Police and SD operating in the field behind the armies. When police control had been sufficiently established in newly occupied territory, the mobile Einsatz Groups were eliminated, and they became regional offices under the commanders of the Security Police and the SD in occupied territories. The Einsatz Groups were a part of the office of the Security Police and SD, the RSHA, and as such were a part of the SS, limited only by the fact that some personnel assigned to the groups were not SS members. In 1939, the main offices of the SD and the Gestapo were consolidated in the RSHA, but the SD at all times preserved its independent identity.

The SD as a part of the SS was composed of SS men with special qualifications. The deeds of this organisation best explain the nature of these special qualifications, for the record in this case in replete with horrible tales of their doings. The SD man was simply a surcharged SS man. If the membership of the SS was basically and fundamentally voluntary, then it follows automatically that the SD membership was likewise voluntary.

The Gestapo was at all times a State organisation, a branch of the Government similar in all usual respects to other branches of the Government. In considering the voluntary character of its membership, all other considerations are secondary to this basic determination of the Gestapo as an agency of State. If membership in the Gestapo was compulsory, membership in the Order Police, and in the Department of Safety, and in the Department of Finance must have been compulsory. When the Gestapo was created, following the seizure of power, it is true that many members of the previously existing political police system of the various Lander were transferred to it. But they were under no legal compulsion to join. As the Gestapo affiant Losse stated, "If they had refused, they would have had to reckon with a dismissal from the service without pension, so that unemployment would have threatened them." The witness Schellenberg stated that new members of the Gestapo were taken on a voluntary basis. Any one of them could have resigned and sought employment in other branches of the Government. The witness Hoffman, in testifying before the Commission, stated that he applied for a job in three branches of the Government, of which the Gestapo was one. The Gestapo accepted his application and in that way he became a member of the organisation. There was nothing to prevent a Gestapo official from resigning his position if the aims and activities and methods of the organisation became repugnant to him. The witness Tesmer testified before the Commission that if an officer refused to carry out a criminal order he probably would be removed from his employment. Even after the war began, when all Government officials were more or less frozen in their positions, members of the Gestapo were able to resign. The witness Tesmer himself resigned from the Gestapo during the war, and the witness Straub testified that a person could resign his position in the Gestapo at the risk of going to the front on active military service. Surely this was not compulsion in any legal sense. The sacrifices which members of the political police might face upon resignation, such as loss of seniority and forfeiture of pension rights, may have seemed decisive to those who remained in the Gestapo, but such considerations could under no circumstances be construed as legal compulsions justifying continued membership in an organisation of such notorious criminality. There may be particular instances where some members of the army secret field police were later transferred from the military to the Gestapo. In such instances, these individuals may have gained, on the basis of military orders, a personal defence to the crimes committed by the Gestapo during the period of their membership. But such special instances, justifiable in subsequent proceedings, can in no way affect the basic character of the Gestapo as a single department of the Government, with no greater degree of compulsion to join and no greater legal restraint from resigning than any other department of the State.

From the establishment of the Nazi Party in 1920, until the conclusion of the war in 1945, these organisations were used by the conspirators for the execution of their schemes, and each committed one or more of the crimes described in Article 6 of the Charter, and participated in the general conspiracy. The Leadership Corps was the first of the organisations to appear on the stage. The next step was the creation in 1920 of a semi-military organisation, the SA, to secure by violence a predominant place for the Party in the political scene. Out of this group, the more select and fanatical SS was formed in 1925, to replace the SA while the latter was banned, and then to join with it in laying the groundwork for the revolution. Upon the seizure of power in 1933, the next organisation, the Reich Cabinet, took its place in the conspiracy. With the Government in their hands, the conspirators hastened to suppress all potential opposition, and to that end they created the Gestapo and the SD. Internal security having been guaranteed, they then obtained for promotion of their plans of aggrandisement the last of their implements - in the form of the military.

Each of these was necessary to the successful execution of the conspiracy - the Leadership Corps to direct and control the Party through which political power had to be seized; the SA and SS to oppose political opponents by violence and, after 1933, to fasten the Nazis' control on Germany by extra-legal activities; the Cabinet to devise and enact the laws needed to insure continuance of the regime; the Gestapo and the SD to detect and suppress internal opposition; and some servile soldiery to prepare and carry out the expansion of the regime through aggressive war.

When it was a question of enforcing laws, of detecting, apprehending, imprisoning and eliminating opponents or potential opponents, the SD, the Gestapo, the SS and the machinery of concentration camps came into play. The close relationship between the SD and the Gestapo, and the importance of the former in selection of Nazi officials, is disclosed by the defence affidavit of Karl Weiss, who averred that all political police officials were screened by the SD before being accepted into the Gestapo, and the SD violated the integrity of German elections by reporting how the people voted in secret ballots. Special units of the SA were used to supplement the police in arresting Communists and in the course of interrogations, men were beaten to death. Such brutal conduct was consistently excused by decrees of amnesty, under which the purposes of the interrogators were alone decisive. When the policy called for war, the paramilitary organisations like the SA and SS laid the foundation, and top militarists prepared the plans for a powerful German Army. When it became a question of exterminating the population of conquered territories, of deporting them for slave labour and confiscating their property, the OKW and the SS had to plan joint operations and, in collaboration with the Gestapo, to carry them into effect. Thus, the Party planned, the Cabinet legislated, and the SS, SA, Gestapo and the military leaders executed.

The oppression, persecution, discrimination and brutality at the hands of the Leadership Corps, the Reich Cabinet and the SA were only the beginnings of the dreadful fate that the Nazis prepared for the Jews. In this fashion, the way was paved for the sinister activities of the Gestapo when it came into play. Now these secret policemen moved in with their wraith-like methods. Trembling Jews were hauled from their beds in the middle of the night and dispatched without semblance of accusation to concentration camps, and often their family awoke to find them missing. Thousands of Jewish people so disappeared never to be seen or heard of again, and all over Europe today surviving family remnants with aching hearts are seeking clues or indications of the fate that befell them. Sad to relate, the only answer to most of the searching is to be found in the records of this Tribunal, in the captured documents of the SS, the SD and the Gestapo, and in the death books of the gas chambers, the mass graves and the crematoria.

It was Goering who ordered Heydrich, as chief of the Security Police and SD, to work out a "complete solution" of the Jewish problem in the areas occupied by the Reich. And it was Heydrich, as chief of the Security Police and SD and acting upon Goering's order, who instructed the Gestapo to murder all Jews who could not be used for slave labour. Gestapo men, under the leadership of Eichmann, went into the occupied territories and, with the assistance of local officers of the Security Police and SD, succeeded in herding virtually all of the Jews of Europe into concentration camps and annihilation centres. With unabated fury the Nazis plunged from Goering's "complete solution" to Himmler's "final solution."

To the Gestapo and the SD was given the first responsibility for carrying out the barbaric Commando Order of 18th October, 1942, and its subsequent amendments calling for the summary execution of allied commandos and paratroopers. Nor should it be forgotten that throughout the war the Gestapo screened prisoner-of-war camps for Jews and those of the Communist political faith, who were then deliberately murdered. The Tribunal will recall the document concerning the screening of prisoner-of-war camps, introduced in the later stages of the Trial, which proved conclusively that local Gestapo offices at Munich, Regensburg, Furth and Nuremberg screened prisoner-of-war camps in Bavaria for classes of prisoners of war to be sent to Dachau for liquidation by SS guards, and that these Gestapo offices were criticised by the High Command for failure to screen as effectively as the High Command desired. This crime has been carefully avoided by counsel in pleading the case for the implicated organisations. It is one of the clearest cases of willful premeditated murder of prisoners of war in violation of established International Law. It is positive demonstration of the complete savagery of the responsible organisations with respect to the treatment of prisoners of war. The infamous Bullet Decree, under which the Gestapo sent recaptured officer prisoners of war to Mauthausen Concentration Camp for execution by SS guards, is additional proof of the criminal character of these organisations.

The two organisations which were most directly concerned with and implicated in the concentration camp system were the Gestapo and the SS. In the early days the concentration camps were under the political direction of the Gestapo, which issued orders for punishment to be inflicted upon the inmates. The decree of 1936 declared that the Gestapo should administer the concentration camps, but it was the SS which furnished guards from the Death's Head Battalions, and ultimately became responsible for all internal administration of the camps. The Gestapo remained the sole authority in the Nazi State empowered to commit political prisoners to concentration camps, although the SD joined the Gestapo in committing Poles who did not qualify for Germanisation. The Gestapo sent thousands upon thousands of persons to concentration camps for slave labour and shipped millions of persons to annihilation centres for extermination.

The Gestapo and officers of the OKW conceived and carried out the hellish "Night and Fog" Decree, by which hapless civilians of occupied countries disappeared into the Reich, never to be heard of again. Thus, by a crime of which only the Nazis were capable, the awful anguish of relatives and friends was added to wanton murder.

In no respect can the criminal activities of these organisations be better illustrated than in the murderous work of the Einsatz Groups of the Security Police and the SD, which were first organised by the SS in September of 1938 in anticipation of the invasion of Czechoslovakia. With their leaders drawn from the SD and the Gestapo and staffed by members of the Waffen SS, they coordinated slaughter and pillage with military manoeuvres, and reports of their activities were forwarded to the Political Leaders through the Reich Defence Commissioners. Even the SA participated in these jackal anti-partisan expeditions in the East.

When the German armies broke into Czechoslovakia and Poland, into Denmark and Norway, the Einsatz bandits followed, for the purpose of striking down resistance, terrorising the population, and exterminating racial groups. So well did these terror specialists do their work that four new units were set up before the attack on the Soviet Union, one of them headed by the infamous Chief of the SD Ohlendorf, who testified in this courtroom to the incredible brutality of his accomplishments, and to the shocking details of the operations carried out in co-ordination with branches of the Army. His testimony will be remembered for its cold account of callous murder, enslavement and plunder, and most of all for the horrible programme of destroying men, women, and children of the Jewish race. Mankind will not soon forget his sickening story of the murder of women and little children in gas vans, nor of the evil, hardened killers whose stomachs turned at the awful sight when they unlatched the doors of the death cars at gravesides. These were the men who sat at the edge of anti-tank ditches, cigarette in mouth, calmly shooting their naked victims in the back of the neck with their machine guns. These were the men who, according to their own corpse accountants, murdered some two million men, women and children. These were the men of the SD. The organisation chart of the Security Police and the SD now before the Tribunal was prepared and certified to by SD official Schellenberg, the Chief of Office VI of the RSHA, and by SD official Ohlendorf, Chief of Office III of the RSHA. This chart shows that these Einsatz Groups were an integral part of the Security Police and SD under the supreme command of the defendant Kaltenbrunner and not, as has been argued, independent organisations responsible directly to Himmler. The officers of these groups were drawn from the Gestapo and the SD, and, to a lesser extent, from the Criminal Police. They received their orders from the various offices of the RSHA, that is, from Office III or VI as to matters pertaining to the SD and from Office IV as to matters pertaining to the Gestapo. They filed their reports with these offices and these offices made up consolidated reports which were distributed to higher police officials and Reich Defence Commissioners, and several examples of these have been introduced in the course of these proceedings.

Counsel for the Gestapo argued that the Gestapo was erroneously blamed for the crimes committed in the occupied territories and that the SS was responsible for them. Counsel for the SS said that the SS was erroneously blamed and that the SD was to blame. Counsel for the SD said that the SD was erroneously blamed and the Gestapo was really to blame. Counsel for the SS said that the Gestapo also wore the feared black uniform and that therefore Gestapo men were frequently mistaken for SS men. Counsel for the SS blamed the Gestapo for the running of the concentration camps, and counsel for the Gestapo blamed the SS. The fact is that all of these executive agencies participated in the commission of these vast Crimes Against Humanity. Counsel do not point to any agencies other than those indicted here as the guilty organisations; the defence of each organisation has been simply to fasten the responsibility on one of the other indicted organisations. The conclusion is irresistible: that all of the organisations participated in the commission of these great crimes.

It is a strange feature of this Trial that counsel for the respective organisations have not sought to deny these crimes, but only to shift responsibility for their commission. The military defendants blame the Political Leaders for initiating wars of aggression; the Gestapo blames the soldiers for the murder of escaped prisoners of war; the SA blames the Gestapo for concentration camp murders; the Gestapo blames the Leadership Corps for anti-Jewish pogroms; the SS blames the Cabinet for the concentration camp system; and the Cabinet blames the SS for exterminations in the East.

The fact is that all of these organisations united in carrying out the criminal programme of Nazi Germany. As they complemented each other it is unnecessary to define as a matter of precise proof the borders of their own devilry. When the Reich Cabinet promulgated the decree for "securing the unity of the Party and State," it insolubly bound those organisations for good and evil. When the membership of those organisations swore an unconscionable oath of obedience to Hitler, they united themselves for all time with him, his work, and his guilt.

The objectives of the Gestapo were laid down by law and discussed time and time again in semi-official publications such as Der Volkischer Beobachter, and Das Archiv, the magazine of the German Police, and Best's basic handbook on the German Police. Every member knew that the Gestapo was the special police force set up by Goering and developed by Himmler to strike down potential opponents of the tyranny. Every member knew that the Gestapo operated outside the law, that the Gestapo could arrest on its own authority and imprison on its independent judgment. Every member knew that the Gestapo was the agency which filled the concentration camps with political opponents. All knew that the Gestapo was organised for the specific purpose of persecuting the victims of Nazi oppression - the Jews, the Communists, and the Churches. The right to use torture in interrogations must have been known to all who interrogated.

There could be no secrecy as to the criminal aims of the Gestapo or the criminal methods by which this primary agency of terror carried out its work. That it was an instrument of terror was known not merely by its members - it was known throughout Germany and Europe, and in every country of the world, where the very name Gestapo became the watchword of terror and fear.

FRIDAY, 30TH AUGUST, 1946

M. AUGUSTE CHAMPETIER DE RIBES (Chief Prosecutor for the French Republic): Mr. President, Your Honors:

We have asked you to condemn the leaders responsible for the drama which has bathed the world in blood. Today, when we ask you to declare as criminal the organisations which served as instruments for their designs, we seek from your justice the moral condemnation of an entire coherent system, which has brought civilization into the gravest danger it has known since the collapse of the Roman world.

We have shown who those were who were principally guilty of all the crimes of National Socialism. But to realize their diabolical plan of universal domination, not only of territories but of men's consciences, they needed collaborators inspired with the same faith, trained in the same school, and that is why the leaders, the "Fuehrer," conceived and brought into being, little by little, this complicated and coherent system of leadership, coercion, and control, which constitutes the whole of the organisations of the State and of the National Socialist Party.

Executive bodies were necessary, from which emanated, by virtue of the "Fuehrerprinzip," general orders and directives; and they were the Reich Cabinet and the Leadership Corps of the Nazi Party.

Instruments were needed for control, for propaganda, for Police and for the execution of orders, and they were the Gestapo, the SA, the SD, and the SS.

I should only like to reply, briefly to two of the arguments to which the Defense Counsel, and particularly those for the Gestapo, the SD and the High Command, appear to attach the greatest importance.

It is possible, they say at first, that abuses were committed in the heat of the struggle, which had become pitiless in the course of the war which had become total, but, it was never a question of anything but individual crimes, which might involve the responsibility of the persons who committed them, but not that of the groups which censured them.

Watertight compartments, says the Defense in the second place, separated the various organisations of the Reich. For this reason the activity of each organisation should be examined separately and this examination does not reveal a criminal intention or activity in any of them.

First argument: In order to determine whether or not an organisation is criminal, it is necessary, says the Defense, to examine the essential principles of its structure. Now, there is nothing criminal in these. So that the crimes, should any have been committed, can only be attributed to individuals, and do not permit the conclusion to be drawn that the character of the group as a whole is criminal.

Thus the Gestapo, according to the terms of its constitution, was a State Police, charged, like the police of all civilized states, with aiding in the work of justice and protecting the community against individuals who might threaten its security. It is possible that it may sometimes have received and carried out orders from above which were not directly relevant to its essential mission of protection, such as mass arrests of Jews, the extermination of Russian prisoners of war, the murder of recaptured prisoners who had escaped. But such accidental activities did not fall within its competence as an institution. They would not alter the essential character of the organisation which had nothing criminal about it.

Thus the SD is constitutionally simply a service for obtaining information and sounding public opinion, a sort of Gallup poll, harmless in itself.

It is possible that members of the SD accidentally collaborated in the repressive measures of the Gestapo. It is true that members of the SD held a number of high positions and indulged in a number of questionable activities, but they were not acting then as functionaries of the SD and could not compromise the organisation, the institutional character of which had nothing criminal about it.

Thus the High Command was charged institutionally only with the defense of the Reich, and solely with that defense. It did not deal with politics and had nothing to do with the Police. It is possible that it may sometimes have overstepped its mission. It is true that it signed orders to deport to an unknown destination those who resisted, to hand over to the Police for extermination the commandos and escaped prisoners, which was contrary to military honor, but it acted then merely as an intermediary for Hitler's or Himmler's orders. This accidental activity outside its own province could not change its essential character, which was not criminal in any way.

Thus the Defense always tries to distinguish between the institutional character of the organisation, which it believes it has shown to be non-criminal, and the practical activity of the group which, it admits, is open to criticism, a distinction which is understandable in a democratic regime, where pre-established institutions limit the arbitrary nature of governments, and the autonomy of the individual and the liberty of the citizen are protected from the misuse of power, but which is incomprehensible in the Hitler regime.

Did Best, the police theorist, trouble himself about respecting a principle when he wrote that the methods of the Police are prescribed by the enemy? Does the decree of 28 February 1933 trouble itself about principle, when it allows the all-powerful state to ignore all legal restraints?

Did Hitler make any distinction between principle and practice, when, at the conference of 23 May 1939 held in the Chancellery and attended by the members of the High Command, he stated:

> "The principle of avoiding the solution of problems by adaptation to circumstances must be banished. Rather must circumstances be adapted to necessities.... It is no longer a question of justice or injustice, but of the existence or nonexistence of 80 million people."

In reality, under the Hitler regime no pre-established institutions, no legality, no limitation to arbitrariness, no excesses of power were possible. There is no other principle than the "Fuehrerprinzip," no other legality than the good pleasure of the chief, whose orders must be executed without any possible dissension all the way down the scale.

The concept of a so-called institution which was supposed to have presided over the constitution of the collective organisations and given them a certain character, is merely an a posteriori construction originating in Defense Counsel's ingenuity.

The concrete activity of the collective organisations is the only thing which counts, and we have proved that it was criminal.

Moreover, the Defense seeks grounds for the exculpation of the collective organisations in the fact that the members of the Gestapo, the SS, or the SD who indulged in these criminal acts did not perform them in the name of their original organisation, but were temporarily detached from them.

Has it not been proved, on the contrary, that in the general organisation of the National Socialist system these groups played the role of reserves and preparatory schools from which the leaders, for their work of domination, drew executives who were perfectly prepared for the criminal deeds entrusted to them?

And is not the fact that Hitler often conferred on his accomplices the dignity of honorary membership in one of these organisations also proof of the importance which he attached to the evidence of orthodoxy implied by membership of one or other of these groups?

Thus, whatever point of view one may take, the first argument of the Defense cannot be maintained.

THE PRESIDENT: M. Champetier de Ribes, I think you can hardly finish your speech before the adjournment; I think perhaps we had better adjourn now.

M. CHAMPETIER DE RIBES: Yes, Sir.

(A recess was taken until 1400 hours.)

M. CHAMPETIER DE RIBES: Mr. President and Gentlemen, the Defense submits a second argument.

The organisations, it says, were independent and did not know each other. Some were subject to the State, others to the Party; and State and Party were active in different domains. The various sections within the organisations themselves were watertight compartments and acted quite independently. And at the risk of sacrificing the most compromised cells, Defense Counsel are trying to clear from responsibility the greatest possible number of these supposedly isolated groups.

But this argument is contradicted by all we know of the general organisation of the Reich's administrative services. In establishing the personal responsibility of each individual defendant, M. Dubost showed that the close interlocking of the organisations and the services is beyond discussion.

The National Socialist State is totalitarian. Its officials, as well as its services, derive their inspiration from a common ideology and pursue common aims. Unity of action is ensured by the penetration of the Party, the expression of the political will of the people, throughout the whole State machine.

This unification of State and Party was effected by the law of 1 December 1933: "The National Socialist Party has become the representative of the conception of the German State and is indissolubly bound to the State." (Article 1.) Public services must cooperate with the Party services. In fact, this interpenetration and unification of State and Party was effected by the concentration into the same hands of the powers emanating from both. Hitler was simultaneously head of the State, the Army, and the Party. Himmler, as Chief of the SS, which is subject to the Party, was simultaneously head of the Police, which was subject to the State. The Gauleiter, Party functionaries, in most cases also represented the State in their capacity of Reich Governors or Chief Administrators of Prussia. The Chief of the Party Chancellery had a part in the elaboration of important laws and in appointing higher State officials. The law of 7 April 1933 provides for the purging of State officials suspected of insufficient devotion to the Party, and we know with what brutality this purging was carried out in the High Command.

Thus, in their acts as in their writings, the interdependence of State, Party, and Army is realized to the fullest extent, and in the sum total of their activity it is impossible to distinguish what share of responsibility belongs to the one or to the other.

Is it necessary to give examples of this? We have already furnished many and fear to weary the Tribunal.

It will suffice to recall the close co-operation between the Gestapo, the SD, the SS, and the Army in the common elaboration of general instructions and in the execution of operations against resistance forces, reprisals against civil population, and the extermination of the Jews.

Do we not find convincing proof of it in Hitler's instruction of 30 July 1944, which has frequently been quoted:

> "All acts of violence committed by non-German civilians in the occupied territories, against the Wehrmacht, the SS and the Police, and against the installations which they use, must, as acts of terror or sabotage, be fought in the following way:
>
> "a) The troops and each individual member of the Wehrmacht, SS, and Police must kill on the spot terrorists and saboteurs caught in the act.
>
> "b) Anyone caught afterwards must be transferred to the nearest local station of the Security Police and the Security Service..." (F-673).

By mentioning the Wehrmacht, the SS, and the, Police three times, side by side, does not Hitler stress the close co-operation existing between these organisations?

Is it necessary to recall once more Keitel's numerous instructions, Marshal Kesselring's order of 14 January - 1944, and General Von Brodowski's diary of operations, which place the Army at the disposal of the Police, or the Police at the disposal of the Army, for the savage repression of the resistance forces? Is it necessary to recall Keitel's orders to the commanding generals in France, Holland, and Belgium that the Army should participate in the pillage of art treasures organised and directed by Rosenberg?

Did not, the witness Hoffmann - quoted by the Gestapo - declare to the Court on 1 August that the "Nacht und Nebel" decree was the work of collaboration between the High Command and the Ministry of Justice?

The Defense therefore tries in vain to lessen these responsibilities by dividing them between the State and the Party agencies, between the so-called independent organisations.

It is no more successful when it tries to establish the existence of watertight compartments separating within the same organisation the various sections composing it. For example, whom does it expect to believe that the administrative officials of the SD (Security Service) and of the Gestapo were unaware of the vast scale of the deportations, when they had to solve the difficult problem of arranging the convoys; or that the maintenance offices could fail to know of the exterminations carried out by chemical means, when they had to repair the gas vans?

In fact, all the departments of the Gestapo, the SD, the SS, and the High Command are jointly responsible for the crimes committed in common; and what is true of these organisations is true also of the Reich Cabinet and the Political Leaders, as has been shown by my honorable colleagues of the Prosecution.

Are organizers less guilty than those who committed the deeds; is the brain less responsible than the arm? We therefore consider we have proved the joint culpability of all those organisations which we request you to declare as criminal.

Does that mean that our purpose is to obtain from the competent tribunals the most severe sentences against all members of these organisations? Certainly not. In requesting of your justice the moral condemnation of the organisations, without which the crimes of National Socialism could not have been perpetrated, we are not asking you to condemn without hearing men who can indeed plead their cases in person before the competent tribunals.

Moreover, although the Charter of your Tribunal decrees that "in cases where a group or organisation is declared criminal lay the Tribunal.... such criminal nature is considered proved and shall not be questioned," it does not say anywhere that all members of such groups or organisations must be arraigned before competent authorities, and in our opinion only those should be prosecuted who, having knowledge of the criminal activity of the group or organisation, deliberately joined it, thus participating personally in the crimes committed by all collectively.

We think, on the other hand, that in the interest of serene justice and in the hope of universal pacification, the penalties must be made proportionate to the gravity of the offences charged, and that if the most severe penalties are justly attendant upon the crimes of which a member of an organisation is found personally guilty, mere affiliation, even voluntary, to- one of these groups should only be punished by penalties involving loss of freedom or even only by loss of all or some civil or political rights.

And if the Tribunal share this opinion, nothing in the Charter prohibits them from saying so in whatever form they deem most fitting. Your verdict therefore will not be, as Dr. Steinbauer seemed to fear in his final pleading for Seyss-Inquart, the conclusion of a "trial of the vanquished by the victor." It will be the solemn and serene manifestation of eternal justice.

In this same final pleading, trying to contrast the words of M. de Menthon with the attitude of one of the most heroic chiefs of the French Resistance, who has since become President of the Government of the Republic, Dr. Steinbauer recalled M. Georges Bidault's words while visiting severely wounded Germans after the liberation. "Comrades," he said to them, "I wish you a speedy recovery and a happy return to your country."

Seyss-Inquart's counsel was wrong. There is no contradiction between the words of Francois de Menthon and those of Georges Bidault; and the French people, just as, I am sure, the free citizens of the United Nations, can all reconcile the severity necessary for the culprits with pity for those who perhaps were only the victims.

In declaring the collective organisations criminal in order to enable the competent authorities to punish the guilty, but only the guilty, in solemnly reminding the world that before the arbitrary rule of men and governments a moral law existed, incumbent on public figures as well as on private persons, on nations as well as on individuals, a law which cannot be broken with impunity, your sentence will contribute greatly to the great work of universal peace which is being undertaken in the organisation of the United Nations as well as at the Peace Conference, in New York as in Paris, by the representatives of the free peoples, "anxiously awaited by sincere men of upright heart."

GENERAL R. A. RUDENKO:

The Gestapo was founded by defendant Goering on 26th April, 1933, at the time when he was Prime Minister of Prussia. During the early period of its existence it was directed by him in person.

Gradually, however, Reichsfuehrer of the SS Heinrich Himmler centred all direction of the political police of the Federal territories in his own hands. The law of 10th February, 1936, declared the Gestapo a "special police" organisation for the entire Reich. By his decree of 17th July, 1936, Hitler appointed Himmler as Chief of the German Police, thus legitimising the "personal union" which had already largely been achieved by the SS and the police.

In harmony with this principle of "personal union" Himmler, by his very first decree on the structure of the German Police, dated 25th June, 1936, appointed Reinhardt Heydrich as Chief of the Sipo (Security Police) which already included within the same system both the Gestapo and the Criminal Police. Heydrich's successor, after his death, was the defendant Kaltenbrunner.

A rearrangement of the central security organisations took place in 1939, in consequence of the consolidation of the leading role of the SD in the general security plan of the Nazi State, and for further unification of the police under a single leadership. This resulted in the fusion of the "Chief SS Security Administration" with "Chief Administration of the Security Police" in one single SS semi- government, semi-party organisation - the "Reich Security Head Office," i.e., the RSHA.

Thus the Secret State Police, then briefly known as the "Gestapo," and up to then existing as part of the "Chief Administration of the Sipo," became Section IV of the RSHA.

(a) TASKS OF THE GESTAPO

The tasks of the Gestapo, in the general system of the security organisations of the Third Reich, were clearly outlined by the same Heydrich in an article published in the German periodical The German Police. While defining the role of the SD as that of political intelligence within both the Nazi Party and the Nazi State, whose task included the study and analysis of the political atmosphere and of the political trends and tendencies both inside and outside the bounds of the Reich, for the purpose of informing the Nazi leadership, he considered that the task of the Secret State Police lay in the definite revealing and rendering harmless of such political elements within the Nazi regime as were both hostile and unreliable.

The entire Gestapo, with its system of central, regional, penal and other special branches and formations, was geared to the accomplishment of this cardinal point of its programme.

The fulfillment of this task demanded the most careful individual selection of Gestapo personnel. These were selected from among the most experienced cadres of the general police and of the administration, who were already proved to be the fanatical adherents of the Hitlerite regime, and also from among the staff employees of the SD. The latter were usually given supervisory positions in the Gestapo.

The affidavit submitted by the former chief of Section IV of the RSHA, Walter Schellenberg, declares that 75 per cent of Gestapo officials were also members of the SS. They had either been members of the SS prior to entering the Gestapo or else they became members as they began their service in this punitive and terroristic organisation.

The number of Gestapo employees in the period 1943 to 1945 amounted to forty to fifty thousand. Such a staff, to quote Fouche, allowed the Gestapo "to have eyes to see everywhere and hands to seize anyone."

The criminal activities of the Gestapo did not confine themselves exclusively to the territory of the Reich.

During the period of preparation for aggression it was the Gestapo that received the task, jointly with the SD of organizing one of the first operational groups, the "Einsatzgruppen," intended to function in the territory of the Czechoslovak Republic.

With the opening of hostilities and in conformity with a plan already prepared and approved, the Gestapo placed at the disposal of the armed forces a certain percentage of its experienced workers to organise the so-called "Secret Field Police," the GFP. The GFP units in the Army combined the functions of both the Gestapo and the Sipo in the Reich, and were also endowed with far-reaching police and punitive rights, directed against the civilian population and the guerrilla fighters in theatres of military operations.

From the very beginning of its existence the Gestapo had wide powers in connection with extra-legal measures of reprisal directed against elements "threatening" the Nazi State or the Nazi Party.

One of the main types of reprisal used against such elements was the utilisation of the right of "preventive arrest" and "preventive custody" which the Gestapo used widely both in the territory of the Reich and in the areas later annexed or occupied by Germany.

The places of preventive arrest were the widely-known and notoriously gloomy German concentration camps. Confinement in a concentration camp could take place on the strength of a simple written directive from the Chief of the Security Police and the SD, Heydrich, whose place was later taken by Kaltenbrunner, or by order of the Chief of Section IV of the RSHA, Muller. In many cases the order for confinement in a concentration camp was issued personally by the Reichsfuehrer of the SS, who was simultaneously Chief of the German Police - Heinrich Himmler.

Never did the victim of preventive arrest know for just how long he would be condemned to torture and suffering - the length of confinement depended entirely on the arbitrary decision of the Gestapo. Even when the Gestapo knew the length of time during which it planned to keep the man in prison, it was still strictly forbidden to disclose this either to the prisoner or to his kin.

These concentration camps were the prototype of the extermination camps which materialised in the subsequent period of aggressive operations, and which generations to come are bound to remember with horror, namely, the camps of Maidanek, Auschwitz, Treblinka and many others.

As the punitive executive organisation of the Nazi State, the Gestapo was in close connection with the Nazi Party.

In the appendix to the decree of the Reich and Prussian Cabinet Minister, dated 20th September, 1936, it is stated without any ambiguity that "the special functions of the Security Police demand the closest and fullest mutual understanding and collaboration ... also with the Gauleiter of the NSDAP..." In studying the decree of 14th December, 1938, concerning the collaboration of the Party organisations with the Gestapo, it is easy to see that there existed the closest contact among the various organisations of the Fascist conspirators, more particularly between the Gestapo and the Party Leadership. Defendants Hess and Bormann were always careful to maintain close contact between the Party and the Gestapo.

(b) PARTICIPATION OF THE GESTAPO IN PLANS FOR AGGRESSION

As I have already stated, together with other criminal Fascist organisations, the Gestapo actively participated in preparing plans for the seizure of territory belonging to other States.

The list of 4,000 Yugoslav citizens, compiled in 1938 and seized in May, 1945, in the Gestapo quarters at Maribor, testifies beyond doubt to the participation of the Gestapo, on its own lines, for the preparation of the invasion of Yugoslavia. We also see from the testimony of the Yugoslav Quisling, Dragomir Jovanovich, a former chief of the Serbian Police during the German occupation, that leading circles of the Fascist conspirators had planned the Gestapo organisations for Yugoslavia beforehand. In accordance with a preconceived plan the police posts were distributed among the German residents in Yugoslavia.

Prior to the seizure of Czechoslovakia by the Fascists, the chief security branches of the Reich planned the development of the functions of the SD and the Gestapo in the territory of this country.

The report of the Czechoslovak Government establishes yet another form of participation of the Gestapo organisations in the preparation for aggression. The Reich Security Main Office also landed in Czechoslovakia their agents for assassination or for kidnapping and carrying off to Germany of anti-Fascists.

The facts of the participation in and elaboration of aggressive plans by the Gestapo are also confirmed by a series of documents which show that long before the treacherous attack on the USSR, the Hitlerite assassins compiled lists, and investigation files, and had collected information regarding leaders of government organisations and social workers, who according to their plans were doomed to annihilation. For instance, together with the SD and the Criminal Police, the Gestapo prepared for these criminal purposes the "Special Intelligence Guide for the USSR," "The German Intelligence Guide," "Lists of Persons whose Residence must be Determined," and other similar intelligence investigation files and lists of persons.

173 Lidice men shot to death by the Gestapo in the garden of the Horákova estate.

The criminal activities of the Gestapo in the preparation and realization of plans far aggression both within the Reich itself and in the Western States have already been dealt with by my respected colleagues. For that reason I shall proceed to the subject of the Gestapo crimes in the territories of the USSR, Yugoslavia, Poland and Czechoslovakia, temporarily occupied by the Hitlerites.

(C) CRIMES OF THE GESTAPO IN CZECHOSLOVAKIA, YUGOSLAVIA AND POLAND

The crimes which the Hitlerites had committed with the help of the executive police organisations in the temporarily occupied territories of Czechoslovakia, Yugoslavia and Poland have many features in common.

The various Gestapo organisations represented the executive machinery which served to realize the majority of these crimes.

The very first mass "action" for the annihilating of the Polish intelligentsia, the so-called "Operation AB," was conceived by Frank, approved by Hitler, and directly perpetrated by the Gestapo. It was the agents of the Gestapo who, with the aid of several SS units and under the direction of the SS and Police Chief for Poland, Obergruppenfuehrer Kruger, as well as Brigadefuehrer Strechenbach, exterminated several thousand Polish intellectuals in the execution of this savage mass operation.

In accordance with Frank's decree of 9th October, 1943, "Standgerichte" (Summary Courts) of evil fame, created "to suppress attacks on German construction in the Government General," also included agents of the Secret Police, i.e., the Gestapo.

Again it was the Gestapo in Poland which put into effect as far back as January, 1941, the terrible reprisal against the clergy which resulted in the murder of some 700 and the imprisonment of 3,000.

As is thoroughly proved by the documents submitted by the Soviet prosecution, the Gestapo established on Polish territory special mass extermination centres for the Jewish population.

In contrast to extermination camps such as Maidanek and Auschwitz, which were under the jurisdiction of the Administrative and Supply Command of the SS, the secret extermination camp in Chelmno, where over 340,000 Jews were done away with in the death vans, was both founded by and directly subordinate to the Gestapo and was known as "Sonderkommando Kulmhof."

This Gestapo Sonderkommando was under the supervision of Braunfisch, Gestapo Chief of the city of Lodz.

It was also the Gestapo which founded Treblinka, prototype of all subsequent extermination camps.

Eichmann's "Essay" for the extermination of the Jews in Europe by special extermination camps created for the purpose by Section "D" of the SS originated in the Gestapo where Eichmann worked as a direct subordinate of the Gestapo Chief Muller.

It was the Gestapo that was responsible for the annihilation of 3,200,000 Jews in Poland, 112,000 in Czechoslovakia and 65,000 in Yugoslavia.

It was the Gestapo that introduced and practised, in the occupied territories of Eastern Europe, the criminal system of hostages and the principle of collective responsibility, thus arbitrarily and constantly widening the circle of persons liable to reprisals. For instance, it was the Gestapo that, together with defendant Frank, issued the notorious decree of mass reprisals with regard to the "families of saboteurs," the decree which stated that "not only should the saboteurs seized be executed on the spot but also that all male relatives of the offenders should be shot immediately and all female relatives over 16 years of age be confined in concentration camps."

What went on in Poland does not typify the Gestapo behaviour in Poland alone, but applies in the same degree to Czechoslovakia and Yugoslavia.

200,000 persons passed through the Gestapo prison in Brno, Czechoslovakia, during the period of occupation alone. Only 50,000 of these were freed, and the others were killed or sent to a lingering death in the concentration camp.

The order of 9th March, 1942, gave the Gestapo the right to apply both "preventive confinement" and "protective custody."

Thousands of Czech patriots, particularly doctors, teachers, lawyers and clergy et alia, were arrested even prior to the war. In addition, lists were compiled in each region of persons liable to be arrested as hostages at the first sign "of disturbance of the social order or security." Karl Hans Frank, addressing "leaders of the movement for national unity," announced in 1940 that 2,000 Czech hostages - then in concentration camps - would be shot unless the Czech leaders signed a declaration of fealty.

After the attempt on Heydrich's life many of these hostages were executed.

In 1939 the Gestapo called together factory directors and warehouse supervisors of the various Czech industrial concerns. They were made to sign the following statement: "I am cognizant of the fact that I shall be shot immediately if the plant stops work without a justifiable cause."

Schoolteachers in Czechoslovakia similarly had to sign declarations rendering themselves responsible for the loyalty of their pupils.

It was the Gestapo which was responsible for that crime unparalleled in its cruelty - of the annihilation of the village of Lidice and of its population.

The Gestapo terror in Yugoslavia assumed a particularly vicious character.

A confirmation of this fact can be found in the following brief quotation from the Report No. 6 of the Yugoslav State Commission for the Investigation of War Crimes:

"A group of hostages was hanged in Celje (Zilli) on hooks used by butchers for suspending meat. In Maribor the condemned victims, working in groups of five, placed the bodies of the hostages shot into cases and then loaded them on to trucks. As each team of five finished its task, it was shot, and the next group of five replaced it in the loading job. This went on continuously. The Sodna Street in Maribor was soaked with blood from these lorries. The number given, of 50,000 victims, appears too small, as several hundred were shot each time; in Granz even as many as 500 being murdered at once."

Numerous documents have been submitted to the Tribunal dealing with the mass shooting of hostages and signed by the corresponding regional chiefs of the Gestapo in Yugoslavia. I shall not dwell upon the details of these documents, since I suppose that the Tribunal still bears them clearly in mind.

(d) CRIMES OF THE GESTAPO IN THE TEMPORARILY OCCUPIED TERRITORIES OF THE USSR

The legal proceedings have thoroughly revealed those monstrous crimes which the Gestapo had committed in the temporarily occupied territory of the USSR. There the Gestapo personnel functioned either in the operational units, i.e., the Einsatzgruppen, the Einsatzkommandos, and the Sonderkommandos of the SD and of the Security Police, or else it comprised the staff of the Secret Field Police (GFP), which was usually complemented by employees both of the Gestapo and the Criminal Police.

As a rule, it was the Gestapo official who on all these occasions directly carried out the inhuman "executions" and "mass actions," acting under the general political leadership of members of the SD staff and with the assistance of officials of other police organisations, as well as units of the Waffen SS, widely used for these purposes.

Numerous cases of mass murder and torture of peaceful Soviet citizens by the Gestapo have been established at the Tribunal. As an example I shall content myself with the description of individual characteristic acts only. In the small town of Vyasma alone, by order of the chief of the Gestapo, several thousands of peaceful citizens were killed or tortured to death. The Fascist monsters not only killed their victims but made them dig their own graves.

In the village of Zaitchiki, in the Smolensk district, the men of the Gestapo drove into one house 23 old men, women and children, set the house on fire and burned alive all those inside.

In the psychiatric hospitals of Riga the Gestapo men exterminated all the inmates of these asylums.

As stated in the report of the Extraordinary State Commission on the crimes of the German Fascist usurpers in the town of Rovno, and in the Rovno district, men of the Gestapo resorted to mass murder as a retaliation for each act of resistance.

When a German judge was killed by an unknown person in November, 1943, in Rovno, the Gestapo shot over 350 prisoners detained in the town prison.

It is known, from the report of the Extraordinary State Commission on the crimes of the German Fascist usurpers, that the Gestapo men used death vans for the extermination of Soviet citizens. In the town of Krasnodar, and in the Krasnodar region, the Gestapo people who formed part of operational groups exterminated by carbon monoxide poisoning over 6,700 Soviet citizens, including women, old men and children who were under treatment in Krasnodar hospital, as well as persons held in the Gestapo prison.

In the outskirts of the town of Krasnodar, in a big anti- tank trench, were buried several thousand bodies of Soviet citizens who had been poisoned by gas and thrown there by the Gestapo.

In the Stavropol region 54 children, who were seriously ill and were being treated at the health resort of Tiberda, were poisoned by gas in the death vans, as were 660 patients of the Stavropol psychiatric hospital.

The evidence given by Kovaltchouk, who lived in the Stavropol region, gives us an idea of the tortures practised by the Gestapo. They interrogated only at night. These interrogations were made in a special room, where special torture devices had been set up, including chains with metal bars fixed in the concrete floor, to which the prisoner's arms and legs were fastened. The arrested person was first of all stripped naked, then laid on the floor, his hands and legs shackled, after which he was beaten with rubber sticks. Sometimes a wooden board was placed on the victim's back and sharp blows were then inflicted with heavy weights on the board.

The torture chamber was so arranged that when an arrested person was tortured, the other arrested people in an adjoining ward awaiting torture were able to follow the scene. After the tortures the unconscious prisoner was temporarily thrown aside by the "modern inquisitors" and the next victim, in most cases already in a half-unconscious condition, was dragged into the room.

These unheard-of tortures were used by the Gestapo even on women.

I shall mention one example only. Such tortures during interrogation were most extensively used throughout the occupied territories of the USSR.

Recourse to medieval tortures during interrogation followed special orders emanating from the RSHA and Muller, chief of the Gestapo. In one of those top secret orders the authorities issued the following instructions: "Third degree can include the following treatment: a very simple diet (bread and water); a hard berth, a dark cell, deprival of sleep, exhausting drill and beating with birch rods."

The intelligentsia, including distinguished men of science and art who were in the Soviet territories temporarily occupied by the Germans, were likewise subjected by the Gestapo to unheard of ill-treatment and persecution.

Persecution by the Gestapo of representatives of the intelligentsia was carried out according to a plan which had been elaborated beforehand. For instance, before the German troops had occupied Lwow, detachments of the Gestapo had in their possession lists of the principal representatives of the Lwow intelligentsia who were to be exterminated. The occupation of Lwow by the Germans immediately marked the beginning of mass arrests and shootings of professors, physicians, lawyers, writers and artists. Paying no heed to the human dignity of their victims, the Gestapo subjected the arrested scientists to the mast refined tortures, after which they shot them.

An investigation carried out by units of the Red Army, after Lwow had been freed from the German occupants, showed that over 70 prominent scientists, technicians and artists had been killed by the Germans, their bodies being subsequently burned by the Gestapo.

Fearing to be held responsible for these acts, the Fascist jackals painstakingly endeavoured to conceal the fact of the extermination of the Lwow intelligentsia.

The Gestapo also took part in the torturing and killing of prisoners of war.

During the court proceedings we heard a directive of Department IV of the Reich Security Main Office, dated 17th June, 1941; it concerned the activities of detachments of the Security Police and SD in the camps of the prisoners of war.

Your Honours also know of the Muller directive dated 9th November, 1941, addressed to all the departments of the Gestapo, which dealt with the disposal of the bodies of such people as had died on their way to the execution ground.

The written testimony of Kurt Lindorf, a former employee of the Gestapo, is at the disposal of the Tribunal. This document concerns the execution of Soviet political commissars and military employees of Jewish origin, and also deals with an order of the chief of the Security Police and SD, transmitted to the local organs of the Gestapo, concerning the transfer of certain categories of escaped officers from prisoner-of-war camps to the Mauthausen concentration camp for the carrying out of the "Kugel" (bullet) action.

The Tribunal is acquainted with the order of the commander of the 6th Military District, dated 27th July, 1944, stating that recaptured escaped prisoners of war lose their rights and are to be turned over to the Gestapo, and also with Keitel's order to the armed forces, dated 4th August, 1942, which stated that the adoption of action against individual paratroopers and groups of paratroopers falls under the jurisdiction of the SD and the Gestapo.

The Gestapo actively co-operated in the deportation to German slave labour of thousands of peaceful citizens from the territories temporarily occupied by Germany and inflicted cruel repressive measures upon these persons on their arrival in Germany. In a like manner Muller, the chief of the Gestapo, in his telegram of 16th December, 1942, stated that the Gestapo could arrest some 45,000 Jews to serve as workers in the concentration camps.

In a directive of 17th December, 1942, Muller writes about this in connection with 35,000 Jews.

In the secret order of 18th July, 1941, Muller instructed the Gestapo about the necessary measures to be taken in order to prevent agitation among foreign workers.

The criminal activity of the Gestapo is of particular importance in the extermination of the Jews.

The affidavit of Wilhelm Hoettl dated 7th November, 1945, establishes the fact that the Gestapo exterminated some 6,000,000 Jews.

In the reports of the Extraordinary State Commission set up for the investigation of German Fascist atrocities in the territory of the USSR, and in other documents as well, innumerable facts of torture, of various outrages and mass murder of Jews by the Gestapo are brought forward.

The proceedings of the Court have fully confirmed the charge submitted against the criminal activities of the Gestapo.

As an organisation for bloody mass terror, the Gestapo must be recognised as a criminal organisation.

THE SECURITY SERVICE - "SD"

The Security: Service or "Sicherheitsdienst" was usually referred to in official Hitlerite police documents under the conventional abbreviation "SD." It originated as a profoundly conspiratorial espionage organisation of German Fascism within the Party and the SS. The SD, as well as the SS, was organised by Himmler.

The SD was that secret organisation within the SS system which, after the seizure of power by the Hitlerites, had been the first to merge with the police agencies, and had promptly been appointed to leading positions in the secret police, created in the system of the SD and security detachments, playing both before and after the organisation of the RSHA - the Reich Security Main Office - the decisive role in the political intelligence system and "preventive annihilation" of elements displeasing to the Hitlerites.

The SD stood in the closest possible proximity to the Central Headquarters at the criminal Nazi conspirators, i.e., the Hitlerite Party Leadership. And that is precisely why the SD participated most actively in planning those police activities which invariably accompanied all the Hitlerite plans of aggression.

As will be shown below, it was the SD which created the first Einsatzgruppen, stood at the head of these predatory organisations of German Fascism, and organised the preparation of those atrocities which were later committed in the occupied territories of Poland, Yugoslavia, the Soviet Union and other countries.

In an attempt to exonerate this criminal organisation from the responsibilities with which it is charged, the defence started an argument about the meaning of the very term SD.

We understand the reason why the defence started this terminological discussion. The defence needs it in its endeavour to support Kaltenbrunner's version of SD as an organisation with functions strictly limited to the "inter-Reich information services," and entirely alien to all police activities.

The defence, having admitted nothing but the more apparent part of the criminal activities of the SD, began this argument in order to conceal by the term "General information concerning trends and tendencies in individual circles" the remaining political and police functions practised by the SD as the peak organisation of the police SS machinery.

In reality, however, the SD was a widely spread espionage organisation of German Fascism which actively contributed to the realisation of the criminal plans of aggression and operated inside Germany, as well as in the occupied regions and abroad.

Along with the Gestapo, it was the SD cadres who formed the backbone of the Einsatzgruppen, where the SD personnel always occupied the principal posts.

The functions of the SD can be subdivided as follows:

(1) "General Information," which literally covered everything, as shown by the SD official documents - the "Lebensgebiete" or spheres vital to the Fascist "Reich," all government offices, and social circles in Fascist Germany.

(2) The "Special Functions" referring to the elaboration of special files and lists of persons (primarily in countries which were to be invaded). The filing cards and lists contained names of people who were to be subjected to the "special treatment," i.e., either to be physically destroyed or confined in concentration camps.

(3) The function of supplying personnel for the special criminal organisations directly concerned with the realization of the Hitlerite plans for the annihilation of the politically undesirable elements and of the intellectuals in the occupied territories, and for conducting savage "executions" and "actions."

The entire staff of the SD consisted of SS men. This is understandable, seeing that the SD was an offspring of the SS and was referred to, up to the very last, as the SD of the Reichsfuehrer SS.

German Gestapo agents arrested after the liberation of Liège, Belgium, are herded together in a cell in the citadel.

The widespread system of the SD included the following: Department III of the RSHA (i.e., Amt III, which consisted of the Political Intelligence Service at home and in the occupied regions); Department VI of the RSHA (Amt VI, consisting of the Foreign Intelligence Services and headed by one of Himmler's closest associates - Walter Schellenberg - whose testimony is well known to the Tribunal); and Department VII (Amt VII), sometimes called the "Department for Ideological Warfare," which in addition included a number of very important subsidiary institutions which constituted the analytical machinery both for the foreign and domestic espionage activities of the SD.

In order to rebut the statements of the defence, I should like to refer to one of the documents showing the actual position of the SD in the police and SS machinery of Hitlerite Germany.

I am now speaking of the document entitled: "Employment of the SD in the case of Czechoslovakia." The document is marked: "Secret - Of State Importance" and is dated June, 1938, i.e., more than nine months before the actual seizure of Czechoslovakia. It was found by the Red Army in the Berlin files of the SD and has been submitted to the Tribunal by the Soviet prosecution.

The contents of this document leave no doubt, first, as to the facts of the active participation of the SD in the preparation and realization of the criminal Hitlerite plans of aggression, and second, in the fact that it was specifically the SD that both initiated and organised the Einsatzgruppen.

I quote some excerpts from this document. It is stated there that:

"The SD should be held in readiness to act in case of complications between the German Reich and Czechoslovakia. The SD should follow, whenever possible, on the heels of the entering troops and take over duties similar to those it held in Germany, ensure the security of political life and, as far as possible, the security of all enterprises indispensable for the national as well as for the war economy."

The entire territory of Czechoslovakia, in accordance with the territorial structure of the SD in Germany, was, beforehand, separated into large (Oberabschnitt) and small (Unterabschnitt) territorial units, and for each of these units special Einsatzgruppen and Einsatzkommandos were prepared and staffed. In the text of the document we can read that a system of Oberabschnitte for Prague, Bohemia, Moravia, Silesia, and others, was prepared and planned. The staffing of the Einsatzgruppen and Einsatzkommandos was entirely a matter within the competence of the SD. In the text of the document we can read in this connection:

"The staffing of the SD agencies should be conducted with the following considerations in mind:

1. Requirements of the SD per se.
2. Requirements of an economy nature."

An entire programme for training agents of the Einsatzgruppen recruited from collaborators in foreign countries and Germans from the Sudetenland was prepared. The utilisation of "suitable persons" of German origin living in Czechoslovakia was equally envisaged, and special mention was made of the point that: "one must bear in mind that in spite of all precautionary measures we shall not have many such people at our disposal since, under certain conditions, a considerable number will be arrested, deported or killed."

The Einsatzgruppen, organised and prepared in German territory, were to concentrated near the German-Czechoslovak border in order to move info Czechoslovak territory jointly with the invading armies. In this connection document says:

"2. As soon as any district is free from the enemy, i.e., when occupied, the allocated groups are immediately sent to the district administration centre, following the leading troops. With them at the same time, definite groups appointed for the next regions to be freed from the enemy, in order to gain a hold there."

For refuting the statement of the defence concerning the relations between the SD and the Gestapo, the fifth part of the document is of considerable interest, this passage being specially dedicated to the delimitation of the activities of the SD and the Gestapo. It says there: "Measures in the Reich are carried out under the direction of the Gestapo. The SD assist them. Measures in the occupied regions are under the leadership of a senior SD leader. The Gestapo officials are appointed to certain special purpose staffs."

There is therefore no possible doubt that it was precisely the members of the SD who played the leading role in the activities of the Einsatzkommandos in Czechoslovakia. They were to stand at the head of the Einsatzkommandos, executing directly the tasks assigned to them by the Reichsfuehrer SS, for the extermination of the Czech patriots, the annihilation of the intellectuals and the suppression of any kind of national movement of liberation in the occupied country.

We have to pay special attention to the fact that members of the SD specially detailed to the Einsatzgruppen had to establish, as we can see from Paragraph 7 of the document, a liaison with the units of the armed SS forces, or with the SS units of special task units called the "Totenkopf." The Einsatzkommando, specially formed by the SD before the invasion of the Czechoslovak territory, had to accomplish, in Germany, a preparatory criminal task. This consisted in the creation of the so-called "M Index Card." These index cards were prepared in duplicate for each district. The names of persons who for one reason or another were to be eliminated were entered on these "M Index Cards." Questions of life and death were decided by a simple note entered on the index cards by an agent of the SD.

In the document quoted by me it is said in this respect:

"(c) The card index, when filled in, must bear the references: arrest, dismissal, removal from office, observation, confiscation, police surveillance, deprival of passport, etc."

The compiling from the card index of all kinds of reference books in which were entered the names of these people captured in the temporarily occupied territories, who were to be physically eliminated, was in general one of the inalienable tasks of the SD. The direct physical elimination was realized later by the Gestapo or by the special SS units, by the Sonderkommandos, and the regular police.

In preparing the aggression against the Soviet Union, the members of the SD carefully compiled a whole series of reference books and investigation lists, in which were entered the names of the representatives of the Soviet intellectuals and political leaders who were to be exterminated in accordance with the inhuman directives of the Hitlerite criminals.

Appendix No. 2 to Operational Order No. 8 of the Chief of Security Police of the SD, dated 17th July, 1941, said that long before the beginning of the war against the Soviet Union, the Security Service had compiled the "German Research Book," "Lists of the Addresses," and a "Special Research Book for the USSR," in which are entered all the names of "Soviet Russians considered as dangerous."

We know from these instructions of Heydrich what the intentions of the Hitlerite criminals in respect to those "dangerous Russians" were.

All of them, without any judicial sentence whatsoever, were to be exterminated by the Sonderkommandos in conformity with instructions No. 8 and No. 14 of the RSHA, dated 17th July and 29th October, 1941, respectively.

The same criminal task was carried out by the SD prior to the invasion of Yugoslavia. The Soviet prosecution presented to the Tribunal a "Research

Book" prepared by the German Balkan Institute; the so-called "Sud-Ost Deutches Institut," pertaining to the SD. This book contained the names of over 4,000 Yugoslav citizens who were to be arrested immediately after the invasion of Yugoslavia. The book, previously prepared by the SD, was transmitted to the executive police, i.e., the Gestapo, which was to operate these arrests directly.

The book was found in the registry office of the Gestapo at Maribor and bore the following stamp made by an SD member: "The persons mentioned in the text are to be arrested and the RSHA to be informed immediately about the completion of the task."

This institute of the SD carried on a special and undermining activity by preparing Fifth Column agents in Yugoslavia. A fellow worker in the SD, a lecturer in Graz University, Hermann Ibler, prepared on this occasion a special work entitled Des Reiches Sudgrenze, which bears the stamp "top secret" and includes a list of Fifth Column agents in Yugoslavia.

It was the SD who staged political provocation abroad. The former Chief of the Security Police and SD, Kaltenbrunner, had to confess to this, when interrogated by the representative of the Soviet prosecution. He could not even deny his signature on the letter to Ribbentrop, concerning the allocation by the Ministry for Foreign Affairs of one million tomans for bribing voters in Iran.

The workers in the SD fully understood the part assigned to them in the occupied territories for the realization of the inhuman Hitlerite plans for the extermination of the enslaved nation.

From this point of view a German document captured by the units of the Polish Army in the Blockstelle of the SD at Mogilno (Poland) and presented to the Tribunal by the Soviet prosecution is most characteristic.

In this letter addressed to the intelligence agents of the SD, a certain chief of a Blockstelle, a Hauptsturmfuehrer SS, informs them of Himmler's speech of 15th March, 1940, in which the latter requested the commanders of the concentration camps scattered over Poland first to utilise the qualified Polish workers in the system of the military industries of the concentration camps, and later to exterminate all these Poles. In his turn this Hauptsturmfuehrer SS from Mogilno, therefore, requested all his "trusted intelligence agents" of the SD to prepare lists of Poles whom they considered as dangerous in order to exterminate them at a later date.

The SD was one of the most important links in the inhuman SS police machinery of German Fascism. It was an espionage and intelligence organisation spread over the entire territory both of the "Old Reich," as well as throughout all the temporarily occupied regions and countries. In certain instances it was the agents of the SD who initiated the most cruel police measures of the Hitlerites.

For this reason the Soviet prosecution, supported by irrefutable evidence, considers that the entire system of the SD is to be declared criminal.

The Judgment

STRUCTURE AND COMPONENT PARTS

The Prosecution has named Die Geheime Staatspolizei (Gestapo) and Der Sicherheitsdienst des Reichsfuehrer SS (SD) as groups or organisations which should be declared criminal. The Prosecution presented the cases against the Gestapo and SD together, stating that this was necessary because of the close working relationship between them. The Tribunal permitted the SD to present its defense separately because of a claim of conflicting interests, but after examining the evidence has decided to consider the case of the Gestapo and SD together.

The Gestapo and the SD were first linked together on 26th June, 1936, by the appointment of Heydrich, who was the Chief of the SD, to the position of Chief of the Security Police, which was defined to include both the Gestapo and the Criminal Police. Prior to that time the SD had been the intelligence agency, first of the SS, and, after 4th June, 1934, of the entire Nazi Party. The Gestapo had been composed of the various political police forces of the several German Federal states which had been unified under the personal leadership of Himmler, with the assistance of Goering. Himmler had been appointed Chief of the German Police in the Ministry of the Interior on 17th June, 1936, and in his capacity as Reichsfuehrer SS and Chief of the German Police issued his decree of 26th June, 1936, which placed both the Criminal Police, or Kripo, and the Gestapo in the Security Police, and placed both the Security Police and the SD under he command of Heydrich.

This consolidation under the leadership of Heydrich of the Security Police, a State organisation, and the SD, a Party organisation, was formalised by the decree of 27th September, 1939, which united the various State and Party offices which were under Heydrich as Chief of the Security Police and SD into one administrative unit, the Reichs Security Head Office (RSHA) which was at the same time both one of the principal offices (Hauptamter) of the SS under Himmler as Reichsfuehrer SS and an office in the Ministry of the Interior under Himmler as Chief of the German Police. The internal structure of the RSHA shows the manner in which it consolidated the offices of the Security Police with those of the SD. The RSHA was divided into seven offices (Amter), two of which (Amt I and Amt II) dealt with administrative matters. The Security Police were represented by Amt IV, the head office of the Gestapo, and by Amt V, the head office of the Criminal Police. The SD were represented by Amt III, the head office for SD activities inside Germany, by Amt VI, the head office for SD activities outside of Germany and by Amt VII, the office for ideological research. Shortly after the creation of the RSHA, in November, 1939, the Security Police was "coordinated" with the SS by taking all officials of the Gestapo and Criminal Police into the SS at ranks equivalent to their positions.

The creation of the RSHA represented the formalisation, at the top level, of the relationship under which the SD served as the intelligence agency for the Security Police. A similar coordination existed in the local offices. Within Germany and areas which were incorporated within the Reich for the purpose of civil administration local offices of the Gestapo, Criminal Police, and SD were formally separate. They were subject to coordination by Inspectors of the Security Police and SD on the staffs of the local Higher SS and Police Leaders, however, and one of the principal functions of the local SD units was to serve as the intelligence agency for the local Gestapo units. In the occupied territories, the formal relationship between local units of the Gestapo, Criminal Police, and SD was slightly closer. They were organised into local units of the Security Police and SD and were under the control of both the RSHA and of the Higher SS and Police Leader who was appointed by Himmler to serve on the staff of the occupying authority. The offices of the Security Police and SD in occupied territory were composed of departments corresponding to the various Amts of the RSHA. In occupied territories which were still considered to be operational military areas or where German control had not been formally established, the organisation of the Security Police and SD was only slightly changed. Members of the Gestapo, Kripo, and SD were joined together into military type organisations known as Einsatz Kommandos and Einsatzgruppen in which the key positions were held by members of the Gestapo, Kripo, and SD and in which members of the Order Police, the Waffen SS and even the Wehrmacht were used as auxiliaries. These organisations were under the over-all control of the RSHA, but in front line areas were under the operational control of the appropriate Army Commander.

It can thus be seen that from a functional point of view both the Gestapo and the SD were important and closely related groups within the organisation of the Security Police and the SD. The Security Police and SD was under a single command, that of Heydrich and later Kaltenbrunner, as Chief of the Security Police and SD it had a single headquarters, the RSHA; it had its own command channels and worked as one organisation both in Germany, in occupied territories, and in the areas immediately behind the front lines. During the period with which the Tribunal is primarily concerned applicants for positions in the Security Police and SD received training in all its components, the Gestapo, Criminal Police, and D. Some confusion has been caused by the fact that part of the organisation was technically a formation of the Nazi Party while another part of the organisation was an office in the Government, but this of no particular significance in view of the law of 1st December, 1933, declaring the unity of the Nazi Party and the German State.

The Security Police and SD was a voluntary organisation. It is true that many civil servants and administrative officials were transferred into the Security Police. The claim that this transfer was compulsory amounts to nothing more than the claim that they had to accept the transfer or resign their positions, with a possibility of having incurred official disfavour. During the war a member of the Security Police and SD did not have a free choice of assignments within that organisation and the refusal to accept a particular position, especially when serving in occupied territory, might have led to serious punishment. The fact remains, however, that members of the Security Police and SD joined the organisation voluntarily under no other sanction than the desire to retain their positions as officials.

The organisation of the Security Police and SD also include three special units which must be dealt with separately. The first of these was the Frontier Police or Grenzpolizei which came under the control of the Gestapo in 1937. Their duties consisted in the control of passage over the borders of Germany. They arrested persons who crossed illegally. It is also clear from the evidence presented that they received directives from the Gestapo to transfer foreign workers whom they apprehended to concentration camps They could also request the local office of the Gestapo for permission to commit persons arrested to concentration camps. The Tribunal is of the opinion that the Frontier Police must be included in charge of criminality against the Gestapo.

The border and customs protection or Zollgrenzschutz became part of the Gestapo in the summer of 1944. The functions of organisation were similar to the Frontier Police in enforcing border regulations with particular respect to the prevention of smuggling. It does not appear, however, that their transfer was complete but about half of their personnel of 54,000 remained under the Reich Finance Administration or the Order Police. A few days before the end of the war the whole organisation was transferred back to the Reich Finance Administration. The transfer of the organisation to Gestapo was so late and it participated so little in the over-all activities of the organisation that the Tribunal does not feel that it should be dealt with in considering the criminality of the Gestapo.

The third organisation was the so-called Secret Field Police which was originally under the Army but which in 1942 was transferred by military order to the Security Police. The Secret Field police was concerned with security matters within the Army in occupied territory, and also with the prevention of attacks by civilians on military installations or units, and committed War Crimes and Crimes against Humanity on a wide scale. It has not been proved, however, that it was a part of the Gestapo and the Tribunal does not consider it as coming within the charge of criminality contained in the Indictment, except such members as may have been transferred to Amt IV of the RSHA or were members of organisations declared criminal by this Judgment.

CRIMINAL ACTIVITY

Originally, one of the primary functions of the Gestapo was the prevention of any political opposition to the Nazi regime, a function which it performed with the assistance of the SD. The principal weapon used in performing this function was the concentration camp. The Gestapo did not have administrative control over the concentration camps, but, acting through the RSHA, was responsible for the detention of political prisoners in those camps. Gestapo officials were usually responsible for the interrogation of political prisoners at the camps.

The Gestapo and the SD also dealt with charges of treason and with questions relating to the press, the churches and the Jews. As the Nazi program of anti-Semitic persecution increased in intensity the role played by these groups became increasingly important. In the early morning of 10th November, 1938, Heydrich sent a telegram to all offices of the Gestapo and SD giving instructions for the organisation of the pogroms of that date and instructing them to arrest as many Jews as the prisons could hold "especially rich ones," but to be careful that those arrested were healthy and not too old. By 11th November, 1938, 20,000 Jews had been arrested and many were sent to concentration camps. On 24th January, 1939, Heydrich, the Chief of the Security Police and SD, was charged with furthering the emigration and evacuation of Jews from Germany, and on 31st July, 1941, with bringing about a complete solution of the Jewish problem in German dominated Europe. A special section of the Gestapo office of the RSHA under Standartenfuehrer Eichmann was set up with responsibility for Jewish matters which employed its own agents to investigate the Jewish problem in occupied territory Local offices of the Gestapo were used first to supervise the emigration of Jews and later to deport them to the East both from Germany and from the territories occupied during the war. Einsatzgruppen of the Security Police and SD operating behind the lines of the Eastern Front engaged in the wholesale massacre of Jews. A special detachment from Gestapo headquarters in the RSHA was used to arrange for the deportation of Jews from Axis satellites to Germany for the "final solution."

Local offices of the Security Police and SD played an important role in the German administration of occupied territories. The nature of their participation is shown by measures taken in the summer of 1938 in preparation for the attack on Czechoslovakia which was then in contemplation. Einsatzgruppen of the Gestapo and SD were organised to follow the Army into Czechoslovakia to provide for the security of political life in the occupied territories. Plans were made for the infiltration of SD men into the area in advance, and for the building up of a system of files to indicate what inhabitants should be placed under surveillance, deprived of passports, or liquidated. These plans were considerably altered due to the cancellation of the attack on Czechoslovakia, but in the military operations which actually occurred, particularly in the war against USSR, Einsatzgruppen of the Security Police and SD went into operation, and combined brutal measures for the pacification of the civilian population with the wholesale slaughter of Jews. Heydrich gave orders to fabricate incidents on the Polish-German frontier in 1939 which would give Hitler sufficient provocation to attack Poland. Both Gestapo and SD personnel were involved in these operations.

The local units of the Security Police and SD continued their work in the occupied territories after they had ceased to be an area of operations. The Security Police and SD engaged in widespread arrests of the civilian population of these occupied countries, imprisoned many of them under inhumane conditions, subjected them to brutal third degree methods, and sent many of them to concentration camps. Local units of the Security Police and SD were also involved in the shooting of hostages, the imprisonment of relatives, the execution of persons charged as terrorists and saboteurs without a trial, and the enforcement of the "Nacht und Nebel" decrees under which persons charged with a type of offence believed to endanger the security of the occupying forces were either executed within a week or secretly removed to Germany without being permitted to communicate with their family and friends.

Offices of the Security Police and SD were involved in the administration of the Slave Labor Program. In some occupied territories they helped local labor authorities to meet the quotas imposed by Sauckel. Gestapo offices inside of Germany were given surveillance over slave labourers and responsibility for apprehending those who were absent from their place of work. The Gestapo also had charge of the so- called work training camps. Although both German and foreign workers could be committed to these camps, they played a significant role in forcing foreign labourers to work for the German war effort. In the latter stages of the war as the SS embarked on a slave labor program of its own, the Gestapo was used to arrest workers for the purpose of insuring an adequate supply in the concentration camps.

The local offices of the Security Police and SD were also involved in the commission of War Crimes involving the mistreatment and murder of prisoners of war. Soviet prisoners of war in prisoner of war camps in Germany were screened by Einsatz Kommandos acting under the directions of the local Gestapo offices. Commissars, Jews, members of the intelligentsia, "fanatical Communists" and even those who were considered incurably sick were classified as "intolerable," and exterminated. The local offices of the Security Police and SD were involved in the enforcement of the "Bullet" decree, put into effect on 4th March, 1944, under which certain categories of prisoners of war, who were recaptured, were not treated as prisoners of war but taken to Mauthausen in secret and shot. Members of the Security Police and SD were charged with the enforcement of the decree for the shooting of parachutists and commandos.

CONCLUSION

The Gestapo and SD were used for purposes which were criminal under the Charter involving the persecution and extermination of the Jews, brutalities, and killings in concentration camps, excesses in the administration of occupied territories, the administration of the slave labor program, and the mistreatment and murder of prisoners of war. The defendant Kaltenbrunner, who was a member of this organisation, was among those who used it for these purposes. In dealing with the Gestapo the Tribunal includes all executive and administrative officials of Amt IV of the RSHA or concerned with Gestapo administration in other departments of the RSHA and all local Gestapo officials serving both inside and outside of Germany, including the members of the Frontier Police, but not including the members of the Border and Customs Protection or the Secret Field Police, except such members as have been specified above. At the suggestion of the Prosecution the Tribunal does not include persons employed by the Gestapo for purely clerical, stenographic, janitorial, or similar unofficial routine tasks. In dealing with the SD the Tribunal includes Amts III, VI, and VII of the RSHA and all other members of the SD, including all local representatives and agents, honorary or otherwise, whether they were technically members of the SS or not.

The Tribunal declares to be criminal within the meaning of the Charter the group composed of those members of the Gestapo and SD holding the positions enumerated in the preceding paragraph who became or remained members of the organisation with knowledge that it was being used for the commission of acts declared criminal by Article 6 of the Charter, or who were personally implicated as members of the organisation in the commission of such crimes. The basis for this finding is the participation of the organisation in war crimes and crimes against humanity connected with the war; this group declared criminal cannot include, therefore, persons who had ceased to hold the positions enumerated in the preceding paragraph prior to 1st December, 1939.

Discover Your History

Ancestors • Heritage • Memories

Each issue of *Discover Your History* presents special features and regular articles on a huge variety of topics about our social history and heritage – such as our ancestors, childhood memories, military history, British culinary traditions, transport history, our rural and industrial past, health, houses, fashions, pastimes and leisure ... and much more.

Historic pictures show how we and our ancestors have lived and the changing shape of our towns, villages and landscape in Britain and beyond.

Special tips and links help you discover more about researching family and local history. Spotlights on fascinating museums, history blogs and history societies also offer plenty of scope to become more involved.

Keep up to date with news and events that celebrate our history, and reviews of the latest books and media releases.

Discover Your History presents aspects of the past partly through the eyes and voices of those who were there.

Discover Your History is in all good newsagents and also available on subscription for six or twelve issues. For more details on how to take out a subscription and how to choose your free book, call 01778 392013 or visit **www.discoveryourhistory.net**